To: Paul Blu-
With Best Wishes Forever
From Kwan Loo (2015)

Y KWAN LOO

Zodiac GUIDE TO SUCCESSFUL RELATIONSHIPS AND CAREERS

How research-based Western and Chinese astrology can help you make the big decisions in life

MEREO
Cirencester

Mereo Books

1A The Wool Market Dyer Street Cirencester Gloucestershire GL7 2PR

An imprint of Memoirs Publishing www.mereobooks.com

Zodiac Guide to Successful Relationships & Careers: 978-1-86151-202-4

First published in Great Britain in 2014
by Mereo Books, an imprint of Memoirs Publishing

A CIP catalogue record for this book is available from the British Library.

The address for Memoirs Publishing Group Limited can be found at www.memoirspublishing.com

The Memoirs Publishing Group Ltd Reg. No. 7834348

The Memoirs Publishing Group supports both The Forest Stewardship Council® (FSC®) and the PEFC® leading international forest-certification organisations. Our books carrying both the FSC label and the PEFC® and are printed on FSC®-certified paper. FSC® is the only forest-certification scheme supported by the leading environmental organisations including Greenpeace. Our paper procurement policy can be found at www.memoirspublishing.com/environment

Typeset in 8/12pt Helvetica
by Wiltshire Associates Publisher Services Ltd. Printed and bound in Great Britain by Printondemand-Worldwide, Peterborough PE2 6XD

CONTENTS

Introduction

Cloaked in deep mysteries. My aim here is to help simplify the subject, biased towards the basic personalities/characteristics and particularly how these can supposedly affect people's lives, in their relationships and especially your career success. I must stress that this book is not about forecasting and predicting of your destiny, career wise. It is basically about familiarising yourself with your astrological strengths and weaknesses (mainly research based) so that you are better able to select the most 'appropriate' profession and relationship for likely success. You will also get the added reassurance from proven successes of celebrities, whose birthdays you might share.

Having a good, basic understanding of astrology as a unique 'system' or 'framework' of knowledge will prove invaluable in your critical understanding of everyone around you – yourself, your partner/spouse, your boss and your children.

This book contains the professions of celebrities, both past and present. More than 800 different professions are mentioned. The contents are based on my personal interviews, experiences, research and extracts from many established astrologers (references to their books are included) and from my research on over 24,000 people. My book is therefore, mainly factual and research based, having statistically good correlations with real people gathered for many years. It has a fresh, concise approach, dealing with your basic personalities and professions that might suit you. Many books have been written using classic astrological delineations, making it difficult for the layperson to have good faith in their accuracies and relevance. Effectively, this means that my book is based on my deductions based on comparing astrological fundamentals with real people.

From a practical view point, people have commented that much of my book can be easily obtained by a quick search on the internet. However, you would need to bear in mind that there are many inherent inaccuracies in such searches – who would you believe? In my case, I have endeavoured to confirm or double check as much of my data as possible. Also, you will find here a huge amount of interesting information in one source, which you can take along, without taking much time spent in accessing the internet.

If you are a purist, this may prove interesting to you. In the late 1950s and 1960s, French statistician Michel Gauquelin and his wife Francoise had researched into the subject of vocations and temperament. He had used over 19000 birth records. However, his conclusions would be too advanced for discussion here. Suffice to say, he had found some interesting data relating to the areas just after the Midheaven, an area just above the Ascendant. More details are in Noel Tyl's book.

Just as there are cynics to religious beliefs, there will be many cynics to astrology amongst you. My message to cynics is simple: keep an open mind. Check your date of birth to find out your Sun and Moon signs and read their characteristics. You will probably be amazed at the accuracies. Many of my previously sceptical contacts were unconvinced till I managed to pinpoint theirs or their friends' key personality traits with surprising accuracy.

The structure is simple; there is a chapter on Western astrology for all the 12 Sun signs where I have listed some key words (both positive and negative traits) to describe each sign relevant to success in careers and relationships. The chapter ends with a list of professions that are attributed in reality to each sign. The professions listed are not in any priority order. This format is repeated for the second chapter on Chinese astrology. The third chapter contains careers that are attributed to a combination of both Western and Chinese star signs. This was mainly compiled from my database of over 24,000 names (from publicly available sources and their accuracies were confirmed wherever possible) with their professions, Sun and Moon signs and Chinese sign in chronological order.

Some of you might well ask this question: "Why is my book different from the many already written by professional astrologers?" My answer is that this book is written by a non astrologer, based on facts or data - birth dates, people's careers and comparatively concise deductions. It is a challenge to you to make your own useful conclusions. Not being an astrologer myself would mean that I have been extra careful and critical in including information that may appear spurious to a lay person. The names were selected to give a maximum variety of nationalities, careers and dates, thereby offering a broad, global approach.

If you were a novice to astrology, a quick sum up here would enlighten. Astrology is a complex subject; sometimes regarded as a pseudo science but it has a clear-cut reference to its bible, the ephemeris (tables of planetary positions, e.g. www.khaldea.com/ehemcenter.shtml). The all important Sun sign (determined from your day, month and your year of birth), such as those published in your daily newspaper would describe your primal, vitalising, conscious/thinking, outer life, natural self and could account for around 50% of you. Your Moon sign, mainly from your year of birth would describe your hidden, 'feeling' subconscious self, like your inner nature of habit that would modify your basic Sun sign, For completeness, your Rising or Ascendant sign (physical character and temperament) is basically calculated from your time and place of birth. Other more advanced astrological books or software will be able to supply you with these amongst your horoscope/natal chart quite easily. Since I am able to include both the Sun and Moon signs, I should be more than 55% accurate or complete. Moreover, many of my descriptions in chapters 1 and 2 are based on my personal deductions with reference to classical/traditional astrology from meeting real people. I must also emphasise one important principle on astrology. We have our free will and hence reasonable control over our destiny although our natural personalities can be strongly influenced by the planetary energies attributed to astrology and some events seem fated to occur. The latter is mainly about the predisposition of an individual to develop certain abilities, supposedly based on the planetary and aspects at his time of birth. Personally speaking, I do believe that our personalities and characters have largely been predetermined by astrology; hence the strong emphases on the key personality traits in this book.

The above paragraph mentions the Sun, Moon and Rising/Ascendant signs. From all the interviews and analyses, I believe that these alone are sufficient to offer you a good enough profile to base your career choice. Not everyone knows his time or place of birth, hence knowing that to give you your Ascendant sign would be a real bonus. However, your Chinese star sign can usefully supplement this missing piece of information.

For determining your Chinese star (Animal) sign, you will need your day, month and year of birth, especially near the cusp around Chinese New Year (around January and February). I have included the elements of wood, fire, earth, metal in the birthday list and a summary of their characteristics in chapter 2. This is because I wanted to keep things simple and my research into these finer elements has not proved conclusive enough. The excellent book by Theodora Lau (see References) has excellent details.

Perhaps you might be interested in my background. I am a professionally trained Chartered Engineer, with a MBA from London Business School. My career (since 1989) was in management consulting, helping organisations with their business and management challenges. Since I was trained to be analytical and logical, many of you might be surprised by my strong interest in astrology, which may seem rather obscure to some people.

Just to confirm, my interest in astrology started off as a mild sceptic but over time, I was surprised to find much truth and evidence in the basics after a prolonged period of analysing the many people I have met. For you who are keen to know, my Sun sign is Aries, Moon in Scorpio and Rising sign in Pisces. There is definitely 'more than something' in astrology. Notable practitioners and consumers of astrology have apparently included Hippocrates, John Dryden, Sir Isaac Newton, Nancy & Ronald Reagan, Caruso, Heinrich Himmler,

Adolph Hitler, Princess Diana, Popes Sixtus IV, Sylvester II and Paul III, Montezuma, King Louis XI, King Edward VII, Benjamin Franklin, Benito Mussolini, Boris Yeltsin, James Pierpont Morgan, George Washington, and Kepler.

Like me, you may well be on your way to discover the fascinating facts of astrology and how they (e.g. planetary energies and influences) can be applied to promote good career and relationship success. For completeness, your career success will also depend on your upbringing, social environment, education, personal experiences, innate abilities and genetic makeup.

Finally, it is inevitable that there will be inaccuracies amongst the thousands of birthdays listed or calculations. Hopefully, there will be very few of these and I will be grateful if you can notify me accordingly to be corrected in future editions.

However, a very high percentage of the data has been verified. Also, my unreserved apologies for any outdated entries or comments, which may offend. My email address is: kwan@k-lassociates.com or ykwanloo@gmail.com. However, I might be unable to enter into detailed astrological discussions.

With best wishes,

Y Kwan Loo, BSc (Eng) MBA CEng MIET MIMechE MCMI MCIM FRSA

PS. As much of the contents of this book have been based on personal research and inferences made from observations, the author is not responsible for any loss or consequential damage caused as a result of any reader following the published advice in this book.

E & O E.

How to use this book

Depending on your aim and interest, the following steps and choices are available:-

Using an ephemeris book or reliable/reputable online astrological programmes and websites, determine your Sun (main/basic Star) sign, Moon ('subconscious' sign, Ascendant(Rising) sign and Chinese Star sign. Your Chinese sign, Sun and Moon signs will be determined by your day, month and year of birth. For the Ascendant/Rising sign, you will need to know your time and place of birth as additional information.

If your birthday is not on a cusp (change point for signs), you should find your Sun sign from the approximate days given in Chapter 1.

You can easily determine your Chinese Star sign from the Lunar Tables in Chapter 2.

To understand your basic personalities (Sun, Moon or Ascendant signs), find your appropriate Western sign in Chapter 1. You can always determine your Signs using one of the well established astrological website or ephemeris table.

To get basic examples of possible careers, using just Western astrology, go to Chapter 1 under your appropriate sign. For more detailed guidance using Western astrology (Sun and Moon) and Chinese astrology, go to Chapter 3.

For the most compatible signs, using Western astrology, go to Chapter 1 under your appropriate sign.

To understand your basic personalities (Chinese signs), find your appropriate sign in Chapter 2.

This chapter will also give you basic examples of possible careers, using just Chinese astrology, under your appropriate Chinese sign.

For the most compatible signs, using Chinese astrology, go to Chapter 2 under your appropriate sign.

For well known people with combined Western and Chinese astrological signs, go to Chapter 3

Having obtained a good grasp of what each star sign's personality could be like, you can pick on a listed person you know of, note their combination of signs and check for correlations between your knowledge and what's stated here. You may be pleasantly surprised!

ACKNOWLEDGEMENTS

I am deeply indebted to the countless people I have met over the past 30 years. These people have shared their birthdates and engaged in dialogues about the accuracy of astrological principles in describing their personalities and behaviours. My family and friends have played a large part in allowing me to indulge in this fascinating subject.

There are also an infinite number of sources of data, which I have learned from and utilised. The main ones are from the obituary columns of newspapers, renowned websites and various astrological publications or books (some are listed in the bibliography) which are too numerous to mention.

Also my thanks to my editor, Chris Newton, and his team at Memoirs Books for their patience and expertise in producing this book to a high standard.

CHAPTER 1

WESTERN ASTROLOGY FOR RELATIONSHIPS

To determine your Sun sign accurately, especially at the change points around 18th to 23rd, use one of the popular astrological websites.

Aries (c20 Mar – 18 Apr)	Cardinal Fire element
Taurus (c19 Apr – 19 May)	Fixed Earth element
Gemini (c 20 May – 20 June)	Mutable Air element
Cancer (c21 June – 21 July)	Cardinal Water element
Leo (c22 July – 21 Aug)	Fixed Fire element
Virgo (c22 Aug – 21 Sept)	Mutable Earth element
Libra (c22 Sept – 22 Oct)	Cardinal Air element
Scorpio (c23 Oct – 21 Nov)	Fixed Water element
Sagittarius (c22 Nov – 20 Dec)	Mutable Fire element
Capricorn (c21 Dec – 18 Jan)	Cardinal Earth element
Aquarius (c19 Jan – 17 Feb)	Fixed Air element
Pisces (c18 Feb – 19 Mar)	Mutable Water element

NB. The exact date relevant for each sign varies according to the year etc. For the correct sign, you may find it from another astrological source (e.g. an ephemeris). It is important that you have determined the correct Sun sign, especially if your birthday falls around the cusp (18 – 23).

Not all the following traits would be present in every Star sign. The aim is to enable you to form a prominent and distinctive profile for each sign; if available, by combining the Sun, Moon and Ascendant (Rising) signs.

If available, and for completeness, compatibility from Eastern astrology for the respective sign (e.g. Rabbit etc in Chapter 2) should be considered when reading compatibility from Western astrology below.

If you know your Chinese sign, Western Sun and Moon signs, Chapter 3 will give you examples of successful people and their professions for your particular combination.

A useful tip to gauge how compatible you might be is to read the positive and negative traits of the suggested 'compatible' sign and check how you feel and think. There may well be additional influences from the person's upbringing, culture and genes that can play an important part.

You will also gain useful insights if you are aware of the well known people listed under each sign.

Aries (warrior, dare devil or pioneer)

Positive/neutral Traits:

pioneering	courageous	sexually magnetic
passionate	lives in the mind	self motivated
natural leader	positive	enterprising
energetic	ideas man	ambitious
enthusiastic	competitive	generous
quick	creative	sharp witted direct

Negative Traits:

impulsive	non trusting	fickle
wilful	excess	very impatient
poor finisher	foolhardy	untidy short fuse
easily bored	apparently selfish	egoistic
forceful	brusque	aggressive

Suitable professions:

inventor farmer dentist entrepreneur self employed leader magician finance actor metal worker military police politician surgeon butcher carpenter conductor musician chemist nurse teacher civil servant tailor dancer

Most compatible with (descending order, being less precise down the line):

Leo Sagittarius Pisces Libra Aquarius Gemini Cancer Taurus Aries Capricorn Virgo Scorpio

Well known Arians:

Isambard Kingdom Brunel Marlon Brando Doris Day Norah Jones Eddie Murphy Washington Irving Otto von Bismarck Sergei Rachmaninoff Susan Boyle Toshirô Mifune Giovanni Casanova Emile Zola Charlemagne Hans Christian Andersen Alec Guinness Jack Brabham Walter Chrysler Maya Angelou David Blaine Lalique Isoroku Yamamoto Muddy Waters C.W. Siemens Tony Benn Graham Norton Agnetha Faltskog Bette Davis Raphael Thomas Hobbes Joseph Lister Ian Paisley Dwain Chambers Myleene Klass Anthony Fokker André Previn Paul Daniels Jackie Chan Billie Holiday William Wordsworth Russell Crowe Vivienne Westwood Mary Pickford Freddie Ljungberg Spike Milligan Wilbur Wright Raphael Benitez Tamerlane Linda Goodman Sophie Ellis Bextor Gloria Hunniford Joseph Pulitzer Tom Clancy Jeremy Beadle Garry Kasparov Thomas Jefferson Christiaan Huygens Emma Watson Jeffrey Archer Henry James Victoria Beckham J P Morgan Descartes Edward Jenner Clare Francis Sirimavo Bandaranaike Maria Sharapova Céline Dion Jayne Mansfield Vincent van Gogh Francisco de Goya Maimonides Rolf Harris Jean-Sébastien Bach Franz Joseph Haydn Neil Kinnock Michael Parkinson Elle Macpherson Jennifer Capriati John Major

Taurus (builder or producer)

Positive/neutral Traits:

Stable/predictable
likes food
creative/artistic
practical
loving
dependable
intelligent/sensible
systematic
kind
hardworking
bulldog tenacity
level headed
good natured/sincere
patient
home maker
reliable
endurance

Negative Traits:

stubborn
fixed (security need)
prejudiced
conservative
materialistic
unimaginative
dogmatic
self indulgent/sloth
pleasure loving
temper tantrum
slow/inertia/plodding
self centred
complacent
possessiveness
dependable/level headed

Suitable professions:

architect (opera) singer entrepreneur draftsman doctor bookkeeper finance electrician entertainer car mechanic lawyer police dentist radio technician art/antique dealer metal worker/fitter nurse composer teacher author artist poet

Most compatible with (descending order, being less precise down the line):

Virgo Capricorn Scorpio Libra Leo Pisces Cancer Taurus Aries Aquarius Gemini Sagittarius

Well known Taureans:

Florence Nightingale Adolf Hitler Tony Blair Léonardo de Vinci Joanna Lumley Bing Crosby Calamity Jane Antony Worrall-Thompson David Beckham Lily Allen Manfred von Richthofen Benjamin Spock Alan Titchmarsh Jerome K Jerome Brian Lara Machiavelli Golda Meir Henry Cooper Ben Elton Audrey Hepburn

Hosni Moubarak Karl Marx Queen Anne Boleyn Tammy Wynette Socrates Pierre Curie Zara Phillips Andy Murray Madeleine Albright Liberace Enya Ayatullah Khomeini Omar Khayam Margot Fonteyn Chow Yun-Fat Cher Tchaikovsky Johannes Brahms Robert Browning Harry S Truman Katherine Hepburn Malcolm X Grace Jones Ho Chi-Minh Pol Pot Nancy Kwan Kirsten Dunst Duke of Wellington Renée Zellweger Guglielmo Marconi Ella Fitzgerald Oliver Cromwell Eric Bristow Jet Li Rudolf Hess Ludwig Wittgenstein Eugène Delacroix Ferdinand Magellan Sheena Easton Ulysses G Grant Sigmund Freud Tony Blair Maximilien Robespierre Orson Welles Pol Pot Andreas Baader Eva Peron Salvador Dali Irving Berlin Valentino Garavani Jonah Lomu Edward Lear Catherine Tate Stevie Wonder Daphne Du Maurier Joe Louis George Lucas Eric Morecambe Thomas Gainsborough Malcolm X Ho Chi-Minh Nellie Melba Joan Miró Charlotte Brontë Alistair MacLean Jack Nicholson Vladimir Ilyich Lenin Prophet Mohammed Yehudi Menuhin Sergei Profokiev William Joseph Turner William Shakespeare Jean Paul Gaultier Edmund Cartwright Anthony Trollope Saddam Hussein W R Hearst Lonnie Donegan Oskar Schindler Harper Lee Terry Pratchett Michelle Pfeiffer Emperor Hirohito Duke Ellington

Gemini (chatterbox, artist or inventor)

Positive/neutral Traits:

Versatile (multitasker)	clever	artistic	sexy
born communicator	quick witted/alert	perceptive	
dexterous/agile	curious (things)	lively	
adaptable	people person	gregarious/sociable	

Negative Traits:

easily bored ('boring')	changeable	inconsistent
talkative	restless	split personality
impulsive	self deceptive	impatient
superficial	mischievous	lacks focus ('too many irons in fire')
dishonest	outspoken	nervous
unemotional	not detailed	

Suitable professions:

artist teacher actor singer salesman business baker nurse doctor radio technician reporter/journalist entertainer linguist car mechanic accountant secretary writer travel related composer electrician draftsman marketer lawyer computer scientist architect carpenter teacher lecturer tax consultant musician vicar psychologist physiotherapist politician waiter student

Most compatible with (descending order, being less precise down the line):

Libra Aquarius Leo Sagittarius Aries Gemini Scorpio Virgo Capricorn Cancer Taurus Pisces.

Well known Geminis:

John Fitzgerald Kennedy Ian Fleming Edward Elgar George Stephenson (rails) Jordan Rudolph Giuliani Kylie Minogue Thora Hird John F Kennedy Noel Gallagher Mel B Bob Hope Harry Enfield Clint Eastwood Walt Whitman Dante Marilyn Monroe Hergé Justine Henin Heidi Klum Jason Donovan Norman Foster Brigham Young Alexander Pope Bob Monkhouse John Masefield Marquis de Sade Johnny Weissmuller Edward Elgar Peter Sutcliffe Thomas Hardy Rafael Nadal Angelina Jolie Jade Goody John Maynard Keynes Franz Mesmer Anatoly Karpov Bob Dylan Eric Cantona Jamie Oliver Adam Smith Bjorn Borg Velasquez Geronimo David Blunkett Dean Martin Arnold Bennett Anna Kournikova Daniel Fahrenheit Queen Victoria Stanley Baxter Julian Clary Boy George Nikolaus Otto Jacques-Yves Cousteau Richard Strauss Jackie Stewart John Constable Alastair Campbell Yasuhiro Nakasone Johnny Depp Charles Saatchi Elizabeth Hurley Tom Jones Paul Gauguin Damien Hirst Frank Lloyd Wright Shilpa Shetty Joan Rivers Tim Berners-Lee Paul McCartney Thabo Mbeki Venus Williams Igor Stravinsky Stan Laurel Phil Mickelson Enoch Powell W B Yeats Ban Ki-Moon Mike Yarwood Arthur Conan Doyle aomi Campbell Richard Wagner Albrecht Durer Gustave-Gaspard Coriolis George Best Joan Collins Richard Dimbleby John Wayne Peter Cushing Zola Budd Matt Busby

Christopher Lee Cilla Black Paul Gascoigne Dashiell Hammett Wild Bill Hickock Judy Garland Che Guevara Donald Trump Charles de Coulomb Paul O'Grady Rowan Williams Lakshmi Mittal Edvard Grieg Blaise Pascal Salman Rushdie Boris Johnson Radovan Karadzic Aung San Suu Kyi Nicole Kidman Errol Flynn Jacques Offenbach Jean-Paul Sartre

Cancer (protector, prophet or teacher)

Positive/neutral Traits:

Sensitive(feeling) tenacious (bounces back)
imaginative intuitive sympathetic
strongly domesticated fiercely protective (family)
nurturing/caring

Negative Traits:

broody/irritable	inconsistent	dramatic
fame/respect seeker	possessive	emotional extremes
moody	sarcastic	introverted/shy
depressive	stubborn	insular
non confrontational	clannish	worrier
easily hurt		

Suitable professions:

social worker teacher business musician salesman bank clerk actor draftsman engineer antique dealer caretaker historian researcher chef nurse PA/secretary architect entrepreneur computer scientist politician counsellor consultant manager car mechanic hairdresser doctor sailor baker teacher architect police journalist dentist housewife caterer hotelier tax consultant psychologist vicar

Most compatible with (descending order, being less precise down the line):

Scorpio Pisces Virgo Aquarius Taurus Capricorn Cancer Aries Libra Sagittarius Gemini Leo

Well known Cancerians:

Sir Edmund Hillary Erno Rubik Julius Caesar Amedeo Modigliani Jennifer Saunders Zinedine Zidane Alan Turing Alfred Kinsey Jack Dempsey George Michael Louis Mountbatten George Orwell Antonio Gaudi Ricky Gervais Pearl S Buck Helen Keller Michael Ball A A Gill Fabien Barthez Jean-Jacques Rousseau Peter Paul Rubens Mel Brooks Jonny Wilkinson Mike Tyson Cheryl Cole Pamela Anderson Princess Diana Missy Elliott Sydney Pollack Carl Lewis Ruud van Nistelrooy Louis Blériot Amy Johnson Estée Lauder René Lacoste Imelda Marcos Jerry Hall Alec Douglas-Home Franz Kafka Ken Russell Giuseppe Garibaldi Calvin Coolidge Jean Cocteau Georges Pompidou Phineas T Barnum Paul Smith Ringo Starr Marc Chagall John D Rockefeller Jean de La Fontaine Marty Feldman Ellen MacArthur David Hockney Edward Heath Camille Pissarro Jack La Motta Giorgio Armani Yul Brynner Walter Raleigh Harrison Ford Gustav Klimt Emmeline Pankhurst Gerald Ford Shelley von Strunckel Roald Amundsen Joshua Reynolds Fatboy Slim Angela Merkel Nelson Mandela Nick Faldo Edgar Degas Sandra Oh Cat Stevens Ernest Hemingway Meryl Streep Dan Brown

Leo (Sun king, boss or president)

Positive/neutral Traits:

magnanimous	energetic	charismatic
optimistic/hopeful	stable	warm/big-hearted
generous	very organised	enterprising
loyal	bold	witty

Negative Traits:

Proud/pompous	bossy	domineering
bully	control freak	vain
"Leo knows best"	easily flattered	practises favouritism
condescending	melodramatic	easily slighted/hurt
snobbish	too trusting	

Suitable professions:

boss/manager teacher actor entertainer dancer singer salesman engineer draftsman bookkeeper machinist architect painter chemist bank clerk dentist fashion designer politics monarch organiser baker police hotel manager architect computer programmer hairdresser PA/secretary metalworker/fitter psychologist insurance broker nurse chemist waiter clerk writer

Most compatible with (descending order, being less precise down the line):

Sagittarius Aries Gemini Taurus Aquarius Leo Capricorn Virgo Libra Cancer Scorpio Pisces

Well known Leos:

Benito Mussolini Madonna Barack Obama Louis Armstrong Queen Mother Percy B Shelley Neil Armstrong William Wallace John Huston Andy Warhol Geri Halliwell Alexander Fleming Michelle Yeoh Alfred Tennyson Mystic Meg Jo Durie Johann Bernoulli Jackie Onassis Benito Mussolini Arnold Schwarzenegger Emily Brontë Henry Ford J K Rowling Shimon Peres Yves Saint Laurent Roger Federer Princess Beatrice of York Nigel Mansell Whitney Houston Antonio Banderas Henri Nestlé Lawrence Dallaglio Pervez Musharraf Alex Haley Enid Blyton Steve Wozniak Pete Sampras Erwin Schrodinger Robert Southey Alfred Hitchcock P D James Fidel Castro John Logie Baird Alan Shearer Annie Oakley Domenico Dolce Makarios III Phil Taylor Halle Berry Napoleon I Sir Walter Scott Oscar Peterson Lawrence of Arabia Robert Redford Roman Polanski Max (Francis) Factor Bill Clinton Gabrielle (Coco) Chanel Orville Wright Gene Roddenberry Ogden Nash John Flamsteed John Dryden Peter O'Toole Aldous Huxley George Bernard Shaw Elisha G Otis Stanley Baldwin Claude Debussy Slobodan Milosevic David Walliams Alexandre Dumas Amelia Earhart Arthur James Balfour Deng Xiaoping Gene Kelly Mick Jagger Carl Gustav Jung Stanley Kubrick Helen Mirren

Virgo (perfectionist, craftsman or critic)

Positive/neutral Traits

Hardworking/diligent	detailed	methodical
analytical/rational	helpful	logical
good with handicrafts	accurate/precise	scientific
discriminating	critical	fastidious
dutiful	curious (people)	accepts subordination
thoughtful	commercial	quiet dignity
practical	perfectionist	tidy

Negative Traits

nit picking	pedantic/fussy	spendthrift
cold	poor delegator	blameful
depressive	negative	idealistic/perfectionist
worrier	dislikes decisions	shy/retiring
conservative	harsh	

Suitable professions:

service industry bricklayer writer teacher entrepreneur engineer salesman sportsman dancer banker accountant bookkeeper craftsman chemist car mechanic insurance broker journalist actor sports radio technician draftsman architect scientist secretary/PA inspector critic carpenter painter dentist film producer hotel manager interior designer dietician musician farmer healer clerk politician

Most compatible with (descending order, being less precise down the line):

Capricorn Taurus Cancer Scorpio Libra Aquarius Gemini Virgo Leo Aries Pisces Sagittarius

Well known Virgoans:

Hugh Grant Cardinal Richelieu Leo Tolstoy Rachel Hunter Natasha

Kaplinsky Antonin Dvorak Peter Sellers Harry Secombe Queen Elizabeth 1 Grandma Moses Johann Bach Cherie Blair Beyonce Knowles Rocky Marciano Twiggy Kate Adie Julio Iglesias Ray Charles John Woo Aldo Moro Linda McCartney Maurice Chevalier Jesse Owens Richard Gatling Bertie Ahern Michael Ondaatje Ángel Cabrera Roald Dahl Stella McCartney Arnold Schoenberg Man Ray Antonia Fraser C S Rolls Samuel Goldwyn Shania Twain Johann von Goethe H G Wells John McAdam Cameron Diaz Edwin Moses Maria Montessori Stephen Fry W H Taft Ettore Bugatti David Copperfield Greta Garbo Lance Armstrong James Gandolfini J B Priestley M S Hershey Amy Winehouse Dmitri Medvedev Nicol Williamson Agatha Christie James Fenimore Cooper Sol Campbell Sophia Loren Stephen King Liam Gallagher Gustav Holst Andy Roddick Mary Shelley Padraig Harrington Jorge Luis Borges Sean Connery Claudia Schiffer Ivan the Terrible Martin Amis George Stubbs Mother Teresa Yasser Arafat Michael Jackson Ingrid Bergman Lenny Henry Ronaldo Michael Faraday Anne of Cleves Dame Christabel Pankhurst Antonin Dvoräk King Richard I Siegfried Sassoon Peter Sellers Mungo Park Jean Foucault James Fenimore Cooper

Libra (harmoniser, statesman, diplomat or manager)

Positive/neutral Traits:

versatile	intelligent	fair
courteous/nice	charming	diplomatic
artistic sense/creative	idealistic	relaxed
graceful	selfless	persuasive
cooperative	sociable	balanced argument
harmonious		

Negative Traits:

flirtatious	suffers stress (nerves)	indecisive
inconsistent	procrastinate	indiscriminating
quarrelsome	manipulative	needs acceptance
likes to please (can't say NO)		lazy
self serving	problem/conflict avoidance	

Suitable professions:
baker bricklayer tailor interior designer manager actor artist hairdresser solicitor bookkeeper bank clerk diplomat PR judge negotiator draftsman engineer hotel manager machinist radio technician composer decorator architect chemist auctioneer agent insurance broker receptionist hairdresser entrepreneur journalist carpenter author beautician teacher politician singer counsellor

Most compatible with (descending order, being less precise down the line):

Gemini Aquarius Taurus Aries Sagittarius Virgo Libra Pisces Cancer Leo Capricorn Scorpio

Well known Librans:

Roger Moore Mahatma Gandhi Margaret Thatcher Kate Winslet Sting Pelé Richard III Groucho Marx Donna Karan Gore Vidal Chubby Checker Susan Sarandon Ann Widdecombe Run Run Shaw Terence Conran Kate Winslet Bob Geldof Lady Jane Grey Britt Ekland Thor Heyerdahl Gerry Adams Heinrich Himmler Simon Cowell Yo Yo Ma Virgil Alesha Dixon Desmond Tutu Canaletto Juan Peron Jesse Jackson Eddie Rickenbacker Ray Reardon John Lennon Camille Saint-Saëns Annika Sorenstam Ashanti David Cameron Giuseppe F Verdi Harold Pinter Daniel Defoe Paul Kruger Dawn French Michelle Wie Luciano Pavarotti Ramsay MacDonald Sasha Baron Cohen Paul Potts Lillie Langtry Cliff Richard William Penn Friedrich Nietzsche Evangelista Torricelli Eminem Mario Puzo Oscar Wilde Angela Lansbury David Ben Gurion Max Bygraves Ernie Els Lee Iacocca Chris de Burgh P G Wodehouse Marie Stopes David Trimble Yitzhak Shamir Robert Stephenson Evel Knievel Peter Stringfellow Robert Atkins Martina Navatilova Jean-Claude Van Damme Pierre Trudeau Nicholas Culpeper John le Carré Franz Liszt John Dewey Mickey Mantle Alfred Nobel Samuel Taylor Coleridge Catherine Deneuve Dannii Minogue Christopher Columbus Christopher Wren Geoffrey Boycott Arsène Wenger Doris Lessing Ang Lee Antonie Van Leeuwenhoek Roman Abramovitch Wayne Rooney Reggie & Ronnie Kray Catherine Zeta Jones Christopher Reeve Patrick Walker Barnes Wallis Dmitri Shostakovich Ronnie Barker George Gershwin T S Eliot Ivan Pavlov Anne Robinson

Brigitte Bardot Confucius Mika Hakkinen Miguel de Cervantes Silvio Berlusconi Tintoretto Horatio Nelson Caravaggio Martina Hingis Truman Capote Deborah Kerr Candice El Greco Vladimir Horowitz Marc Bolan Lillian Gish E E Cummings Caroline Ann Southey Samuel Johnson Omid Djalili Julie Andrews Thomas Attwood Louis Botha

Scorpio (governor, detective or inspector)

Positive/neutral Traits:

determined	committed	penetrating
observant	astute	magnetic
charismatic	independent	judgemental
protective	loyal	courageous
patient	passionate	confident
intuitive	crisis buster	strong willed

Negative Traits:

vindictive	unyielding	brusque
secretive	exacting	intimidating
sneaky	ruthless (sting)	fanatic
easily hurt	suspicious/paranoid	resentful
manipulative	complicated	emotional
begrudging	jealous	

Suitable professions:

inspector administrator baker painter bricklayer hairdresser tailor bookkeeper entrepreneur detective computer programmer surgeon chemist hotel manager carpenter decorator machinist engineer physiotherapist psychiatrist architect doctor nurse computer scientist insurance broker sociologist actor politician

Most compatible with (descending order, being less precise down the line):

Pisces Cancer Capricorn Taurus Virgo Gemini Aquarius Scorpio Sagittarius Aries Leo Libra

Well known Scorpios:

Marie Curie Christiaan Barnard Pablo Picasso Georges Bizet Richard E Byrd Hilary Clinton François Mitterrand Jaclyn Smith Domenico Scarlatti Theodore Roosevelt James Cook Niccolo Paganini John Cleese Dylan Thomas Simon Le Bon Julia Roberts Bill Gates Erasmus Francis Bacon Bernie Ecclestone Evelyn Waugh Auguste Escoffier Diego Maradona Cheiro John Adams Charles Atlas Chiang Kai-Shek John Keats Hokusai Gary Player Voltaire Marie Antoinette Lulu Puff Daddy Luis Figo Vivien Leigh Art Garfunkel Adolphe Sax Jerry Yang Albert Camus Léon Trotsky Billy Graham Christiaan Barnard Edmond Halley Bram Stoker Ken Dodd Luis Felipe Scolari Ivan Turgenev Leonardo DiCaprio Demi Moore Fyodor Dostoyevsky George Patton George Blake Charles Manson Grace Kelly Ted Turner Auguste Rodin Nadia Comaneci Sun Yat-sen Chad Varah Whoopi Goldberg Robert Louis Stevenson King Edward III Condoleezza Rice Claude Monet Bjork Stefano Gabbana Aaron Copland Robert Fulton Erwin Rommel William Herschel Frank Bruno Oswald Mosley Martin Scorsese Bernard Montgomery Soichiro Honda Emperor Vespasian Kim Wilde Louis Daguerre Jodie Foster Indira Gandhi Ferdinand de Lesseps Kelvin Klein James Garfield Bo Derek Edwin Hubble Charles Berlitz René Magritte George Eliot Peter Drucker Martin Luther William Hogarth Lady Caroline Lamb Emperor Vespasian Louis-Jacques Daguerrre Emperor Tiberius Sir Samuel Cunard Thomas Cook Sainsbury (Lord) Daniel Boone James Gregory Isaac Singer Angelica Kaufmann James Boswell Oscar Pistorious

Sagittarius (archer, adventurer, happy-go-lucky)

Positive/neutral Traits:

candid	sporty	independent
philosophical	mental vigour	optimistic
adventurous	energetic	forgiving/broad minded
eclectic	succinct	courteous
friendly	generous	outgoing/upbeat
far sighted	adaptable	

Negative Traits:

dismissive	disloyal	inconsiderate
dislikes restrictions	overpromises	rebellious
unreliable	reckless	impetuous
outspoken	tactless	insensitive
restless	impatient	superficial
indiscriminate	easygoing	freedom/fun seeking
not holistic	gambler	

Suitable professions:

farmer sportsman teacher politician artist bricklayer gardener electrician comedian priest philosopher writer explorer entertainer lawyer actor playwright composer hairdresser engineer painter counsellor carpenter hotel manager computer scientist police bank clerk waiter tailor tax consultant astrologer computer programmer baker

Most compatible with (descending order, being less precise down the line):

Leo Aries Gemini Aquarius Sagittarius Libra Pisces Scorpio Taurus Capricorn Virgo Cancer

Well known Sagittarians:

Sir Winston Churchill Gianni Versace Giacomo Puccini Joe DiMaggio Andrew Carnegie Imran Khan Karl Benz Charles Kennedy Tina Turner Bruce Lee Jimi Hendrix Anders Celsius Alexander Dubcék Ernie Wise William Blake Rose West Hector Berlioz Robert Koch Nero Frank Sinatra Dionne Warwick Edvard Munch Tracy Austin Woody Allen Bette Midler Georgy Zhukov Britney Spears Maria Callas Gianni Versace Georges Seurat Alexander Haig Ozzy Osbourne Katarina Witt Joseph Conrad Franz Klammer Jay Z Thomas Carlyle Ronnie Corbett Crazy Horse Walt Disney Ronnie O'Sullivan José Carreras George Custer Eddie (the Eagle) Edwards Marie Tussaud Dave Brubeck Ira Gershwin Nick Park Satoru Iwata Kim Basinger Jean Sibelius Eli Whitney Sammy Davis Jr James Galway Lucian Freud Donny Osmond John Milton Jean-Claude Juncker Robert

Hawke Dorothy Lamour Edith Piaf Boris Karloff Leonid Brezhnev Uri Geller Billy Bragg Dr Mahathir bin Mohamad Boris Becker Billy the Kid Harpo Marx Flo-Jo Chris Evert Samuel Crompton William Cowper Benjamin Disraeli Jonathan Swift Manolo Blahnik Friedrich Engels Michael Owen Henri Becquerel J Paul Getty Ludwig van Beethoven Wassily Kandinsky Jane Austen Benny Anderson Philip K Dick Noël Coward Arthur C Clarke Humphrey Davy Brad Pitt Steven Spielberg Paul Klee Jonathan Cainer Ty Cobb Scarlett Johansson Charles de Gaulle Jane Fonda Catherine of Aragon Warren Hastings J L Gay-Lussac Geoff Hurst Mary, Queen of Scots Charles Wesley Joseph Grimaldi

Capricorn (go-getter, priest, ambassador, conqueror or scientist)

Positive/neutral Traits:

ambitious	diplomatic	very persevering/tough
financially shrewd	organised	industrious
risk averse/careful	serious	reliable/dutiful
patient	sure footed	conscientious
enjoys challenge	competitive	funny
wise		

Negative Traits:

pessimistic	introspective	conservative
traditional	(anti-innovation?)	snobbish
overly serious	controlled	manipulative
plodding	megalomaniac	demanding/controlling
obnoxious	miserly	sultry
neurotic/insecure	self conscious	unapproachable
suspicious	reserved/shy	

Suitable professions:

farmer bricklayer engineer gardener boss investor carpenter metal worker/fitter actor draftsman computer scientist police nurse diplomat civil servant lawyer politician liaison manager teacher dentist scientist administrator tailor entrepreneur author

Most compatible with (descending order, being less precise down the line):

Virgo Taurus Pisces Scorpio Cancer Capricorn Leo Gemini Aries Aquarius Sagittarius Libra

Well known Capricorns:

Richard Nixon Mao Zedong Sir Isaac Newton Jacob Grimm Nostradamus Grock Carla Bruni Sarkozy Emperor Akihito Helmut Schmidt Ava Gardner Howard Hughes Carol Vorderman Anil Kapoor Ignatius Loyola Humphrey Bogart Annie Lennox Conrad Hilton Charles Henry Babbage Marlene Dietrich Louis Pasteur Stan Lee Johannes Kepler Ratan Tata Thomas Woodrow Wilson Nigel Kennedy Maggie Smith Pablo Casals William Ewart Gladstone Rudyard Kipling Tiger Woods Ben Johnson Anthony Hopkins Henri Matisse Donna Summer Elizabeth Arden J D Salinger Bonnie Prince Charlie Kim Philby Paul Revere Elvis Presley David Bowie Jamelia Stephen Hawking Shirley Bassey Simone de Beauvoir Richard M Nixon Wilbur Smith Gracie Fields Rod Stewart Barbara Hepworth Gunther von Hagens Arthur Scargill Hermann Goering Melanie Chisholm Maharishi Mahesh Yogi Joe Frazier P W Botha Orlando Bloom Stephen Hendry Ll Cool J Albert Schweitzer Harold Shipman Martin Luther King Moliere Gamal Abdel Nasser Ivor Novello Kate Moss Sade Adu Muhammad Ali Benjamin Franklin Cary Grant Kevin Costner Al Capone King John James Watt Jenson Button Martin Bashir Federico Fellini Gary Barlow Stonewall Jackson Lord Byron Charles Macintosh Sir Richard Arkwright Philippe Starck Oliver Hardy Dolly Parton Paul Cézanne Michael Crawford St Ignatius of Loyola Keith Floyd Will Young Nigella Lawson

Aquarius (water bearer, truth seeker or free spirit)

Positive/neutral Traits:

humane/caring	probing	popular/likeable
visionary	inventive	ingenious
friendly	sociable	individualistic
free thinking	truthful	all rounder
enjoys change	original	charismatic
enthusiastic	focused	

Negative Traits:

detached	unsentimental	distant
perverse	cool/insensitive (feelings)	eccentric
cranky	enigmatic	reforming
weak memory	impractical	dogmatic/fanatical
rebellious	abstract thinker	idealist
unpredictable	needs independence/freedom	

Suitable professions:

farmer priest teacher nurse doctor physiotherapist psychologist scientist engineer TV reporter dancer reformer church minister campaigner/reformer researcher draftsman musician TV host inventor social worker teacher anthropologist artist astrologer clairvoyant florist politician horse trainer publisher

Most compatible with (descending order, being less precise down the line):

Gemini Libra Sagittarius Aries Cancer Virgo Leo Scorpio Aquarius Pisces Capricorn Taurus

Well known Aquarians:

Ronald Reagan Vanessa Redgrave Russell Grant Charles Darwin Cristiano Ronaldo Andre Citroen Eva Braun Charles Dickens Thomas More John Grisham John Williams John Ruskin Bertold

Brecht Charles Lamb Harold MacMillan Jennifer Aniston Tom Baker Thomas Edison Burt Reynolds Abraham Lincoln Anna Pavlova Virginia Woolf Corazon Aquino William Somerset Maugham Robert Boyle Robert Burns Paul Newman José Mourinho Jacqueline de Pré Wayne Gretzky Douglas MacArthur Wolfgang Mozart Marat Safin Lewis Carroll Mikhail Baryshnikov Edith Cresson Mohamed Al-Fayed Stendhal Nicolas Sarkozy Elijah Wood Colette Jackson Pollock Arthur Rubinstein Michael Jordan Charles George Gordon Oprah Winfrey Anton Chekhov W C Fields Christian Bale Vanessa Redgrave Justin Timberlake Franz Schubert Norman Mailer Philip Glass Edouard Manet Charles E.O. Carter Shakira Valéry Giscard d'Estaing James Joyce Carolina Kluft David Jason Nell Gwyn Clark Gable Robbie Williams Jerry Springer Matt Groening Charles 'Chuck' Yeager Kevin Keegan Michael Praetorius Ernest Shackleton Ramakrishna Heinrich Steinway Jeremy Bentham Graham Hill John McEnroe Kim Jong Il Paris Hilton Barry Humphries Ruth Rendell John Travolta Alessandro Volta Enzo Ferrari Mary Tudor Helen Fielding Dick Emery Edwin Buzz Aldrin André-Marie Ampere Christian Dior Emma Bunton Benny Hill Jack Nicklaus Francis Bacon Grigori Rasputin

Pisces (dreamer, poet, healer or interpreter)

Positive/neutral Traits:

Kind/thoughtful	sympathetic	chameleon like
helpful	artistic/creative	versatile
perceptive	touchy/feely	creative imagination
religious	receptive	intuitive/psychic
empathic	visionary	

Negative Traits:

indecisive	moody	dreamy
fatalistic	emotional/clingy	elusive
very sensitive	deceptive ('fishy')	fearful
gullible	carefree	escapist
compliant	vague	

Suitable professions:

farmer caring professions actor engineer poet artist singer doctor counsellor carpenter fiction author musician teacher nurse draftsman physiotherapist hypnotherapist metalworker/fitter vicar clerk fortune teller electrician dancer warden criminal

Most compatible with (descending order, being less precise down the line):

Scorpio Cancer Aries Capricorn Taurus Pisces Libra Sagittarius Aquarius Leo Gemini

Well known Pisceans:

Rudolf Diesel Elizabeth Taylor Patrick Moore Jon Bon Jovi Daniel Craig Harold Wilson Mikhail Gorbachev Alexander Graham Bell Antonio Vivaldi Hans Eysenck Gerardus Mercator King Henry 2 Cyrano de Bergerac Kiri Te Kanawa Frankie Howerd Maurice Ravel Ivan Lendl Lord Snowdon Thomas Wolsey Juliet Binoche Bobby Fischer Yuri Gagarin Amerigo Vespucci Molotov Sharon Stone Osama bin Laden Prince Edward George Harrison Lleyton Hewitt Wilhelm Grimm Pierre-Auguste Renoir Rudolf Steiner Anthony Burgess John Saul Zeppo Marx Victor Hugo Johnny Cash Emile Coué Buffalo Bill Sandie Shaw Fats Domino Christopher Marlowe Levi Strauss John Steinbeck Ariel Sharon Enrico Caruso Paddy Ashdown Nicolas Copernicus Rupert Murdoch Jack Kerouac Laurence Llewelyn-Bowen Vaslav Nijinsky Ron L Hubbard Albert Einstein Johann Strauss Georges de La Tour Pam Ayres Eva Longoria Fabio Kurt Cobain Cindy Crawford Gordon Brown Robert Mugabe Douglas Bader Jilly Cooper Steve Irwin Christine Keeler Julie Walters Kenneth Williams Bruce Forsyth Vijay Singh Heinrich Hertz Jesus Christ Linus Pauling Michael Dell Samuel Pepys Frédéric Chopin

CHAPTER 2

CHINESE ASTROLOGY FOR RELATIONSHIPS

The Chinese star sign can be obtained by checking your birthdate against the list below:
For e.g. for someone born on 3rd February 1908, i.e. 2.3.08, the Chinese sign will be that of a positive Earth Monkey.

Sign	*From*	*To*		*Element*
Rat	1.31.1900	2.18.1901	(+)	Metal
Ox	2.19.1901	2.7.1902	(-)	Metal
Tiger	2.8.1902	1.28.1903	(+)	Water
Rabbit/Cat	1.29.1903	2.15.1904	(-)	Water
Dragon	2.16.1904	2.3.1905	(+)	Wood
Snake	2.4.1905	1.24.1906	(-)	Wood
Horse	1.25.1906	2.12.1907	(+)	Fire
Goat	2.13.1907	2.1.1908	(-)	Fire
Monkey	2.2.1908	1.21.1909	(+)	Earth
Rooster	1.22.1909	2.9.1910	(-)	Earth
Dog	2.10.1910	1.29.1911	(+)	Metal
Pig	1.30.1911	2.17.1912	(-)	Metal
Rat	2.18.1912	2.5.1913	(+)	Water
Ox	2.6.1913	1.25.1914	(-)	Water
Tiger	1.26.1914	2.13.1915	(+)	Wood
Rabbit/Cat	2.14.1915	2.2.1916	(-)	Wood
Dragon	2.3.1916	1.22.1917	(+)	Fire

Snake	1.23.1917	2.10.1918	(-)	Fire
Horse	2.11.1918	1.31.1919	(+)	Earth
Goat	2.1.1919	2.19.1920	(-)	Earth
Monkey	2.20.1920	2.7.1921	(+)	Metal
Rooster	2.8.1921	1.27.1922	(-)	Metal
Dog	1.28.1922	2.15.1923	(+)	Water
Pig	2.16.1923	2.4.1924	(-)	Water
Rat	2.5.1924	1.23.1925	(+)	Wood
Ox	1.24.1925	2.12.1926	(-)	Wood
Tiger	2.13.1926	2.1.1927	(+)	Fire
Rabbit/Cat	2.2.1927	1.22.1928	(-)	Fire
Dragon	1.23.1928	2.9.1929	(+)	Earth
Snake	2.10.1929	1.29.1930	(-)	Earth
Horse	1.30.1930	2.16.1931	(+)	Metal
Goat	2.17.1931	2.5.1932	(-)	Metal
Monkey	2.6.1932	1.25.1933	(+)	Water
Rooster	1.26.1933	2.13.1934	(-)	Water
Dog	2.14.1934	2.3.1935	(+)	Wood
Pig	2.4.1935	1.23.1936	(-)	Wood
Rat	1.24.1936	2.10.1937	(+)	Fire
Ox	2.11.1937	1.30.1938	(-)	Fire
Tiger	1.31.1938	2.18.1939	(+)	Earth
Rabbit/Cat	2.19.1939	2.7.1940	(-)	Earth
Dragon	2.8.1940	1.26.1941	(+)	Metal
Snake	1.27.1941	2.14.1942	(-)	Metal
Horse	2.15.1942	2.4.1943	(+)	Water
Goat	2.5.1943	1.24.1944	(-)	Water
Monkey	1.25.1944	2.12.1945	(+)	Wood
Rooster	2.13.1945	2.1.1946	(-)	Wood
Dog	2.2.1946	1.21.1947	(+)	Fire
Pig	1.22.1947	2.9.1948	(-)	Fire
Rat	2.10.1948	1.28.1949	(+)	Earth
Ox	1.29.1949	2.16.1950	(-)	Earth
Tiger	2.17.1950	2.5.1951	(+)	Metal

Rabbit/Cat	2.6.1951	1.26.1952	(-)	Metal
Dragon	1.27.1952	2.13.1953	(+)	Water
Snake	2.14.1953	2.2.1954	(-)	Water
Horse	2.3.1954	1.23.1955	(+)	Wood
Goat	1.24.1955	2.11.1956	(-)	Wood
Monkey	2.12.1956	1.30.1957	(+)	Fire
Rooster	1.31.1957	2.17.1958	(-)	Fire
Dog	2.18.1958	2.7.1959	(+)	Earth
Pig	2.8.1959	1.27.1960	(-)	Earth
Rat	1.28.1960	2.14.1961	(+)	Metal
Ox	2.15.1961	2.4.1962	(-)	Metal
Tiger	2.5.1962	1.24.1963	(+)	Water
Rabbit/Cat	1.25.1963	2.12.1964	(-)	Water
Dragon	2.13.1964	2.1.1965	(+)	Wood
Snake	2.2.1965	1.20.1966	(-)	Wood
Horse	1.21.1966	2.8.1967	(+)	Fire
Goat	2.9.1967	1.29.1968	(-)	Fire
Monkey	1.30.1968	2.16.1969	(+)	Earth
Rooster	2.17.1969	2.5.1970	(-)	Earth
Dog	2.6.1970	1.26.1971	(+)	Metal
Pig	1.27.1971	2.15.1972	(-)	Metal
Rat	2.16.1972	2.2.1973	(+)	Water
Ox	2.3.1973	1.22.1974	(-)	Water
Tiger	1.23.1974	2.10.1975	(+)	Wood
Rabbit/Cat	2.11.1975	1.30.1976	(-)	Wood
Dragon	1.31.1976	2.17.1977	(+)	Fire
Snake	2.18.1977	2.6.1978	(-)	Fire
Horse	2.7.1978	1.27.1979	(+)	Earth
Goat	1.28.1979	2.15.1980	(-)	Earth
Monkey	2.16.1980	2.4.1981	(+)	Metal
Rooster	2.5.1981	1.24.1982	(-)	Metal
Dog	1.25.1982	2.12.1983	(+)	Water
Pig	2.13.1983	2.1.1984	(-)	Water
Rat	2.2.1984	2.19.1985	(+)	Wood
Ox	2.20.1985	2.8.1986	(-)	Wood
Tiger	2.9.1986	1.28.1987	(+)	Fire
Rabbit/Cat	1.29.1987	2.16.1988	(-)	Fire

Dragon	2.17.1988	2.5.1989	(+)	Earth
Snake	2.6.1989	1.26.1990	(-)	Earth
Horse	1.27.1990	2.14.1991	(+)	Metal
Goat	2.15.1991	2.3.1992	(-)	Metal
Monkey	2.4.1992	1.22.1993	(+)	Water
Rooster	1.23.1993	2.9.1994	(-)	Water
Dog	2.10.1994	1.30.1995	(+)	Wood
Pig	1.31.1995	2.18.1996	(-)	Wood
Rat	2.19.1996	2.6.1997	(+)	Fire
Ox	2.7.1997	1.27.1998	(-)	Fire
Tiger	1.28.1998	2.15.1999	(+)	Earth
Rabbit/Cat	2.16.1999	2.4.2000	(-)	Earth
Dragon	2.5.2000	1.23.2001	(+)	Metal
Snake	1.24.2001	2.11.2002	(-)	Metal
Horse	2.12.2001	1.31.2003	(+)	Water
Goat	2.1.2003	1.21.2004	(-)	Water
Monkey	1.22.2004	2.8.2005	(+)	Wood
Rooster	2.9.2005	1.28.2006	(-)	Wood
Dog	1.29.2006	2.17.2007	(+)	Fire
Pig	2.18.2007	2.6.2008	(-)	Fire
Rat	2.7.2008	1.25.2009	(+)	Earth
Ox	1.26.2009	2.13.2010	(-)	Earth
Tiger	2.14.2010	2.2.2011	(+)	Metal
Rabbit/Cat	2.3.2011	1.22.2012	(-)	Metal
Dragon	1.23.2012	2.9.2013	(+)	Water
Snake	2.10.2013	1.30.2014	(-)	Water
Horse	1.31.2014	2.18.2015	(+)	Wood
Goat	2.19.2015	2.7.2016	(-)	Wood
Monkey	2.8.2016	1.27.2017	(+)	Fire
Rooster	1.28.2017	2.15.2018	(-)	Fire
Dog	2.16.2018	2.4.2019	(+)	Earth
Pig	2.5.2019	1.24.2020	(-)	Earth
Rat	1.25.2020	2.11.2021	(+)	Metal
Ox	2.12.2021	1.31.2022	(-)	Metal
Tiger	2.1.2022	1.21.2023	(+)	Water
Rabbit/Cat	1.22.2023	2.9.2024	(-)	Water

Dragon	2.10.2024	1.28.2025	(+)	Wood
Snake	1.29.2025	2.16.2026	(-)	Wood
Horse	2.17.2026	2.5.2027	(+)	Fire
Goat	2.6.2027	1.25.2028	(-)	Fire
Monkey	1.26.2028	2.12.2029	(+)	Earth
Rooster	2.13.2029	2.1.2030	(-)	Earth
Dog	2.2.2030	1.22.2031	(+)	Metal
Pig	1.23.2031	2.10.2032	(-)	Metal

Metal Element
ambitious persevering self sufficient money focused intense feelings materialistic stubborn selfish opinionated success oriented

Water Element
influential communicative good exploiters aware adaptable penetrate (like water) inconsistent conciliatory dependent passive over-reliant

Wood Element
ethical self confident cooperative convincing compassionate progressive enthusiastic generous impractical over ambitious

Fire Element
leadership decisive positive assertive dynamic risk taker doer forceful impulsive destructive inconsiderate restless

Earth Element
pragmatic methodical organiser prudent disciplined intelligent constructive reliable conservative unimaginative over critical

The following traits should be modified by the above characteristics due to their respective element (e.g. by metal, water, wood, fire or earth) when reading the descriptions below. It will become obvious as to how each element can, in practice, affect the behaviour/personality.

If available, for completeness, compatibility from Western astrology for the respective sign (e.g. Aries etc) should also be used when reading compatibility from Eastern astrology below.

By examining the positive and negative traits, it should be obvious why some signs are incompatible. This may be the result of your strong personal preferences for certain types of behaviour or character.

Note: The compatibility ranking is put in descending order, i.e. the sign mentioned on the left should be most compatible. Hence, for the RAT, the most compatible Chinese sign should be a Dragon and the least compatible with a Horse. Due to limited and less research done by myself, compatibility using Chinese astrology is slightly less accurate than with the Western signs.

RAT

Positive/neutral Traits:

crafty charming financially shrewd/thrifty
sociable efficient opportunistic
industrious level headed full of ideas
quick tempered

Negative Traits:

frugal clannish critical
over ambitious calculating possessive selfish

Suitable professions:

actor artist business musician author politician historian journalist detective financial adviser lawyer

Most compatible with (descending order, being less precise down the line):

Dragon Monkey Pig Ox Rat Dog Rabbit Snake Goat Rooster Tiger Horse

Well known Rats:

Richard Nixon William Shakespeare Leo Tolstoy Jules Verne Charlotte Brontë Mozart Prince Charles Marlon Brando Yves St Laurent

OX

Positive/neutral Traits:

disciplined	hardworking	patient
plodding	resolute	tenacious
down to earth	leader	conscientious
risk averse	serious	responsible

Negative Traits:

phlegmatic	traditional	slow
proud	uncompromising	tactless
unsympathetic	loner	stubborn

long memory (unforgiving)

Suitable professions:

politician actor artist dictator president manager administrator philosopher composer chef teacher

Most compatible with (descending order, being less precise down the line):

Snake Rooster Rat Rabbit Monkey Dog Ox Pig Horse Tiger Dragon Goat

Well known Oxen:

Adolf Hitler Margaret Thatcher Meryl Streep Pandit Nehru Emperor Hirohito Charlie Chaplin Richard Burton Peter Sellers Walt Disney Marlene Dietrich

TIGER

Positive/neutral Traits:

dynamic ultimate optimist daring
warm/hot live wire charismatic assertive

Negative Traits:

defiant impulsive untrusting
temperamental obstinate hot-headed
loud sensitive restless

Suitable professions:

writer actor entrepreneur boss musician academic politician

Most compatible with (descending order, being less precise down the line):

Horse Dog Dragon Goat Rabbit Rooster Tiger Pig Ox
Snake Rat Monkey

Well known Tigers:

Isambard Kingdom Brunel Stevie Wonder Beethoven Charles de Gaulle Ho Chi Minh Marilyn Monroe Hugh Hefner Queen Elizabeth 2 Diana Rigg

RABBIT (Cat)

Positive/neutral Traits:

kind	business acumen	thorough
gracious	wise	strong willed
peaceable	artistic	likeable
intelligent	suave	observant
discreet	sensitive	

Negative Traits:

moody	superficial	self indulgent	
inscrutable	conflict avoiding	conceited	
self preserving	cautious	procrastinate	
fixed	a little reserved	fickle	aloof

Suitable professions:

doctor scientist actor politician research administrator military author artist accountant librarian decorator philosopher adviser

Most compatible with (descending order, being less precise down the line):

Goat Pig Ox Dog Rabbit Tiger Snake Rat Dragon Horse Monkey Rooster

Well known Rabbits:

Marie Curie Roger Moore Kate Winslet John Cleese Bob Hope Ingrid Bergman Albert Einstein Queen Victoria Orson Welles Fidel Castro Benjamin Spock

DRAGON

Positive/neutral Traits:

energetic	decisive	magnanimous
strong	enthusiastic	purposeful
doer	dutiful	super positive
open	sincere	vibrant
resilient	self reliant	wise

Negative Traits:

proud	eccentric	egoistic
impetuous	irrational	naïve
abrasive	uncompromising	

Suitable professions:

boss actor singer musician prime minister author composer psychologist salesperson

Most compatible with (descending order, being less precise down the line):

Rat Monkey Snake Tiger Rooster Pig Horse Goat Rabbit Ox Dragon Dog

Well known Dragons:

Cliff Richard Florence Nightingale Charles Darwin Salvador Dali Joan of Arc Placido Domingo John Lennon Mae West Ché Guevara Ringo Starr Yehudi Menuhin Jeffrey Archer

SNAKE

Positive/neutral Traits:

thinking	graceful	self reliant
cautious	mesmerizing	cunning
intelligent	intuitive/canny	determined
opportunistic		

Negative Traits:

vindictive	suspicious	ruthless
possessive	presumptive	reserved
jealous	secretive/plotting	lazy

Suitable professions:

theologian financier politician philosopher author scientist business/entrepreneur artist actor clairvoyant PR linguist

Most compatible with (descending order, being less precise down the line):

Ox Rooster Dragon Dog Rabbit Snake Goat Rat Horse Monkey Tiger Pig

Well known Snakes:

John Fitzgerald Kennedy Mahatma Gandhi Muhammad Ali Tony Blair Mao Zedong Jacqueline K Onassis Franz Schubert Indira Gandhi Howard Hughes Princess Grace Kelly Rainier Pablo Picasso

HORSE

Positive/neutral Traits:

quick witted
open minded
affable
tireless
autonomous
problem solver
lively
sociable
flexible
expressive
happy-go-lucky
eloquent

Negative Traits:

headstrong
temper
self centred
unpredictable
forgetful
unscrupulous
showy
independent
insensitive
fiery

Suitable professions:

actor artist astronaut sports evangelist politician singer cowboy psychologist composer writer sales driver teacher counsellor therapist

Most compatible with (descending order, being less precise down the line):

Tiger Dog Goat Horse Rooster Dragon Ox Pig Monkey Snake Rabbit Rat

Well known Horses:

Rudolf Diesel David Cameron Jackie Chan Kevin Costner Barbra Streisand Neil Armstrong Rembrandt Leonard Bernstein Billy Graham Nick Clegg

GOAT (Sheep)

Positive/neutral Traits

sincere	creative	artistic
generous	patient	soft seller
kind	discerning	easygoing
considerate	inventive	

Negative Traits

emotional/moody	subjective	indirect
conflict avoiding	worrier	needs guidance
dependent	fickle/trivial	lacks foresight

Suitable professions:

artist actor priest inventor politician business scientist author composer investor

Most compatible with (descending order, being less precise down the line):

Rabbit Pig Horse Goat Tiger Snake Monkey Dragon Rooster Rat Dog Ox

Well known Goats:

Edmund Hillary Benito Mussolini Paul Gascoigne Michelangelo Leonardo da Vinci Andrew Carnegie Charles Dickens Catherine Deneuve Pierre Trudeau

MONKEY

Positive/neutral Traits:

inventive	charming	fast learner	
quick witted	flexible	persuasive	
competitive	versatile	unsinkable	
resourceful	fine memory	strategist	amusing

Negative Traits:

superiority complex	egoistic	jealous
untrustworthy	cunning	hedonistic
very critical	snobbish	mercenary
impulsive		

Suitable professions:

actor writer diplomat lawyer sports teacher business politician PR storyteller film director artist

Most compatible with (descending order, being less precise down the line):

Dragon Rat Monkey Ox Goat Dog Horse Pig Rooster Snake Rabbit Tiger

Well known Monkeys:

Kylie Minogue Elizabeth Taylor Erno Rubik Ian Fleming Paul Gauguin Bette Davis Federico Fellini Kiri Te Kanawa

ROOSTER

Positive/neutral Traits:

sharp intellect	organised	decisive
direct	competitive	flamboyant
stamina	efficient	meticulous
patient	helpful	honourable
orderly	vocal	

Negative Traits:

tactless	opinionated	cocky
miserly	aloof or noisy	perfectionist
over ambitious	unreasonable	eccentric
candid	conservative	

Suitable professions:

teacher investigator actor/comic guru politician singer military composer

Most compatible with (descending order, being less precise down the line):

Snake Ox Horse Pig Dragon Tiger Goat Rooster Monkey Rat Dog Rabbit

Well known Roosters:

Michelle Pfeiffer Deborah Kerr Peter Drucker Elia Kazan Alexander Dubcek

DOG

Positive/neutral Traits:

intelligent
forthright
practical
logical
adventurous
loyal
open minded
fearless
resilient
diligent
egalitarian
responsible
good judge
constant

Negative Traits:
critical
pessimistic
anxious
non trusting
cold
impatient
moody
dogged
outspoken
self righteous
demanding

Suitable professions:

military lawyer teacher judge doctor boss missionary martyr psychologist singer politician researcher scientist composer author

Most compatible with (descending order, being less precise down the line):

Horse Tiger Rabbit Snake Ox Pig Monkey Rat Dog Rooster Goat Dragon

Well known Dogs:

Christiaan Barnard Winston Churchill Gianni Versace Madonna Sharon Stone Golda Meir Brigitte Bardot Pierre Cardin Cher Zhou En-Lai Alphonse Capone

PIG (Boar)

Positive/neutral Traits:

honest	jovial	natural
harmonious	patient	loyal
sincere	guileless	calm
magnanimous	cultured	hardworking
trusting	helpful	curious

Negative Traits:

condescending	naïve	over trusting
soft hearted	thick skinned	can't say 'NO'
fatalistic/pig headed	inflexible	over promise
wrath		

Suitable professions:

actor statesman military author singer film director composer artist civil servant researcher personnel manager chef social worker fundraiser

Most compatible with (descending order, being less precise down the line):

Goat Rabbit Rat Dog Pig Rooster Dragon Ox Horse Monkey Tiger Snake

Well known Pigs:

Ronald Reagan Patrick Moore Julie Andrews Fred Astaire Montgomery of Alamein Steven Spielberg Alfred Hitchcock Lucille Ball

CHAPTER 3

Typical Professions using Western & Chinese Astrology

This chapter gives you some of the actual professions (from publicly available sources of celebrities and the famous/infamous) associated with specific combinations of Western and Chinese astrology. The Sun and Moon signs are used here. Both the Sun and Moon signs are determined from your day, month and year of birth.

Instances where at least two examples of the same professions are found, these are displayed with the number of occurrences in brackets (). For example, engineer (3) means that the profession of 'engineer' has 3 known examples up till now, in my database under that unique astrological combination (Chinese animal, Western Sun & Moon signs).

For example, Rat - Aries/Taurus will denote a Rat Chinese sign combined with the Sun in Aries and Moon in Taurus. Just below the list of professions are listed names of well known people who have this specific combination of birth signs. In some cases, the profession of the 'academic' is also mentioned under the same sign combination to provide further information. The same applies to 'boss', 'Admiral' etc. If two professions relate to the same person, these words are separated by **/**. For example, academic/chemist means that this person is likely to be a Professor who is (or was previously) also a chemist; hence appearing on the right. Hence, if there are 2 or more professions given separated by /, the ones on the left are the latter professions of the person. A 'blanket' profession may be used to include several subsets. Some common examples of - 'politician' may include a MP/MEP, President, Governor,

Prime Minister. 'Boss' may include MD, Chairman, CEO, Director, Chief, Head, governor etc. Academics may include Professor, Reader, lecturer, and teacher.

If you want more examples under your own specific combination, I would suggest looking under just your Chinese sign and the Sun signs. For example, if you are a Rat and have the Sun sign of Aries, you may wish to omit the Moon signs. This should give you at least 10 times as many professions.

Rat - Aries/Aries

Accountant (2) | businessman | actor (5) | actress | author (2)
journalist | aviator | boss/accountant | Dean/Canon
environmentalist | novelist | priest | printer (screen)
film star/singer | singer/actress | Capt

Bettine Le Beau | Emile Zola | Marlon Brando | Doris Day

Rat - Aries/Taurus

Actor | bishop | boat designer | boss | boxer
diplomat | educationist | pilot | rocket pioneer/engineer
2-politician | presenter (TV)/columnist | stockbroker/farmer
writer | trade unionist (2)

Lord Alport | Jeremy Beadle | Karl Marden | Wernher von Braun | Leif Mills

Rat - Aries/Gemini

Actor | athlete | broadcaster/writer/cartoonist
University principal/accountant | tennis | Capt/aviator | General
Maj-Gen | Lieut-Gen | educationist/teacher/musician | industrialist

Baron Thyssen-Bornemisza | Linford Christie | Mario Vargas Llosa
Ted Harrison | Conchita Martinez | Spencer Tracy

Rat - Aries/Cancer

Academic | actress | ambassador | boss (4)
boss (cars) | commentator | composer/pianist | Constable (Chief)
PR consultant | historian (2) | art historian | lawyer | physician
police (2) | politician (2) | surveyor | composer (2)/songwriter

James Callaghan | Prof Ernst Gombrich | Jonathan Agnew

Rat - Aries/Leo

Archivist boss (film festival) college master comedian composer film director lawyer painter QC/barrister singer spy Vice Admiral

Andrew Lloyd Webber | Peter Ustinov | Maurice Vlaminck

Rat - Aries/Virgo

Academic (5) academic/University master academic/archaeologist actor architect boss (3) boss (bank) boss (paints) conductor cook/teacher cricketer geographer journalist otolaryngologist pianist/composer politician QC/engineer/arbitrator Admiral

John Harvey-Jones | Henry Mancini

Rat - Aries/Libra

Actress headmaster composer journalist/broadcaster receiver (police) singer (3) singer/musician soprano video game designer violinist

Michel Ance | Kyung-Wha Chung | Jeremy Clarkson

Rat - Aries/Scorpio

Academic/economist accountant/boss (2) actor/comedian auctioneer boss (health) composer conductor economist politician (leader) puppeteer scientist (research)

Rat - Aries/Sagittarius

Academic ambassador boss economist headmistress manager (football) physiologist politician (2) Rear Admiral/hydrographer

Erich Fromm | Albert Gore Jr | Raphael Benitez

Rat - Aries/Capricorn

Ambassador Assyriologist explorer/naval officer/businessman
nurse printmaker/painter registrar (council) singer
skater/actress Capt/college bursar Commander Lieut-Gen

Sonja Henie

Rat - Aries/Aquarius

Academic ambassador bassist/boss (artists') boss (3)
boss (insurance) editor founder headmaster novelist
ichthyologist journalist musician scientist Air Marshal
seaman /etcher

F W Woolworth

Rat - Aries/Pisces

Academic (2)/chemist actor administrator boss (2) (fire) boss (gas)
businessman/sociologist cellist footballer gardener singer
historian/teacher lawyer poet politician (2) writer
tennis (2) watercolourist Maj-General
academic/sociologist

Mario Ancic I Kim Il Sung I Denis Rooke I Milos Sádlo

Rat - Taurus/Aries

Academic (3) academic (sculptor) actor boat builder
boss (retail) conductor lecturer (neo natal) medical consultant
novelist (2) organist (2) pianist TV producer
psychiatrist writer/teacher

Dennis Hopper

Rat - Taurus/Taurus

Academic/provost actor administrator astronomer composer diplomat drummer editor poet/founder (Pre-Raphaelite)/painter writer reformer singer

Roy Orbison | Irving Berlin | Dante Gabriel Rossetti

Rat – Taurus/Gemini

Actress (2) administrator boss (2) boss (research) comedian/voice artist golfer musician politician (2) novelist Maj-Gen actress/model/dancer/businesswoman businessman/wrestler

Perry Como | Jill Ireland | Ian Rankin

Rat - Taurus/Cancer

Organ builder composer judge manager model/TV personality/singer(4) poet screenwriter/ film director surgeon

Lord Belper | Justice Cazalet | Carmen Electra | Piotr Ilyich Tchaikovsky

Rat - Taurus/Leo

Actor astronomer athlete boss (3) editor chess grandmaster conductor/boss (orchestra) educator lawyer/adviser musician boss (medical research)

Tony Hancock | Elizabeth Peabody | Charlotte Lessing

Rat - Taurus/Virgo

Academic boss (3) boss (education) boss (collection) broadcaster genealogist politician paediatrician sheriff singer/ composer composer (2)

Judy Finnigan | Conrad Swan | Engelbert Humperdinck

Rat - Taurus/Libra

Actor Archbishop Archdeacon boss ballerina
biologist cricketer economist/sociologist historian/art critic novelist
photographer poet singer Vice Admiral

Nigel Barker | Grace Jones | Max Weber

Rat - Taurus/Scorpio

Actor boss (4) boss (health) cartoonist dean (U)
explorer headmaster (2) industrialist journalist/editor judge
physicist politician rector singer (2) soprano surgeon
trainer vexillologist engineer/development expert

Phil May | Bono | Samuel Courtauld

Rat - Taurus/Sagittarius

Academic (2) actor (2) actress barrister boss (CBI)
boxer cleric composer conductor theatre director
engineer footballer journalist poet politician (5)
politician/consultant (PR) politician/boss (bank) wrestler
Lieut-Gen Admiral architect/town planner

Ayatollah Khomeini | Dwayne Johnson | Albert Finney | Glenda Jackson

Rat - Taurus/Capricorn

Actor author boss (4) 2-businessman cellist
civil servant founder (research) poet fashion designer magnate
manufacturer missionary stockbroker Vice Admiral Lieut-Cdr
politician/writer/cook/journalist

Clement Freud | Peter Abeles | Terry Pratchett

Rat - Taurus/Aquarius

Academic (psychiatry) actor (2) actress administrator boss (3)
boss (paints) chess cameraman Chief Constable
film director prison governor headmaster (2) trade unionist judge
lawyer politician (2)/QC politician (leader) singer/songwriter/actor
priest writer

Charlotte Brontë | Bobby Darin | Dr Kenneth Kaunda

Rat - Taurus/Pisces

Academic (2) boss (2) boxer cartoonist
comedian (2) dancer darts designer/muse diplomat editor
founder (Red X)/businessman/activist headmaster mountaineer
physicist (2) tennis

Eric Bristow | Jean Henri Dunant | Lloyd Honeyghan | Roy Hudd
Zizi Jeanmaire | Wolfgang Pauli | Phil Silvers | Edward Whymper

Rat - Gemini/Aries

Academic (2) academic/mathematician archaeologist biologist
boss (3) editor engineer entrepreneur glaciologist lawyer
politician tenor writer

Edward du Cann | Mary Lavin | Prof Peter Fowler

Rat - Gemini/Taurus

Academic (otolaryngology) actor (2) actress ballerina
boss (2) boss (planes) broadcaster conductor cricketer
engineer journalist politician registrar
Rear Admiral

Paula Yates | Kristin Scott Thomas

Rat - Gemini/Gemini

Athlete, boss (2), boss (Trust), ballerina, diplomat, editor/author, TV/film director, TV personality, politician (leader), publisher, General

Anthea Turner | Bryony Brind | Kenneth Loach

Rat - Gemini/Cancer

Architect, author (2), boss (2), diplomat, fisherman (fly), headmaster, journalist, novelist, nurse, politician

Enoch Powell | Thomas Hardy

Rat - Gemini/Leo

Academic, author/politician, Bishop, boss (banking), Vice-Chancellor (U)/physicist, lawyer, librarian, organist, politician, rector, rugby, Air Marshal, Admiral

Peter Winterbottom

Rat - Gemini/Virgo

Academic/QC, actor, author (2), boss (games), comedian, composer, jockey, lawyer, missionary, novelist/journalist, rapper/producer/actor, reformer

Richard Strauss

Rat - Gemini/Libra

Artist (2), boss, comedian, racing driver, golfer, novelist, pianist, politician (2), psychiatrist

Rubens Barrichello | Sam Snead | Heinrich von Kaan | Gerald Scarfe
George Bush Sr | Alois Alzheimer

Rat - Gemini/Scorpio

Academic archaeologist banker Bishop
composer/bandleader cricketer diplomat (2) headmaster lawyer
librarian (2) novelist oncologist pharmacologist philologist
politician Maj-Gen

Leo Sayer

Rat - Gemini/Sagittarius

Academic bookseller boss (packaging) boss (2) conductor
novelist physicist singer surgeon thinker

Ian McEwan | Nick Hucknall

Rat - Gemini/Capricorn

Actress/singer literary agent architect astrophysicist
boss (insurance brokers) broadcaster composer (2) drummer/bandleader
editor industrialist (2) journalist pilot/industrialist politician
singer (3) singer/dancer writer

Charles Aznavour | Stevie Nicks | Otto Luening

Rat - Gemini/Aquarius

Bishop advertising boss (3) boss (training)/inspector
boss (Nazi) boxer cartoonist composer golfer
journalist college master musician priest publisher
singer soldier Admiral (Fleet)

Martin Bormann | Wally Fawkes

Rat - Gemini/Pisces

Academic (5) academic (vet surgery) actor (2) actress
artist boss climber composer Dean
diplomat 2-management consultant expert nurse
painter radiologist Maj/academic/rider

Lynda Bellingham | Mikhail Glinka | I S Dhingra

Rat - Cancer/Aries

Actor boss (2) comedienne/singer
international affairs consultant diplomat headmaster
art historian keeper (Privy Purse) novelist/playwright
Ombudsman police priest philosopher
yachtsman Air Chief Marshal Brigadier/administrator
General/politician

Anthony Barrowclough | Baroness Prashar | Frank Wedekind
Herbert Marcuse

Rat - Cancer/Taurus

Academic chaplain cricketer theatre director
headmaster judge naval officer/yachtsman
politician saxophonist sociologist

Albert Ayler

Rat - Cancer/Gemini

Accountant/boss (2) administrator boss racing driver
forester/ornithologist haematologist photographer politician (3)
politician/diplomat singer writer (2)

Louis Mountbatten | Nathaniel Hawthorne | René Arnoux

Rat - Cancer/Cancer

Actor (3) actress economist (2) academic/economist founder journalist/author mountaineer singer singer/songwriter

Duffy | Kris Kristofferson | Prof Michael Beesley | F S Smythe

Rat - Cancer/Leo

Academic (2) academic/cellist actor/singer/songwriter artist aviator/writer conductor civil servant footballer headmistress librarian theatrical producer/theatrical agent

Antoine de Saint-Exupéry | Robert King | Kris Kristofferson

Rat - Cancer/Virgo

Academic (2) academic/musicologist boss/publisher/dealer broadcaster (2) broadcaster/author boss/engineer Canon cartoonist cellist costume designer drummer/bandleader engineer chief fire inspector metallurgist politician (3) politician/barrister

Emma Porteous

Rat - Cancer/Libra

Academic actor architect civil servant conservationist cricketer sound designer diplomat racing driver engineer folklorist geologist chief monuments inspector journalist/astrologer/graphologer mathematician musician/songwriter paediatrician politician skier

Alan Turing | Antonio Gaudi | John Inman | Garry Sobers
Bernd Arnulf Mertz | Ben Burtt | Vince Clarke | Perrine Pelen

Rat - Cancer/Scorpio

Biographer/journalist broadcaster footballer novelist (2) painter
surgeon violinist writer Maj-Gen/boss

Mary Wesley | Brian Yale | Zinedine Zidane | Pinchas Zukerman

Rat - Cancer/Sagittarius

Actor actuary anatomist boss (2) boxer
conductor cricketer dancer diplomat journalist
magistrate painter poet scholar/teacher Air Chief Marshal

Dennis Lillee | Gerald Norden | Richard Owen | Wayne Sleep

Rat - Cancer/Capricorn

Actress author bishop cyclist
economist (polit) educationist Classics master novelist (2)
neuro surgeon painter politician (leader) squash player principal
singer(2) singer/songwriter/guitarist teacher college warden
writer/cartoonist

Robbie McEwen | Margot Gordon | Raymond Chandler

Rat - Cancer/Aquarius

Academic/Vice Chancellor (2) boss comedian footballer
headmaster politician priest singer/songwriter/educator
sportswoman surgeon writer

Dave Allen | Kate Cruise O'Brien | Cat Stevens

Rat - Cancer/Pisces

Academic/surgeon academic (2) actress (2) actor
boss (2) (charity) boss (nurse) editor gastroenterologist judge (2)
mogul (movie) musician novelist surgeon Maj-Gen

Kathy Bates I Brian Hitchen I Louis Burt Mayer

Rat - Leo/Aries

Actor (2) author Commissioner (church) engine designer dramatist
editor golfer novelist painter philosopher poet
saxophonist singer statesman

Antonio Banderas I Wilfrid Scawen Blunt I Roland Kirk I Baron Selwyn Lloyd
Kenny Perry I J M Pienkowski I Frank Wedekind

Rat - Leo/Taurus

Boss (2) boss (textiles) darts diplomat
environmentalist farmer neuro-psychiatrist psychologist
secretary singer (2) poet TV presenter
publisher Vice Admiral

Sir William Coats I Sarah Brightman I Arthur Janov I Phil Taylor

Rat - Leo/Gemini

Academic/lawyer boss (4) (chemicals) boss (insurance)
boss (medical services) boss (music) Bishop musical director
econometrician gardener politician (3) scientist soprano
Commander

Robert Holdstock

Rat - Leo/Cancer

Accountant, actor/film director, businessman
designer (stage), obstetrician/gynaecologist, philosopher, playwright
politician (2), singer, writer

Geri Halliwell | Sean Penn | Jean-Pierre Raffarin | Lord Weinstock

Rat - Leo/Leo

Academic/vet/neurophysiologist, accountant/boss, actress, architect
boss (2), chemis, IT consultant, stage designer, golfer
guitarist, impresario, journalist/author, mountaineer
politician, psychoanalyst, police, publisher, singer

Ben Hogan | Catherine Destivelle | Johnny Jones | Ismond Rosen
Barbara Flynn | S T Sweetman | Geri Halliwell | Ben Hogan

Rat - Leo/Virgo

Academic, actor (2), actress, Chief Constable, cook
cricketer, diplomat, founder, lawyer, politician
printer, rugby, tennis, wrestler, writer

Julia Child | Lawrence Dallaglio | Jo Durie | Robert Redford
Takanohana Kóji | Leon Uris | Greg Chappell

Rat - Leo/Libra

Academic (anaesthesia), actor/boss, basketballer, Bishop
businessman, chess master, cinematographer, commissioner (Guides)
dancer, footballer, headmaster, journalist, judge
politician, songwriter

Mikhail Botvinnik | Wilt Chamberlain | Mario Fazio | Carla Fracci

Rat - Leo/Scorpio

Actor broadcaster conductor/composer/musicologist
civil servant correspondent cricketer impresario journalist
judge obstetrician pioneer college principal swimmer
teacher

**Sir Garfield Sobers | John Logie Baird | Ben Affleck | Kenneth Kendall
Ryan Lochte**

Rat - Leo/Sagittarius

Academic (Japanese) administrator archaeologist architect
boss (retailing) ceramicist consultant cricketer editor
founder art historian philosopher politician publisher
singer (2) soldier tennis

**Gottlieb Duttweiler | Martin Jean-Jacques | Jean-François Lyotard
T E Lawrence**

Rat - Leo/Capricorn

Academic (3) academic/art historian biologist
bookmaker composer/violinist/conductor dancer fashion
designer diplomat mountaineer musician
politician (leader)/lawyer representative (quango) sociologist

Sir Richard Greenbury | Gene Kelly

Rat - Leo/Aquarius

Actor Archbishop author (2) boss (2) (cement)
boss (news) boxer friar glamour model
headmistress novelist playwright politician/academic
tennis producer (record)

**Raymond Chandler | Sir Christopher Hogg | Anne Ridler | Robert Bolt
David Duchovny**

Rat - Leo/Pisces

Academic/economist academic (2) acupuncturist architect artist author boss (2) diplomat drama critic footballer guitarist judge neuro-psychiatrist priest/physicist/theologian psychiatrist singer zoologist

Michael Coveney | Bobby Mitchell | Hamish Orr-Ewing | Prof Milton Friedman Robert Plant | Frank Richards | Robin Soderling | Colin Thoms

Rat - Virgo/Aries

Academic boss businessman composer fencer heptathlete matron physicist physiologist politician(3) politician (leader) tennis singer (2) surgeon wrestler

Frank Boidin | Rosemary Casals | Gwynfor Evans | Jeremy Irons Jean-Michel Jarre | Great Khali | Denise Lewis

Rat - Virgo/Taurus

Actress (4) actor ambassador architect author theatre director engineer headmaster historian judge lawyer novelist pianist medical researcher singer (3) equestrian trainer racehorse trainer trade unionist/nurse ventriloquist

Lauren Bacall | Amy Black | Cameron Diaz | Colin Firth | Hugh Grant Keith Harris | Katie Melua | Capt Mark Phillips

Rat - Virgo/Gemini

Academic/econometrician adviser (to PM) boss civil servant clerk composer editorial director musician historian/boss (galleries) journalist judge singer/songwriter/guitarist college warden writer Vice Admiral Air Chief Marshal

Carol Bartz | Buddy Holly | Collin Wilcox | John Cage

Rat - Virgo/Cancer

Architect boss (3) boss (electric) businessman climber
composer defence consultant fashion designer politician (2) footballer
novelist publisher trade unionist/politician/historian writer

Glen Johnson | George Richardson | Charles Stanford

Rat - Virgo/Leo

Academic/mathematician/economist astronomer author
boss (museum) advertising director driver (racing)
geographer/explorer harpist mathematician politician
scientist/author singer

Herbert Henry Asquith | Damon Hill | S Radharkrishnan

Rat - Virgo/Virgo

Academic (2) academic/physician actor(2) architect
author boss (2) baseballer diplomat/civil servant
doctor/biochemist politician (leader) priest singer/actress retailer
teacher (dance) tennis hymn writer

Ira Sankey | James Scullin | Count Leo Tolstoy

Rat - Virgo/Libra

Academic (2) academic/geratologist astronomer actress
boss (licence) boss (2) cartoonist financier judge
lawyer (2) newscaster photographer/artist politician
saxophonist/composer/bandleader singer

Horace Babcock | Peter Clarke | Jennifer Dickson | Richard Gaskell
Natasha Kaplinsky | Simon Marks (M&S) | Eduard Möricke

Rat - Virgo/Scorpio

Actor (2) actress financial adviser impresario lawyer lecturer
missionary novelist (2) novelist/playwright pharmacist poet
writer

Dame Antonia Byatt | Emma Samms | Giovanni Verga

Rat - Virgo/Sagittarius

Actress cardiologist matron painter philosopher
politician (5) politician (leader) singer solicitor
racehorse trainer

Dr Raphael Balcon | Judy Geeson | John Martyn | Maurice Chevalier
Urho Kekkonen | Arnold Toynbee

Rat - Virgo/Capricorn

Baseballer boss/industrialist/metallurgist US footballer judge
politician (2) poet/singer/lawyer psychologist
singer/guitarist trade unionist

John McCain | Sir Ian MacGregor | Elsie Osborne

Rat - Virgo/Aquarius

Academic boss (2) Vice-Chancellor engineer founder
guitarist hockey ice hockey metallurgist
novelist/playwright scientist speed skater tennis Capt

W O Bentley

Rat - Virgo/Pisces

Archbishop academic (music) boss (4) boss (broadcasting)
composer (2) diplomat (2) drummer lawyer
novelist intelligence officer photographer physicist

Maurice Jarre | Terence Donovan | Kenny Jones | Dr Andrew S Grove
James Hilton

Rat - Libra/Aries

Actress (2)/dancer actress architect (2) theatre designer diplomat
footballer headmaster pianist

Duncan Edwards | Margot Kidder | Geoffrey Jellicoe

Rat - Libra/Taurus

Academic (archaeology)/writer actress baritone
boss/industrialist cartoonist chemist composer engineer
golfer novelist/scriptwriter novelist (2) politician

Laura Davies | Lee Iacocca | Elinor Glyn | William Ramsay | Bob Kane

Rat - Libra/Gemini

Academic actress (2) Bishop burlesque artist cricketer
educationist poet pathologist/reformer/lecturer
pharmacist politician (leader)/playwright Lieut-Col

Václav Havel | T S Eliot | Gwyneth Paltrow | Dita von Teese

Rat - Libra/Cancer

Academic (4) actress banker Bishop
boss (4) boss (insurance) boss (TV) film director/film producer
economist/writer originator priest rugby trade unionist
Admiral

Ernest Swinton | Olivia Newton-John | Sumantra Ghoshal
Michele Dotrice | Gerry J Robinson

Rat - Libra/Leo

Academic/philosopher actress (2) agriculturalist artist athlete
chemist theatre director film editor footballer historian
journalist (2) journalist/commentator judge (2)
musician/curator (instruments) painter politician (2) TV presenter
college principal publisher skier sportswoman
racehorse trainer Air Marshal

Odilon Redon | Ray Clemence | Norman Ayrton | Judith Chalmers
Steve Cram | Lindsey Vonn

Rat - Libra/Virgo

Academic (molecular medicine)/biologist actor (3)
actress/singer adviser martial artist/actor author boss (2)
boss (pests) cricketer historian judge pianist/broadcaster
poet Colonel/astronaut Colonel/pilot/cartoonist

Shakti Gawain | Miguel de Unamuno | Michael Gooley

Rat - Libra/Libra

Academic (2) academic/scientist (polymer) bookseller cricketer
fashion designer footballer headmistress pharmacist
poet/sociologist politician music writer writer
Air Vice Marshal

Ian MacDonald | Donna Karan | Trevor Brooking | Steve Cram
Truman Capote

Rat - Libra/Scorpio

Actor banker boss (intelligence) composer impresario
monk nephrologist singer (2) singer/musician

Avril Lavigne

Rat - Libra/Sagittarius

Academic/archaeologist boss (2) businesswoman
race horse trainer interpreter chief Ombudsman politician (2)
scientist (boss) Brigadier

Urho Kekkonen | Gerry Adams

Rat - Libra/Capricorn

Academic (3) academic (Greek) boss (2) boss (tribunals)
actress/dancer coroner cricketer/teacher explorer guitarist
judge tea master psychiatrist rapper teacher
tenor trade unionist writer (2)/dramatist General

Victor Serebriakoff | Thomas C Wolfe | Kate Losinska | Jackson Browne
Juliet Prowse | Lil Wayne

Rat - Libra/Aquarius

Academic boss/accountant boss (2) coroner
broadcaster/author ice hockey TV presenter (2) singer (3)
singer/guitarist tenor writer

Rick Parfitt | Katherine Mansfield | Eminem | Georg Solti
Gordon Honeycombe

Rat - Libra/Pisces

Boss (3) boss (orchestra)/conductor dancer/choreographer/boss musician photographer politician (2) politician (leader)/entrepreneur rapper

Pras | Heinrich Himmler | Silvio Berlusconi

Rat - Scorpio/Aries

Academic athlete baseballer civil servant rugby coach composer conductor Chief Constable rugby/cricketer/rugby journalist poet politician film/TV producer rugby (2) scientist trade unionist violinist Colonel

Carl Davies | Nigel Dempster | John Pullin | Said Ouita | Anne Bolt

Rat - Scorpio/Taurus

Athlete Bishop boss (2) comedienne composer economist painter politician (leader) specialist researcher singer yachtsman/writer Colonel

Gordon Beningfield | Conlon Nancarrow | Col Paul Rivière | Steve Smith Oliver Tambo | Se7en

Rat - Scorpio/Gemini

Academic (cancer) author chess player civil servant (2) QC civil servant archaeologist/author novelist politician sculptor surveyor Rear Admiral explorer/aviator

Richard E Byrd | Auguste Rodin | Prince Charles | Jose Raul Capablanca Margaret Mitchell

Rat - Scorpio/Cancer

Academic (medicine)/pioneer (heart disease) actor boss
businessman engineer/inventor (Rotomatic) journalist painter
rugby saxophonist sculptor tennis

Claude Monet | Stanley Hiller Jr

Rat - Scorpio/Leo

Athlete bacteriologist bandmaster boss
composer/pianist dictator editor (2) engineer
musician/editor/writer physicist singer

Joseph Swan | Cristina Odone | Alfredo Stroessner | Hideyo Noguchi
Baron Aaron Copland

Rat - Scorpio/Virgo

Academic actress boss geneticist playwright
politician (2) rugby sculptor soprano writer
Air Commandant

Akio Makigawa | Mary Travers

Rat - Scorpio/Libra

Actor adviser (population) boss (music school)
businessman choreographer composer footballer politician

Krzysztof Penderecki | Luis Figo

Rat - Scorpio/Scorpio

Academic (Slavonic) actress author broadcaster
businessman drag performer singer/gardener poet sculptor
skater surgeon

Monica Edwards | Sasha Cohen | Zbigniew Herbert | Jonathan Ross
RuPaul | Kim Wilde | Bill Woodrow

Rat - Scorpio/Sagittarius

Academic (3) ballerina boss consultant
histopathologist painter physician politician
computer scientist/author (2) singer writer

Kelly Osbourne | Lulu | C V Raman

Rat - Scorpio/Capricorn

Academic/Vice Chancellor banker boss Colonel
lyricist/composer physicist trumpeter writer
Brigadier/farmer

Maurice Roche

Rat - Scorpio/Aquarius

Boss coach (football) guitarist (2) historian judge
musician/teacher poet/storyteller racehorse trainer
Air Vice Marshal Rear Admiral/naval engineer

John Horder | Peter Liddle

Rat - Scorpio/Pisces

Academic (2)/violinist academic (medicine)/scientist actress (2)
actor/writer biologist boss (army) footballer
guru/orator/philosopher historian/Rabbi musician Air Marshal

Sai Baba | Prof György Pauk | Lady Baden-Powell | Diego Maradona

Rat - Sagittarius/Aries

Barrister fashion designer economist gynaecologist headmaster
organist physiologist politician radiologist Air Marshal

Dr M A N L Soares | John Galliano

Rat - Sagittarius/Taurus

Boss (2) management coach commentator dramatist racing driver footballer linguist/ethnomusicologist pathologist philosopher politician (leader) politician (2) QC novelist Air Commandant

Abraham Viktor Rydberg | Gary Lineker | Raul Boesel

Rat - Sagittarius/Gemini

Actress (5) bassist boss kick boxer drummer heptathlete ice hockey musician playwright

Julianne Moore | Daryl Hannah | Alyssa Milano

Rat - Sagittarius/Cancer

Activist/trade unionist basketballer bassist canoeist/physiologist comedian golfer impresario landowner/politician mayor/lawyer pioneer (child care)/politician racehorse breeder vocalist walker General

Ed Koch | Harpo Marx

Rat - Sagittarius/Leo

Badminton financial analyst/investor civil servant management coach model musician politician (4) politician (leader) college principal TV reporter racehorse trainer

Briton Rivière | Franklin Pierce | Benjamin Disraeli

Rat - Sagittarius/Virgo

Actor (2) actor/film director President's aide artist headmaster fashion designer magazine editor politician writer racehorse trainer

Samuel L Jackson | Kenneth Branagh | John Ehrlichman

Rat - Sagittarius/Libra

Actor boss (2) (orchestra) boss (art) comedian engineer painter theatrical producer shipping solicitor writer Brigadier/boss (nursing)

David Carradine | Jimmy Jewel | Henri Toulouse-Lautrec | Ernst von Siemens

Rat - Sagittarius/Scorpio

Actress (2) boss editor/conservationist footballer Lord Lieut/councillor shipping magnate college mistress/mathematician sculptor

Pat van den Hauwe | Scarlett Johansson | Lord Rotherwick

Rat - Sagittarius/Sagittarius

Artist (2) artist/sculptor ballerina baseballer Bishop/theologian cricketer cyclist economist politician/press secretary/researcher

Geoffrey Clarke | Patricia Hewitt

Rat - Sagittarius/Capricorn

Academic actress (2) actor artist boss (2) boss (music) comedian architect High Commissioner historian politician reporter vocalist General

Maxwell Hutchinson | Ozzy Osbourne | Edward Stourton

Rat - Sagittarius/Aquarius

Actor (3) actress boss boxer broadcaster businessman composer (2) musical director/composer racing driver editor physicist politician (2) merchant seaman typographer/writer/teacher Major Maj-Gen General

Henri Becquerel | Manuel de Falla | Keke Rosberg | Tommy Steele Gen Alexander Haig | Deanna Durbin

Rat - Sagittarius/Pisces

Academic (2)/historian accountant author boss (3)
boss (trust) boss/accountant editor
politician (leader)/economist/academic

Rat - Capricorn/Aries

Actor (2)/manager actress astrologer boss (2)
dictator/politician diplomat editor politician (3)
politician (leader) silversmith/goldsmith/designer Commander/pilot

Idi Amin Dada I Steven Forrest

Rat - Capricorn/Taurus

Actor (5)/film producer/martial artist 3-actress baseballer
boss (newspaper) boxer cricketer dancer/teacher
entrepreneur headmaster ice hockey mathematician/code breaker
ship owner politician/QC film producer (2) warlord

James Caan I George Foreman I Linda Lovelace

Rat - Capricorn/Gemini

Actor ceramic artist author (2) cellist/conductor/composer
circus director engineer guide (religious) journalist/playwright
magistrate (boss) medical officer test pilot playwright
pool player writer zoologist

Haruki Murakami I John Delorean

Rat - Capricorn/Cancer

Actor artist Bishop boss (2)
boss (TV)/actress climber racing driver novelist sculptor
singer

Lewis Hamilton I Lee van Cleef

Rat - Capricorn/Leo

Academic (2) academic (elect engineering) astrologer cantor
cartoonist footballer historian (2) industrialist

Baron Arthur Rank | Noel Tyl | Lynn Hill | Charles Addams

Rat - Capricorn/Virgo

Political agent athlete civil servant/diplomat cyclist designer
racing driver historian researcher singer (2) writer (2)

Philippe Starck | Yukio Mishima | Eddie Cheever

Rat - Capricorn/Libra

Academic actor/film producer actress (2) barrister boss
civil servant cricketer metallurgist politician singer
tennis Air Marshal

Pat Rafter | Jude Law

Rat - Capricorn/Scorpio

Academic/scientist (chemistry) actress boss (2) actor
andrologist geographer transport consultant novelist
screenwriter Air Marshal

Gerard Dépardieu | Ian La Frenais | Fulgencio Batista y Zaldivar
Alexander Keith Johnston

Rat - Capricorn/Sagittarius

Academic (classics) actress civil servant college principal
composer Dean (religious) diplomat historian (2)
historian mountaineer painter printmaker politician
Brigadier/matron General/dictator

Robert Hall

Rat - Capricorn/Capricorn

Academic (2)/economist | academic/composer/conductor | actress (2)
ambassador | bandleader | cartoonist/businessman | cricketer
headmaster | organist | IQ test pioneer | singer | writer
Maj-Gen/physician

Donna Summer | Shirley Eaton | Keith Dawson | Lewis Terman
Loretta Young

Rat - Capricorn/Aquarius

Actress | boss (2) | farmer | footballer
mathematician | photographer | politician (3) | politician (leader) | QC
college principal | poet

Hilary Heilbron | Earl of Drogheda | Richard M Nixon | Gustáv Husák
Peter Beardsley

Rat - Capricorn/Pisces

Author | boss (3) | broadcaster | fashion designer
politician (2) | prison governor | scientist | singer | surgeon | witch

Margaret Marshall | Filippo Marinetti | Carol Vorderman
Doreen Valiente

Rat - Aquarius/Aries

Actor/film director | architect | racing driver | golfer
musicologist/composer | pianist | politician (2) | college principal
rower | trade unionist

Alan Alda | Malcolm Binns | Lord Bill Jordan

Rat - Aquarius/Taurus

Academic (2)/college principal actress ambassador author (2)
boss (bank)/politician critic/teacher/poet drummer engineer
historian show jumper singer statesman tennis
treasurer writer General

Natassja Kinski | Hjalmar Schacht | Adlai Stevenson | Clark Tracey
Edwad 'Budge' Patty

Rat - Aquarius/Gemini

Academic (2) academic/psychiatrist actress architect
author chaplain conductor cricketer film director/designer/painter
headmaster hockey (ice) model phrenologist politician/QC

Sinead Cusack | Wayne Gretzky

Rat - Aquarius/Cancer

Ambassador architect/theorist boss judge nurse
poet/journalist politician violinist writer
Maj-Gen/boss (Household) Capt

A B (Banjo) Paterson

Rat - Aquarius/Leo

Actor (2) actress archivist astronaut
headmaster ice hockey judge scholar (Byron)
businessman politician footballer golfer (2)

Lee Marvin | Lana Turner

Rat - Aquarius/Virgo

Academic/theologian actor (2) actress/dancer/ballerina
boss (2) (museum)/curator boss (retail) composer film composer
musician/writer/educationist painter politician Vice Admiral

Rat - Aquarius/Libra

Actor psychic healer boss (2) headmaster journalist
lawyer host (TV/radio) singer surgeon surveyor
umpire (cricket) sculptor author

Don Everly | Burt Reynolds

Rat - Aquarius/Scorpio

Academic/U principal actress chemist politician
designer/animator/producer singer (3)
drummer/multi-instrumentalist gardener/broadcaster
singer/guitarist singer/songwriter

Holly Johnson | Vince Neil | Percy Thrower | Joan Walley

Rat - Aquarius/Sagittarius

Academic boss designer engineer
financier/investor lawyer test pilot poet
Air Marshal

Jean Auel | Georges Simenon

Rat - Aquarius/Capricorn

Actress boss (radio/TV) cinematographer diplomat (2) civil rights
activist editor engineer politician lawyer
poet/dramatist writer (2)/broadcaster writer

Ronald Eastman | Jenny Greene | Peter Jay | Rosa Parks

Rat - Aquarius/Aquarius

Academic/writer/historian actor auctioneer baseballer
Chief Constable historian hockey judge fashion
model saxophonist publisher singer/composer violinist
Wing Commander

Sean Kerly

Rat - Aquarius/Pisces

Academic (2) actress boss architect composer
footballer humorist inventor (auto m/c gun, cordite)
mathematician neurologist aviation pioneer pioneer (pneumatic tyre) (2)
psychoanalyst/author teacher/activist trombonist

G U 'Scotty' Allan | Leon Alberti | John Boyd Dunlop | Ian Murray

Rat - Pisces/Aries

Composer/violinist diplomat theatre director/producer Maj-Gen
pianist bass player pilot (fighter) politician
singer writer (self help)/speaker

Virginia Bottomley | Johann Strauss the Elder

Rat - Pisces/Taurus

Actor (2) actor/writer/comedian anthropologist baseballer
boss (industrials) correspondent dramatist historian
photojournalist/photographer physician psychiatrist lawyer
Pope QC Air Vice Marshal

Billy Crystal | Gavin Stamp | Henrik Ibsen | Pope Pius XII

Rat - Pisces/Gemini

Accountant academic (history) astronomer boss (6)
conductor founder (dance company)/ballerina judge physician
pioneer (computing)/designer/mathematician political scientist rower

Dame Marie Rambert | Greg Searle

Rat - Pisces/Cancer

Author baseballer basketballer/coach boss (2) boss (TV)
composer engineer swimmer Admiral/industrial consultant

John Tusa

Rat - Pisces/Leo

Actress boss boss (pharma) diplomat
theatre director racing driver founder politician (2)
politician (leader) college principal secretary (press) Brigadier/Lord Lieut

Dennis Waterman | Lord Melchett | Canaan Banana | Jim Clark

Rat - Pisces/Virgo

Academic (applied maths) actress bassist biochemist
boss (2)/conservationist charity worker diplomat judge
QC tenor painter pharmacologist writer
Rear Admiral Maj-Gen

Takashi Ishihara Robert Mugabe

Rat - Pisces/Libra

Actress/singer/author (2) astrophysicist boss (3) editor
footballer parachutist/gymnast painter physicist playwright
politician surgeon writer/photographer Admiral

Steven Chiu | Daren Anderton | Klaus von Bismarck

Rat - Pisces/Scorpio

Academic (4) academic/biologist academic/botanist actress
banker boss (TV) painter spectroscopist rector show jumper

Noboru Takeshita

Rat - Pisces/Sagittarius

Banker boss (3) (charity) boss(TV) boss (quango)
2-civil servant composer(2) cyclist drummer/composer
film director judge physiologist politician (leader) school principal

Heinrich Haussler

Rat - Pisces/Capricorn

Academic/astronomer archaeologist astronaut bassist cartoonist
dramatist/poet prison governor industrialist judge
pioneer (submarine) politician psychiatrist singer

Prof Alexander Boksenberg | Edgar Bowers | J P Holland | Shakin Stevens

Rat - Pisces/Aquarius

Actor (2) actress academic (2) academic author
boss (HR) designer (fashion) guitarist judge musician
poet politician Rabbi

Gyles Brandreth | Dr Jonathan Sacks | Ursula Andress

Rat - Pisces/Pisces

Academic (3) academic/physiologist actor editor
footballer musician (3) /singer/songwriter musician/songwriter
politician (2) politician (leader) singer/radio host tennis traveller

Prof Enid Mumford

Ox - Aries/Aries

Actress broadcaster founder (party)/politician illusionist
jockey (2) lecturer/musicologist politician (2) producer (TV comedy)
psychoanalyst QC/politician/judge saxophonist scholar/translator
racehorse trainer/jockey

Jill Gascoigne I Michael Brecker I Pauline Marois I Sue Cook I David Blaine

Ox - Aries/Taurus

Actor artist boss/ businessman fashion designer
diplomat footballer painter
philosopher/dramatist/scientist solicitor storyteller

Edward Fox I Hans Christian Andersen I Bella Freud

Ox - Aries/Gemini

Academic/anthropologist actor historian newscaster
pentathlete physician politician trade unionist

Earl Russell I Richard Phelps

Ox - Aries/Cancer

Academic accountant actor author boss (2)
conductor consultant/engineer cricketer poet politician
potter proprietor/founder (bridge club)/journalist racehorse trainer
Air Vice Marshal

Gabriela Mistral I Adrian Boult I Sir Henry Peat

Ox - Aries/Leo

Academic boxer fashion designer flying instructor
industrialist politician (4) politician (leader) priest
restaurateur rugby singer

Ellery Hanley | Lord Aberconway | Antonio Carluccio | Andre Giraud
William Hague | Anthony Wedgewood Benn | Teddy Taylor

Ox - Aries/Virgo

Academic (2) academic (photography) accountant baritone boss
campaigner civil servant dancer textile designer engineer
expert judge librarian musician/ keyboarder/ trombonist
college principal singer writer

Dorothy Fosdick | Leona Lewis

Ox - Aries/Libra

Actress author (2)/journalist boss footballer golfer
guitarist pianist hairdresser politician
singer (3) singer/songwriter singer/drummer figure skater trade
unionist writer (2) Captain

Susan Boyle | Tom Jackson

Ox - Aries/Scorpio

Actor (2) actor/comedian astrologer boss (3) diplomat
mathematician soprano civil rights activist

Warren Beatty | Charlie Chaplin | Linda Goodman | Eiddwen Harrhy
Ian MacLaurin | Eddie Murphy

Ox - Aries/Sagittarius

Academic boss (2) boss (engineering)/inventor
broadcaster designer impressionist singer (2)/entertainer
soprano surgeon racehorse trainer

Rory Bremner | William Gaunt | Vincent van Gogh | Elihu Thomson | Tiny Tim

Ox - Aries/Capricorn

Academic actor (2) boss designer diplomat
painter trade unionist politician singer (2) wrestler

Paloma Picasso | Jessica Lange | William Gaunt | Eddie Fatu | Jack Jones
Hyman Bloom | Rod Steiger

Ox - Aries/Aquarius

Academic/principal/metallurgist academic (2) actress Bishop
boss (3) diplomat golfer lawyer
metallurgist (2) theatre producer Capt/chief matron General/politician

Angela Bonallack | Gen Colin Powell

Ox - Aries/Pisces

Academic accountant actor artist/humorist/musician
author boss broadcaster/writer judge priest singer

Gerard Hoffnung | F H Tate | Muddy Waters | Valerie Singleton

Ox - Taurus/Aries

Academic (3)/historian academic/boss (health body) academic/chemist
actor author boss (US Muslims) dictator/politician
politician (2) tycoon (oil)/explorer Maj-General Air Marshal

Malcolm Little (Malcolm X) | Antonio d'Oliveira Salazar

Ox - Taurus/Taurus

Academic/political scientist
actor (2)/film director
actress
basketballer
boss (2) (museum)
boss/founder
businessman/farmer
coach (ice hockey)
commissioner/bursar
politician
steward (Jockey Club)
writer/journalist

Ox - Taurus/Gemini

Actor
artist
Bishop
boss (shipping)
comedian
cyclist
engineer
horticulturist/broadcaster
impresario
singer
trade unionist
wrestler
writer/broadcaster

Enya | Dr Miriam Stoppard | Alan Titchmarsh

Ox - Taurus/Cancer

Actor/ screenwriter/ composer
boss/accountant
boss (3)
boss/economist
chef/TV presenter
golfer
headmaster
inventor
physician/neuroscientist/author/academic
politician
typographer

Trevor Baylis | Ken Hom | Peter Oosterhuis | Alan Titchmarsh

Ox - Taurus/Leo

Academic (engineering)
actress
footballer
actor(2)/director
hairdresser
politician (2)
politician (leader)
2-singer

Madeleine Albright | M S Rattan

Ox - Taurus/Virgo

Actor (2)
actor/director/producer
ambassador
banker/writer
boss (defence)
dancer
boss (4)
boss/consultant
composer/arranger
diplomat
headmaster
singer/songwriter

Fred Astaire | Sir William Batty | Jack Nicholson | George Takei

Ox - Taurus/Libra

Archdeacon author boss (2) boss (food)
engineer/inventor magician/actor musician/clarinettist pistol shooter singer

Natalie Appleton | Franck Dumoulin | Billy Joel

Ox - Taurus/Scorpio

Archbishop/Primate boss (retail clothes) farmer inventor/researcher
judge neurologist photographer politician (leader) (2)
politician (leader)/lawyer

Alphonse Bertillon | Sanjiva Reddy

Ox - Taurus/Sagittarius

Academic/architect actress boss (2) (council) boss (analysis) conductor
cricketer poet politician (leader) writer

'Tich' Freeman | Saddam Hussein Zöe Wanamaker

Ox - Taurus/Capricorn

Academic/geologist actor/director/screenwriter actress (2)
archaeologist boss (3) (association) boss (electronics) boxer
golfer rugby Vice Admiral/engineer
General/chief of police

George Clooney | Una Stubbs | Lee Westwood

Ox - Taurus/Aquarius

Actress boss/publisher baritone composer broadcaster
creator (books) editor jewellery designer philosopher politician (3)
TV presenter

Charles Warrell | Stafford Cripps | Paul Heiney | Jessica Lange
Rick Wakeman | Stephen Varcoe

Ox - Taurus/Pisces

Actor/boss (2) boss (TV) Canon editor educator
novelist pioneer (cybernetics) potter gospel singer(2) soprano

Ludwig Wittgenstein | Andrew Neil | Rosalind Plowright

Ox - Gemini/Aries

Architect boss (2) broadcaster couturier editor
3 day eventer judge naval officer rugby singer/songwriter
solicitor

Lionel Richie | Mary Thompson | Richard Baker

Ox - Gemini/Taurus

Academic/biologist/conservationist archaeologist aviator (2) actor
comedian composer builders' merchant politician publisher
singer writer/historian Commander/aviator

Michael J Fox | Nadine Coyle

Ox - Gemini/Gemini

Author boss bowler comedian sculptor/priest politician (2)
politician/businessman tennis trade unionist

Ian Spurling | Robert Crow

Ox - Gemini/Cancer

Actress boss (3) comedian theatrical director linguist
mariner pathologist politician singer racehorse trainer

Boy George | Geronimo | C K Ogden

Ox - Gemini/Leo

Administrator (artistic) comic book artist literary agent astronomer/ broadcaster (2) author/broadcaster boss/diplomat editor pioneer gynaecologist singer

Alison Moyet I Patrick Steptoe

Ox - Gemini/Virgo

Academic/chemist boss (electricity) comedian/author conductor/composer dancer/teacher editor expert (tax) farmer GP painter politician (2) mountaineer reporter/publisher mezzo-soprano

V F Desvignes I John Millais

Ox - Gemini/Libra

Academic/ (2) academic/writer actor (2) Archbishop artist/teacher author boxer ballet designer journalist painter politician QC 2-vet Vice Admiral

Tony Curtis I King George V I Ken Follett I Luis Rodriguez

Ox - Gemini/Scorpio

Boss (2) boss (newspapers) businessman college principal dancer headmaster/administrator/educationist musician/composer philosopher/writer politician Reverend singer

Isadora Duncan I André Glucksmann

Ox - Gemini/Sagittarius

Academic/philologist boss accountant boss (2) cricketer journalist lyricist politician sculptor tenor trombonist

Ox - Gemini/Capricorn

Administrator boss (3) (broadcasting) boss (petroleum)
boss (NHS) entrepreneur pilot politician (2) skier
show jumper Air Commodore

Dominique Gisin

Ox - Gemini/Aquarius

Actor (2) architect Bishop boss (foods) dramatist
drummer novelist/essayist politician (2) politician (leader) singer
Lieut-Col/surgeon

Simon Callow | Sukarno | W B Yeats

Ox - Gemini/Pisces

Boss (3) consultant/bookseller composer judge novelist
painter/textile designer restaurateur teacher
Vice-Chancellor (court)

David Gestetner | Frederick (Fritz) Loewe | Colleen McCullough

Ox - Cancer/Aries

Academic/scientist actress authoress boss racing driver
high master engineer judge politician revolutionary
trade unionist

Elspeth Thomas | Dame Barbara Cartland

Ox - Cancer/Taurus

Actress (2) boss (2) /accountant 2-boss/engineer judge playwright
poet politician novelist/Reverend

Lindsay Wagner | Meryl Streep | Tom Stoppard

Ox - Cancer/Gemini

Academic	boss (tax)	designer fashion	cricketer	chaplain
civil servant	college principal	historian	lens designer	judge
politician	pianist/conductor	racing driver	worker (social)	writer
Rear Admiral	General			

Betty Jackson | Henry Thoreau | Michael Kidger | Vladimir Ashkenazy

Ox - Cancer/Cancer

Actress	boss (shipping)	boss (stats)	statesman (2)/financier
conductor/musicologist	novelist	pioneer	nuclear scientist
politician	tennis	college warden	Vice Admiral

Anders Jarryd | Cecil Rhodes

Ox - Cancer/Leo

Ambassador	architect	artist	bedchamber lady
boss (trust)	comedian	art dealer	diplomat
editor/gastronome	journalist	physicist	politician
producer (theatre)	surgeon	General/engineer	

David Hockney | Peter Kay

Ox - Cancer/Virgo

Academic (4)/philosopher	academic	obstetrician	academic/boss
academic/theologian	actor	artist	boss (publisher)
curator/archivist	drama critic	dramatist	prison governor
headmaster	art historian	industrialist	oncologist
politician	Recorder		

Lionel Jospin | Edward Schofield

Ox - Cancer/Libra

Actress activist boss (3) painter
poet/novelist/film director scholar/archaeologist/educator soprano
tennis Commander Maj-Gen

Jean Cocteau | John Gilbert | Malala Yousafzai

Ox - Cancer/Scorpio

Academic businessman civil servant comedian/author
designer politician (leader) 2-singer/songwriter activist/salesman

Ricky Gervais

Ox - Cancer/Sagittarius

QC academic (3) academic/cardiologist architect boss (2)
novelist (2) judge politician (2) rugby singer
writer

George Hamilton IV | Gerald Ford

Ox - Cancer/Capricorn

Academic (immunology) astrologer administrator boss (3)
boss/botanist comic actor ballerina textile designer engineer
Lord-Lieut/farmer footballer museum keeper novelist
politician (2) singer writer/consultant (PR)

Sunil Gavaskar | Keizo Obuchi | Joseph Hooker | Lady Hilda Swan

Ox - Cancer/Aquarius

Academic/biologist art consultant astronaut athlete boss
cricketer cyclist economist/anthropologist novelist
politician (2) politician/journalist singer/broadcaster

Carl Lewis | Princess Diana | Sheila McCarthy

Ox - Cancer/Pisces

Boss (2) (airport) boss (TV co)/ civil servant broadcaster
consultant (Br art) film director headmistress physician/hypnotist
poet/novelist (2) skier/race organiser writer Major/ saboteur

Cyril Fletcher | Earl Stanley Gardner | Hermann Hesse | Vittorio De Sica

Ox - Leo/Aries

Academic/ educationist boss composer diplomat film maker
musician/trumpeter physicist politician secretary
songwriter/guitarist Brigadier

Mark Knopfler | Louis Armstrong

Ox - Leo/Taurus

Accountant boss (race course) boxer
dancer/ choreographer entrepreneur HM Inspector/management consultant
inventor/physicist politician (3) politician (leader) General

Barack Obama | Jeremy James | Ernest Lawrence | Nikolai Valuev
Sergey Brin

Ox - Leo/Gemini

Actor/director Bishop comedienne boss/investor
editor/compiler engineer consultant/designer (2) Reiki founder
Gestapo officer/shop owner Orientalist poet writer/illustrator

Nicola Bayley | Kristen Wiig | Norris & Ross McWhirter | Mikao UsuiDame
Mary Gilmore

Ox - Leo/Cancer

Actor (2) actress boss tennis coach/tennis
composer (2) dancer diplomat drummer jockey
politician (leader) Air Vice Marshal

Walter Swinburn

Ox - Leo/Leo

Actor (3) actress boss (3)/catalogue) boss (water)
journalist (music)/Dylanologist engineer psychologist/hypnotist
shot putter singer/songwriter writer

**Geoff Capes | Shelley Long | Rick Springfield | Helen Wambach
Barbara Windsor**

Ox - Leo/Virgo

Academic (architecture)/scientist actor (2) actress athlete
boss (2) cricketer historian/politician music writer/broadcaster
orator reporter (investigative)

Dustin Hoffman | Prof Henning Larsen

Ox - Leo/Libra

Academic (polymer) 2-actress boss (2) (bank)
boss (newspaper) boxer/trainer/manager dean/cathedral minister
industrialist college master philosopher poet politician

Anna Massey | Telman Ter-Petrossian | Honor Blackman

Ox - Leo/Scorpio

Academic arbitrator/scholar (industrial relations) boss/publisher composer
TV journalist judge obstetrician poet/prostitute runner
writer/editor

Ox - Leo/Sagittarius

Boss (council/quango) TV controller church minister (2)
engineer 2-footballer judge/barrister singer writer

Ernst Jandl

Ox - Leo/Capricorn

Academic/economist actor/comedian (2) author/comedian
boss (3) boss (electronics) broadcaster law
consultant editor engineer wood engraver poet
politician (3)/broadcaster snooker

**Matthew Parris | Walid Joumblatt | William Rushton | Fred Davis
Richard Ingrams | Gary Mabbutt | Archbishop Makarios III | Alan Whicker
Joseph Locke**

Ox - Leo/Aquarius

Architect academic/surgeon Archbishop boss
businessman industrialist diplomat engineer
photographer politician (3) politician/dissident TV press officer
wrestler Air Vice Marshal Colonel

**Prof Simon Domberger | Donald Dewar | Menachem Begin | Harry Smith
Aleksandur Staliiski**

Ox - Leo/Pisces

Academic/QC actress artist bassist Bishop
boss (2) boss (museum) dancer golf architect/correspondent
painter politician property developer songwriter

Sir Michael Foot | C R W Nevinson | D MacLennan | A Steel | A K Glazunov

Ox - Virgo/Aries

Bishop boss (2) boss (airports) businessman/mgr
coach (basketballer) footballer industrialist illustrator/caricaturist
journalist/dog breeder lawyer motoring pioneer painter
politician surgeon writer

Roger Uttley | C S Rolls | Fabio Cannavaro

Ox - Virgo/Taurus

Actor boss designer discus journalist
physicist rugby singer solicitor

Amy Black | Laura Ashley | Peter Sellers

Ox - Virgo/Gemini

Academic (3)/climatologist academic/dean academic/philologist actor
boss (3) boss/engineer boss/politician chemist/physicist composer
geologist physicist (2) politician Major

Tony Newton | Antonin Dvoräk

Ox - Virgo/Cancer

Academic (4) academic/historian academic/writer/critic
anaesthetist author/film director artist boss (3) boss (CID)
bridge player civil servant cricketer diplomat footballer
guitarist (2) guitarist/singer organist philosopher/writer
politician (3) singer

Peter Shilton | Hendrik Verwoerd | Mel Tormé | Charles Haughey

Ox - Virgo/Leo

Academic (3) academic/ theologian
academic/principal/economist actress/model artist boss (2)
boss/lawyer chemist critic theatre director painter
percussion player/author physicist politician

Twiggy

Ox - Virgo/Virgo

Academic/critic/novelist adviser artist boss (2) boss/astronomer/physicist broker (reinsurance) cricketer football mgr guitarist (2) guitarist/singer photographer politician scriptwriter Maj-General

Martin Amis | B B King | Sir Bernard Lovell | Steve O'Shaughnessy

Ox - Virgo/Libra

Academic actor adviser architect boss (3) (finance) boss (insurance)/banker/Mandarin co-founder film/TV director footballer headmaster karate journalist/TV host judge photojournalist politician rugby/boss school keeper singer/songwriter trumpeter/composer/bandleader

David Packard | Mylène Farmer | Lisa Ling

Ox - Virgo/Scorpio

Architect banker/politician boxer head teacher mathematician judge pianist rugby Capt sculptor/painter writer yachtsman

Francis Chichester | Imogen Cooper | Alun Pask | Kenzo Tange Billy 'Bombardier' Wells

Ox - Virgo/Sagittarius

Academic/entomologist actor (3) actress Bishop boss cricketer editor/writer publisher secretary singer/guitarist

Richard Gere

Ox - Virgo/Capricorn

Actor architect athlete boss/industrialist
businessman chief fire officer civil servant footballer
historian/ceramicist judge politician (2) researcher/surgeon tennis
General/hospital governor

Jean-Claude Decaux | James Gandolfini | Greg Rusedski

Ox - Virgo/Aquarius

Academic (2)/musician academic/ pathologist actress adviser
Archbishop athlete biologist Bishop chess chaplain
choreographer/dancer diarist golfer industrialist judoka
journalist/playwright poet/translator

Tom Watson | Ingrid Berghmans | Jack Dee | Jesse Owens
Eiji Toyoda

Ox - Virgo/Pisces

Academic/physician medical researcher archaeologist
actor (2)/fashion model actress artist (graffiti) boss (2) chaplain
fashion designer diplomat (2) industrialist jockey
inventor (vacuum cleaner) journalist librarian/curator mountaineer/engineer
physician (2) pianist/composer police inspector QC politician
trade unionist vet officer General

Russ Conway | Tom Ford | Dr Liam Fox | Speedy Graphito

Ox - Libra/Aries

Actress author/journalist artist (2) boss magazine editor
diplomat TV host lexicographer/encyclopaedist
musician/impresario philosopher/artist/poet physicist swimmer
Colonel/adviser

Penny Junor | Enrico Fermi | Pierre Larousse

Ox - Libra/Taurus

Actress dramatist/poet editor/novelist historian
manufacturer (clothing)/salesman politician film producer/singer
Vice Admiral

Andy Lau

Ox - Libra/Gemini

Actress Archdeacon boss (2) composer/diplomat
mercenary pioneer (space)/scientist/engineer model/singer poet
politician (leader) publisher QC writer
Field Marshal

John Blackwell | Kiki de Montparnasse | Rosamund John

Ox - Libra/Cancer

Actor/director anatomist boss (2) (insurance) boss (survey)
cinematographer cricketer diplomat footballer politician
surgeon TV personality tennis

Ox - Libra/Leo

Academic (philosopher) author businessman cartoonist
comedian (satirical) guitarist/vocalist physicist/politician (3) poet
politician (leader) scientist (agric)

C R Giles | Joe 'Guitar' Hughes | Baroness (Margaret) Thatcher

Ox - Libra/Virgo

Author(2) boss (telecom) editor journalist (2) (radio)
journalist/author judge paleoanthropologist physicist politician
publisher Capt

Ox - Libra/Libra

Accountant actress commentator (sports) editor
journalist footballer/manager novelist philosopher
show jumper singer Capt

Harry Carpenter | Jackie Collins | Angela Lansbury | Benjamin Netanyahu
Bruce Springsteen | Arsène Wenger

Ox - Libra/Scorpio

Archaeologist author (2)/journalist author/surgeon boss (2)/accountant
boss/ballerina haematologist novelist (2) historian
politician (2) politician (leader) printer Brigadier

William Faulkner | Lord Nuffield | Emmuska Orczy (Baroness)
Dame Merle Park

Ox - Libra/Sagittarius

Actor ambassador boss golfer jockey
car manufacturer college master physicist psychotherapist/writer

Brian Blessed | William Morris (Lord Nuffield)

Ox - Libra/Capricorn

Academic (2)/physiologist academic/physicist actor (2) actress
composer dancer diplomat US footballer footballer (3)
prison governor novelist pharmacist/journalist QC
scientist (Kevlar vest) singer Admiral Vice Admiral

Bobby Charlton

Ox - Libra/Aquarius

Academic/biologist college principal/QC cricketer critic/historian
film director/painter journalist photographer physician trumpeter

Annie Leibovitz

Ox - Libra/Pisces

Actress boss (2) cartoonist clerk comedian engineer footballer naval officer politician/physician scientist singer Commander

Jean de Brunhoff | Jack Dee | Georges Clemenceau | Lillie Langtry

Ox - Scorpio/Aries

Academic (junior psychiatry) actress (3) actor/writer actor/theatre manager/producer architect boxer boss (2) band leader economist film maker/poet (2) poet politician (2) politician (leader)

Warren Harding | Larry Holmes | Alan Budd | Meg Ryan

Ox - Scorpio/Taurus

Academic (2)/rheumatologist academic (medicine) actress diplomat/SOE politician/physician satirist/writer/comedian singer

Su Pollard | Peter Cook

Ox - Scorpio/Gemini

Academic actor ballerina Bishop conductor correspondent/TV personality environmentalist farmer/businesswoman pianist psychologist reporter trade unionist

Tadaaki Otaka

Ox - Scorpio/Cancer

Academic actor (2) baseballer bassist/singer/record producer boss (2) (DIY) boss coach/footballer/goal keeper hurdler/athlete ice hockey novelist (2) writer/designer

Ox - Scorpio/Leo

Academic (2) academic/historian anarchist boss (3)
boss/physicist airman/politician/writer (2) author/historian cricketer (2)
drummer film maker painter politician (2)
lead burning specialist trade unionist

Jawaharlal Nehru | Larry Mullen

Ox - Scorpio/Virgo

Actress (2) boss (2)/trade unionist boss comedian (2)
comedian/actor composer/conductor/pianist cricketer film director
jockey/trainer designer/explorer malariologist neurophysiologist
singer/songwriter Rear Admiral

K D Lang | Viscount Linley | Lord Scanlon | Benjamin Britten
June Whitfield

Ox - Scorpio/Libra

Astronomer chemist/inventor malariologist/microscopist
musician/actor/singer painter/illustrator politician
stage director/actor (2) treasurer (Queen) viola/teacher/composer

Lillian Fuchs | Edwin Hubble | Otto Wichterle

Ox - Scorpio/Scorpio

Boss (2) chef/restaurateur diplomat editor film director
headmaster (2) headmistress impresario pianist politician
school master snooker trade unionist

Gerald Ratner | Raymond Blanc | Dennis Taylor | Jill Dando
Ferdinand de Lesseps

Ox - Scorpio/Sagittarius

Actor Bishop boss (2)/accountant boss/industrialist/engineer
conductor educationist politician (2) sculptor
Capt/horseman Lieut-Colonel/politician

Rock Hudson

Ox - Scorpio/Capricorn

Academic/geographer academic (3) actor (2)/trapeze actress
attorney/adviser boss (2) boss (airports) composer editor
gymnast journalist (3) musician neurologist/lecturer poet
TV presenter Rear Admiral/engineer

Burt Lancaster | Virna Lisi | Nadia Comaneci

Ox - Scorpio/Aquarius

Actress (2) actor artist/TV presenter Bishop
boss/publisher film director/acting mentor editor/journalist golfer
judge politician pioneer/statistician sports medicine practitioner

George Gallup | Vivien Leigh

Ox - Scorpio/Pisces

Actress boss (3)/businessman boss boss (museum)
boxer broadcaster footballer dancer
diplomat (2) equerry/secretary novelist painter
politician (2) singer/preacher solicitor Group Capt

Frank Bruno | Albert Camus | Hedy Lamarr | Wayne Rooney
Serge Tchuruk

Ox - Sagittarius/Aries

Actress (2)/model (2) artist/writer/broadcaster comedian composer
diplomat (2) drug dealer engineer photographer
politician (2) singer Colonel

Ox - Sagittarius/Taurus

Actor (2) athlete conductor (2)
conductor/composer cricketer prison governor
headmaster film producer vocalist writer

Jeff Bridges | John Akii-Bua | Jean Marais | Carlo Ponti

Ox - Sagittarius/Gemini

Actor (s) actress/singer boss (2) boxer
broadcaster/writer composer cricketer/umpire golfer
cricketer (2) politician radio presenter
Lieut-General Commander General

Kerry Packer

Ox - Sagittarius/Cancer

Academic (German) actor boss (3) boss (council)
boss/politician journalist gallery owner mountaineer nurse
physicist

Edith Cavell

Ox - Sagittarius/Leo

Actress/campaigner actress (2) boss (4) college bursar composer
historian pilot musician politician (4) film director (2) TV/film
producer solicitor Lieut-Colonel/comptroller

Jane Fonda | Samantha Bond | Willy Brandt | Jean Sibelius

Ox - Sagittarius/Virgo

Academic/civil servant/secretary actor (2) actress boss
Commissioner (films) headmaster politician singer/entertainer trade unionist

Paula Wilcox | Sammy Davis Jr

Ox - Sagittarius/Libra

Actor (2)/boss actor ambassador athlete
cartoonist/film producer cellist conservationist physicist painter
priest

Walt Disney | Werner Heisenberg | Paula Radcliffe

Ox - Sagittarius/Scorpio

Broadcaster chaplain/Canon composer film director
TV presenter/film maker pianist poet/writer pole vaulter polymath

Ridley Scott | Caroline Amel | Dick Van Dyke | Michael Ingrams

Ox - Sagittarius/Sagittarius

Columnist/commentator/author (2) composer/pianist/conductor
Deaconess/writer equestrian/painter poet QC singer

Aiko Kayo | Anton Rubinstein

Ox - Sagittarius/Capricorn

Actress (3) actor ambassador athlete boss (3) (chemist)
boss/adviser chemist civil servant footballer
art historian rower singer (2)/actress singer/dancer

Steve Nicol | Ryan Giggs

Ox - Sagittarius/Aquarius

Academic anthropologist author barrister chef
cricketer textile designer footballer judge
shipping magnate mountaineer musician/song writer (2) politician (3)
politician (leader) politician/parliament speaker QC sculptor
singer/songwriter

Robin Gibb | Maurice Gibb | Marco Pierre White

Ox - Sagittarius/Pisces

Academic/publisher/humanist actor (2)/dancer actor/writer caricaturist fashion designer model/TV presenter sculptor swimmer tennis writer (2) writer/ screenwriter

Alexander Godunov | Raphael Maklouf | Dr Mahathir bin Mohamad
Monica Seles

Ox - Capricorn/Aries

Academic/criminologist actress (3) boss (2)/businessman boss/accountant college principal composer (2) dramatist footballer headmaster politician publisher soldier/civil servant

Clive Hunting | Eric Liddell | R S Unwin | Jane Wyman

Ox - Capricorn/Taurus

Activist academic/clarinetist boss (creative) boss (3) composer conductor Dean docker guitarist/singer/songwriter luge politician trade unionist

Arthur Scargill

Ox - Capricorn/Gemini

Actress (2)/ entertainer actress/writer author/poet Bishop boss/trade unionist bookseller boss (2) broadcaster/author/diplomat businessman/gardener calligrapher chief inspector comedian correspondent equestrian judge politician (2) publisher Recorder singer writer (4) writer/politician/farmer

Jack Jones | Jim Carrey | Rose Louise Hovick (Gypsy Rose Lee)
Rudyard Kipling

Ox - Capricorn/Cancer

Academic ambassador (2) attorney Bishop
boss art critic Dean (hosp) Chief inspector medical officer
pianist/conductor politician (2) TV presenter scholar writer

Carol Smillie

Ox - Capricorn/Leo

Academic (3)/college master actress (4) author (2) baseballer
Chief Constable art historian/teacher governess/teacher
model/actress politician (2) writer/dramatist

Marlene Dietrich

Ox - Capricorn/Virgo

Academic (3) academic/classicist academic/geneticist
actor boss (2) FBI agent boss/accountant
composer/record producer diplomat footballer/manager journalist
politician singer (2) Brigadier/boss

Melanie Chisholm

Ox - Capricorn/Libra

Actor athlete boss (games) chess champ cricketer
footballer journalist politician (3) TV presenter/journalist singer

Ben Johnson | Elaine Pritchard

Ox - Capricorn/Scorpio

Boss (3) creator (Desert Island) fashion designer geologist
hydrographer super model novelist politician (2)
Brigadier

Ratan Tata | Gavin Hastings | Kate Moss | Roy Plomley

Ox - Capricorn/Sagittarius

Actor artist boss (3) boss (investment) boss/administrator
diplomat editor fashion designer footballer
hoaxer/stuntman journalist rugby Air Commodore/boss

Gordon Banks | Anthony Hopkins

Ox - Capricorn/Capricorn

Academic (3) academic academic/ philosopher actor (2)
legal adviser/lawyer athlete boss (2)/conductor boss (bank)
composer creator (Paddington Bear)/author racing driver
expert (preservation) financier/socialite founder (Mormons)
mathematician poet murderer painter (2) photographer politician
psychiatrist psychologist/philosopher/doctor rugby trombonist

Gilles Villeneuve | David Bailey | Ian Brady | Michael Bond
Warren Mitchell | Joseph Smith

Ox - Capricorn/Aquarius

Abbot academic/engineer actress anthropologist
astrophysicist boss (3) boss (civil service) chief engineer
guitarist journalist/horsewoman politician (3)
QC singer/songwriter singer/teacher

Liza Goddard | Chuck Berry

Ox - Capricorn/Pisces

Actress academic/obstetrician broadcaster
art dealer/boss (Air Liaison – SOE) cricketer headmaster politician
psychologist rugby scriptwriter comedy writer (2) writer/artist

Sissy Spacek | Moira Shearer

Ox - Aquarius/Aries

Academic cricketer/footballer dancer doctor/ musician founder (Lettrism)/poet entrepreneur/author (2) headmaster novelist politician (3) computer scientist/inventor tennis Lieut-Commander

Duncan Bannatyne | "Patsy" Hendren | Isidore Isou

Ox - Aquarius/Taurus

Academic (2)/historian academic/expert (dementia) actor (2) actor/body builder ambassador bailiff boss (radiology) broadcaster (2) conductor (2) conductor/composer/organist design engineer novelist/critic photographer politician tennis virologist Maj-General/engineer

Manuel Orantes | Steve Reeves

Ox - Aquarius/Gemini

Academic (2) actor baritone boss college principal driver (racing) film director politician surgeon writer Lieut-Colonel Air Chief Marshal

Jody Sheckter | Paul Girolami

Ox - Aquarius/Cancer

Actor architect/educationist/conservationist/historian boss (3) broadcaster (2)/writer (3) broadcaster/musician entertainer chief inspector (air) registrar novelist (3) writer/translator writer campaigner General

Ox - Aquarius/Leo

Academic (5) academic (medicine)/physician/researcher academic (paediatrics) academic/physicist academic/art historian actor/comedian actress (2) athlete broadcaster/columnist civil servant cricketer racehorse trainer writer (hymn)

Gundappa Viswanath | Libby Purves | Cathy Freeman | Jack Lemmon

Ox - Aquarius/Virgo

Astrologer basketballer boss (shipbuilding) cricketer
film director footballer novelist singer (3)
singer/actress singer/songwriter skateboarder Vice Admiral

W H Harrison | Claude Makelele

Ox - Aquarius/Libra

Anthropologist arranger (composer) choreographer chief coastguard
comedian/actor editor headmaster judge
mountaineer/educationist politician (4) 2-politician (leader)
college principal singer

Valéry Giscard d'Estaing | Ken Maginnis

Ox - Aquarius/Scorpio

Academic (2) academic (biophysics) artist/banker businessman (3)/guru
businessman/restaurateur boss (3) boss/college master poet (2)
poet/soldier arts promoter publisher trade unionist
Rear Admiral

H S Lanier

Ox - Aquarius/ Sagittarius

Actress artist aviator boss (2)
boss (farmers) conciliator space engineer/cosmonaut media executive
QC/prosecutor swimmer Air Commodore

Mark Spitz | Charles Lindbergh

Ox - Aquarius/Capricorn

Actress boss (2) boss (council) film composer cricketer lawyer
poet politician (leader) singer/songwriter theatre producer trombonist

Dr Garret FitzGerald | Peter Gabriel

Ox - Aquarius/Aquarius

Academic/rector actor archaeologist boss (2)
boss/publisher boxer critic jockey pioneer (hair transplant)
politician (2) politician university principal writer/ campaigner

Peter Hain | Oscar de la Hoya | Paul Hamlyn

Ox - Aquarius/Pisces

Academic athlete actor Bishop
boss (2)(Arts) boss/editor (Press) civil servant consultant (polit)
designer (stage) diplomat guitarist headmistress lawyer (2)
politician (2) book searcher solicitor/Speaker Admiral Marshal

Paul Newman

Ox - Pisces/Aries

Academic/ anaesthetist boss (3) boss (TV) cricketer
college master footballer (2) historian (2) historian/librarian painter
photojournalist QC/politician rugby/surgeon medical missionary
author/yachtswoman Air Chief Marshal Major

Dame Naomi James | Justin Fashanu | Pierre-Auguste Renoir

Ox - Pisces/Taurus

Actress art dealer boss (2) boss (festival) geneticist
hotelier optometrist/contact lens pioneer painter/sculptor
playwright/poet politician (3) rugby

Miou-Miou | Reo Stakis

Ox - Pisces/Gemini

Actor (2) actress/super model comedian diplomat
editor college master sculptor tennis

Eva Herzigova | Jelena Jankovic | Zeppo Marx

Ox - Pisces/Cancer

Academic (2) (chemistry) academic/principal (2) assassin (polit) author (2)
boss (3) boss (charity) boss (construction) businessman curator
dancer/teacher lawyer politician university principal runner
scientist/activist singer writer/translator

Jilly Cooper | Ron Clark | Linus Pauling | Laxmishanker Pathak

Ox - Pisces/Leo

Actor broadcaster/politician boss/lawyer
boxer film director founder/hospital mountaineer (2)/author
mountaineer/hotelier politician/engineer politician (2) typographer
writer Lieut-General

David Mellor | Barry McGuigan

Ox - Pisces/Virgo

Academic/priest/archaeologist actor (2) actress
comedian/author conductor film director
racing driver laryngologist/otologist poet/essayist/translator
saxophonist silversmith

Ox - Pisces/Libra

Academic/economist artist archaeologist boss (3) (quango)
boss (business body) boss/secret police film composer
cyclist nurse photographer trumpeter
Maj-General Air Vice Marshal

Ox - Pisces/Scorpio

Actor boss (brewery) entrepreneur (golf) footballer
kayaker politician/Mayor singer (2)/songwriter (2) snooker
softball player volleyball

Alex Higgins | Juninho

Ox - Pisces/Sagittarius

Academic (2)/paediatrician academic/ zoologist architect athlete actor astronaut barrister boss cricketer (2) entrepreneur fashion model founder (Levi Strauss) musician politician/campaigner priest saxophonist/composer Major/politician

Ivana Trump | Levi Strauss | Stephen Fitz-Simon Valentina Nikolayeva-Tereshkova

Ox - Pisces/Capricorn

Academic actress (porn)/sex educator consultant (physiotherapy)/pioneer cricketer film director racing driver politician/Chief Whip Lieut-General

Niki Lauda | Robert Altman

Ox - Pisces/Aquarius

Boss (3) boss (property)/shipping broker/courtier boss/surveyor politician soprano surgeon trade unionist urologist writer/illustrator Brigadier

Ox - Pisces/Pisces

Academic (2)/ archaeologist actress auctioneer boss microbiologist/pathologist novelist (2) nurse author/journalist soprano teacher/editor

S C Whitbread | Stephanie Beacham

Tiger - Aries/Aries

Academic (animal behaviour)/provost actress (2) actor/engineer/activist Canon/librarian clarinettist novelist (2)/screen writer novelist/writer poet politician (4) politician (leader) robber senator Vice Admiral

Butch Cassidy | Ali MacGraw | Benito Juarez | Sir David Steel

Tiger - Aries/Taurus

Barrister/QC boss (orchestra) controller editor headmaster (3) headmistress journalist politician (leader) rector politician film producer

Tiger - Aries/Gemini

Academic (2) (philosophy) actor (2) boss cricketer driver educationist headmaster High Commissioner historian magician poet/essayist/ambassador politician/founder (antiseptic) solicitor/boss (legal)/QC college tutor

Paul Daniels | Graham Barlow | Alec Guinness

Tiger - Aries/Cancer

Boss (quango) diplomat footballer founder (opera co.) geneticist journalist (2) novelist player (keyboard)/songwriter politician film producer provost singer

Kofi Annan | Tony Banks | Maria Ewing | Carl Rosa

Tiger - Aries/Leo

Actor boss boxer clarinettist headmistress judge musician physicist politician QC

Robbie Coltrane

Tiger - Aries/Virgo

Academic (2) (psychology) academic/pathologist actor boss (3)/accountant boss/industrialist boss/barrister/author judge neurologist pathologist/campaigner Vice Admiral

Tiger - Aries/Libra

Academic (law) aviator/designer boss (retailing) comedian diplomat economist entrepreneur/founder head teacher photographer/pioneer oarsman/consultant reporter rugby trade unionist Lieut-Colonel Maj-General/boss Rear Admiral/training officer

Lord Rayner | Ingvar Kamprad | John Fowles | Anthony Herman Fokker Eadweard Muybridge | Steven Redgrave

Tiger - Aries/Scorpio

Academic (2) (endocrinology) academic/neurologist actor actress (3) artist boss (2) Chief Constable civil servant (2) civil servant/writer racing driver politician sculptor singer solicitor wrestler writer Air Vice Marshal General/politician Wing Commander

Jack Brabham | M G Rizzello | James Hertzog | Agnetha Faltskog Dame Flora Robson

Tiger - Aries/Sagittarius

Actor astronaut boss (3)(banking)/accountant boss composer headmistress horticulturist journalist minister/Mayor pianist poet/artist University principal politician surgeon tennis college warden writer/ illustrator Brigadier

Virgil Grissom | William Walton

Tiger - Aries/Capricorn

Academic (2)/cardiologist academic (studies) actor administrator athlete boss (2) biographer/poet broadcaster dancer/boss/writer educationist industrialist photographer rugby scholar songwriter soldier/diplomat

J H Haynes | Hoyt Axton | Rev Ian Paisley | Rodolphe Peugeot Peter Snow

Tiger - Aries/Aquarius

Academic (2)/ pathologist academic/social scientist activist boss (3) boss (cars)/salesman boss (TV) expert (jazz)/writer/promoter pianist singer (2) singer/guitarist TV presenter Admiral

David Cassidy | Phillip Schofield | Victoria Beckham Maruyama Masao | Lord Stokes

Tiger - Aries/Pisces

Academic/ radiologist actor (2) agronomist boxer broadcaster chemist lawyer artist's model/investigator politician (leader) QC University principal

Lord Fitt | Hugh Hefner

Tiger - Taurus/Aries

Academic (addictions) boss (2) boss/ investor comedian broadcaster conductor cricketer diplomat film director high mistress judge naturalist politician/HGV driver QC/writer singer (2)/musician singer/composer snooker writer (2) writer/journalist

David Attenborough | Bernard Madoff | Stevie Wonder | Peter Gabriel Jimmy White

Tiger - Taurus/Taurus

Academic/composer boss (2)/accountant boss/revolutionary business developer comedian medical consultant headmistress mathematician/physicist politician 2 (leader) politician/trade unionist publican theorist

Karl Marx | Ho Chi-Minh | Bud Abbott

Tiger - Taurus/Gemini

Academic actor (2) actor/comedian broadcaster/wine writer
composer fashion designer farmer hurdler
philosopher/economist

Eric Morecambe

Tiger - Taurus/Cancer

Actress/dancer boss (2) boxer composer engineer
rugby/boss composer editor novelist/historian playwright (2)
restaurateur singer (2) soprano Lieut-General

Penelope Cruz

Tiger - Taurus/Leo

Boss broadcaster chancellor chaplain/Canon
composer dancer/choreographer prison Governor librarian politician
QC trade unionist

David Jacobs

Tiger - Taurus/Virgo

Academic (2) (statistics) academic/lawyer actor Bishop
judge (2) chief judge politician (2) politician/QC
singer/campaigner TV presenter Major-General/boss

Tyrone Power

Tiger - Taurus/Libra

Academic/artist actress literary agent/publisher
ambassador boss (3) (bank) accountant boss (charity)
boss/ barrister jockey politician
press secretary/writer tennis

Tony McCoy | Susan Hampshire | Rudy Narayan | Michael Shea

Tiger - Taurus/Scorpio

Academic (3) (paining) academic/principal academic/chemist boss conductor graphic designer founder QC singer (2) writer

W G Fargo

Tiger - Taurus/Sagittarius

Accountant footballer historian college master pilot/farmer politician (2) QC (2) QC/recorder volcanologist/geologist Capt

Barbara Calvert

Tiger - Taurus/Capricorn

Academic/economist 2 -bishop boss (2) boss/ yachtsman boxer broadcaster toy designer founder (beauty) lawyer activist musician/historian novelist/poet/playwright photographer sailor trade unionist Air Marshal

Clive Jenkins | Mary Spillane | Joe Louis

Tiger - Taurus/Aquarius

Academic (2) academic (immunology) actor (2)/TV presenter actor bassist boss (2) (hospital) boss/farmer cricketer official/farmer civil servant Maj-General/pilot

Matthew Kelly

Tiger - Taurus/Pisces

Actor (3) architect/painter bassist biologist bowler broadcaster coal miner guitarist politician psychologist singer (2)/actress rugby solicitor writer/poet

Duane Eddy | Jeremy Paxman | Andrea Corr

Tiger - Gemini/Aries

Actress actor author (1)
bandleader/arranger/keyboard player boss (charity) bodyguard
civil servant conductor engineer/port builder
headmaster (2) headmistress lyricist/musician novelist
politician/paymaster trade unionist (2)/author trade unionist

E W Hornung | David Troughton

Tiger - Gemini/Taurus

Academic/physicist author (3)/journalist actress Bishop boss (5)
boss (church) boss (investment) chemist comedian police
Commander composer/singer nurse/historian politician (3)
politician (leader) tennis (2) writer/advertising exec writer/activist
Rear Admiral/politician

Gemma Craven | Rafael Nadal | Lindsey de Paul

Tiger - Gemini/Gemini

Actor (2) Archbishop barrister boss (2) (bank)
boss (personnel)/management consultant comedian economist
engineer industrialist lecturer pianist poet/novelist
politician Brigadier/lecturer Wing Commander

John Masefield | Dr Rowan Williams | Stan Laurel | Ahmed Sukarno
Lakshmi Mittal

Tiger - Gemini/Cancer

Academic/entomologist boss (2) (airline) boss (orchestra) climber
zoo owner engineer/inventor/entrepreneur politician (2)
politician (leader) violinist Group Capt/ace pilot

Tenzing Norgay | John Prescott

Tiger - Gemini/Leo

Academic (2)/philosopher academic/physician actress (2) actress/TV hostess agronomist boss (2) (council) businessman expert (church architecture) guerrilla leader headmaster (2) headmistress keyboard player singer (2) Air Marshal Major-General/boss

Denise van Outen

Tiger - Gemini/Virgo

Academic/economist diplomat diver/cameraman engineer politician soprano Vice Admiral actress/singer/author

Tiger - Gemini/Libra

Academic/ boss actor entrepreneur golfer QC pilot politician psychologist singer/songwriter/record producer

Chad Campbell | Alanis Morissette

Tiger - Gemini/Scorpio

Actress/singer archaeologist biographer/incunabulist boss (3) businessman chess designer (yacht)/editor martial arts novelist scientist 2-singer sprinter Lieut-General

Tiger - Gemini/Sagittarius

Academic (2) academic/palaeontologist bandleader boss (2) businessman cartoonist composer dramatist/novelist physician politician (leader) 2-rugby singer (2) singer/bassist songwriter racehorse trainer

Guy Lombardo

Tiger - Gemini/Capricorn

Actor anthropologist boxer correspondent
designer (jewellery)/singer (2)/choreographer inventor (steam turbine)
pilot (fighter) pioneer (aviation) politician saxophonist/flautist
singer/bassist tennis urologist

Suzi Quatro | Paula Abdul | Charles Parsons

Tiger - Gemini/Aquarius

Actor (3) actress biographer/author/translator boss (2)
comedian conservator cricketer dancer/ ballet master/boss
pilot (fighter) film-maker historian (2) journalist/historian
politician surveyor Lieut-General

Marilyn Monroe | Bobcat Goldthwait

Tiger - Gemini/Pisces

Academic (2)/archaeologist academic/administrator/tenor artist
barrister/copyright consultant boss boss/surveyor
businessman campaigner cricketer dancer
designer (furniture) diplomat editorial director headmistress judge
poet politician (leader) General

Yuri Andropov | Allen Ginsberg | Ravi Shastri

Tiger - Cancer/Aries

Academic (2)/house warden actress (3) composer trumpeter
academic/engineer boss environmentalist politician
TV presenter wrestler/model company secretary scriptwriter

Sarah Kennedy | Natalie Wood

Tiger - Cancer/Taurus

Academic/educationist actor/director attorney general boss
clarinettist cyclist footballer judge
politician (2) singer surgeon writer

Tony Leung | Chiu Wai | Terence Stamp | Michael Ball

Tiger - Cancer/Gemini

Archbishop boss (2) (airport) boss (insurance)/actuary
cinematographer correspondent comedian librarian
psychiatrist (2) writer/broadcaster

Elisabeth Kubler-Ross | Jean-Yves Escoffier

Tiger - Cancer/Cancer

Actor adviser/civil engineer ambassador/senator
boss/engineer designer hostess (polit) politician (leader) U principal

Tom Cruise | Bruce Oldfield

Tiger - Cancer/Leo

Academic (2)/archaeologist academic/physicist actress
boss (4) (construction) boss (charity) boss (oil) Chief Constable
civil servant GP illustrator poet/author tennis writer/historian

Pam Shriver

Tiger - Cancer/Virgo

Academic (3)/psycho-linguist academic (Greek)
academic/scientist/conservationist actor (3) actress apothecary
archaeologist architect barrister boss (4) (HR) boss (artistic – plays)
boss (conglomerate) boss (jeans) conductor (2) conductor/composer
artistic director diplomat politician (3) racehorse trainer

Richard Branson | General Leopoldo Galtieri | Shami Ahmed
Karisma Kapoor

Tiger - Cancer/Libra

Academic/biochemistactor (2) actor/singer author
boss (2)(manufacture) boss (retailing) chef/restaurateur composer
editor/politician civil engineer headmaster civil servant
rugby/soldier General

Leos Janácek

Tiger - Cancer/Scorpio

Academic/Vice Chancellor aerodynamicist athlete boss (2) (tourism)
boss (TV) boxer car designer physicist

Nuccio Bertone | George Ohm

Tiger - Cancer/Sagittarius

Academic/surgeon actor architect archaeologist
film director (3) novelist politician QC showman
soldier/administrator

Bill Pertwee

Tiger - Cancer/Capricorn

Academic (2) (statistics) 2-academic/educationist boss (2) (law)
boss impresario photographer politician (2) football referee
singer

Tiger - Cancer/Aquarius

Actress (2) ambassador actor/director aviatrix boss
boss (TV)/accountant camera pioneer (photography)/manufacturer founder
aerobatic pilot/stunt driver publisher politician(2)
politician (leader) surgeon youth worker/ administrator

Mel Brooks | Susan Penhaligon | George Eastman

Tiger - Cancer/Pisces

Academic (2) (composition)/composer academic/historian (econ) boss/engineer/manufacturer explorer TV/radio host/doctor disc jockey journalist musician/songwriter painter tenor

Camille Pissarro

Tiger - Leo/Aries

Actress (2) actress/film producer/photographer/writer boss/engineer (2) campaigner chemist engineer/inventor (ultrasound)/doctor gymnast judge pharmacologist sculptor/goldsmith vet surgeon

Tiger - Leo/Taurus

Academic (4)/engineer academic/philosopher academic (pathology)/virologist academic/physician athlete boss (food) chief inspector/reformer politician (leader) sculptor

Tiger - Leo/Gemini

Academic (2)/boss academic artist/goldsmith author (2) ballerina boss (5) businessman/lawyer commentator (2) cricketer diplomat journalist/broadcaster singer/entertainer politician (1) singer (2) ballet teacher/boss vocalist/songwriter writer/broadcaster Air Marshal

Tony Bennett

Tiger - Leo/Cancer

Academic (3) academic/GP academic/scientist actor astrologer Chief Constable computer engineer/founder (2) polo entrepreneur judge circus performer poet/novelist politician singer Air Marshal Vice Admiral/surgeon Maj-General

Emily Brontë | **Frank Finlay** | **Kenny Rogers** | **Steve Wozniak**

Tiger - Leo/Leo

Boss (2) (research) boss/soldier cartoonist composer cricketer headmaster magnate (shipping) production manager meteorologist politician (leader) (2) skier theatre proprietor satirist writer Vice Chancellor/QC Commandant/boss

Chuan Leekpai | Emperor Franz-Joseph I | Didier Cuche | Ian McCaskill

Tiger - Leo/Virgo

Academic/geneticist actor/film director biochemist boss (2) boss (TV)/judo teacher dramatist/poet entrepreneur/founder/engineer cricketer photographer physician/overseas worker tennis Col-Commandant/chief matron

Princess Anne | Giovanni Agnelli | Terry O'Neill

Tiger - Leo/Libra

Actress (3)/dancer author/humorist boss (3) graphic designer actor/film director 2-physicist pianist (2) pianist/singer politician (leader) scientist singer (2)/actor tenor violinist

Fidel Castro | P A M Dirac | René Goscinny | Buddy Greco
Michelle Yeoh | Zino Francescatti

Tiger - Leo/Scorpio

Academic/geologist artist Bishop boss (2) (telecoms) boss/correspondent broadcaster fashion designer High Commissioner diplomat/journalist novelist engineer police commissioner singer winemaker Maj-General

Terry Wogan

Tiger - Leo/Sagittarius

Academic/physiologist actress (2) boss (2) (supermarkets)
boss (hotels) businessman/journalist athletics coach
author/watch maker camera man engineer historian politician
rugby singer (2) singer/model/songwriter model (2)/actress

Susan George | Felix Wankel | Lord Sainsbury | Hilary Swank

Tiger - Leo/Capricorn

Academic/chemist boss car designer judge librarian novelist
ophthalmologist (consulting) physician/medium/surgeon (psychic) rugby
school master/educationist hall principal reformer tennis
Vice Admiral

Georgette Heyer | Rod Laver

Tiger - Leo/Aquarius

Boss(2)(football) boss (council) dietitian/nutritionist
fashion designer gangster novelist/dramatist writer(2)
ornithologist politician record producer soldier/colonial servant
trade unionist Lieut-Colonel/game warden

John Galsworthy | Harriet Harman | Ogden Nash

Tiger - Leo/Pisces

Academic/composer actress artist (2) boss (insolvency)/mayor/accountant
economist judge (2) politician (2) politician (leader) musician/producer
songwriter sprinter theologian racing trainer

Usain Bolt | Anthony Jolliffe | Wycliffe 'Steely' Johnson

Tiger - Virgo/Aries

Actress (4) actor architect bank governor lecturer computer scientist golfer hockey player model/actress TV personality/actress pianist/bandleader poet polymath college principal sculptor sociologist/historian
2-tennis (champ/scoring)

Lord Eddie George | Pat Coombs | Gustavo Kuerten

Tiger – Virgo/Taurus

Actor artist baseballer boss (3)/businessman boss (catalogues) boss (food, finance) boxer footballer/TV presenter founder (books) neurologist novelist poet politician politician (leader) sculptor tennis Air Vice Marshal/boss

James J Corbett (Gentleman Jim) | John Fashnu | Tim Henman
Allen Lane | John Smith

Tiger - Virgo/Gemini

Academic/chemist Bishop boss (auctioneers) businesswoman/author/model/TV host choreographer college master/engineer (2) editor/astrologer patriarch politician (leader) singer
Squadron Leader/pilot

Tiger - Virgo/Cancer

Academic/writer archaeologist author/physician boss (council) university principal (2) university principal/civil servant/administrator banker boss (charity) powerboat designer footballer novelist politician publisher singer/actress writer (5) UN worker

Tiger - Virgo/Leo

Academic accountant boss (2) (prison) boss/businessman/founder dep police Commissioner engineer footballer guitarist (2)/composer guitarist/songwriter oarsman politician (4) politician (leader) schoolmaster soprano statesman

Tiger - Virgo/Virgo

Architect/conservationist bookseller boss (3) boss (research) boss (radio) car body designer diplomat film director/cameraman historian songwriter (2) motorcyclist novelist/commentator solicitor/consultant pathologist priest

Frederick Forsyth | Barry Sheene

Tiger - Virgo/Libra

Academic (2) academic/agronomist actor (2) fashion designer footballer (2) footballer/manager/TV commentator judge novelist (2) town clerk painter film producer writer (2) writer/TV commentator

Beryl Cook | Dame Agatha Christie | Ruud Gullit | Sol Campbell Kenneth More

Tiger - Virgo/Scorpio

Academic/boss athlete bookseller/publisher boss (2) broadcaster/writer organist/composer ship owner politician QC yachtswoman

Tracy Edwards | Loyd Grossman

Tiger - Virgo/Sagittarius

Actor (2)/TV presenter actress/activist administrator architect biographer boss choreographer diplomat journalist painter (2} playwright politician Group Capt/pilot

Glyn Worsnip

Tiger - Virgo/Capricorn

Academic (2)/medical officer academic (psychiatry) actor administrator boss judge photographer/painter/film maker restaurateur civil servant Air Marshal

Man Ray

Tiger - Virgo/Aquarius

Actress advertiser boss (2) (prosecutions) boss (bank)
cameraman composer/organist diplomat marine engineer
gun inventor golfer gynaecologist/researcher novelist politician
psychologist/astrologer records keeper soprano

Richard Gatling | Fay Wray | H G Wells

Tiger - Virgo/Pisces

Academic/college master architect artist Bishop boss (2)
boss (trust) Chief Constable fashion designer diplomat
editor/lexicographer headmaster inventor/philosopher glamour model
novelist physicist(2) physicist/neurobiologist/inventor
police/wrestler politician (leader) (2) Intelligence officer/sailor rugby
trainer (racehorse)/jockey trumpeter

Karl Lagerfeld | Sir James Dewar

Tiger - Libra/Aries

Academic/boss actor/comedian ambassador Bishop
boss (2) (council) boss (quango) astrologer/ psychotherapist
shaman boss (5) designer/pianist entrepreneur diplomat
industrialist/politician politician (4) civil servant skier tennis
wrestler/ entrepreneur zoologist

Lord Montague of Beaulieu | Leonard Rossiter

Tiger - Libra/Taurus

Actor author/anthropologist/explorer bassist engineer
journalist/author (2) theatre director/writer (2) politician (leader)
politician (2)/protester registrar skier baritone
trainer (horse)/breeder Chief Marshal Colonel

Chester Arthur | Thor Heyerdahl

Tiger - Libra/Gemini

Actor (2) actress/model academic (aerodynamics) baritone boss (2) economist journalist painter/designer poet politician singer (3) singer/songwriter/instrumentalist Air Commodore/chief matron

Groucho Marx

Tiger - Libra/Cancer

Academic (education) baritone boss(2) boss (insurance) boss/bursar boxer businessman/banker Chief Constable educationist expert (aviation safety) illustrator/cartoonist lawyer/postmaster politician (leader) scholar/producer singer/activist

Marv Johnson | Baron Edmond de Rothschild | Evander Holyfield

Tiger - Libra/Leo

Legal academic conductor furniture designer impresario TV personality/columnist fighter pilot/designer bridge player politician soldier/engineer stuntman rugby tennis writer (2)

Evel Knievel | Ann Jones | Eddie Rickenbacker | Oscar Wilde

Tiger - Libra/Virgo

Archbishop author (2)/journalist creator (Superman) diplomat Governor General judge/QC otolaryngologist/physician/surgeon pipe major public servant trade unionist writer

Earl of Dalhousie | Bill Morris | Jerry Siegel

Tiger - Libra/Libra

Academic/boss (2)/engineer actor (3) boss cinematographer golfer mountaineer playwright/scriptwriter poet violinist General/politician (leader)

Derek Jacobi | Ray Tindle | Gen Dwight Eisenhower | Arthur Rimbaud

Tiger - Libra/Scorpio

Academic/ gerontologist actor ballerina boss comedian (2)
TV comic/ game show host footballer co-founder/bookseller
industrialist inventor (crash dummy) politician (2) politician/patriot
college provost tennis

Vera Dushevina | Larry Fine | Ray Kroc

Tiger - Libra/Sagittarius

Architect boss (3) clarinettist/conductor/teacher comedian engineer
monk/teacher/activist bomber (suicide) politician (2) politician (leader)
PR officer TV presenter vet/chief inspector

Ramsay MacDonald | Claude Gill | Mohammad Sidique Khan

Tiger - Libra/Capricorn

Academic (2)/playwright academic/psychiatrist author/psychic boss
High Commissioner founder (books) journalist mountaineer
writer/politician singer swimmer

John M Menzies

Tiger - Libra/Aquarius

Astronaut athlete designer book editor/author (3)
guitarist/songwriter/singer lawyer novelist philosopher/lecturer
pianist politician (leader) Rabbi/astrologer rugby swimmer (2)

Tiger - Libra/Pisces

Academic/engineer boss (2) guitarist/singer headmaster historian
skier college warden water polo writer/broadcaster Air Chief Marshal

Chuck Berry

Tiger - Scorpio/Aries

Academic boss (accounting) boss (cars – finance) chief chaplain management consultant cricketer (2) economist High commissioner musician novelist/dramatist palaeontologist Admiral

Ivan Turgenev | Martin Scicluna | Michael Vaughn

Tiger - Scorpio/Taurus

Academic/physicist academic (2) activist actress boss author (2) composer/writer journalist/broadcaster politician (2) trainer (racehorse) Brigadier

Demi Moore | Mariella Frostrup

Tiger - Scorpio/Gemini

Actress govt adviser (counter terrorism) boss entrepreneur/founder fashion designer (2) historian (research) musician/composer (2) composer/conductor Ombudsman/lawyer TV producer/novelist psychoanalyst/scholar publisher music publisher QC soprano rapper

Koji Tatsuno | Stefano Gabbana | Edouard Leclerc | Nelly | J P Sousa

Tiger - Scorpio/Cancer

Activist architect (2) baseballer college fellow comedian jockey musician musicologist/psycho-analyst politician (2) politician (leader)

Tiger - Scorpio/Leo

Architect author boss (hospital) boxer gardener historian huntsman police film producer runner singer surgeon/teacher winemaker

Hedy Lamarr

Tiger - Scorpio/Virgo

Actress author (2) boss (2) boss (fire brigade)
broadcaster film maker footballer palmist/clairvoyant
politician (leader) priest theologian/author rugby saxophonist
singer/songwriter/guitarist songwriter (2) swimmer General

Cheiro | Thorbjørn Jagland | Jodie Foster | James Savile

Tiger - Scorpio/Libra

Actor (2) boss (clothing) businessman/founder property developer
editor milliner/antiques dealer nematologist slalom
surgeon/educator (2) teacher (Zen)

Ted Turner | Leonardo DiCaprio

Tiger - Scorpio/Scorpio

Academic author/critic/painter boss (4) comedian
designer (theatrical) prison governor motor mechanic
TV presenter/campaigner spy Air Chief Marshal

Frank Carson | Herbert Austin | Ralph Halpern

Tiger - Scorpio/Sagittarius

Boss footballer photographer politician
singer (2)/impersonator/humorist soprano swimmer/presenter

Dame Joan Sutherland | Sharron Davies | Paul Scholes

Tiger - Scorpio/Capricorn

Broadcaster designer (photographic) founder (Boys' Brigade)
historian lecturer linguist/teacher pioneer (software)
playwright poet politician (4) politician/revolutionary film producer
trainer (racehorse) Air Vice Marshal Maj-General

Charles Berlitz | David Dimbleby | Sun Yat-sen | Jacqui Smith
Sir William Smith

Tiger - Scorpio/Aquarius

Academic (history) actor (2) actress boss (court) baritone
composer diplomat film director poet
politician (leader) radio presenter/producer tennis

Dylan Thomas

Tiger - Scorpio/Pisces

Academic/judge colonial administrator boss (health)/QC civil servant
discoverer/microbiologist hydrographer Press officer Ombudsman
painter physicist politician singer (2)/songwriter soprano
writer/restaurateur Rear Admiral/hydrographer Maj-General

Jonas Salk

Tiger - Sagittarius/Aries

Academic (4)/consultant academic/historian (religion)
academic/Vice-Chancellor (U) author boss (photocopier)
counsellor (European) ecologist/editor 2-historian industrialist
judge painter poet police/adviser politician (2)
teacher/campaigner Brigadier General/statesman Lieut-General/boss (security)
Lieut Commander/pilot

Charles de Gaulle

Tiger - Sagittarius/Taurus

Actor (2)/writer actress attorney general/QC
eventer (3 day) herald journalist poet 2-politician
General Rear Admiral Vice Admiral

Charles Hawtrey | **Richard Meade**

Tiger - Sagittarius/Gemini

PR consultant TV controller designer (theatrical) engineer
maker (car) politician college principal soprano
tennis

Anke Huber

Tiger - Sagittarius/Cancer

Boss (quango) cricketer 2-economist model/actress
poet/author politician QC (2) QC/Recorder tennis

Tracy Austin

Tiger - Sagittarius/Leo

Actor (2) architect boss diplomat footballer
poet rugby singer/actress/impersonator
singer (2) Brigadier/church registrar Group Capt/pilot

Connie Francis | Sir Ralph Richardson

Tiger - Sagittarius/Virgo

Academic (biology) actress Chief Constable executive (newspaper)
fighter (resistance) film director poet/playwright polymath/harpsichord maker
politician QC singer teacher/conservationist tennis
Lieut-Colonel/golfer/administrator

Nicole Appleton | Dorothy Lamour | Max Manus

Tiger - Sagittarius/Libra

Actress (2) actor boss (2) comedienne
historian/college master novelist/biographer/translator racing driver rugby
poet theatre director Major

Liv Ullmann | Michael Bogdanov | Emily Dickinson | Pamela Stephenson
Paul Thorburn

Tiger - Sagittarius/Scorpio

Actor athlete boss (banking) boss (4)
boss (arts centre) boss (music)/civil servant conductor
curator (museum) musician/owner (nightclub) painter politician
principal Lieut-Commander/pilot

Ralph Fiennes | Ronnie Scott

Tiger - Sagittarius/Sagittarius

Artist archbishop boss (3) disc jockey/TV presenter
model/actress musician politician (2) politician 2-singer
Vice Admiral/submariner

Joan Armatrading | Sara Cox

Tiger - Sagittarius/Capricorn

Actor accountant/adviser baseballer/football
boss (2) (tribal) boss (MI5) diarist college principal GP
rugby trainer (racehorse) Admiral

Victor Kiam | Crazy Horse

Tiger - Sagittarius/Aquarius

Academic/physicist actor boss (3) boss (U) bullfighter
civil servant racing driver politician film producer QC
sculptor secretary (quango)

Tiger - Sagittarius/Pisces

Accountant baseballer boss/teacher clerk school dean/GP
political counsellor college principal (2) founder/doctor
wine merchant politician geographer/anarchist sculptor
TV newscaster/anchorman trade unionist

Joe DiMaggio

Tiger - Capricorn/Aries

Academic/psychoanalyst actor (3) actress/comedienne/singer (2) boss (2) entrepreneur/nurse film producer/impresario journalist house master/priest novelist politician (2) driver (racing) saxophonist show jumper singer star (film, stage) virologist (vet) wrestler

G S Babra | Elizabeth Arden | E M Forster | Harvey Smith | Jon Voight Richard Widmark

Tiger - Capricorn/Taurus

Academic/engineer actress basketballer bassist biologist boss racing driver gymnast judge politician/farmer 2-singer/songwriter trade unionist Commander-in-Chief Lieut-Col/astronaut

Robert E Lee

Tiger - Capricorn/Gemini

Academic/pharmacologist boss conductor cosmonaut engineer/author film maker/cameraman footballer journalist radio controller sculptor writer (2)

Barbara Hepworth

Tiger - Capricorn/Cancer

Academic/historian actress/singer author/agitator boss (2) boss (computers) boss (quango) critic/editor pilot poet TV producer

Eartha Kitt

Tiger - Capricorn/Leo

Academic (2) academic/ statistician actor
boss (3) (tax) boss/engineer boss (3) (research project)
consultant/physician coxswain diplomat inventor (safety razor)
politician (2) civil servant writer Air Commodore

K C Gillette

Tiger - Capricorn/Virgo

Actress boss (ports) college head commando
composer designer (fashion) surgeon trade union leader
violinist writer/activist writer (2)

David Horowitz | Susannah York

Tiger - Capricorn/Libra

Academic/politician announcer Archdeacon boss/accountant
businessman/politician historian instructor (dance)/dancer model
TV presenter umpire (cricket) Vice Admiral

Piers Merchant

Tiger - Capricorn/Scorpio

Academic accountant actress (porn) boss (2) boss/fire officer
theatre director founder/designer (fashion) journalist
college master/economist landowner physicist
Speaker (Hse of Commons) sprinter theologian translator

John Bercow | James Joule | Jeanne Lanvin | Martin Bashir

Tiger - Capricorn/Sagittarius

Author/estate agent/property developer boss (4) (museum) composer pilot politician/miner college provost publisher rocker Wing Commander (2)/pilot/flying instructor

Tiger - Capricorn/Capricorn

Academic/astronomer accountant actress (2) actress/singer aviator/boss Chief Constable journalist novelist pianist politician singer Lieut-Commander

Phil Everly | Michel Petrucciani | Barbara Rush

Tiger - Capricorn/Aquarius

Academic/vet ambassador boss (hotels) bank governor playwright/critic politician TV producer/director/writer singer tennis

Una Dillon

Tiger - Capricorn/Pisces

Academic (3) (physics) academic (archaeology) academic (classics) talk show host boss (econ body) founder (Dillons) poet landowner politician (leader) producer (theatrical) publisher writer (2)/musician writer/photographer Lieut-Commander

Tiger - Aquarius/Aries

Actor ambassador/socialite boss (2) boss/accountant boxer canon/provost film director headmaster judge philosopher politician provost/doctor

John Schlesinger | Jemima Khan | Christian Bale

Tiger - Aquarius/Taurus

Academic artist author (2) boss/accountant civil servant designer (theatrical) editor/campaigner engineer (radio) expert (dialect)/broadcaster headmaster murderer (2) owner (racehorse) singer/ songwriter trumpeter TV producer/novelist/lecturer writer Air Marshal Air Vice Marshal/engineer

Robert Stroud (Birdman of Alcatraz) | Sheryl Crow | Elizabeth Montgomery Ian Huntley

Tiger - Aquarius/Gemini

Academic/master (college) author clarinettist High Commissioner critic (TV, radio) journalist politician (leader) skier (2) racehorse trainer stockbroker/musicologist violinist

Michael Mair | William Burroughs | Robert Cecil

Tiger - Aquarius/Cancer

Actress (2)/radio DJ actress ambassador author (2)/ dissident cricketer/footballer driver (racing) drummer jazz player/bandleader politician (3) politician/lawyer/judge public servant writer/farmer

Edward Carson (Baron) | Jemima Khan

Tiger - Aquarius/Leo

Academic/economist/writer (2) actor (3) actress boss/accountant diplomat/SOE footballer harmonica player tennis writer/radio producer Brigadier/politician

Oliver Reed | Hana Mandlikova | Stanley Matthews | John Profumo

Tiger - Aquarius/Virgo

Actor (3) actor/musician academic adviser (nursing)/nursing officer
boss (2) (HR) boss (TV) critic (theatre) high mistress (school)
judge politician runner saxophonist/bandleader
civil servant

Mike Farrell

Tiger - Aquarius/Libra

Academic (3) academic (nursing) academic/biologist actress
ambassador astronaut athlete Bishop comedian catcher (spy)
cricketer geologist/ palaeontologist pioneer (music)/TV star
poet/novelist politician (2) politician/paediatrician/lawyer trade unionist

Janet Suzman | Gordon Prentice | Boris Pasternak | Norman Wisdom

Tiger - Aquarius/Scorpio

Anaesthetist boss (2) boss/musician boxer curator
guitarist horticulturist/engineer QC/prosecutor politician (2)
politician/writer 2-singer/drummer singer/artiste (variety) singer (5)
singer/songwriter/model Admiral of the Fleet

Roberta Flack | Phil Collins | Naseem Hamed | Phil Manzanera
Robbie Williams | Natalie Imbruglia

Tiger - Aquarius/Sagittarius

Academic (2) (Islamic) academic/chemist/vice chancellor artist/magician
basketballer broadcaster Canon economist
investigator (war crimes) musician 2-politician surgeon

Olof Palme | Hakeem Olajuwon

Tiger - Aquarius/Capricorn

Actor artist/critic author (3) author/traveller boss (3)
boss (museums) boss/TV editor curator (gallery)
neurophysiologist painter politician producer/theatre director tennis

Yevgeny Kafelnikov

Tiger - Aquarius/Aquarius

Actress (3) actor administrator ambassador astrologer
editor founder (books)/publisher headmistress politician (leader)
producer (TV) scientist writer Commander in Chief/General

Una Dillon | Russell Grant | William McKinley

Tiger - Aquarius/Pisces

Actress (3) actress/singer/model Archbishop architect/goldsmith/artist
boss/surveyor boss (3) comedian (2) film director/producer/writer
industrialist judge magistrate physicist pianist poet
politician singer (2)

Jean Becquerel | André-Gustave Citroën | Cybill Shepherd
Eddie Izzard

Tiger - Pisces/Aries

Academic/scientist/administrator actor (3) adviser (medical)
biochemist/embryologist boss (2) (HR) boss/accountant driver (rally)
drummer editor singer/model/actress Maj-General

William Hurt | Vanessa Kelly | Jerry Lewis | Sébastien Loeb

Tiger - Pisces/Taurus

Academic (3)/zoologist academic/linguist actress (2) actor artist artiste (variety)/singer bacteriologist boss (5) boss (cars) consultant (business) film maker headmaster pianist civil servant

August von Wasserman | Jamie Bell | Julie Walters

Tiger - Pisces/Gemini

Actress boss (3) boss/chaplain consultant (business) journalist (TV) model poet politician (leader) politician (2) potter Rabbi surgeon Vice Admiral

Jayde Nicole | Arthur Pearson | Helen Clark | Dame Myra Hess R T (Bobby) Jones | Julia Neuberger

Tiger - Pisces/Cancer

Actor designer (fashion) golfer judge (2) politician (3) politician (leader) proprietor (newspaper) Rabbi statesman singer (2) singer/boxer

Charlotte Church | Kenneth Williams | Franco Moschino Julia Neuberger

Tiger - Pisces/Leo

Academic (2)/ philosopher academic/vice chancellor biochemist boss (2) correspondent (foreign) headmaster QC/ warden (college) lawyer master (college)/headmaster musician/guitarist photographer politician singer Captain

Ansel Adams | Karen Carpenter

Tiger - Pisces/Virgo

Administrator biochemist designer (fashion)
businessman (2)/banker headmaster hostess (talk show) lawyer
pathologist politician writer/ founder (co- Private Eye) Capt/ship owner

Paul Ehrlich | Vanessa Feltz | Andrew Osmond

Tiger - Pisces/Libra

Academic (2)/ Vice-Chancellor academic/chemist
actor (2)/playwright/lyricist actor/manager Archbishop
architect/town planner bacteriologist 2-bassist /composer
clerk (Privy Council) boss commentator (TV, radio) dancer
expert (wildlife)/personality (TV) poet producer (operatic) soprano
statesman/diplomat trainer (racehorse) Lieut-Col

Steve Irwin | Elizabeth Barrett Browning | Vyacheslav Molotov
Rudolf Nureyev

Tiger - Pisces/Scorpio

Boss golfer (2) Lady-in-Waiting novelist pianist/ conductor
saxophonist swimmer tennis trainer (racehorse)

Thomas Enqvist | John Steinbeck

Tiger - Pisces/Sagittarius

Academic/haematologist actor (2) boss (4) boss/economist
boss (water) boss (museum)/engineer high commissioner
dancer/ choreographer film/theatre director head gardener
musicologist/author principal (college) Reverend singer

Alan Greenspan | Vaslav Nijinsky

Tiger - Pisces/Capricorn

Academic (music) accountant/librarian actor athlete
cricketer rugby boss (3) boss/expert (aviation) boxer
cellist/conductor dean/rector film producer/scriptwriter/journalist
High Commissioner musician/businessman pianist politician
scholar (music) Commandant Maj-General/qtr master

Joe Bugner | Willie Duggan | Jon Bon Jovi

Tiger - Pisces/Aquarius

Academic/virologist activist (civil rights) architect boss (2) (newspapers)/editor
boss/midwife boxer cartoonist keeper (gallery)/artist school master
trade unionist writer Air Marshal

David Langdon | Terry Spinks | Bridget Rowe

Tiger - Pisces/Pisces

Academic/biologist commentator (TV, radio) conductor engraver (wood)
inspector (Constabulary) poet politician (2)/lawyer/economist
politician (leader) rugby solicitor (2) tenor

R Lagos Escobar

Rabbit - Aries/Aries

Author Bishop Bishop (Assistant) boss (2)
chess player (2) educationist film maker/cameraman
governess Mayor physician/pulmonologist
Colonel Maj-General

Rabbit - Aries/Taurus

Academic/boss actor (2) actress/ singer/ TV presenter (2)
boss (oil) 2-chess critic (cinema)/TV host/author
film director footballer mayor model/photographer
politician singer (2) soldier

Gary Stevens | Quentin Tarantino

Rabbit - Aries/Gemini

Academic/poet boss (resistance) headmistress librarian model/actress oculist/surgeon painter politician (4) composer/saxophonist writer

Elle Macpherson

Rabbit - Aries/Cancer

Academic (Italian) actor boss chaplain cricketer educator (theatre) musician pianist politician/QC singer trade unionist writer

Dorothy Squires

Rabbit - Aries/Leo

Actress (3) actress/singer (2) baritone biochemist boss civil servant dealer (antiquities) playwright/screenwriter QC TV presenter/comedian writer/film-maker

Israel Horovitz | Olivia Hussey | Graham Norton

Rabbit - Aries/Virgo

Academic (chemistry) actress businessman/pilot politician QC psychologist/administrator scientist (conservation) singer (2) trade unionist trombonist/humorist trumpeter/composer

Marvin Gaye

Rabbit - Aries/Libra

Boss (2) (bank) boss (TV)/novelist cartoonist cricketer disc jockey film star historian musician pianist/conductor/founder (orchestra) pioneer (2) (aviation) pioneer (Br Chinese trade) singer

Charles Hallé | Wilbur Wright

Rabbit - Aries/Scorpio

Bandleader/musician (2) banker broadcaster
conductor/musician criminal (war) hairdresser judo
management consultant/engineer film director rheumatologist writer
Lt-Commander

Karen Briggs | Francis Ford Coppola | Sir David Frost | Henry James
Y Kwan Loo | Arturo Toscanini

Rabbit - Aries/Sagittarius

Academic (3) (materials) academic/QC academic (neurology) actress
Bishop boss (2) boss/architect chess dancer film maker
physicist

Garry Kasparov

Rabbit - Aries/Capricorn

Academic/psychologist agent (special - FBI) boss (2)/consultant (fire)
boss (promotion) cellist/conductor historian painter/sculptor
playwright singer tennis trainer (racehorse) writer

Alan Ayckbourn | Billie Holiday | Mohammed Fadhil Jamali
Jimmy Osmond | Maria Sharapova

Rabbit - Aries/Aquarius

Academic/gynaecologist actor (2) actress boss (2) civil servant
comedian/host (TV) pharmacologist poet politician (leader)
scholar/bibliographer singer (2) tenor Wing Commander/engineer

Seamus Heaney

Rabbit - Aries/Pisces

Academic (3) academic/scientist (political) academic/boss actress (2)
adviser (medical) boss (2) broadcaster cartoonist diver
driver (racing) guitarist inventor (Lego) oarsman
reporter (news) sculptor singer trade unionist

O K Christiansen | Jeremy Hands | Dusty Springfield
Rachel Whiteread

Rabbit - Taurus/Aries

Actor (2)/film director (2) actress businessman
consultant (engineering management) cricketer film/theatre director
footballer politician driver (racing) singer

Jackie Jackson

Rabbit - Taurus/Taurus

Academic (housing studies) actor (2) biochemist
boss (3)/musician (2)/composer/pianist boss (water) boss /civil servant (2)
conductor diplomat hostess (political) organist/choirmaster
politician(3) college principal Colonel/Lord Mayor

Lady Nancy Astor | Jet Li

Rabbit - Taurus/Gemini

Actor (2) artist (martial)/actor boss (2)/accountant
boss (shipbuilding) civil servant economist director (film, TV) footballer
rugby Brigadier Capt Maj-General

Nancy Kwan | Jonah Lomu | Lee Majors

Rabbit - Taurus/Cancer

Academic (4)/author academic/biochemist academic/engineer academic/pianist/critic actor boss editor diplomat expert (childcare)/psychologist founder (neurology) journalist judge manager pioneer (telephony) rugby sailor/sail maker/boat designer deputy Speaker (Hse of Lords)

Anthony Quinn | Elisabeth Söderstrom | Dr Benjamin Spock

Rabbit - Taurus/Leo

Actor author (3)/schoolmaster/ archaeologist boss (3) broadcaster conductor editor (newspapers) singer (2) soprano writer/printer/painter Field Marshal

Thomas Beecham | Bing Crosby | Moshe Dayan | Sir Arnold Hall Selina Scott | Rosie Boycott

Rabbit - Taurus/Virgo

Actor boss (2) comedian designer (fashion) editor judge painter politician (3) politician/judge sociologist

James Fox | Christian Lacroix

Rabbit - Taurus/Libra

Ballerina banker Bishop boss (3)/accountant boss/chief engineer/scientist composer golfer politician restaurateur singer/songwriter trade unionist Vice-Chancellor

Sergei Prokofiev

Rabbit - Taurus/Scorpio

Academic/engineer boss (2) boss/solicitor radio presenter sculptor singer (2) writer singer/songwriter

Joey Ramone

Rabbit - Taurus/Sagittarius

Academic/architect actor (2) actress author/poet boss (3)
boss/judge boss/pharmacist curator (museum) composer
educator (2) engineer politician (2) tennis General

Andy Murray | Natasha Richardson

Rabbit - Taurus/Capricorn

Academic (2)/historian academic (law) archaeologist astronaut
boss (2)/nurse boss (quango) composer dealer (antique) editor
footballer guitarist/vocalist mathematician/politician (2)
oarsman/doctor politician psychiatrist singer

Rajendra Persaud | Helen Sharman

Rabbit - Taurus/Aquarius

Academic/paediatrician actor/director boss businessman
diplomat racing driver footballer Lieut-General

David Beckham | Orson Welles

Rabbit - Taurus/Pisces

Actor architect boss/designer (graphic)
critic (2) (music) critic (theatre) bicycle designer footballer musician
politician restaurateur trainer (racehorse)

Norman Shaw | Antony Worrall-Thompson

Rabbit –Gemini/Aries

Academic (2)/physicist academic/venereologist actor (2) actress
ambassador cricketer (2)
cricketer/consultant (PR & sports marketing)/journalist/broadcaster (2)
headmaster politician (2) sculptor/painter swimmer
writer/broadcaster General

Angelina Jolie | Jackie Stewart

Rabbit - Gemini/Taurus

Actress barrister/judge boss (5) boss/surgeon composer/cellist designer (stage) inventor lexicographer poet rugby singer Vice-Chancellor writer

Saul Bellow | Jacques Offenbach | Shilpa Shetty | Frederick Tennyson Rory Underwood | Noah Webster

Rabbit - Gemini/Gemini

Actor banker boss (3) cameraman designer diplomat painter politician (2) tennis trumpeter/poet/politician

David Rockefeller | David Yip

Rabbit - Gemini/Cancer

Artist boss (management school) Canon comedian (2)/screenwriter judge lyricist naval officer/pilot painter proprietor singer virologist writer/poet/reformer Lieut/General Maj-General/signal officer General/politician

Bob Hope | J C Maxwell | Mike Myers | Cole Porter | Bonnie Tyler

Rabbit - Gemini/Leo

Academic (linguistics) actor (2) boss (3) composer/pianist cricketer driver (racing) fire fighter headmistress Ombudsman physician physicist (2) physicist/mathematician poet/essayist politician provost

Red Adair | Ramakant Desai | Ukyo Katayama | Ian McKellen Walt Whitman

Rabbit - Gemini/Virgo

Activist anaesthetist architect barrister/writer boss (4) Chief Constable dramatist editor (2) physicist fashion teacher Air Commodore

Frank Lloyd Wright | Gerald Ronson

Rabbit - Gemini/Libra

Actress boss civil servant driver (racing) hostess (literary) physicist politician surgeon Maj-General/chief scout

J C Adams | Anne-Sophie Mutter | Nanette Newman | Paul Boateng John Redwood

Rabbit - Gemini/Scorpio

Academic (developmental cardiology) actor adviser ballerina bookseller boss composer librarian/writer novelist (2) politician singer

Marcus Fox | Aram Khatchaturian | Terry Waite | Tim Waterstone Herman Wouk

Rabbit - Gemini/Sagittarius

Academic (2)/vet academic/ geneticist actor ambassador astronomer (discovered Neptune) boss/surveyor editor engineer/pioneer (concrete) nephrologist (consultant paediatric) novelist politician (2)

Johnny Depp | Ian Hargreaves

Rabbit - Gemini/Capricorn

Academic/college master actor (2) secret agent author boss chef chess consultant (nutrition) cricketer dancer/ballet master style guru painter politician (2)/journalist politician (leader) QC rugby singer/actress town planner Brigadier

Mel B | Paul Eddington | Joe Clark | Gustave Courbet | Anatoly Karpov Jamie Oliver

Rabbit - Gemini/Aquarius

Academic astronaut actor boss (supermarket composer/pianist developer (property) 2-diplomat editor (2) headmaster journalist naturalist novelist/clergyman politician (2) politician (leader) rugby writer (2)/editor Rear Admiral/Chief of Staff Air Marshal/pioneer (radar)

Andrew Farrell | Edvard Grieg | Charles Kingsley | Sally Ride

Rabbit - Gemini/Pisces

Academic (radiological sc) barrister (2) Bishop boss (2) boss (furniture) High Commissioner businesswoman boxer dancer film/TV director QC/Recorder novelist philosopher (moral) physicist politician (2)/Mayor politician rugby solicitor tennis

Arnold Bennett | John Conteh | Novak Djokovic | Rachel Heyhoe Flint Queen Mary of Teck

Rabbit - Cancer/Aries

Actress boss (newspaper)/author clarinettist dancer/choreographer/director entertainer headmaster jockey painter politician (3) trainer (racehorse)

Paul Eddery

Rabbit - Cancer/Taurus

Academic (2)/ archaeologist   academic/ astronomer   actress (2)
adviser (agricultural)/college principal   boss (3)/company founder   dramatist
musician   painter   Colonel

Brigitte Nielsen | Luigi Pirandello | Fatboy Slim

Rabbit - Cancer/Gemini

Academic (2) (meteorology)   academic/chemist   actor
author   boss   Chief Constable   cricketer
economist   novelist/poet   playwright/screenwriter   politician
sailor/writer   singer   soldier (2)/patriot   writer (4)
Vice Admiral

Saul Bellow | Giuseppe Garibaldi | Richard Hadlee

Rabbit - Cancer/Cancer

Actor (3)   actor/ broadcaster   ambassador   boss   cricketer (2)
cricketer/footballer   engineer   official (UN)   politician   QC/judge
zoologist/boss (research)/expert

Yul Brynner

Rabbit - Cancer/Leo

Academic (2)   boss (3)   curator (museum)   Lord Chancellor
playwright   rapper   film/TV director
stage director/choreographer   headmaster   college principal
trade unionist   Air Commodore/pathologist

Lil' Kim

Rabbit - Cancer/Virgo

Academic/engineer actress aviator cameraman film director footballer college master Moderator (church) playwright politician/chief whip

Amy Johnson | Ken Russell

Rabbit - Cancer/Libra

Academic actress (2) boss headmaster journalist musician politician (2) singer soldier (4)/art dealer solicitor/biographer surgeon violinist Rear Admiral Vice Admiral Colonel/Commandant (school)

Jill Halfpenny | Cheryl Ladd

Rabbit - Cancer/Scorpio

Academic (3)/architect (naval) academic/boss (research) academic/astronomer broker (insurance) football manager lawyer/Mayor murderer nursing officer viola player politician/principal (theology college) writer Maj-General

Dame Jill Knight

Rabbit - Cancer/Sagittarius

Actor (4) actress actress/singer architect cricketer/sociologist/author footballer historian physicist/inventor politician/deputy Speaker satirist/scriptwriter/actor songwriter/arranger tennis

Lorraine Chase | Henri Leconte | Frank Windsor

Rabbit - Cancer/Capricorn

Boss cricketer journalist (2) owner/writer playwright/ theatre director politician (2) politician/tennis Reverend

Rabbit - Cancer/Aquarius

Academic (soil) actor adviser (legal) author/ illustrator
boss (3) boss/dentist boss/Reverend civil servant
harpsi-chordist historian (art) inventor journalist (2)
violinist/composer tenor Commander/boss

Elias Howe | Tobey Maguire

Rabbit - Cancer/Pisces

Academic/biologist actor/ comedian aerodynamicist anaesthetist athlete
boss (2) boss/engineer cartoonist conductor dancer
designer/ furniture maker driver (racing) novelist (2) owner (racehorse)
politician (3) politician (leader) (2) politician (leader)/lawyer
publisher (music) rugby translator Vice Admiral

Mary Peters | Ralf Schumacher | Irving Stone | Robin Williams

Rabbit - Leo/Aries

Academic (2) (epidemiology) academic (geography)/ Vice-Chancellor
actress/singer boss (2) disc jockey 2-driver (rally) film director
novelist physician/mountaineer politician saxophonist singer (2)
surgeon

Lynda Carter | Whitney Houston

Rabbit - Leo/Taurus

Academic/microbiologist actor/ wrestler anaesthetist broadcaster (2)
founder (Avis) disc jockey painter sculptor Maj-General

Warren Avis | Sridevi

Rabbit - Leo/Gemini

Academic (2)/archaeologist academic (Chinese) actress (3) boss (2)
boss/consultant (2)` composer boss/ pioneer (air transport) composer traveller

Kate O'Mara

Rabbit - Leo/Cancer

Academic (3)/boss/college master academic/bursar
academic (farm business mgt) actress author boss (5)
boss/ architect boss (bank) boss/founder civil servant composer
consultant (marketing) engineer entertainer/artist (cabaret drag)
journalist /trade unionist librarian (2) poker player college principal
politician (3) scientist sociologist/ innovator (social) tennis

Evonne Cawley | Danny La Rue | Philip Snow

Rabbit - Leo/Leo

Academic (2)/geneticist academic (horticulture) actor (4)
actress/model (fashion) boss/banker headmaster journalist
obstetrician pharmacist rugby solicitor writer/cathedral Dean
Air Marshal

Tom Felton | Charlize Theron

Rabbit - Leo/Virgo

Archbishop broadcaster painter physician/rugby playwright
poet politician/trade unionist politician (2) violinist/composer writer/
botanist Field Marshal/Governor General

Stanley Baldwin | Viscount William Slim | Graham Sutherland
Trevor McDonald

Rabbit - Leo/Libra

Academic (2)/haematologist academic/mathematician
activist (polit)/theorist bookseller/author boss consultant (PR) cricketer
drummer college master film maker/screenwriter
founder (Theosophical Soc) QC schoolmaster/expert (space) pianist/singer

Tori Amos | Ginger Baker | Helena Blavatsky | Richard Illingworth
Lord Mishcon

Rabbit - Leo/Scorpio

Academic (astronomy) artist/surveyor boss broadcaster
civil servant/author co-ordinator journalist college principal
TV presenter/producer

William Woollard

Rabbit - Leo/Sagittarius

Academic (3)/pathologist academic/ epidemiologist
academic/surgeon/businessman boss (3) choral director/composer
entrepreneur (2) footballer headmaster healer politician (2)
rapper restaurateur writer/sailor Major/equerry

Habib Bourguiba | Coolio | J W Howard | Herman Melville
Mark Wright

Rabbit - Leo/Capricorn

Academic/Vice-Chancellor actress boss/civil servant
author/organiser conductor/ harpsichordist/composer
explorer/archaeologist/sculptor film director politician (2)
politician /lawyer QC/gynaecologist reformer (social)/activist (2)
activist (welfare rights) Vice Admiral Air Chief Marshal

Peter Bogdanovich | Katie Leung

Rabbit - Leo/Aquarius

Academic (2)/Bishop academic/geographer actor
archaeologist/anthropologist boss/consultant/lecturer boxer carver/artist
conductor guitarist politician tenor

Alan Minter

Rabbit - Leo/Pisces

Actress (2)/model (2) guitarist/songwriter judge model/actress musician/film composer/film producer politician (3) sculptor singer writer

Rabbit - Virgo/Aries

Actress author/consultant (publishing) boss (3) broadcaster consultant (management) critic/journalist entertainer (TV) entrepreneur footballer impresario (theatrical) politician rugby writer (2) writer/essayist

Ingrid Bergman | Andy Irvine

Rabbit - Virgo/Taurus

Academic author boss (2) driver (racing) screenwriter songwriter/bassist surgeon/physician Lieut-General Maj-General Major/QC/judge

Rabbit - Virgo/Gemini

Academic (Spanish) actor (2) actress Archdeacon High Commissioner stage director doctor headmaster illustrator manager (football) musician novelist presenter (TV) singer

Pamela Armstrong | Peter Falk | Arthur Rackham

Rabbit - Virgo/Cancer

Agent (literary) ambassador boss (2) boss/accountant cricketer critic (literary) judge musician obstetrician/gynaecologist intelligence officer pianist/composer pioneer (cinema)

John Dankworth | W Friese-Greene

Rabbit - Virgo/Leo

Academic/historian (art) actor (2) actor/film producer
antiquary/historian ice hockey QC/ barrister chess player
singer swimmer Vice-Chancellor Major

Dana

Rabbit - Virgo/Virgo

Actor archaeologist coach (tennis) cricketer crofter
designer (consultant) diplomat (2) dramatist judoka
musician/teacher operative (MI5) physicist statesman Rear Admiral

David Bairstow | Jean-Bernard | Léon Foucault | Richard Kiel
Victorien Sardou | Ry ko Tamura

Rabbit - Virgo/Libra

Academic actor (2) actress archaeologist/explorer ballerina
boss (3) boss/accountant detective/founder (detective agency) footballer
historian (ballet) politician 2-singer trade unionist Maj-General/boss

Jarvis Cocker | Marie-Agnès Gillot | Michael Keaton | Allan Pinkerton
David Seaman

Rabbit - Virgo/Scorpio

Academic (business) bassoonist bowler footballer journalist
physicist singer trainer (racehorse)

Prince Albert | Michael Buble | Armand Hyppolyte

Rabbit - Virgo/Sagittarius

Actor boss broadcaster/consultant (financial) businessman
coach (football) economist/adviser engineer headmaster
politician (leader)/lawyer surgeon trombonist/composer

Paul Volcker

Rabbit - Virgo/Capricorn

Academic (2)/theologist artist director (music)/violinist
engineer (2) golfer headmistress exile leader pilot (acrobatic) tutor (Fr)

Rabbit - Virgo/Aquarius

Actor administrator/intelligence officer/ornithologist
architect/designer (theatre set) Bishop headmaster judge
physician politician Vice-Chancellor

Bertie Ahern

Rabbit - Virgo/Pisces

Academic (3) (education) academic/ (govt/public administration)
academic/urologist/surgeon actor aide to Senator artist
boss (assurance) broadcaster broker (insurance)
consultant (cardiologist) driver (racing) headmaster
politician/soldier soprano violinist Capt/historian (naval)

Arthur Lowe | Juan Pablo Montoya | John Peel

Rabbit - Libra/Aries

Archaeologist boss/ broadcaster clerk (barrister's)/Mayor
film producer musician/composer painter poet politician
college principal singer/songwriter surgeon tennis

Roscoe Tanner

Rabbit - Libra/Taurus

Academic/ (operative dental surgery) activist (Greenpeace) artist baritone
cartoonist/creator (Batman) GP golfer scholar (textiles) solicitor

Laura Davies | Bob Kane

Rabbit - Libra/Gemini

Academic/chemist actor (2) actress boss/ solicitor (2)
broadcaster US governor journalist lawyer
colonial officer physicist pioneer (dance) QC speedway (champ)

James Chadwick | Sir Roger Moore | Anneka Rice

Rabbit - Libra/Cancer

Academic (2)/ chemist academic/ anaesthetist actor (3) actress
boss (2) 2-broadcaster/writer news cameraman expert (aviation)
headmaster musician 2-rugby scientist writer (3)/ playwright
Rear Admiral

Melvyn Bragg | Gunter Grass | Clive James | William Whiteley | A M Yurko

Rabbit - Libra/Leo

Academic/film producer (2) actor (2) athlete author (2)
author/surgeon boss diplomat editor (film) journalist/film maker
judge pioneer (dept store) poet politician psychologist sculptor

Paul Hogan | George C Scott

Rabbit - Libra/Virgo

Actor ballerina (prima) boss carver (netsuke) conductor
dancer/ ballet master consultant (quality management) novelist
principal (music sch)/musician/teacher publisher (2) tennis
Lieut-Colonel/intelligence officer

Maria Bueno | Nathanael West

Rabbit - Libra/Libra

Academic (2)/ sociologist academic/nephrologist actress (2) chef/hotelier 2-judge novelist philosopher/research fellow/literary critic physicist/Reverend sculptor singer/composer statesman/industrialist vibraphonist Capt/boss

Parminder Nagra | Sting | Kate Winslet

Rabbit - Libra/Scorpio

Bishop boss (2)/electrical engineer designer (fashion) painter/printmaker psychiatrist rugby solicitor/boss trumpeter Brigadier General

Phil Davies | Ralph Lauren | Mark Rothko

Rabbit - Libra/Sagittarius

Academic (2)/ paediatrician academic (physics) architect (2) architect/ planner (town artist boss broadcaster civil servant critic (music)/editor painter singer/ initiator (Band Aid) figure skater translator Vice Admiral Air Chief Marshal

Sandy Gall | Bob Geldof

Rabbit - Libra/Capricorn

Architect artist assassin/sailor boss (4) boss (electronics) footballer government chief whip pianist politician (4)

Sebastian de Ferranti | Lee Harvey Oswald | Yitzhak Shamir

Rabbit - Libra/Aquarius

Artiste (music hall) boss (4) boss (retail) boss/QC cricketer editor novelist/journalist pianist playwright/essayist psychiatrist Recorder/magistrate singer/actor Admiral/Governor

Sir Leon Brittan | Vladimir Horowitz | Arthur Miller

Rabbit - Libra/Pisces

Accountant actor biologist/biochemist consultant (design) designer (interior) diplomat golfer QC/ college provost midwife

Rabbit - Scorpio/Aries

Academic (3)/ (social geography) academic/scientist (space) actor (3)/comedian actress (2) boss (2) entrepreneur (holiday)/lecturer conductor/composer golfer minister (Methodist) politician/ambassador college rector/Reverend rugby savant singer/actress swimmer trainer (racehorse) Air Marshal Brigadier/boss

John Cleese | Jimmy Hoseason | Faye Tozer | Yuki Uchida

Rabbit - Scorpio/Taurus

Administrator/ambassador basketballer comedian/singer 2-film maker manager (football) rapper singer swimmer tennis Commander Maj-General/politician

Ken Dodd | James Garfield | Mark Hughes | Patti Page
Erwin Rommel | Zhang Yimou

Rabbit - Scorpio/Gemini

Academic/educationist/historian actress adviser (education) boss/engineer boss (4) broadcaster/ footballer theatre director/writer drummer entertainer glider (champ) headmaster/Reverend judge zoologist

Tatum O'Nea | Lord Wolfson | Ian Wright | Lena Zavaroni

Rabbit - Scorpio/Cancer

Archbishop boss (3) boss/engineer guitarist/composer
picture framer producer (TV) politician (2) QC/politician
teacher (spiritual)/writer/artist

John Barnes I Lawrie Barrat I Lord Falconer

Rabbit - Scorpio/Leo

Academic (3)/ physician academic (medicine) academic/physicist
actor (2) boss/ accountant footballer hypnotist/broadcaster
judge leader (Russian Revolution) merchant (clothing) politician (2)
QC/solicitor spymaster

Paul McKenna I Wallace Rowling I Léon Trotsky

Rabbit - Scorpio/Virgo

Actress/singer boss (4) boss (banking) judge
meteorologist politician priest college
principal/lecturer/sociologist rugby sociologist Maj-General/banker

Fanny Brice I John Egan I Marie-Hélène de Rothschild

Rabbit - Scorpio/Libra

Boss (2) broker (insurance) cartoonist deputy editor
lecturer (sc history) librarian politician (2) politician (leader)
psychoanalyst sociologist

Edgar R H Bowring I Chong Jin Wee

Rabbit - Scorpio/Scorpio

Academic administrator boss (TV)/Dean/Reverend climber
entrepreneur journalist / TV/radio host singer (2) tennis (2) trombonist
vocalist

Zina Garrison-Jackson

Rabbit - Scorpio/Sagittarius

Ambassador Archbishop boss (2) dancer educationist (environmental) 2-footballer headmaster novelist photographer politician presenter (TV) Reverend singer (2) soprano solicitor tennis Brigadier General/private secretary

Dame Cleo Laine | Sir Timothy Raison | Peter Schmeichel Lisa Scott-Lee

Rabbit - Scorpio/Capricorn

Academic (3) academic (biochemistry) academic/boss/economist actress (3) actress/fashion model boss (newspaper) economist musician novelist rugby

George Eliot

Rabbit - Scorpio/Aquarius

Actor advocate athlete boss (2) editor/author (2) Egyptologist entrepreneur (arts) meteorologist novelist (2) politician promoter (boxing) spy/writer

Margaret Atwood | Mary Bancroft | Nigel Havers | Tom McKean Lord Sainsbury | David Saul | Auberon Waugh | Evelyn Waugh

Rabbit - Scorpio/Pisces

Actor/bodybuilder campaigner (for Palestine) chemist diplomat house builder leader (Hindu nationalist) journalist/broadcaster politician

Marie Curie | Lou Ferrigno

Rabbit - Sagittarius/Aries

Academic (3)/campaigner academic (materials) footballer (2) founder (orchestra) jockey judge leader (Soviet) politician teacher (dance) secretary Admiral Field Marshal/Governor General

Joseph Stalin

Rabbit - Sagittarius/Taurus

Academic (3)/ (maths) academic (engineering) academic/ Vice-Chancellor actor (2) actress banker/ antiquary boss civil servant/ adviser (legal) diplomat nurse playwright/poet politician (2) saxophonist singer

Abdullah Badawi | John Gummer | Tina Turner

Rabbit - Sagittarius/Gemini

Academic (2)/college master academic/archaeologist boss cardiologist historian model (fitness)/wrestler musician/writer/broadcaster Mayor physician (consultant) politician Lieut-Colonel Squadron Leader/pilot/engineer

Arthur Marshall

Rabbit - Sagittarius/Cancer

Boss (research)/politician (2) counsellor (spiritual)/author designer (lighting) educationist (physical) governor (bank) poet rugby General/dictator/politician

Nigel Heslop | Augusto Pinochet

Rabbit - Sagittarius/Leo

Actress bacteriologist boss golfer inventor (microchip) manufacturer (aircraft) ski jumper potter singer writer/politician

Richard Cassilly | Eddie (the Eagle) Edwards | Robert Koch | Lee Trevino

Rabbit - Sagittarius/Virgo

Academic (2)/pioneer (computer software) Academic/Vice-Chancellor adviser (tech) author boss (2)/politician boss/ publisher composer footballer (2) nationalist novelist QC/judge rugby/administrator singer (2) tenor

Max Reinhardt

Rabbit - Sagittarius/Libra

Bishop boss (2)/accountant boss (quango) broadcaster/writer
civil servant engineer footballer guitarist rugby squash

Jahangir Khan | Michael Owen

Rabbit - Sagittarius/Scorpio

Academic (zoology) author boss (3) broadcaster
paediatrician flute player politician (2) presenter (radio/TV)

James Galway | Young Sam Kim

Rabbit - Sagittarius/Sagittarius

Academic (2)/ antiquary academic (history) boss footballer
journalist (2) novelist/journalist politician QC tenor writer General

Karim Benzema

Rabbit - Sagittarius/Capricorn

Actor/ film producer actor (2) banker immune geneticist physician
politician snooker soprano trainer (racehorse) writer (2)
Air Marshal Vice Admiral

Clyde Cessna | Ronnie O'Sullivan | Brad Pitt | Eli Wallach

Rabbit - Sagittarius/Aquarius

Actress (2) ambassador athlete basketballer diplomat
racing driver journalist/translator judge model/actress
musician/songwriter police (boss) (2) singer wrestler (2)
Commandant/boss

Rabbit - Sagittarius/Pisces

Actress (2)/singer ballerina boss (2) boxer
manager (football)/footballer painter politician (2) singer (3)
singer/actor Commodore

Paul Klee | Frank Sinatra | Balthazar Vorster | Andy Williams

Rabbit - Capricorn/Aries

Academic/paediatrician actor cellist chaplain/headmaster
comedienne/writer darts film producer/ creator (Keystone Cops) geologist
governor (bank) judge optician poet politician (2) runner
scientist/inventor Brigadier/boss

Caroline Aherne | P W Botha | Kip Keino

Rabbit - Capricorn/Taurus

Academic (2)/vet actor (2) actor/comedian boss broadcaster
inspector (chief - Fire Services) musician/disc jockey politician (2)
politician/journalist/editor priest/teacher wrestler

Michael Barratt

Rabbit - Capricorn/Gemini

Academic/geologist astronomer civil servant/lawyer
management consultant (arts) golfer (2) politician (4)
Air Marshal

Zulfikar Ali Bhutto | Walter Mondale | Jack Nicklaus

Rabbit - Capricorn/Cancer

Athlete boss/farmer golfer journalist pastor poet
producer/director (TV) writer Capt/pilot

Mohammad-Ali Jamalzadeh

Rabbit - Capricorn/Leo

Architect/editor boss college master editor headmaster
assistant inspector politician (2) priest producer (radio drama)
saint/visionary surveyor

Bernadette of Lourdes

Rabbit - Capricorn/Virgo

Academic (2) (archaeology) academic/(psychiatry) actor artiste (variety)
Bishop boss (2)
historian (art) judge politician QC/barrister
Air Chief Marshal

Oliver Hardy

Rabbit - Capricorn/Libra

2-Academic /college master actor athlete (marathon)
bassist boss (2) consultant (engineering/safety) cricketer
diplomat judge lobbyist (political) poet singer
Maj-General/boss

Nicolas Cage | Richard Nerurkar

Rabbit - Capricorn/Scorpio

Academic (2)/ physicist academic (physics) editor (2)
editor/journalist engineer novelist soprano hair stylist General

Henry Miller | Vidal Sassoon

Rabbit - Capricorn/Sagittarius

Actor boss (3) boss (investments)
boss/soldier clown composer dancer disc jockey
editor journalist photographer/designer (theatre) pilot (test)
politician(2) producer (radio) financial secretary singer

**Maxene Andrews | Cecil Beaton | Edmund de Rothschild | Cary Grant
Grock**

Rabbit - Capricorn/Capricorn

Actor artist/scriptwriter Bishop boss (2) cartoonist/painter Constable (Chief) critic (dance, music) designer (fashion) 2-film director golfer politician (militant) singer (gospel) Capt/solicitor

Beaverbrook (Lord) | John Glashan

Rabbit - Capricorn/Aquarius

Artist author/dramatist boss/politician diplomat industrialist (Fiat) lawyer model painter priest tennis

Edoardo Agnelli | Bob Hewitt | Michelle Obama

Rabbit - Capricorn/Pisces

Actor (2) actress boss coach (weightlifting) coach (US football)/US footballer educationist theatre director painter writer/scholar

Cary Grant | Jane Horrocks | Trevor Nunn | J R R Tolkien

Rabbit - Aquarius/Aries

Actress (3) actress/film producer ambassador athlete/skier boss (2)/businessman civil servant novelist/actress politician (2) politician/boss tennis undertaker/organist/singer

Bharrat Jagdeo | Lucie Safarova

Rabbit - Aquarius/Taurus

Academic/ (2) Vice-Chancellor academic/sculptor boss (3) boss (freight) boxer comedian footballer painter/sculptor pianist poet rugby statesman

Nigel Benn | Howard Davies | Dick Emery | Gary Neville

Rabbit - Aquarius/Gemini

Academic (2) academic (music) actor (2) actress
astrologer/author boss golfer manager (football)/footballer
magnate (media)/publisher pioneer (adding machines) politician
skater (figure) skier soprano Field Marshal

William Seward Burroughs | John Hurt | Kevin Keegan | Jane Seymour
Gillian Shephard | Pirmin Zurbriggen

Rabbit - Aquarius/Cancer

Actress biographer/critic boss
Deputy Commissioner (police) Constable (Chief) editor matron in chief
politician trade unionist writer/poet/artist Rear Admiral/boss

Lois Maxwell | John Ruskin

Rabbit - Aquarius/Leo

Academic (2) (family research) academic (electrical engineering) actress
baritone/teacher boss (2) cricketer (Capt) diplomat
Governor (prison) humorist/writer physicist psychologist (child) rugby
General

June Brown | John Gallagher | Douglas MacArthur

Rabbit - Aquarius/Virgo

Academic (3) academic/chemist academic/planning consultant actor
agent (intelligence)/politician (2) astrologer/author boss (2)
Commander composer diplomat engineer
guerrilla/politician/poet musician painter (2) pharmacist
physician/explorer scientist singer Maj-General/boss

Emma Bunton | Airey Neave | W C Fields

Rabbit - Aquarius/Libra

Academic/philosopher farmer model painter
pioneer (typewriter) rapper/actor/radio personality ventriloquist writer/politician

Edouard Manet

Rabbit - Aquarius/Scorpio

Actor bassist boss (2) theatre director TV host industrialist
novelist/critic tennis vocalist General

Marcel Dassault | William Sherman

Rabbit - Aquarius/Sagittarius

Academic/statistician actor author (3) basketballer boss (bank)
bursar maker (instrument) soprano theatre director rugby
writer/poet

Lewis Carroll | David Jason | Michael Jordan

Rabbit - Aquarius/Capricorn

Actor (2) actress ambassador martial artist/wrestler
athlete (2) athlete/footballer baseballer boss (2)(charity)
boss (chemists)/scientist film director TV, radio host/author/entrepreneur
education officer singer/musician soccer player

Jimmy Tarbuck

Rabbit - Aquarius/Aquarius

Actor (4) actress boss (2) counsel
engineer (electrical) manager (football) model/actress college master
muralist/designer songwriter Colonel/boss

José Mourinho

Rabbit - Aquarius/Pisces

Actor (2) actress campaigner choreographer physicist poet/percussionist/sound artist politician (leader) Reverend/broadcaster saxophonist surgeon

Lord Soper

Rabbit - Pisces/Aries

Academic/Vice-Chancellor (2) academic/principal (LBS) actor (2) actress/model boss (4) boss/consultant boss/academic chess (grandmaster) judge nutritionist rector scholar (2) scholar (Sanskrit)/Bard trade unionist Lieut-General

Eva Longoria | D D Sieff

Rabbit - Pisces/Taurus

Academic (5) academic/anatomist academic/engineer academic/gastroenterologist architect/consultant (design)/writer boss (3) boss (bank) boss/physics cartoonist composer (2) college master diplomat hairdresser church minister pianist policeman politician (2) singer Admiral/politician (leader) Air Vice Marshal

Prof George Bain | Sviatoslav Richter | Trevor Sorbie

Rabbit - Pisces/Gemini

Academic/principal (U) (2) ballerina (prima) designer (fashion) Vice-Chancellor/principal (U) driver (racing) editor/boss lexicographer/engineer politician (2) politician/chief whip surveyor trainer (racehorse) Brig-General/pilot

Kenzo Takada | Sebastian Vettel

Rabbit - Pisces/Cancer

Actor (3) actress cartoonist academic/college principal judge physician/teacher politician saxophonist scientist (environmental) surveyor trade unionist

Drew Barrymore

Rabbit - Pisces/Leo

Academic/architect (2) administrator athlete civil servant/ consultant (telecoms) cricketer footballer (US) politician economist footballer player (cornet)/composer saxophonist scientist (2) medical scientist statistician/scorer (cricket)

Bix Beiderbecke | Gordon Brown | Bernie Kosar

Rabbit - Pisces/Virgo

Actress (2) actress (porn)/model boss (2) boss/ lecturer choreographer controller (Radio) founder (Tate Gallery) physicist/chemist

Samantha Eggar | Otto Hahn | Sir Henry Tate

Rabbit - Pisces/Libra

2-Academic/philosopher actor/ film director ballerina biologist Bishop boss (2) businessman/engineer businessman/rugby composer consultant (competition) cricketer designer (fashion)/ founder (Givenchy) golfer photographer/ film/video director 2-politician tenor

Hubert de Givenchy | John Joubert | Sidney Poitier | Lynn Seymour

Rabbit - Pisces/Scorpio

Actor/TV producer boss Constable (Chief) expert (wine) inventor (Pullman carriages) journalist/book (reviewer) poet (2) poet/writer principal (U) reviewer singer (2) soprano Vice Admiral

Henry Wadsworth Longfellow | Adelina Patti | George Pullman

Rabbit - Pisces/Sagittarius

Academic (2)/ historian academic/statistician/ criminologist boss (2)/accountant broadcaster consultant (legal)/arbitrator/judge cricketer designer (interior) editor explorer/writer (2) founder photographer physicist playwright/novelist/actor proprietor (newspaper) singer/composer

Albert Einstein | Salim Malik | Neil Sedaka

Rabbit - Pisces/Capricorn

Actor boss (2) investigator (accident)/pilot/engineer novelist (2)/poet (2) poet/ diplomat manager (football)/footballer provost/boss scholar/writer

Kenny Dalgleish

Rabbit - Pisces/Aquarius

Astronomer/ founder (Lovell observatory) boss (3) boss (law)/judge engraver (glass) town planner golfer manager (football) musician (2) politician singer singer/actor winemaker yachtsman General

Harry Belafonte | James Lovell | Vijay Singh

Rabbit - Pisces/Pisces

Academic (2)/ obstetrician academic/artist artist author/founder (battered wives shelter) boss/engineer cricketer designer (fashion) diplomat film-maker novelist Rabbi singer trainer (racehorse)

Michael Deakin | Phil Edmonds

Dragon - Aries/Aries

Academic/Vice-Chancellor/engineer actor (2) actress driver (racing) historian novelist/critic physiologist politician (2) trainer (ice-skating)

Betty Callaway | Maria Schneider | Dmitri Volkogonov

Dragon - Aries/Taurus

Academic/ Vice-Chancellor actress astronaut boxer broadcaster columnist journalist model (super)/actress novelist singer Colonel

Maxim Gorky | Gloria Hunniford | James Lovell

Dragon - Aries/Gemini

Actuary executive assistant comedian/teacher driver (racing) footballer/coach model/actress (2) musician pianist/ composer singer (2)/actress singer/songwriter

Max Mosley

Dragon - Aries/Cancer

Academic/archaeologist actor/playwright Archbishop boss (2) civil servant driver (racing) impressionist painter percussionist/composer politician/author/actor rugby

Jeffrey Archer | Ieuan Evans

Dragon - Aries/Leo

Academic/ educationist architect/town planner athlete mountaineer novelist/satirist poet spy writer (2) writer/broadcaster General

Liz McColgan

Dragon - Aries/Virgo

Academic/physicist academic/Vice-Chancellor ambassador
Archbishop boss cook dancer/ choreographer film star (silent)
GP missionary/civil servant QC/ Recorder writer
Rear Admiral/submariner/businessman

Algy Cluff | Mary Pickford

Dragon - Aries/Libra

Activist/lecturer (2)/leadership develop't specialist actor (4)
architect/ town planner boss (2) /industrialist coach (football) comedian
editor entertainer/producer deputy judge/QC council leader
novelist/singer/actress playwright/scriptwriter/lecturer
politician/boss (print/marketing) producer (TV) QC (2) Maj-General

Sirimavo Bandaranaike | Prof Peter Moore | James Watson

Dragon - Aries/Scorpio

Academic (3)/geneticist/joint discover DNA academic/classicist
academic/historian actor (2) author film director
physicist/ mathematician model/fan dancer rugby statesman (2)
statesman/financier Marshal (RAF)

Dragon - Aries/Sagittarius

Academic (2)/ geologist actress civil servant conductor/composer
cricketer director (artistic, theatre, film, TV) dramatist founder/surveyor
lecturer/songwriter/singer mathematician organist politician (2)
trainer (racehorse)/jockey writer

Reese Witherspoon | Nigel Farage

Dragon - Aries/Capricorn

Conductor/composer cricketer designer (theatre) film director footballer
politician/historian politician (2) sculptor surgeon

Dragon - Aries/Aquarius

Academic (2) (logic) academic(vet anatomy)/environmentalist/activist actor boss college warden diplomat (2) diplomat/Governor General motorcyclist/ driver (racing) politician GP rugby/ printer

Russell Crowe | Penelope Keith

Dragon - Aries/Pisces

Academic (2)/engineer actor/film director/author archaeologist boss (3) composer (3) Constable (Chief) craftsman (forest) jockey/ trainer (racehorse) Buddhist lama lecturer/writer (2) naturalist/writer pilot (test)/ historian (air) producer (theatrical) tennis

Jennifer Capriati | Jung Chang | Ferde Grofé | Franz von Suppé

Dragon - Taurus/Aries

Academic (2)/biotechnologist academic/historian actress (2) actress/model/porn star ambassador boss (opera) civil servant college Dean/Canon curator (gallery) journalist/editor painter QC

Salvador Dali

Dragon - Taurus/Taurus

Academic (2)/scientist chess champion/editor designer (fashion)/presenter (TV) novelist nurse/reformer (hosp) politician/dictator priest/lecturer snooker Rear Admiral Air Chief Marshal

Peter Benchley | Jean Paul Gaultier | Florence Nightingale | John Parrott Pol Pot (Saloth Sar)

Dragon - Taurus/Gemini

Actor (2) actress/diplomat boss (5) broadcaster/ presenter (TV) diplomat (2) explorer (2) society hostess journalist judge/QC politician psychoanalyst/neurologist scholar/poet scientist (forensic) trainer (racehorse) trumpeter chief vet

Shirley Temple Black | Sigmund Freud | Robert Peary

Dragon - Taurus/Cancer

Academic/ statistician   actor (3)   actor/producer (film)
actress/singer   artist   broadcaster   comptroller/auditor
theatre/opera   director   corporate financier   headmaster (2)   physicist
sculptor   saxophonist   secret operations officer   trainer (racehorse)
writer (3)   writer/speaker (public)

N D Cadbury   Sir Huw Weldon

Dragon - Taurus/Leo

Actress/singer   athlete   Bishop   boss (5) (polytechnic)
boss (bank)/engineer   boss (bank)   boss (collection)   composer (2)
geologist   hotelier   chief librarian   musician/teacher   soldier (2)
organist   pianist/ composer   pilot/fighter (air)   politician   writer
yachtsman   Air Vice Marshal

**Milton Babbitt | Chay Blyth | Manfred von Richthofen | Isla St Clair
Thomas 'Fats' Waller | Alan Wells**

Dragon - Taurus/Virgo

Academic (2)/bioengineer   academic/Vice-Chancellor   archer
boss (insurer)   entertainer   essayist/critic   musician/songwriter   politician (2)

Michael Barrymore | Marshal Tito | Prof Heinz Wolff

Dragon - Taurus/Libra

Academic/ physicist   boss (water)   musician   novelist/poet
politician (2)   provost   writer   computer scientist

L Frank Baum | Cecil Day-Lewis

Dragon - Taurus/Scorpio

Academic (2) (maritime archaeology) academic/pathologist
boss (5) (admin) boss (milk) boss (pharmaceuticals)
2-boss/banker criminologist/civil servant engineer
founder (modern ballet)/dancer/choreographer impresario/founder (theatres)
matron-in-chief Mayor photographer/ promoter (circus)
politician publisher singer

Richard D'Oyly Carte | Hosni Moubarak

Dragon - Taurus/Sagittarius

Academic/ Vice-Chancellor/principal/engineer accountant actor (2)
boss Dean/Very Reverend Reverend (2) journalist judge
packer (meat) physician politician film producer violinist/conductor
singer/actress Marshal

Martine McCutcheon | Al Pacino | Henri Philippe Pétain

Dragon - Taurus/Capricorn

Academic (2)/historian/Reverend academic/theologian
author (2)/critic boss (investor) boxer chess/ publisher
correspondent jockey musician novelist nurse
statesman tennis tenor

Gordon Richards | Harold Robbins | Jimmy Wilde

Dragon - Taurus/Aquarius

Broadcaster/ commentator clerk composer/pianist
correspondent film director engineer/aviator farmer novelist (2)
painter/artist (cartoon) General/politician

Burt Bacharach | Saw Maung | Morris West

Dragon - Taurus/Pisces

Actor (s) actress/voice actor boss(2) (NHS) film director founder (Lamborghini) editor/boss US footballer politician (2) surgeon

Cheryl Gillan | Ferruccio Lamborghini

Dragon - Gemini/Aries

Artist/writer (2) author boss (3)/baritone boss/ engineer chaplain/ Archdeacon (Navy) Constable (asst Chief)/detective inventor/astronomer mathematician pathologist physician poet/ musician (street) politician sales person singer (2) Vice-Chancellor

Che Guevara de la Serna

Dragon - Gemini/Taurus

Actress (3) actress/model cricketer editor leader (guerrilla) painter politician (2) 2-singer stuntman/actor/boxer

William Cosgrave

Dragon - Gemini/Gemini

Academic (3) (botany) academic/Vice-Chancellor academic (medieval history) actor (2) boss (poly)/engineer cricketer lawyer novelist/poet/librettist chief medical officer performer (dub & reggae) rugby singer (3) singer/actress solicitor/consultant

Moira Anderson | Vikram Seth | David Shapiro

Dragon - Gemini/Cancer

Actor (3) actress ambassador artist boss cataloguer (picture) consultant (export credit) cricketer driver (racing) engineer horticulturist journalist musician/writer painter politicia singer (2) trainer (racehorse) trade unionist writer (3) writer/broadcaster General

André Derain | Colin Farrell | Tom Jones | Henri Rousseau
Nancy Sinatra

Dragon - Gemini/Leo

Advertising executive boss (2) boss (NHS) comedienne/actress Industrialist/founder (Gevaert) politician (2) singer/songwriter writer General

Kathy Burke | Lieven Gevaert

Dragon - Gemini/Virgo

Academic/biologist/discover (DNA) barrister boss (charity) comedian composer University Dean farmer pathologist physicist politician (leader)/boss (bank, car) TV star Wing Commander

Courteney Cox | Francis Crick

Dragon - Gemini/Libra

2-boss (marketing) journalist (2) civil servant editor/politician/mayor pioneer (disability)/journalist/TV broadcaster politician (leader) politician (3) lyricist singer/comedian tennis

Jefferson Davis | George Formby | Boris Johnson

Dragon - Gemini/Scorpio

Artist broadcaster/comedian civil servant designer (2) (theatre) designer (furniture) golfer industrialist (mining) inventor (4 stroke engine) politician schoolmaster/writer (dictionary) skier (water) swimmer

Paul Goydos | Bob Monkhouse | Adrian Moorhouse
Sir Ernest Oppenheimer | Nikolaus Otto

Dragon - Gemini/Sagittarius

Academic (2)/ bacteriologist academic/philosopher actor (2) boss cinematographer comedian cyclist/politician designer (fashion) explorer headmistress judge musician/composer politician (2) reporter/editor singer/songwriter Rear Admiral

David Baddiel | Lenny Kravitz | Liam Neeson | Robert Falcon Scott
Paul Shane

Dragon - Gemini/Capricorn

Academic (2) academic/ sociologist actor (3) architect boss (2) (banking) boss (flight operations) Canon poet/ essayist swimmer/actor

Charles Rennie Mackintosh | Basil Rathbone | Johnny Weissmuller

Dragon - Gemini/Aquarius

Academic (3)/sociologist academic/scientist (political) academic (Pure Maths) boss (2) boss/accountant 2-composer cyclist/engineer film director dancer/ film-maker/restorer footballer/manager gardener pathologist philosopher physicist (discovered thallium) provost rugby scientist/surgeon witch/journalist/playwright

Roden Cutler

Dragon - Gemini/Pisces

Academic/geographer author (2) ballerina bard broadcaster diplomat founder (JCB Excavators) performer (music hall) Illustrator/writer physicist (2)/engineer physicist/musician Brigadier/boss

J C Bamford | Maeve Binchy | Moondog (Louis T Hardin) | Johnny Morris

Dragon - Cancer/Aries

Actor/singer Archbishop (Cardinal) barber boss (2)/industrialist cricketer economist/banker (founder) founder (museum) politician (2)

Sir Leonard Hutton | Sir Kirby Laing

Dragon - Cancer/Taurus

Author (2) (cookery)/teacher bookseller boss (intelligence) broadcaster (2)/journalist cellar master drummer footballer journalist pilot politician/QC traveller writer (2) writer/broadcaster Capt/pilot

Alastair Burnet | Stewart Copeland | Lord Greville Janner | Patrick Vieira

Dragon - Cancer/Gemini

Author (2)/boss author banker/broadcaster bookseller boss composer judge musician painter pianist QC/politician Recorder restorer (picture)

Kenneth Clarke

Dragon - Cancer/Cancer

Academic/ novelist/ historian (art) academic (3) academic /physician actor (3) actress bacteriologist boss/broadcaster environmentalist/author/administrator environmentalist (3) footballer golfer musician/actress novelist (3) poet/diplomat/politician politician (2) tenor Commander/administrator

Anita Brookner | David Hasselhoff | Olivia de Havilland Courtney Love | Pablo Neruda | Inbee Park | A A Shaikh Alastair Stewart | Gianluca Vialli

Dragon - Cancer/Leo

Ambassador Commissioner (charity) footballer school head historian (social)/museologist journalist musician presenter (TV)/writer squash trombonist

Ruud van Nistelrooy | Ringo Starr

Dragon - Cancer/Virgo

Academic/economist Archbishop bassist boss (car services) cartoonist ecologist headmaster songwriter Lieut-General

Sir Thomas Farmer

Dragon - Cancer/Libra

Academic (3)/Hispanic academic/(oncology) academic/Reverend actor administrator (music)/intelligence officer/broadcaster artist/creator (Smurfs) bandleader/impresario commentator (sports) originator (spoonerisms)/Reverend physicist/inventor/engineer politician (2) publisher regulator/QC Rear Admiral General

Dan Aykroyd | Edward Heath | Jimmy Hill | Peyo (Pierre Culliford) Nikola Tesla

Dragon - Cancer/Scorpio

Accountant actor (3) ambassador author (2) boss (2) (assurance) boss (directors, textiles) editor politician (3) politician/QC writer

Harold Evans | David Morrissey | Sir Cyril Smith | Patrick Stewart Gough Whitlam | Lord Winston

Dragon - Cancer/Sagittarius

Academic (2) (research) academic/obstetrician actor author boss/engineer drummer/musician headmaster journalist/TV host novelist/biographer nurse playwright/critic politician (2) sailor trade unionist

Ellen MacArthur | Dan Brown | Tommy Cunningham | Alvaro Uribe

Dragon - Cancer/Capricorn

Accountant activist/author/lecturer actor (2) actress/entertainer boss (housing) author (3) broadcaster (2) broadcaster/writer businessman/farmer journalist mathematician politician solicitor

Bonnie Langford | Tim Brooke-Taylor | Marianne Williamson

Dragon - Cancer/Aquarius

Archdeacon astrologer/author attaché (military) baritone boss (supermarket) broadcaster/journalist (2) conservationist/journalist herald politician QC/ Lord Chancellor (2) singer/actor/Chancellor Maj-General

Henry Rider Haggard | Lord A A Mackay Irvine | Esther Rantzen

Dragon - Cancer/Pisces

Academic (2)/ paediatrician boss (2) boss (water/waterways) businessman/tennis director (film casting) philosopher/theologian politician/soldier publisher scholar/educator sculptor college warden

Michael Colman | Helen Keller | René Lacoste

Dragon - Leo/Aries

Academic (2)/scientist academic (2) (education) actress architect author (3) author/publisher banker (merchant)/businessman boss (2) boss (construction) cricketer curator (museum) diplomat footballer historian (art) painter physiologist/ psychologist pianist politician singer teacher comedy writer

Jorgen Klinsman | Brian Mawhinney | Andy Warhol

Dragon - Leo/Taurus

Actor/bandleader botanist boss (local council) boxer clown/ringmaster critic (drama) dancer/choreographer journalist keeper (contemporary art museum) lawyer maker (TV documentary) model pilot (pioneering)/engineer surgeon Vicar Commandant

Marie Helvin

Dragon - Leo/Gemini

Academic (psychoanalysis) actress/model boss (2) boss (tobacco) conductor diplomat engineer/founder (Olivetti) fiddler inspector (chief) obstetrician politician

Camillo Olivetti | Clive Sinclair | Abhisit Vejjajiva

Dragon - Leo/Cancer

Academic (industrial relations) artist/photographer boss (arts) clerk composer driver (racing) engineer/inventor (steam hammer) school mistress newsreader/announcer rapper scientist (naval) surgeon tennis umpire (cricket)

Nelson Piquet

Dragon - Leo/Leo

Academic (orthodontics) actor (2) actor/stuntman/boxer clerk cricketer (2) dramaturge jockey missionary politician (2) singer

Martin Sheen | Patrick Swayze

Dragon - Leo/Virgo

Architect boss (auctioneer)/economist headmaster lyricist/singer/guitarist politician (2) solicitor statesman surgeon Vice-Chancellor

Joe Strummer

Dragon - Leo/Libra

Actress artist diver engineer/editor (music dictionary) footballer founder (co-Theosophical Soc) politician (2) snooker solicitor/adviser

Henry Olcott

Dragon - Leo/Scorpio

Academic (2) (engineering) academic (French) banker/QC biochemist boss (2)/designer (consultant) boss/athlete/journalist composer/conductor Constable (Chief) director (prosecutions) manufacturer (cosmetics) politician skater (figure) snooker soldier (2) squash writer/designer (exhibition) Lieut-General

Stephen Blackmore | Max (Francis) Factor | Dom Mintoff | Lisa Opie Michael Weiss

Dragon - Leo/Sagittarius

Actor Archdeacon draughts champion conductor engineer/politician film director Governor head master painter/sculptor politician (2) politician/anthropologist reporter (crime) reporter (TV)

Sang-woo Kwone

Dragon - Leo/Capricorn

Academic (international affairs) engineer manager (football) pianist/bandleader poet politician (2)/whip politician/dictator rugby

James Arbuthnot | Ossie Ardiles | "Count" Basie | Deng Xiaoping

Dragon - Leo/Aquarius

Actress (2) dancer/ choreographer film director ecologist educationist engineer/pilot horticulturist physicist politician tennis

Johan Bruyneel | Sandra Bullock

Dragon - Leo/Pisces

Academic (3)/GP academic/surgeon academic/Vice-Chancellor boss (2) boss (TV) comedian composer (2) guitarist navigator/accountant poet/dramatist/diplomat founder (Party) politician (3) singer teacher/bookseller vet Commander in Chief/politician

Mikko Lindstrom | Hugh McDiarmid | Johnny Nash | Jill St.John Alexei Sayle

Dragon - Virgo/Aries

Boss correspondent designer (fashion) diplomat (2)
headmaster leader (Hse of Lords) novelist (2)/screenwriter
philosopher/scientist pioneer (cardiac catheterisation)/physician
politician (3) QC writer/critic Air Marshal

Zandra Rhodes

Dragon - Virgo/Taurus

Academic (2) academic/physiologist archaeologist boss bowler
businessman/politician cricketer golfer poet sculptor
secretary singer/ record producer suffragette

Guillaume Apollinaire | Dame Christabel Pankhurst

Dragon - Virgo/Gemini

Academic (2) (architecture) academic (superconductivity)
artist/anarchist boss (2) (charities) boss (tourism) chemist
novelist painter politician (2) singer (2) soprano
trade unionist trainer (racehorse)

Tina Ann Barrett

Dragon - Virgo/Cancer

Academic coordinator (cultural) drummer/lyricist/author ice hockey
hurdler model TV presenter/DJ singer (3) vocalist/guitarist
Lieut-Col/mountaineer

Dragon - Virgo/Leo

Academic/surgeon arbiter boss (4) (airports) boss (investment)
boss (council) cardiologist composer politician

Aldo Moro

Dragon - Virgo/Virgo

Academic (2)/geneticist academic actress architect banker/industrialist bank cashier (chief) educationist engineer footballer missionary/Canon photographer Lieut-Commander

Ronaldo Luiz Nazario de Lima

Dragon - Virgo/Libra

Academic (English) actor (2) actress architect astronomer biographer boss (newspapers) civil servant politician tennis writer (2) writer/publisher

Raquel Welch

Dragon - Virgo/Scorpio

Actor boss (company) broadcaster businessman keeper (gallery) principal/Canon singer solicitor

Michel Bisnier | Adam West

Dragon - Virgo/Sagittarius

Academic (2) (pharmaceutics) academic (engineering) Bishop boss Dean author (2) matron-in-chief colonial officer cricketer internet developer journalist/essayist/satirist judge novelist politician (2)

Henry L Mencken

Dragon - Virgo/Capricorn

Academic/historian actor adviser (2) (personal) dancer/choreographer film director drummer engineer osteopath politician solicitor writer

Manuel Pinero

Dragon - Virgo/Aquarius

Academic (2) (histochemistry) anaesthetist boss (5)/adviser boss (dance) boss (investment)/actuary boss (Fraud Office) boss (stds, control) composer consultant (management – arts) golfer painter poet politician/QC rugby show jumper singer music teacher tennis Brigadier/photographer

Jimmy Connors | Darius Milhaud

Dragon - Virgo/Pisces

Actress (3) ambassador boss (2) (oil) boss (Ad council) clairvoyant/astrologer/host (TV/radio) cyclist dancer historian (art)/teacher journalist model (glamour)/actress novelist physicist politician sculptor

Maggie Cheung | Abi Titmus

Dragon - Libra/Aries

Academic (2) academic/writer/activist actor (2) boss (quango) motorcyclist singer skater (figure) Lieut-General

Marc Coma | Sir Cliff Richard

Dragon - Libra/Taurus

Academic (4)/actor academic/boss (3) academic/boss (aerospace) academic/philosopher actress (2) astronomer athlete journalist Ombudsman (Building Societies) pianist/conductor pioneer (helicopter) proprietor (nightclub) singer (2) trade unionist Vice Admiral

Greer Garson | George Peppard | Roland Smith | Peter Stringfellow

Dragon - Libra/Gemini

Actor (2) actress Archdeacon boss (2) (cars) cricketer (2) fencer headmistress journalist/author lawyer/politician (2) musician/keyboardist politician/QC singer surgeon Maj-General/boss

Geoffrey Boycott | Michael Gambon | Manfred Mann

Dragon - Libra/Cancer

Academic/biophysicist boss (4) (cars) boss (econs institute) boss (tribunals) boss (investment) film director/actor/screenwriter creator (the Archers) footballer hotelier Industrialist manager (music)/promoter/presenter (TV) model/actress novelist politician (2) psychiatrist socialite/charity worker 2-Admiral

Graham Greene | Sharon Osbourne | Pelé | Lal Bahadur Shashtri

Dragon - Libra/Leo

Actor (3) actress (2)/ fashion model (2) astronaut businessman (3) Lord Lieut/businessman model/actress/businesswoman politician secretary/registrar (institute) theatre/TV director Capt (submarine) Air Marshal

Dame Josephine Barstow

Dragon - Libra/Virgo

Actor/director/songwriter architect/designer author/editor boss (2) broadcaster coach (rugby) composer painter principal (University) rower surveyor/boss trade unionist Maj-General Marshal (RAF)

Jimmy Knapp | Nicholas Parsons

Dragon - Libra/Libra

Academic (2)/band manager academic/ scientist actor author/explorer boss (2) boss (crime squad) economist manufacturer (food) surfer/board maker Maj-General/boss (marketing)

Henry John Heinz | Leo Woo

Dragon - Libra/Scorpio

Administrator clown/ animal presenter cricketer designer (textile)/Cardinal dramatist film maker footballer (2) footballer (Capt) missionary zoologist

Alan Igglesden | Francesco Totti | Guillermo Del Toro

Dragon - Libra/Sagittarius

Actor (3) author correspondent designer (hi-fi) musician
philosopher politician/QC surfer Field Marshal

Jeff Goldblum | James Herriot | Friedrich Nietzsche | Christopher Reeve

Dragon - Libra/Capricorn

Actress anthropologist architect/author banker (merchant)
boss (2)/jurist botanist designer (dress) engineer
founder (Kenwood)/inventor judge otolaryngologist/Dean (hosp)
physicist psychiatrist publisher/boss

Sylvia Kristel | Kenneth Wood

Dragon - Libra/Aquarius

Academic (4) (polit economy) academic/scientist academic/archaeologist
academic (physiology) boss (3) (tribunals) boss businessman/boss
executive (advertising) judge politician singer/songwriter General

John Lennon

Dragon - Libra/Pisces

Academic (4)/keeper (records) academic (law) academic/physiologist/biophysicist
actor (2) actress artist/teacher boss (research)/consultant Chancellor
classicist/ bridge player compiler (crossword) engineer/designer
film maker healer insurgent judge (2) model/socialite
musician/teacher politician scientist/pioneer (birth control) author
trade unionist trainer (racehorse) translator/author Air Chief Marshal

Dame Anna Neagle | Marie Stopes | Royston Tan

Dragon - Scorpio/Aries

Actor/radio host actress (2) literary agent chauffeur chief clerk
politician (2) rower skater (figure) songwriter Vice Admiral

David 'Screaming Lord' Sutch

Dragon - Scorpio/Taurus

Academic/physicist (2) accountant/boss actress ambassador boss (3)
boss (publishing) financial controller journalist musician/saxophonist
Chief medical officer physicist physiologist/geneticist playwright/lyricist
politician (leader) principal (institute) singer tennis

Mark Philippoussis

Dragon - Scorpio/Gemini

Ambassador arranger (jazz) aviator basketballer Bishop
boss (2) (opera)/administrator boss/industrialist businessman/writer/publisher
coal miner cricketer/ footballer/umpire editor model/presenter (TV)
painter/novelist (2) politician

John Alcock | Lord Carr

Dragon - Scorpio/Cancer

Actor author/journalist boss (3) boss (construction)
boss (museum) businessman consultant editor engineer
Governor General (country) headmaster heptathlete poet
runner scientist songwriter/composer therapist (cancer)/teacher
toxicologist Admiral

Sainsbury (Lord - of Turville) | Kelly Sotherton

Dragon - Scorpio/Leo

Academic (2) (oral medicine) academic/mathematician/founder (co- topology) academic/paediatrician actress film animator/writer (2) artist ballerina boss/founder (records co) boss (4) boss/civil servant boss/dental surgeon painter commentator (sports) principal Procurator General/solicitor writer

Terry Gilliam | Felix Hausdorff

Dragon - Scorpio/Virgo

Academic (common law) 2-actress astronaut/engineer athlete/ administrator/ educator Bishop boss (housing) fashion designer/model drummer football manager/ footballer painter singer wrestler

Dragon - Scorpio/Libra

Academic (2)/geneticist actor/director actress (2) boss (2) civil servant consultant (industrial medicine) diplomat ecologist explorer (Arctic) painter/ pioneer (Intimisme) palaeontologist/teacher politician (2) umpire (cricket) Admiral/boss Maj-General/adviser (govt)

François Mitterrand | Edouard Vuillard

Dragon - Scorpio/Scorpio

Academic (2)/ mathematician ambassador Constable (Chief) designer (3) (fashion) designer (video game) disc jockey/personality (TV)/ model (fashion) novelist (3) diplomat politician (2) producer/writer/cameraman scholar (literary) scientist (2) scientist/inventor/designer (aircraft) writer

Cat Deeley | David Emmanuel | Shigeru Miyamoto

Dragon - Scorpio/Sagittarius

Academic/surgeon actress (3) actress (erotic) boss (4) (airports) boss (army) boss (charity) boss (TV) diplomat (2) film maker (2) film producer super model musician/author politician singer/guitarist/actor

Yasmin Le Bon

Dragon - Scorpio/Capricorn

Academic (3)/critic/educationist academic/physicist actor/film producer/director artist athlete/writer (2)/entrepreneur/show producer baseballer bass player diplomat golfer runner tenor writer/storyteller/lecturer

Debjani Chatterjee

Dragon - Scorpio/Aquarius

Academic (English law) actor/wrestler Archbishop architect broadcaster cricketer judge (2) principal (music school)/educationist singer (2) singer/songwriter

Walter Cronkite | Calista Flockhart | Michael Ramsey

Dragon - Scorpio/Pisces

Academic (neurology) barrister (2) boss (4) boss (quango) boss/editor boss (pools) civil servant DJ (sound system) QC/lawyer Reverend show jumper nursing officer poet sculptor singer/guitarist

Robert Bridges | Jacob Epstein | John Moores

Dragon - Sagittarius/Aries

Actress boss/chief agent composer Constable (Chief) consultant (education)/broadcaster controller (TV programme) joker/painter/author judge/QC singer

Jerry Bock

Dragon - Sagittarius/Taurus

Academic (3) (psychobiology) academic (obstetrics, gynaecology)
accountant/boss artist boss (2) consulting Dean engineer
politician/lecturer producer (children's TV) rugby (2) singer (2)
General Maj-General

John Kirwan | Dionne Warwick

Dragon - Sagittarius/Gemini

Academic (2)/ Vice-Chancellor academic/ mathematician/code breaker
actor boss engineer (2) pioneer (motorcar) engineer
drag race driver expert (architecture) novelist/dramatist
painter/designer (stained glass) playwright wrestler writer (2)
General/politician

Karl Benz | Kirk Douglas | Francisco Franco | Stephen Poliakoff

Dragon - Sagittarius/Cancer

Actor (2) actress/model boss (food) composer cricketer
theatre director (opera, TV) editor school inspector Reverend
2-singer/songwriter singer/songwriter/record producer
Maj-Gen/Prof (systems engineering)/astronaut/pilot

Keith Michell | Mel Smith

Dragon - Sagittarius/Leo

Academic (2)/biophysicist actor (2) boss (2) boss (stationery)
entrepreneur/founder (Craigslist) founder (record co) novelist
painter/designer/lecturer pilot politician Capt/pilot

Nancy Mitford | Peter Myers

Dragon - Sagittarius/Virgo

Boss/pioneer (TV) composer/musician/film director engineer/builder (Eiffel Tower)
footballer/coach Head (schools) headmaster (2) journalist librarian

Alexandre Gustave Eiffel | Roberto Mancini | Joseph John Thomson
Frank Zappa

Dragon - Sagittarius/Libra

Academic/linguist/philosopher actress boss (2) boss/co founder developer (property) essayist/novelist libertarian microscopist physicist/discoverer (electron) poet(2) poet/writer politician spectroscopist trade unionist Maj-General

Naom Chomsky | Betty Grable

Dragon - Sagittarius/Scorpio

Academic/physicist actor (2) Bishop boss (bank) commentator (racing)/jockey founder (Getty Oil Co.)/industrialist journalist publisher singer

John Alderton | John Francome | J Paul Getty | Bruce Lee (Liu Yeun Kam)

Dragon - Sagittarius/Sagittarius

Actor (2) author boss (transport)/businessman cricketer film director (2) film maker economist Governor (Falklands) judge deputy keeper (museum) editor model/actor planner (theorist on transport) politician vocalist/songwriter/drummer

Dragon - Sagittarius/Capricorn

Actor artist/architect boss (2) boss (newspaper) cricketer playwright/producer (TV, radio) surgeon (gynaecologist) violinist

Dragon - Sagittarius/Aquarius

Academic (2)/college provost academic/psychiatrist actress (2) author (3) boss (3) boss/songwriter boss/ bookmaker columnist engineer poet

Jenny Agutter | Louisa May Alcott | Aleksandr Blok | Joe Coral Teri Hatcher | Philip K Dick

Dragon - Sagittarius/Pisces

Academic (2) (anatomy) academic/principal (U) astronomer/mathematician boss broadcaster correspondent cricketer diplomat founder (Firestone) furrier/expert (Venice) pianist politician/QC Major/lawyer Air Vice Marshal

Walter Cronkite | Harvey Firestone | Scott Joplin | Imran Khan

Dragon - Capricorn/Aries

Actor (2) actress boss (2) chess (grandmaster) mathematician philosopher (2) film maker philosopher politician trade unionist writer/adventurer

Tom Mix | Joely Richardson

Dragon - Capricorn/Taurus

Actor agony aunt biologist boss (2) (cars) comedian/scriptwriter/doctor hunter (Nazi) guitarist/pianist/drummer/singer journalist oarsman physician (2) poet/critic politician provost (cathedral) stockbroker land surveyor violinist/boss (music)

Joan Baez | Andrew Johnson | David Knopfler

Dragon - Capricorn/Gemini

Architect boss (3) boss (construction) boxer designer (fashion) lawyer/ entrepreneur poet politician (2) rapper silversmith (designer)/boss singer (2)

Derek B | Brian Merrikin Hill

Dragon - Capricorn/Cancer

Academic/writer (2) actor boss (weather forecast)/scientist photographer pioneer (radio) politician/author college principal/psychiatrist rugby

Dragon - Capricorn/Leo

Academic (vet surgery) actor (3) actress boss editor
computer engineer guitarist/singer inventor (braille) jockey surgeon
yogi

Louis Braille | Prof Victoria Bruce | Bernard Cribbins | Bo Diddley
Faye Dunaway | Herbert Lom | Paramahansa Yogananda

Dragon - Capricorn/Virgo

Academic (3)/physician/preacher (2) academic/psychologist
academic (physics) artist businessman commissioner (UN)/Governor (Mauritius)
guitarist spiritual leader organist politician statistician tennis

Maharishi Mahesh Yogi

Dragon - Capricorn/Libra

Academic (Christian Doctrine)/Reverend architect film director judge (2)
technical officer painter/sculptor singer (2) singer/songwriter
trader (futures)

Dragon - Capricorn/Scorpio

Academic/cardiologist actor anaesthetist biographer/critic
boss (3) boss (funds investment) boss (cars) composer diplomat
criminal leader/ creator (Luftwaffe) ornithologist pilot/prison camp
forger/psychologist politician (3) politician/govt-research officer
film producer (theatrical) singer General

Orlando Bloom | Hermann Goering | Yandel

Dragon - Capricorn/Sagittarius

Academic/geophysicist author composer/dramatist/actor
designer (2) (car) designer (film, theatre) dramatist (2)
historian (2) (urban) historian/college provost QC/lawyer/politician/diplomat
singer songwriter umpire (cricket)/cricketer

Ivor Novello | David Shepherd

Dragon - Capricorn/Capricorn

Boss comedian diplomat golfer rock manager
novelist/critic intelligence officer politician
college provost/Vice-Chancellor socialist General (Marshal Aid)

Dame Rebecca West | Thomas Woodrow Wilson

Dragon - Capricorn/Aquarius

Academic/philosopher actor/footballer actress (2) boss (militant group)
farmer philatelist/publisher singer/songwriter tennis

Guy Forget | Robson Lowe | Vinnie Jones

Dragon - Capricorn/Pisces

Academic (physics) actor boss leader (civil rights)
singer (2)/songwriter singer/TV host trainer (elephant)/circus
artist writer/poet/playwright

Martin Luther King | Edgar Allan Poe

Dragon - Aquarius/Aries

Actor (3)/choreographer/film director boss (3) (electrical) boss (insurance)
boss/solicitor entrepreneur/co founder (Microsoft) headmistress lawyer
saxophonist teacher/soldier/actor writer (gardening) Maj-General

Paul Allen

Dragon - Aquarius/Taurus

Academic (engineering design) actor director (2)/producer
dramatist/judge/author (2) editor mystic physician
pianist/conductor Registrar (appeals)/QC surveyor/sailor writer/director
General/administrator

Myung-whun Chung | Charles George Gordon | Grigori Rasputin

Dragon - Aquarius/Gemini

Academic (2)/physicist   academic/college rector   artist/writer
boss (gallery)   dean (cathedral)   drummer   equerry   politician   GP
sculptor   association secretary   tennis/administrator   writer (3)
writer (cookery)/caterer   yachtsman/barrister

Prue Leith

Dragon - Aquarius/Cancer

Archbishop   artist (visual)   boss (2)   boss (artistic)   musician
military officer (4)   singer (3)   singer/entertainer   singer/songwriter/dancer
town planner/architect   Group Capt   Lieut-Commander/aviator (naval)
Wing Commander/adviser (training)

Smokey Robinson | Shakira | Frankie Vaughan

Dragon - Aquarius/Leo

Boss (2) (cars)   boss (publishing)   curator (house)   designer (fashion)
diplomat   golfer   journalist   keeper (wicket)   playwright/cartoonist
politician (2)   politician (leader)/adviser   publisher   urologist

Christian Dior | Yani Tseng | Yoshifumi Tsuji

Dragon - Aquarius/Virgo

Academic (fluid mechanics)   actor   ambassador   artist   boss (finance)
composer   diplomat   farmer   harpist   headmaster   pathologist
rugby

Felix Mendelssohn

Dragon - Aquarius/Libra

Academic (2) (experimental physics)   academic/engineer   actress   author (2)
boss (3)   boss (engineers)   boss (strategic studies)   Constable (Chief)
musician/composer   physician/author/activist

Kitaro | Jean Simmons

Dragon - Aquarius/Scorpio

Academic author (2) baseballer boss Dean (cathedral
inventor (self focusing camera, ATM) politician (2) tenor wrestler

Placido Domingo | D G Hessayon

Dragon - Aquarius/Sagittarius

Academic (2) (metallurgy) academic/physicist actor (3) actor/comedian
actor/singer contralto banker matron singer (3) tennis

Neil Diamond | Val Doonican

Dragon - Aquarius/Capricorn

Actor adviser (accountancy)/accountant boss diplomat historian
journalist/novelist/playwright naturalist/writer (2) politician (leader)
legal secretary violinist virologist General

Charles Darwin | Abraham Lincoln

Dragon - Aquarius/Aquarius

Actress (3) actor architect/conservationist boss (2)/soldier
composer/writer comedian film director nurse
playwright/actor poet politician/boss producer (TV)
writer (3) (comedy) zoologist/writer

Jean Moreau | Desmond Morris

Dragon - Aquarius/Pisces

Actor boss (insurance) comedian film director drummer
pioneer (women's suffrage) politician (2) singer writer

J M Coetzee | Eartha Kitt | Edvard Schevardnadze | Roger Vadim

Dragon - Pisces/Aries

Academic/educationist (vet) actor architect boss (2) (books) boss (shipbuilding) composer (2) composer/lyricist doctor/politician (2) engineer politician/pilot QC writer

Marshal (RAF)

Dragon - Pisces/Taurus

Academic (2)/boss (lab) academic/legal scholar actor (3) artist/teacher author civil servant dancer/ choreographer/actor engineer/industrialist footballer judge saxophonist singer/pianist/songwriter

Fats Domino | Emile Mathis | Courtney Pine | Ariel Sharon

Dragon - Pisces/Gemini

Actor (2) author/actress engineer/boss philosopher 2-politician (leader) politician trainer (racehorse) violinist

Frank Dobson | Harold Wilson

Dragon - Pisces/Cancer

Academic/boss (4) (cancer research institute) author boss (bank) boss (bank) boss (health) broadcaster/footballer composer cricketer dramatist/screenwriter headmistress/designer (garden) novelist (2) novelist/biographer/poet physicist politician (2) trade unionist

Jimmy Greaves | Viv Richards | Victoria Sackville-West

Dragon - Pisces/Leo

Actor (3) actress author (3) bandleader (3) boss (3) (construction) broadcaster/writer/rugby composer controller (radio) film producer horticulturist/boss (park) judge musician/bandleader neurologist primatologist psychiatrist/boss (hosp) trumpeter/bandleader writer Vice Admiral Capt (submarine)

Jimmy Dorsey | Arthur Honegger | Glenn Miller | Alan Sillitoe

Dragon - Pisces/Virgo

Actress author (2) author/dramatist/musician boss boxer civil servant diplomat editor footballer illustrator/cartoonist journalist teacher (music therapy) tennis trade unionist/politician Admiral

Douglas Adams | Henrik Sundstrom | Sir John Tenniel | Morgan Tsvangirai

Dragon - Pisces/Libra

Academic (literature) artist (stained glass) boss (2) (insurance) boss (radio) caterer/hotelier diplomat organist/conductor soprano trade unionist

Stephen Gately

Dragon - Pisces/Scorpio

Actor/director boss (6) boss/adviser boss (consumers) boss (water) conservationist dramatist driver (racing) economist/boss financier chief inspector (audit/environment) journalist/editor college principal soldier/merchant (wine) surgeon writer

Edward Albee | Mario Andretti

Dragon - Pisces/Sagittarius

Academic (3) (cardiac) academic/Dean (dentistry) academic/soldier/historian Constable (Chief) golfer jockey novelist politician show jumper singer (2) Commander/astronaut/engineer

Frank Borman | David Broome | Pat Eddery

Dragon - Pisces/Capricorn

Academic (2) (chemistry) academic (statistics) actor (2) actress boss (5) boss (polit. campaigning) boss (charity) boss (customs) conductor/composer boss (ports) drummer judge physician politician (2) singer trainer (racehorse)

Juliet Binoche | Lydia Dunn (Baroness) | G P Hinduja | Derek Longmuir

Dragon - Pisces/Aquarius

Actor (2)/writer/director actress (porn)/model biographer (literary) Bishop boss (3) engineer guitarist/musician principal (music academy)

Patrick McGoohan

Dragon - Pisces/Pisces

Academic (4)/Dean academic (management) academic/psychologist actress boss (tax)/conductor caricaturist/painter/sculptor entertainer judge motorcyclist novelist/poet politician schoolmaster singer ventriloquist Air Marshal/ consultant (aviation, defence)

Honoré Daumier | Prof H J Eysenck | Nikolai Rimsky Korsakov

Snake - Aries/Aries

Academic (politics) actor biochemist boss (3) (retailing/sales) boss (teaching/standards) boss (secret service MI6) cheese maker conductor cricketer designer (lock) footballer motor racer pharmacologist politician producer (TV)

Stephen Byers | Freddie Ljungberg | Jack Simmons | Linus Yale

Snake - Aries/Taurus

Academic/ Vice-Chancellor (University) actor (2) actress boss (2) boss/vet civil servant prison governor judge poet/editor Air Commandant/matron-in-chief

Robert Downey Jr

Snake - Aries/Gemini

Author (2) boss (3) boss (Law)/advocate/judge boss (property)/surveyor designer (film) harpsichordist/teacher journalist/broadcaster (2) musician/singer pharmacologist politician (2) (leader) politician/mediator producer (theatrical)/creator (Follies) statesman writer/broadcaster Brigadier/logistics officer

Cyrus Vance | Florenz Ziegfeld

Snake - Aries/Cancer

Academic (2) academic (Info Sc) actor (2) actress/comedian boss (2) chaplain comedian stage director high jumper poet politician

Sir Adrian Cadbury | Ruby Wax

Snake - Aries/Leo

Actor (2) architect bandleader/composer boss (2) commentator High Commissioner Constable (Chief) designer (fashion) librarian politician/boss (petroleum) producer (TV drama) satirist/puppeteer sociologist writer/translator/cartoonist/photographer

Peter Fluck | Georges Eugene Haussmann | Gorden Kaye | James Last Vivienne Westwood

Snake - Aries/Virgo

Actor/director actress (2) actuary (consulting) architect athlete college master judge soprano screen writer Admiral

Roger Bannister | Paul Theroux

Snake - Aries/Libra

Academic (2)/provost (U) academic/physician/analyst (Jungian) actress architect aviator boss (2) (TV) boss (insurance broker) designer (interior)/author (2) footballer journalist author (2) judge novelist/dramatist politician (2) QC/politician translator General

Nikolai Gogol | Edwin Lutyens | Bobby Moore

Snake - Aries/Scorpio

Academic (2) (engineering) academic/ philosopher (religion) actor (2) actress author/ educator (childbirth) boss (council) boss (3) civil servant climber Mayor/boss (furnishings) politician singer trainer (racehorse)

Julie Christie | Leslie Howard

Snake - Aries/Sagittarius

Academic (medical ethics) cricketer (2) musician novelist circus performer softball pitcher politician psychic/musician psychotherapist surveyor

Snake - Aries/Capricorn

Academic/pathologist actress (2) author boss (gallery) historian lawyer mathematician politician singer trade unionist Vice Admiral

Billy Fury | Sarah Jessica Parker

Snake - Aries/Aquarius

Academic (2) (Spanish culture) actor architect chef/ restaurateur composer film director footballer founder (theatre)/teacher historian (2) painter politician (3)

Bela Bartok | Nigel Hawthorne | Michel Roux

Snake - Aries/Pisces

Activist (leader) actress agent (literary) athlete/boss (sports) boss (tax-court) composer conductor/pianist/composer editor art historian gardener/photographer historian (3) film historian politician publisher/consultant (literary) writer Brigadier General Maj-General

Sarah Michelle Gellar | David Moorcroft | André Previn

Snake - Taurus/Aries

Academic (4)/archaeologist academic/historian academic (history) academic/(ophthalmology)/surgeon actress ballerina Bishop boss (2) designer (toy) editor guitarist intelligence officer journalist/editor pianist/entertainer psychologist violinist Air Marshal/boss (engineering) Colonel/manager

Snake - Taurus/Taurus

Academic (4) (geology) academic/economist academic (research) academic (law) activist (socialist) archaeologist artist ballerina boss/accountant boss (2) (insurance) boss (publishing) engineer judge/headmaster model politician/lawyer scholar(manuscripts)/archivist solicitor tenor/broadcaster/writer

Snake - Taurus/Gemini

Academic/theologian/Reverend actor/film producer athlete boss (2) (insurance) boss (leisure) comedian composer (2) composer/ vocalist/ pianist driver (racing) instructor (ski) musician/composer painter politician (2) singer (2) skater squash Vice Admiral

Jonah Barrington | Pierce Brosnan | Ella Fitzgerald | Joan Miró Mike Oldfield

Snake - Taurus/Cancer

Architect author Bishop composer/organist engineer footballer politician (2) skier/journalist stockbroker trade unionist General

I M Pei | Norman Whiteside

Snake - Taurus/Leo

Actor architect (naval) artist author (2) correspondent politician writer/comedienne surgeon swimmer

Victoria Wood

Snake - Taurus/Virgo

Academic (2)/geophysicist boss/politician model (fashion) navigator/judge/diplomat politician (3) scholar (classical)/teacher shipbuilder 2-singer theatrical producer writer/barrister

Hastings Banda | Linda Evangelista

Snake - Taurus/Libra

Academic (2)/author (2) academic/theologian/Reverend actor banker/film producer boss businessman diplomat film director/producer chief inspector (nuclear) novelist/poet college provost violinist Maj-General

Henry Fonda

Snake - Taurus/Scorpio

Actor Archdeacon/Canon academic (2)/parasitologist boss cricketer critic/author (2) editor/scientist/astrologer film director governor (Calif) industrialist lecturer (3) musician/writer/artist playwright/screenwriter poet politician silversmith/designer singer violinist/conductor/teacher Major/ expert (bomb disposal)

Joachim von Ribbentrop

Snake - Taurus/Sagittarius

Legal administrator basketballer boss (2) boss/statistician columnist (humorous) cyclist engineer instructor (Judo) naturalist painter

Johannes Brahms | Harry Campion

Snake - Taurus/Capricorn

Academic (law)/adviser boss (3) boss (foods) engineer prison governor poet/novelist organiser (resistance) politician/leader restorer (mosaics/wall paintings) Air Vice Marshal/boss

Lord Prof Dahrendorf | Jeremy Thorpe

Snake - Taurus/Aquarius

Academic (sociology)/director (U) actor architect author (3) civil servant composer historian (architectural) manager (football) nun/author politician (2) writer Lieut-Colonel

Tony Blair | Ryan O'Neal | Graeme Souness

Snake - Taurus/Pisces

Academic (2) (physics) academic/astronomer actress (2) angler/author (2)/film maker artist Bishop boss (2) boss (drinks) civil servant conductor disc jockey judge organist/conductor screenwriter/director/writer singer writer (2)

Audrey Hepburn

Snake - Gemini/Aries

Academic (maths) actor artist/film maker boss (insurance) QC (2) QC/politician (2) politician scriptwriter tennis (2) writer/broadcaster/chef

Menzies Campbell | Pat Cash | Václav Klaus | Delia Smith

Snake - Gemini/Taurus

Academic (health history) actor architect film director bank governor painter photographer (fashion) politician publisher (newspaper) singer/author/poet veterinarian

Bob Dylan

Snake - Gemini/Gemini

Actress (2) actor ambassador boss (2) (bank)/Lord-Lieut boss (car) councillor director (artistic -theatre) engineer/pioneer QC/politician politician (3) swimmer trade unionist writer/playwright Group Capt/pilot

Derek Barron | Raymond Burr | A A Griffrith | Katie Hoff
Dorothy L Sayers | Brooke Shields

Snake - Gemini/Cancer

Actor astronaut boss (2) (commission) boss (NHS) chess judge mountaineer musician/lecturer philosopher priest physician/pathologist/parasitologist QC/adviser/recorder singer

Snake - Gemini/Leo

Academic (2)/archaeologist academic (nursing) businessman diarist footballer Governor model/host (radio, TV) pianist politician provost/Very Reverend tennis

Anne Frank | Andrea Jaeger

Snake - Gemini/Virgo

Artist (2) artist (Star Wars) chief inspector (Fire) cricketer (2) director (artistic) drummer explorer film producer lawyer/legislator pianist 2-politician Pope Provost/ librarian

Damien Hirst | John Fitzgerald Kennedy | Nigel Short | Charlie Watts

Snake - Gemini/Libra

Boss (housing) boss (3) boss (opera)/administrator chemist co founder/publisher college master composer/conductor Master (King's Musick)/fisherman monologist/actor musician/composer playwright/performer/activist politician (3) tennis trainer (racehorse) trumpeter

Benazir Bhutto | Edward Elgar

Snake - Gemini/Scorpio

Academic/dean (medicine/dentistry) actress (2) architect author (3) boss conservationist (wildlife) conservationist (architectural)/draughtsman diplomat judge planner (party) psychologist/statistician writer (2)/editor shot putter writer/translator

Eva Bartok | Françoise Gauquelin | Elizabeth Hurley | Joachim Olsen Michael Portillo

Snake - Gemini/Sagittarius

Actor artist (2) boss campaigner (polit) diplomat organist dramatist/poet musician/writer (2) sculptor/school principal soprano writer (film.TV)/director/artist Brigadier/artist

Snake - Gemini/Capricorn

Architect Bishop boss (4) boss (sugar) designer (fashion)/actress goal keeper journalist/boss politician pianist/composer

Dean Martin

Snake - Gemini/Aquarius

Actor boxer broadcaster/journalist geographer/author (2) golfer impressionist chief nursing officer college rector writer/ Existentialist/dramatist

Sadie Frost | Jean-Paul Sartre | Mike Yarwood

Snake - Gemini/Pisces

Boss (2) (legal aid) boss (sugar) chef/restaurateur entrepreneur journalist lawyer/diplomat/politician musician/songwriter film producer painter/engraver satirist/historian spy/intelligence officer

Snake - Cancer/Aries

Actress (2)/writer/painter author (2) baseballer cartoonist composer golfer model/actress pianist/teacher politician theologian/Reverend

Elizabeth Emanuel | Reg Smythe

Snake - Cancer/Taurus

Academic (2) (linguistics) academic/astronomer boss (petroleum) cricketer designer (fashion) headmaster historian (art)/curator (museum) librarian politician psychiatrist/psychotherapist singer Vice Marshal (Diplomatic Corps)

Snake - Cancer/Gemini

Actress/artist boss (water) cricketer footballer headmaster (2) photographer/author writer (2)

Snake - Cancer/Cancer

Academic (biology) boss (3) baseballer boxer columnist/writer comedienne/pianist comedian (2) economist founder (Barnardo homes) QC (2) politician (2) principal sheriff/QC singer/bandleader soldier/cricketer/businessman trade unionist

Thomas Barnardo | Eddie Large | Leon Spinks

Snake - Cancer/Leo

Attorney Boss (TV) cricketer designer (yacht) diplomat film-maker golfer headmistress leader (US civil rights) rugby

Stoke Carmichael (Kwame Ture)

Snake - Cancer/Virgo

Actor (2) actress/author/activist baritone baseballer dancer (2)/choreographer dancer/actor doctor/ pathologist politician (5) wrestler

Twyla Tharp

Snake - Cancer/Libra

Actor (2) boss (freight)/accountant brewer farmer/landowner poet/playwright politician (2) (finance) politician (leader) singer/actor swimmer Brigadier/conjuror

David Hasselhof | Ron Hayward

Snake - Cancer/Scorpio

Boss (2) boss (computers) critic (literary) diplomat drummer/musician editor environmentalist journalist/author (2) judge philosopher photographer politician film producer psychiatrist/author rugby scientist (clinical) singer (2) singer/entertainer

Snake - Cancer/Sagittarius

Academic ((oral medicine) actor (3) actor/ornithologist actress/writer/activist ambassador boss footballer (2) football manager/footballer musicologist/editor/astrologer politician/QC singer star (cabaret)/owner (nightclub) trade unionist trainer (racehorse) Lieut-Colonel

Michael Howard | Bill Oddie

Snake - Cancer/Capricorn

Academic/ (3) Vice-Chancellor (U)/rector academic /archaeologist academic (theology)/Reverend actor (2) actress ambassador archaeologist/ broadcaster (2) architect boss (arts/TV) boss/sailor bullfighter campaigner (nuclear disarmament) priest cartoonist/author (2) commentator comedian Constable (Chief) critic college principal co founder drummer metallurgist singer trade unionist writer

Lord Gormley | Bruce Kent | Alan Osmond | Liv Tyler

Snake - Cancer/Aquarius

Academic (2)/boss (research)/ ethnologist/linguist
academic/ Vice-Chancellor (U)/scholar banker counsel/QC
founder (church) historian/educator judge politician writer
anarchist

Mary Baker Eddy | David Milliband

Snake - Cancer/Pisces

Academic (3) (microelectronics) academic (divinity) Reverend
academic/anthropologist author/critic boss (3) (healthcare) boss (news)
boss civil servant diplomat historian/museum curator percussionist
trumpeter/composer Air Chief Marshal Brigadier Maj-General

Evelyn Glennie | Peter Kindersley

Snake - Leo/Aries

Abbot academic (archaeology)/chess actor boss (2) (TV)
choreographer civil servant/boss (TV) editor (2) golfer hymn writer
manager (jazz club) mathematician narrator/voice actor novelist
painter/illustrator publicist/publisher trombonist/leader (orchestra)

Arthur Cayley | Daniel Radcliffe | Jack Teagarden

Snake - Leo/Taurus

Actor (4) actress/model/gymnast actress/director artist boss (info)
comedian/writer rower scholar singer/actor writer (2)

Snake - Leo/Gemini

Actress architect/craftsman composer (2)/musician
entrepreneur/ambassador historian/traveller pathologist/researcher pianist
teacher poet politician college principal violinist/composer

Clara Bow | Alfred Tennyson

Snake - Leo/Cancer

Academic (4)/psychologist (econ) academic/psychiatrist academic/archaeologist boss (museum)/clerk conductor Dean/Very Reverend editor (2) historian (art) army officer politician (4) politician/mystic QC singer surveyor trainer (racehorse) trombonist

Caspar Weinberger | Dag Hammarskjöld | Jack Lynch | Jack Wellings

Snake - Leo/Leo

Boss (2) (bank) boss (engineering) driver (racing) footballer geologist/pioneer (3rd World) pathologist poet politician (2)

Julinho | Nigel Mansell | Slobodan Milosevic

Snake - Leo/Virgo

Archbishop author (2) Bishop (3) consultant (advert) designer lecturer (biblical) college principal/writer/naturalist Maj-General

Dolores del Rio | J K Rowling | Caspar Weinberger

Snake - Leo/Libra

Academic/botanist attorney cryptanalyst economist film director/producer journalist novelist Orientalist politician (leader) boss (electronics) psychiatrist singer (3) singer/composer singer/guitarist Capt/ trainer (racehorse) Major

Sola Akingbola | Paul Anka | Sam Mendes | Carol Thatcher

Snake - Leo/Scorpio

Academic (2)/composer academic/boss (2) actor (2)/writer actress barrister/QC boss/surgeon novelist politician (2) politician (leader) chief registrar (Friendly Soc) revolutionary Air Commodore/engineer

Benjamin Harrison | Mae West

Snake - Leo/Sagittarius

Actress bacteriologist/discoverer (penicillin) Bishop body guard
boss (4) boss (art) boss (engineering)/engineer diplomat
driver (rally) gymnast chief inspector (school) cricketer judge/QC
leader (party) front of house manager/mariner magnate/author/stockbroker
principal (RADA) trade unionist trainer (racehorse) Air Chief Marshal

Alexander Fleming | Graham Gooch | Stéphane Peterhansel

Snake - Leo/Capricorn

Academic ((industrial relations) actor (2) actress boss (insurance)
Deputy High Commissioner head master illustrator politician
TV drama director writer/humorist/poet

Snake - Leo/Aquarius

Academic (2) (corporate law) academic/astronomer boss (3) (confectionery)
boss boss/banker designer (fashion) diplomat film director/producer
2-headmaster bedchamber maid physicist treasurer

John Rocha

Snake - Leo/Pisces

Actor author/illustrator barrister/journalist historian (art)
keeper (museum) musician/vocalist/bassist/keyboardist pianist film producer

Cecil B de Mille | Robert Mitchum

Snake - Virgo/Aries

Academic (2)/humorist academic/philosopher Bishop boss (investment)
cartoonist film director/producer dramatist/actor headmaster
musician/guitarist physician/writer politician (4) politician/party leader
scientist (computer) singer/songwriter Commander/air observer

Yasser Arafat | Otis Redding | Oliver Wendell Holmes

Snake - Virgo/Taurus

Academic/violinist actress (20 Archbishop boss (3)
boss/journalist boss (industrial relations) designer (festival) harpist
musicologist/conductor politician (leader)/businessman
singer/ presenter (radio, TV) soldier/geographer surgeon trainer (racehorse)
Squadron Leader

Greta Garbo | Christopher Hogwood | Dmitri Medvedev

Snake - Virgo/Gemini

Academic (2) (health law, ethics, policy) academic (chemistry) actor
architect driver (truck) boxer chemist designer (car)/manufacturer
photographer poet prosecutor QC/ barrister

Ettore Bugatti

Snake - Virgo/Cancer

Actor/singer body builder chess grandmaster author (2)
cosmonaut film director founder (chocolates) jockey
painter/sculptor politician principal (music/drama) wrestler writer

Tommy Carberry | Milton Hershey | Ferdinand Marcos

Snake - Virgo/Leo

Academic/educationist boss (2) boss (mining) cyclist
doctor/author guitarist/musician pilot/engineer/founder (co) politician (2)
politician inventor (belisha beacons)

Baron Leslie Hore-Belisha | Vincenzo Lancia | Han Suyin | W H Taft

Snake - Virgo/Virgo

Academic (2)/theologian/Reverend academic (geophysics) architect (landscape)
boss (sport) boss (TV) composer (2)/organist diplomat editor
judge lecturer/composer/conductor pentathlete singer/songwriter

Shania Twain

Snake - Virgo/Libra

Actress/pianist boss (detective) broker (insurance) comedian/actor High Commissioner lyricist model/author percussionist trumpeter educator photographer producer (opera) scientist show jumper

Sophie Dahl | Hermann von Helmholtz

Snake - Virgo/Scorpio

Athlete boss (2) (personnel) businessman/company founder diplomat poet saxophonist solicitor/boss/town clerk General

Bernard Ebbers | Edwin Moses

Snake - Virgo/Sagittarius

Academic/clinical virologist actor attorney general/politician/QC author boss (2) boss/ entrepreneur boxer broadcaster dean/Reverend golfer (2) fruit grower/cider maker mariner/fighter (resistance) poet politician/journalist polymath/novelist/critic film producer/director rower surveyor/boss (land/property) toymaker yachtsman General Air Marshal

Glyn Charles | Robert Einke | Knut Haugland | Arthur Koestler Alexander Korda | Lennox Lewis | Sue MacGregor | Arnold Palmer Charlie Sheen | William McEwan Younger

Snake - Virgo/Capricorn

Academic/Vice-Chancellor comedian conductor/orchestrator driver (racing) drummer goalkeeper journalist singer General/historian/governor

David Brabham | General William Jackson

Snake - Virgo/Aquarius

Actress Archbishop author genealogist/author golfer journalist/critic/historian leader (charity) painter writer/broadcaster

Edward Burne-Jones | Sam Torrance

Snake - Virgo/Pisces

Academic (2)/ veterinarian academic/boss (meteorology) artist (2) artist (graphic) ballerina boss (museum) comedian/pianist/singer driver (racing) farmer florist historian jockey philologist poet/novelist politician radiologist/doctor satirist puppeteer Air Marshal

Roger Law | Stirling Moss | Nicholas Witchell

Snake - Libra/Aries

Academic/(chemistry) actor (2) actress Archbishop/reformer (social) boss (savings/investments) cricketer/administrator founder (YMCA)/ reformer (social) pharmacist politician (2) presenter(TV, news) sculptor medallist (portrait) singer trumpeter/bandleader/composer

Henri-Michel | A Capu | Peter Mandelson | Sir George Williams

Snake - Libra/Taurus

Academic (3)/biologist academic/psychiatrist ambassador(2) author politician (2) boss(oil) ambassador Constable (Chief) dancer engineer/boss (2) headmaster lecturer/hostess (society) minister (Baptist)/activist (civil rights) obstetrician chief fire officer/boss politician (leader)

Jesse Jackson | Trent Lott

Snake - Libra/Gemini

Academic (2)/architect academic/Vice-Chancellor Archbishop author (2) ballerina boss (regulator) comedian guitarist host (game show) novelist/playwright politician Air Vice Marshal

Diane Abbott | Steve Coogan | Heather Watts

Snake - Libra/Cancer

Academic (2)/surgeon academic/ zoologist actress artist boss
boxer comedian cricketer diplomat engineer/businessman
advertising executive expert (language/literature) interpreter judge
librarian newscaster (TV) novelist (2) politician (2)
singer/songwriter tennis theatre/TV director writer/journalist

Ronnie Barker | Paul Simon | P G Wodehouse

Snake - Libra/Leo

Actress (3) actress/dramatist boss (gallery) broadcaster/actress
broker (govt) composer critic/historian/writer physicist
pianist/pioneer ('bop') politician (2) politician/leader singer

Felix Bloch | Mahatma Gandhi

Snake - Libra/Virgo-

Boss (6) boss (advert)/adviser (PR) boss (finance)/ accountant
boss (mining) boss (TV) boss/legal adviser/personal agent boxer
clairvoyant 2-judge poet scholar/teacher writer/translator/campaigner

Lord Tim Bell | James McAuley

Snake - Libra/Libra

Academic (physics) actor (5) actress boss composer
drummer/percussionist industrialist (toiletries) founder (charity)
investigator (monuments) journalist/author/astrologer college master
photographer singer/guitarist

Nevill Mott | John Zochonis

Snake - Libra/Scorpio

Actor (2) basketballer boss consultant (research)/historian driver (racing) photographer/musician school master singer (2)

Linda McCartney | Midge Ure

Snake - Libra/Sagittarius

Actor (2) actress comedian (2) comedian/ presenter (TV) interior designer editor journalist/broadcaster Speaker (Commons) theologian/historian/priest trumpeter/bandleader/singer

Betty Boothroyd | Les Dennis | Omid Djalili | Dizzy Gillespie Lillian Gish | David Threlfall

Snake - Libra/Capricorn

Actress cricketer headmaster (2) headmistress killer matron poet horse rider politician painter architect provost (U) singer (3) singer/guitarist tennis Rear Admiral

Joan Fontaine | Tito Jackson | Mir-Hossein Mousavi | Frederick West

Snake - Libra/Aquarius

Actor (Speaking Clock) anthropologist/ psychoanalyst/ philosopher/author bass baritone boss (3) boss (health authority) broadcaster chemist/inventor/engineer fencer judge politician singer Lieut-Colonel/conservationist

Chong Jin Wee | Brian Cobby | Magnus Magnusson | Alfred Nobel Michelle Wie

Snake - Libra/Pisces

Academic/astrophysicist bass baritone boss (2) (industrial relations) coach (basketballer)/basketballer forester/boss (furniture) headmaster mycologist politician (2) politician/reformer (social) producer (dance) singer (2)

Charles Bradlaugh | Chubby Checker

Snake - Scorpio/Aries

Actor actor/comedian columnist drummer footballer (2) guitarist
head master novelist politician rugby vocalist/songwriter writer

Nigel Dempster | John Pullin

Snake - Scorpio/Taurus

Academic/historian/author actor administrator baseballer/coach
boss (2) (radio) boss (Customs/Excise) farmer minister/composer
novelist (2) singer/composer solicitor writer Marshall/engineer

Ed Asner | Art Garfunkel

Snake - Scorpio/Gemini

Comedian cricketer driver (racing) editor engineer
inventor (Technicolor) missionary novelist politician Recorder
singer/composer tenor (3) Capt (destroyer)

Fyodor Dostoyevsky | Eddie Irvine | H T Kalmus

Snake - Scorpio/Cancer

Actor (2) actress boss (2) body builder civil servant
diplomat/politician/author golfer horticulturist/presenter umpire (cricket)
violinist writer/scholar

Charles Atlas | Peter Firth | Nerys Hughes

Snake - Scorpio/Leo

Academic (3)/astrophysicist academic/boss (lab) academic/Vice-Chancellor
Bishop boss (2) clerk (town) headmaster politician (2)
psychiatrist singer trombonist/bandleader Lieut-General

Tommy Dorsey

Snake - Scorpio/Virgo

Academic (2) (anthropology/sociology) academic (political sc) actress
author boss (councils) designer (bathroom fixtures) guitarist skier

Snake - Scorpio/Libra

Actress (2) diplomat footballer TV host pianist
musician/producer politician singer/actress snooker
Air Vice Marshal/pilot

Joan Plowright

Snake - Scorpio/Scorpio

Actor (4) /director/producer) actor/model (photographic) actress
architect (consultant) Bishop boss/lawyer composer/chemist
entrepreneur/ sound engineer Latinist lawyer (2) publisher
singer (2)/actor singer/songwriter 3-day eventer Air Chief Marshal
Maj-General

Bjork | Alexander Borodin | Amar Bose | Lucinda Green

Snake - Scorpio/Sagittarius

Academic (neurological surgery) actress artist boss (quango) boxer
designer (fashion) animation director endocrinologist (consultant)
US footballer mathematical sensation volleyballer

Pablo Picasso

Snake - Scorpio/Capricorn

Academic (2) Vice-Chancellor (University) academic/U principal (2) actor (2)
actress astrologer dancer/ teacher film writer/ wine connoisseur
footballer/entrepreneur harpist maker (watch) politician (leader)
private secretary/police 2-singer/ songwriter singer/ songwriter/guitarist

Milton Black | Tom Conti | Indira Gandhi | Hank Brian Marvin
Helen Reddy

Snake - Scorpio/Aquarius

Editor golfer guitarist inventor/designer (Bell helicopter) politician (leader) skater (fig) sociologist/gerontologist Lieut-Commander/pilot

Snake - Scorpio/Pisces

Accountant/boss actor (3) actress boss (retail) editor/politician keeper (firearms) novelist physiologist politician (2) singer (2) medical writer Maj-General/chief engineer

Griff Rhys Jones | Grace Kelly

Snake - Sagittarius/Aries

Biologist boss (3) (publisher) boss (ambulance) boxer physiologist pianist/bandleader QC/boss sculptor skater (fig) teacher tennis theologian/lecturer/author

Richard Meade | Katarina Witt

Snake - Sagittarius/Taurus

Academic (Egyptology) actor Bishop boss/accountant Constable (Chief) editor/author/mountaineer entrepreneur footballer manager (football) politician/barrister singer Capt Lieut-Commander/aviator (naval)

Mike England | R W ('Tiny') Rowland

Snake - Sagittarius/Gemini

Academic/author (3) author/ broadcaster/actor boss Constable (Chief) footballer murderer politician surgeon writer Air Marshal

Sheridan Morley | Andrew Morton

Snake - Sagittarius/Cancer

Academic (2)/physician/civil servant Bishop boss (3) (council) boss (insurance) boss (trust) editor/lecturer chef/restaurateur diplomat inventor (tape recorder) manager (football) novelist pianist poet scientist singer (2) singer/songwriter/guitarist

Joseph Conrad | Valdemar Poulson

Snake - Sagittarius/Leo

Boss civil servant designer (ceramic) footballer poet/ inventor/scientist novelist publisher (2) rugby sheriff (Scotland) trombonist

Will Carling | Gustave Flaubert | Geoff Hurst

Snake - Sagittarius/Virgo

Abbot academic (econs) actor (2) Bishop boss (3) (bank) boss (foods) boss (electronic) dramatist/poet editor historian judge organist secretary

Alistair Darling | Robert Fellowes | Rosemary West

Snake - Sagittarius/Libra

Archbishop author (3) barrister/QC boss (bank) comedian/writer cricketer golfer hotelier/designer scriptwriter/author Rear Admiral

Anouska Hempel | Luke Donald | Andrew Flintoff

Snake - Sagittarius/Scorpio

Academic (race relations) actor boss (4) boss (association) boss (council) boss (museum) engineer footballer journalist/ broadcaster poet/critic skier Air Commodore (fighter ace) Lieut-General

Derek Jameson | Franz Klammer

Snake - Sagittarius/Sagittarius

Actor boss (2) (charity) boss (wines)/critic musician/scholar musician (2) official (weightlifting) painter politician QC/recorder saxophonist

Geoff Hoon

Snake - Sagittarius/Capricorn

Actor (2) actress ambassador boss (assurance) dep bank governor prison governor footballer journalist keeper (museum) Pope politician singer/record producer/bandleader writer

Kim Basinger | General Kriangsak Chomanan | Arthur C Clarke
John Malkovich

Snake - Sagittarius/Aquarius

Academic/musicologist actor (3) actress actress/teacher boss (2)/accountant boss/producer (theatre) broadcaster/writer (2) dean (music college) diplomat footballer musician writer/librarian Vice Admiral/boss Supreme Commander/politician (leader)

Snake - Sagittarius/Pisces

Accountant actor boss (2) boss (personnel) comedian cricketer footballer prison governor novelist (2) ornithologist/conservationist politician (2) writer

Heinrich Böll | Jim Davidson | Robert Hawke

Snake - Capricorn/Aries

Astrologer/author/editor Bishop boss (3) boss (adviser) consultant (econs) geneticist TV host/author (2) chief medical officer priest 2-trainer (racehorse)

John Cahill | Gong Li

Snake - Capricorn/Taurus

Boss (2) boss (investment) composer designer (fashion) executive (film studio) film director guitarist judge manager (cricket) college president

Brigadier | Maj-General

Snake - Capricorn/Gemini

Actor (2) actress archaeologist diplomat impersonator/singer manager (football) model physician politician QC/economist Air Chief Marshal

Alex Ferguson | Sarah Miles

Snake - Capricorn/Cancer

Actor archer attorney (2) radio host/activist editor/journalist judge Mayor/attorney/police officer politician (leader) scientist teacher/historian (food) wrestler

Albert Hofmann | John Thaw

Snake - Capricorn/Leo

Academic (2) academic (botany) actress broadcaster musician photographer pianist poet politician politician (party founder) writer Colonel Vice Admiral Air Marshal Wing Commander/pilot

Jan Leeming | Mao Zedong (Mao Tse Tung)

Snake - Capricorn/Virgo

Academic/physicist actor (2) actress athlete (paralympist) boss (football)/businessman boss (TV) boxer conductor farmer/politician musician newscaster politician (2) politician (leader)/lawyer writer Field Marshal

William Ewart Gladstone | Prof Stephen Hawking | Tippi Hedren

Snake - Capricorn/Libra

Academic (2) (govt)/author actor (2)/adventurer/yachtsman/singer/cook actress astrologer astronaut/pilot author (3) broadcaster/politician campaigner (right to die)/lecturer diplomat editor (2) headmaster/Reverend pianist surgeon wrestler writer/editor

Edwin Buzz Aldrin | Richard Clayderman

Snake - Capricorn/Scorpio

Academic (dentistry) actress author campaigner (women's rights) prison governor headmaster lawyer organist physicist snowboarder

Snake - Capricorn/Sagittarius

Academic boss film director (2) magnate (shipping) manager (cricket) manufacturer/aviator/film producer painter/sculptor potter presenter/editor stockbroker writer/economist/humorist Lieut-Col (chapel clerk)

Howard Hughes | Henri Matisse | Aristotle Onassis

Snake - Capricorn/Capricorn

Academic/scholar/grammarian cricketer/underwriter fashion designer guitarist/banjoist historian (created Winnie-the-Pooh)/dramatist microbiologist novelist (2) physiologist politician scriptwriter (TV, film) tennis writer

Stefan Edberg | A A Milne

Snake - Capricorn/Aquarius

Academic (2) (astrophysics) academic/statistician actor (2) actress aviator Bishop boss (construction) boxer film director judge obstetrician/gynaecologist pianist/composer/bandleader poet (leader) politician

Muhammad Ali | Earl 'Fatha' Hines | Martin Laing | Anthony Minghella Gamal Abdel Nasser

Snake - Capricorn/Pisces

Academic/QC/college master actor (2) actor/singer actress boss boss (4) (investors) boss (museum) boss (polytechnic) boss (inspector) boxer civil servant journalist/author judge philosopher politician (3) publisher screenwriter/producer singer/songwriter

Michael Crawford

Snake - Aquarius/Aries

Author boss (industrials) businessman/boss (2) comedian judge novelist/critic painter photographer rugby songwriter/singer/musician spy wrestler/manager Squadron-Leader/pilot Vice Admiral Marshal/leader (polit)

Virginia Woolf

Snake - Aquarius/Taurus

Academic/boss (institute) actor /broadcaster author attorney/QC boss (2) (TV) driver (racing) footballer (2) footballer/manager librarian manager (show business) painter/lithographer/ceramicist physician poet statistician (medical)/researcher statistician/boss Lieut-General

Eusebio | Paul Ferris | Graham Hill

Snake - Aquarius/Gemini

Academic/surgeon author (3) actor (3)/writer/composer (2)
actress/singer (2) boss (nuclear)/engineer college warden
composer/vocalist (2) cryptographer musician/comedian
screenwriter/ singer businesswoman actress writer/adviser

Patricia Routledge

Snake - Aquarius/Cancer

Academic (2) (engineer)/QC/arbitrator academic/Vice-Chancellor actor
Archdeacon boss (2) (investigations) commissioner (estates) composer
film director editor/boss 2-politician (leader) politician (2)
songwriter/singer trade unionist/politician

Nicolae Ceausescu | Edith Cresson

Snake - Aquarius/Leo

Actress ballerina boss comedian explorer musician/arranger
novelist (3) poet/ novelist politician (2) politician (leader)
puppeteer/entertainer surgeon writer Brigadier/writer/broadcaster
General

Zsa Zsa Gabor | Terry Jones | James Joyce | Anna Pavlova
Franklin D Roosevelt

Snake - Aquarius/Virgo

Academic (diagnostic radiology) cricketer journalist
model/presenter (TV) politician (3) producer (record)/rapper/actor
2-singer/songwriter statesman wrestler

Dr Dre

Snake - Aquarius/Libra

Artist (comics/graphics)/illustrator author/activist boss (construction) boss (2) Constable (Chief) cricketer film director writer (3) novelist/playwright/publisher photographer politician (2) politician (leader)

Susan Hill | Kim Hughes | Kim Jong Il | Maurice Laing
Dame Muriel Spark

Snake - Aquarius/Scorpio

Academic (2) (physiology) actress (2) actress/singer boss (3) (lawyer) boss (insurance) boss (retailing) boss (theatre) consultant (PR) illustrator Christian minister author poet/playwright politician (2) politician (leader) singer songwriter surgeon teacher

Ben E King | Julia McKenzie | Geoffrey Mulcahy

Snake - Aquarius/Sagittarius

Actress/hostess (talk show) boss (TV) boss (4) correspondent (foreign) dean (dental surgery)/surgeon founder/boss (TV) politician psychiatrist Air Commodore Air Vice Marshal/boss (training)

Oprah Winfrey

Snake - Aquarius/Capricorn

Actor (2)/writer boss (3) boss (charity) politician (2) dean (hosp)/physician developer (property)/boss model (super) musician/actor politician/Reverend politician (leader) singer

Ehud Barak | John Junkin | Peter Tork

Snake - Aquarius/Aquarius

Actor boss chaplain/Reverend chemist commissioner (charity) historian painter physician/co founder (medical school) civil servant/Ombudsman technologist (baking) Group Capt Air Commodore

Elizabeth Blackwell

Snake - Aquarius/Pisces

Abbot academic (2) (Arabic) academic/scientist boss (museum) campaigner/magistrate art dealer/writer/artist golfer novelist/journalist politician (4) physicist politician/TV presenter politician (leader) singer/songwriter

Dick Cheney

Snake - Pisces/Aries

Actor (4) actor/comedian/writer (2)actress architect author/ broadcaster boss/financier Dep Commissioner (Police) critic/novelist/composer poet politician priest psychotherapist/psychologist/pharmacist nosegay supplier

Ian Blair | Anthony Burgess | Emile Coué
Wilfred Owen | Jim Slater

Snake - Pisces/Taurus

Boss (auditing/consulting) boxer conductor/drummer Constable (Chief) golfer historian politician prosecutor scholar (literature) Major/rifle shot

Neville Chamberlain | Floyd Mayweather

Snake - Pisces/Gemini

Academic (2) /anthropologist college mistress academic/ historian actor beadle/sexton boss (3) boss (corporate/info) boss/owner (restaurants) choirmaster harpsichordist/pianist (2) designer (interior)/personality (TV) poet (2) politician (2) U principal/Vice-Chancellor singer/guitarist/pianist Capt Maj-General

Laurence Llewelyn-Bowen

Snake - Pisces/Cancer

Academic (2) (urban planning) academic (moral philosophy) artist author/journalist boss (2) (health boss (polytechnic) boss (TV) composer designer (textile) judge/QC musician/actor/TV producer politician (3) politician (leader) politician/trade unionist singer/guitarist trainer (racehorse)

Desi Arnaz | Jose Maria Aznar | Ernest Bevin | Craig Martin David Wainwright

Snake - Pisces/Leo

Actor author (2) ballerina/choreographer comedian cricketer headmistress novelist/poet philosopher General/politician (leader)

Kemal Ataturk | Frankie Howerd | Ronan Keating

Snake - Pisces/Virgo

Academic/Canon road agent/wrestler artist/potter cricketer/Capt racing driver economist columnist/author historian/curator (museum) politician (2) Scottish Justice Senator Maj-Gen/Lord Lieut

Snake - Pisces/Libra

Academic/physicist actress author (2) journalist boss (2) (charity) boss/founder (party) explorer/scholar film director headmaster maker (glove) photographer physiologist poet/critic/translator politician (2) businessman screenwriter/novelist singer statesman swimmer charity worker

Peter Cazalet | Googie Withers | Richard Burton (explorer)

Snake - Pisces/Scorpio

Academic/biochemistArchdeacon architect artist/painter bassist
boss (3) boss (artistic - theatre) Commissioner (police)
conductor/founder (proms) critic/poet film director editor pianist
politician theologian/pastor/essayist trainer (racehorse)
Admiral/flag officer Capt/boss (car parks) Lieut-General

Bernardo Bertolucci | Frank Gehry | Robert Mark | Sir Henry Wood

Snake - Pisces/Sagittarius

Actress/singer Bishop business man (founded Dell) conductor
Constable (Chief dancer producer (theatre) tennis
Air Chief Marshal

Michael Dell

Snake - Pisces/Capricorn

Actress (2) Bishop (2) Bishop/cricketer boss (airline) diplomat
driver (racing) novelist politician (2)

Snake - Pisces/Aquarius

Academic (2)/physician academic/Vice-Chancellor (u) actress
Bishop boss (2) boss (engineering) engineer founder (scouts)
journalist/writer physicist politician college principal
film producer QC/barrister singer teacher (New Age)/author (2)
writer

Heinrich Hertz | Lembit Öpik | Lord David Puttnam | Dame Vera Lynn
Baron Robert Baden-Powell

Snake - Pisces/Pisces

Boss (4) (research) boss (Equity) boss (tax) cricketer (3) civil servant designer (stage) gardener/photographer novelist official (CIA)/journalist politician (leader) (3) politician (leader)/soldier statesman wrestler/model/actress Air Marshal/boss (training) Maj-General/boss (charity)

Paddy Ashdown | Gail Kim | Brian Mulroney

Horse - Aries/Aries

Actress/psychotherapist advocate/solicitor artist/entertainer boss (2) (engineering) comedian conductor/ boss (musical) economist governor (prison) historian/broadcaster judge politician (2) politician (leader) presenter (TV/radio)/singer/model/pianist Reverend scout (chief)

Rolf Harris | Myleene Klass

Horse - Aries/Taurus

Academic/pathologist actress boss (2) (engineering) boss (engineering) conductor boss (musical) industrial designer instrumentalist/singer/songwriter QC scout (chief) singer (4) writer

Rachel Stevens

Horse - Aries/Gemini

Academic (Spanish) actor/ film director/comedian boss (3) (cars) boss (girl guides) boss (law) footballer headmaster (2) ice hockey ophthalmologist news reporter singer

Jackie Chan

Horse - Aries/Cancer

Actor (4) actor/writer (2) athlete author/comedian Bishop (3) Bishop designate boss (2) (TV) broadcaster/rugby boss (design) designer (fashion) entrepreneur footballer/manager (football) novelist activist public speaker teacher singer

Frank Barlow | William Holden | Spike Milligan | Richard O'Brien | Andrew Sachs | Iain Duncan Smith

Horse - Aries/Leo

Actor (3) actress athlete boss broadcaster dancer film director footballer organist 2-politician (leader) intelligence officer/Russianist/academic/historian college principal psychoanalyst singer writer/mountaineer

Roger Black | Chris Evans | Neil Kinnock | Mélanie Klein | Teddy Sheringham | Bessie Smith | Michael York

Horse - Aries/Virgo

Academic (animal production) actor boss (3) civil servant Constable (Chief) guitarist owner (cinema)/impresario poet/artist/printer politician (2) politician (leader) polar scientist scriptwriter/playwright

Nikita Khrushchev | William Morris | Barbara Roche

Horse - Aries/Libra

Boxer conductor driver (racing) historian (furniture) judge musician/songwriter politician (2) politician (leader) QC wrestler writer

Hugh Gaitskell | Ricardo Patrese

Horse - Aries/Scorpio

Academic (2)/college principal academic/gastro-enterologist biologist boss driver (racing) editor film/TV director footballer/manager matron murderer pioneer (mothercraft)

Trevor Francis

Horse - Aries/Sagittarius

Academic/historian actress (2) author (2) Bishop boss (law institute) diplomat musician QC writer Air Marshal

W Atlee Burpee | Phil Hyams | Emma Watson | Samuel Beckett

Horse - Aries/Capricorn

Academic/engineer actor archaeologist boss businessman composer critic (film)/biographer herald nurse physician/mountaineer 2-politician (leader) scriptwriter/producer singer solicitor origami historian tennis

Victor Herbert | Earl Jellicoe | Steve McQueen | Stephen Sondheim Lisa Stansfield

Horse - Aries/Aquarius

Actor archaeologist boss (2) clarinettist commando correspondent judge model/singer politician college principal yachtsman/administrator

Samantha Fox

Horse - Aries/Pisces

Academic (sociology)/boss actor boss (2) broadcaster/author cricketer cyclist diplomat/historian film director/screenwriter/novelist theatre director/writer driver (racing) editor painter poet solicitor sprinter/rugby Air Vice Marshal Lieut-Colonel/SAS soldier

Dwain Chambers | Arnaud Tournant

Horse - Taurus/Aries

Actor/artist (martial) actor (3) boss (retail) composer (2)/pianist composer/musician founder (newspaper) hall principal film/TV producer/actor schoolmaster (2) schoolmaster/author singer (2) singer/songwriter

Georges Braque | Janet Jackson | Archie Norman | Dev Patel Dawn Primarolo

Horse - Taurus/Taurus

Academic/pathologist boss (2) chemist composer Constable (Chief) designer (fashion) film/TV director politician singer stuntman traitor/propagandist (Nazi)

William Joyce (Lord Haw-Haw) | Franz Lehár | Véronique Nichanian

Horse - Taurus/Gemini

Barrister/QC (2) boss (engineering) businessman/co founder company. equestrian champion entrepreneur politician judge painter QC

Horse - Taurus/Cancer

Academic/biochemist astronomer athlete Bishop boss (2) (TV) boss broadcaster/politician (2) businessman/conductor civil servant Constable (Chief) designer (fashion) diplomat doctor (flying) footballer college master racer (bicycle) General/politician (leader)

Antonio Colom | Lynn Davies | Ulysses G Grant | Robert Kilroy-Silk P (Nobby) Stiles

Horse - Taurus/Leo

Boss (insurance) boss (5) boss (education) dancer/choreographer designer (fashion) expert (naval intelligence) historian film producer footballer golfer (2) governor (country) headmaster politician (2) singer (2)/actress soprano Rear Admiral/engineer

John Daly | Martha Graham | Birgit Nilsson | Barbra Streisand Harry Vardon

Horse - Taurus/Virgo

Actor composer historian football manager/footballer novelist physicist (2) historian physicist/founder (quantum theory) soprano

Max Planck

Horse - Taurus/Libra

Academic (2)/Vice-Chancellor academic (literature) thinker actress boss (4) boss/businessman boss (health) civil servant cricketer psychoanalyst golfer mathematician novelist broadcaster physicist boss producer (TV) pioneer waiter writer/playwright

Joan Sims

Horse - Taurus/Scorpio

Academic (3) (differential psychology) academic (American literature) academic/principal/Vice Chancellor actress film director footballer/manager jockey physician/astronaut

Trevor Francis

Horse - Taurus/Sagittarius

Academic (literature) actress coach (footballer) footballer drummer engineer/boss judo (2) journalist painter (2) pilot principal (U) rector/Canon singer/songwriter writer

Horse - Taurus/Capricorn

Academic (astronomy) ambassador (2) ambassador/politician athlete broadcaster civil servant criminal (Nazi war) editor film producer/author activist librarian organist/master (choristers) pianist/composer politician (4) politician (leader) scientist/boss singer (2) writer Air Chief Marshal Maj-General

Jonathan Edwards | **Rudolf Hess** | **Vladimir Ilyich Lenin**
Tammy Wynette

Horse - Taurus/Aquarius

Academic (2) (literature) academic/gold/silversmith Archbishop banker scientist engineer (2) lawyer police inspector poet/essayist politician

Norman Lamont

Horse - Taurus/Pisces

Academic/scholar (Shakespearean) boss (aircraft) dancer/choreographer politician (3) 2-politician (leader) politician (leader)/writer college president writer (2) Vice Admiral/surgeon

Malcolm Fraser

Horse - Gemini/Aries

Athlete boss (2) boss (art gallery) industrial designer (2) designer (dress) editor engineer GP politician (leader)/dictator snooker Admiral Brigadier Colonel

Doug Mountjoy | Muammar al-Gaddafi

Horse - Gemini/Taurus

Academic (2) (engineering) academic/author actor (3) actress/film director/screenwriter actress/singer astronomer Bishop biochemist consultant (legal) barrister haematologist shot putter swimmer javelin thrower

Horse - Gemini/Gemini

Academic (numerical analysis) agent/producer/owner (theatre) athlete composer (2) composer/lyricist publisher (music) dictator novelist/writer (travel) politician (leader) scholar (biblical) Reverend solicitor

Diane Modahl | Harold Spina

Horse - Gemini/Cancer

Academic actor (2) boss (music) film director/writer footballer hostess judge motorcyclist colonial officer administrator physicist politician college president proprietor (newspaper)

Giacomo Agostini | Eric Cantona | Catherine Cookson

Horse - Gemini/Leo

Actor (2) rodeo rider actress anaesthetist athlete boss (2) boss (museum) 2-businessman cricketer film critic designer (fashion) goldsmith judge novelist painter politician (leader) restaurateur/chef/writer (2) writer

Zola Budd | Helena Bonham Carter | Peter Carl Fabergé
Thabo Mbeki | Paul McCartney | Robert Schumann

Horse - Gemini/Virgo

Boss (insurance) businessman composer/singer consultant (educational) cricketer drummer footballer ice hockey novelist trade unionist Vice Admiral/Lord Lieut

Horse - Gemini/Libra

Academic (2) agent/producer boss (radio) chancellor chemist consultant (environment) cricketer (3) diplomat headmistress journalist/biographer politician (leader) scholar/Reverend sculptor singer

Josephine Baker | Bruce Roberts

Horse - Gemini/Scorpio

Academic (2)/obstetrician/gynaecologist academic/biographer actress Bishop cricketer/author film director journalist model (glamour) personality (TV) poet/dramatist producer (theatrical) singer toolmaker trade unionist bibliophile Maj-General/boss (law)

Jordan (Katie Price)

Horse - Gemini/Sagittarius

Actor (3) actress archaeologist/keeper (museum) Bishop
boss Vice-Chancellor (University) comedian footballer
founder (charity) obstetrician/gynaecologist politician (leader) preacher
singer (2) singer/actress

Daniel Kitson | Frank Lampard | Yasuhiro Nakasone

Horse - Gemini/Capricorn

Academic (2)/economist academic/guitarist (flamenco) musician (2)
actor (2) singer/comedian 2-actress musician/violinist/music historian
politician (2) prosecutor screenwriter wine producer

Horse - Gemini/Aquarius

Actress boxer civil servant/historian diplomat
performer (comic)/dancer pianist politician writer

Marvin Hagler | Dashiell Hammett | Allan Lamb | Kathleen Turner

Horse - Gemini/Pisces

Actor/dramatist cricketer footballer novelist
painter/teacher 2-politician (leader) politician (leader)/philosopher
pilot (test) entrepreneur producer singer/lawyer tenor (2)
trumpeter General

Kenny Ball | David Platt | Jan Christiaan Smuts | Brian Statham

Horse - Cancer/Aries

Academic (primary education) actor Bishop boss (3) boss (finance)
Dean (cathedral)/V Reverend judge publisher secretary surgeon
Air Chief Marshal

Burt Kwouk

Horse - Cancer/Taurus

Author boss (4) (association) boss (racing) chaplain/canon designer/boss historian pop impresario inventor (lava lamp) mountaineer poet politician (3) politician/boss/columnist hall president secretary (cricket) singer/songwriter/dancer writer

Sir Alec Bedser | Nicole Scherzinger

Horse - Cancer/Gemini

Academic/chemist boss (2) (logistics) boss/vet columnist/writer/critic (2) critic (art) dean (medical schools) film director theatre director civil engineer (2) financial journalist (2) pioneer (tabloid City pages) novelist politician (2) politician (leader) Rabbi/broadcaster sailor/engineer umpire (cricket) Lieut-Commander

A A Gill | Hugo Gryn

Horse - Cancer/Cancer

Actor academic (adult education) boss (3) (charity) boss (charity) boss (arts quango) engineer film director film director/writer poet politician (2) politician (leader) weightlifter

Harrison Ford | John Heath-Stubbs | J H Wahlström

Horse - Cancer/Leo

Actor author (2) bandleader editor film director film producer novelist playwright politician (leader) politician (2) showman tennis General

Phineas T Barnum

Horse - Cancer/Virgo

Academic/archaeologist boss (2) (sports) boss/founder (computers) broadcaster (2) cricketer disc jockey headmaster leader (suffragette) painter/etcher Rabbi/broadcaster

Ingmar Bergman | Emmeline Pankhurst | Peter Sissons James McNeill | Whistler

Horse - Cancer/Libra

Academic (2) neuropsychologist academic/astronomer athlete businesswoman politician drummer fencer naturalist/exec (TV)/politician (5) politician (leader) treasurer

Mick Fleetwood | Carlos Menem

Horse - Cancer/Scorpio

Academic/Dean (dental) boss (2) (trust) boss (energy) entrepreneur/investor/author murderess naval officer/ambassador circus/stunt performer photographer politician (2) (leader) producer (film, TV) statesman Rear Admiral

Myra Hindley | Eddie Large | Nelson Mandela | Lady Zuckerman

Horse - Cancer/Sagittarius

Academic(2)(natural history) accountant/boss (council) artist civil servant diplomat founder (Universal Sufism) mountaineer musician politician (2) teacher/writer/broadcaster

Lady Margaret Douglas-Home | Rachel Squire

Horse - Cancer/Capricorn

Baker designer judge novelist/boss painter politician (2) politician (leader) college principal/historian singer writer/playwright trade unionist Vice-Chancellor (U)/rector watercolourist

Charlotte Bingham | Edgar Degas | Lord Rogan | Josephine Veasey

Horse - Cancer/Aquarius

Architect boss (2) (pensions) boss (artistic) engineer journalist/ (2) writer/host (TV, radio) physician/therapist playwright/journalist/author (2) poet politician (2) 2-politician (leader) college principal

G W Goethals | Inayat Khan | Angela Merkel | Willie Whitelaw

Horse - Cancer/Pisces

Academic/zoologist/sociologist actress (2) boss (2) (translation) boss (engineering) footballer Constable (Chief) healer (faith) politician (2) singer/actress

King Edward VIII | Susan Hayward | Alfred Kinsey

Horse - Leo/Aries

Academic (medieval history) architect/historian boat builder broadcaster/businessman comedian dancer/choreographer entrepreneur/founder (Wikipedia) farmer chief prison inspector magistrate novelist (2) optometrist philosopher singer

Bernard Manning | Jimmy Wales

Horse - Leo/Taurus

Basketballer boss (2) (finance) boss (museum/gallery) financier novelist (2) politician politician (leader) prostitute/sex film producer/TV host/editor sportswoman/administrator toastmaster TV weatherman/actor/author

Aldous Huxley | David Lange

Horse - Leo/Gemini

Academic (2)/boss (institute) academic/criminologist actress architect author/storyteller/humorist poet/author (3) boss (hospital) boss (pharmaceutical) boss (4) boss (retailing) boss (finance) boss (health) boss (oil) drummer footballer (2) journalist (2) photographer teacher/writer

Vitas Gerulaitas | Ted Hughes

Horse - Leo/Cancer

Academic/Vice-Chancellor (U) actress architect boss (4) boss (research) civil servant/boss clerk (parliament) consultant (design) film director driver (racing) politician (4) 2-politician (leader) psychiatrist scientist sculptor singer

Auguste Bartholdi | Halle Berry | Hugo Chavez | Princess Margaret

Horse - Leo/Leo

Actor (3) actress/comedienne chief scientific adviser boss cricketer film-maker impresario jurist/historian merchant (wine) QC model/actress musician (2)/composer pianist/musician Capt/boss

Horse - Leo/Virgo

Academic/educationist businessman footballer model (super) physician playwright psychoanalyst/consultant soprano tennis

Christiaan Eijkman

Horse - Leo/Libra

Actress aircrew/consul ballerina boss (books) footballer pioneer (aeronautics) guitarist singer/writer soldier (2) solicitor writer Commander/pilot

Martin Keown

Horse - Leo/Scorpio

Administrator biochemist composer engineer
entertainer (music hall) master (foxhounds) sheriff (high) chief matron
Air Chief Marshal

Lionel Bart

Horse - Leo/Sagittarius

Academic (2)/geographer academic/astronaut artist/keeper (art academy)
civil servant (2) civil servant/printer lawyer/QC
manufacturer (aircraft)/designer rugby statesman violist volleyball

Neil Armstrong | Geoffrey de Havilland

Horse – Leo/Capricorn

Academic actor astrologer/psychic athlete ballerina cricketer
guitarist/ composer (2) historian headmaster radio journalist
novelist pianist/composer politician (2) politician (leader) singer
tennis

Sally Gunnell | Mystic Meg (Margaret Lake)

Horse - Leo/Aquarius

Academic/scientist (food) actress (2) author (2) civil servant
clerk (parliament) diplomat film director economist
guitarist/songwriter planner (town) film star violinist writer (TV)

Clara Bow | Jeff Buckley | Joan Hickson | John Huston

Horse - Leo/Pisces

Artist boss (2)/investor boss (schools) civil servant cyclist
film director politician (2) politician/author ornithologist

Luc Leblanc | George Galloway | George Soros

Horse - Virgo/Aries

Academic (2) (political science) academic/historian 2-actor
Bishop boss chess player composer/conductor/author
designer (hotel) diplomat/UN official editor/journalist engineer guitarist
judge chief matron pilot (wartime) diplomat public servant
politician (2)

Jonathan Aitken | Leonard Bernstein

Horse - Virgo/Taurus

Actor actress arbitrator/mediator boss (2) golfer impresario
judge painter/secret agent surveyor/boss Capt Lieut-General
General/politician

Isao Aoki | Jacqueline Bisset

Horse - Virgo/Gemini

Academic/politician boss (2) (hall) boss/teacher chemist/physicist
inventor (gas mantle) cook/writer (cookery) engineer
pioneer (oil production technology) education inspector politician (3)
singer/guitarist trainer (racehorse) yachtsman/designer (yacht)

Murtaza Bhutto | Al Jardine

Horse - Virgo/Cancer

Astronaut boss (2) (commission) boss (forest) Vice-Chancellor
golfer historian judge lyricist politician singer/songwriter
ventriloquist Air Marshal

Ray Alan | A J Lerner | Karl Böhm | Elvis Costello

Horse - Virgo/Leo

Academic/boss (museum) actor (4) actor/comedian actress boss (3) boss (film) boss (retailing) composer conductor driver (racing) disc jockey ecologist college warden chancellor (U) Lady-in-Waiting model (glamour) musician paediatrician presenter/writer (TV) QC/recorder tennis trainer (racehorse)

Cherie Blair | John Lloyd | Derek Nimmo | Steve Wright

Horse - Virgo/Virgo

Academic (literature) Bishop dancer/choreographer boss (ballet) ecologist/college warden/U Chancellor footballer/manager paediatrician (consultant) painter politician (leader) swimmer trainer (horse) Air Chief Marshal

Sean Connery | Junius Jayewardene

Horse - Virgo/Libra

Academic (4) (social policy) academic/chemist academic (anatomy) college master property developer judge painter photographer college principal politician (leader) politician (2) psychiatrist publisher/author teacher/sportsman Lieut-General

Robert Kocharyan

Horse - Virgo/Scorpio

Actor (2) Bishop boss (2) surveyor boss/treasurer circulation director founder (airlines)/pilot garden manager/horticulturist politician (2) politician (leader) tennis writer Capt

Windsor Davies | Ben Gazzara | Jiabao Wen | Harris Queensway

Horse - Virgo/Sagittarius

Banker (investment) boss (2) broadcaster cricketer historian investor/businessman poet/ musicologist rower

Warren Buffett | Desmond Lynam

Horse - Virgo/Capricorn

Attorney general/QC boss (3) broadcaster cricketer percussionist/composer judge photographer pioneer (grassland sc) politician (3) politician (leader)/statesman politician (leader) writer Lieut-Colonel/diplomat Major/boss Field Marshal

Anne Diamond | Andrew Bonar Law

Horse - Virgo/Aquarius

Artist author boss (2) (opera) boss (trust) kick boxer/actor businessman Constable (Chief) diplomat novelist/critic film producer/pioneer (film) footballer/coach jockey physician

Samuel Goldwyn | Chaim Herzog | Richard Linley | J B Priestley

Horse - Virgo/Pisces

Academic/researcher/administrator film director judge politician skater (ice) trade unionist trainer (racehorse) writer (2) writer/biographer Colonel

King Baudouin

Horse - Libra/Aries

Academic /chemist/inventor (2) actress/singer boss (2)/interpreter/journalist boss (TV) TV presenter composer engineer (acoustics) founder (Body Shop) inventor (Portakabin, Portaloo) judge college principal surgeon photographer poet/painter/essayist politician QC writer lecturer

E E Cummings | John Platts-Mills | Anita Roddick

Horse - Libra/Taurus

Academic (4)/college warden academic (acoustics)
academic/boss/Vice-Chancellor (U) actress author/film producer/doctor
boss (2) (cars) diplomat/boss headmaster interpreter/journalist
inventor (air brake) pilot playwright politician (leader) QC
sculptor teacher/dancer writer/broadcaster technician (nuclear)

Michael Crichton | Frank Delaney | Michael Edwardes
David Goode | Rutherford B Hayes | Jyothika | Harold Pinter
George Westinghouse

Horse - Libra/Gemini

Academic/biochemistactor (2) actress politician (6) politician (leader)
politician (leader)/lawyer politician/teacher screenwriter/playwright

Ian McShane

Horse - Libra/Cancer

Anaesthetist/dean (school) Dr architect banker civil servant
ichthyologist model (fashion) sports woman/personality (TV)
pioneer (rocketry) politician (3) politician (leader)
politician/poet/theorist runner warden/Archdeacon

Jodie Kidd | Alan Williams

Horse - Libra/Leo

Actress adviser (bank) boss (3) boss (council)
boss (publishing) footballer nephrologist/rugby physician (Atkins Diet)
cardiologist 2-politician (leader) college president
Reverend scholar (Hardy)/author Brigadier Capt

Robert Atkins | David Cameron | Britt Ekland | Jhanna Sigurdardottir

Horse - Libra/Virgo

Academic (2)/principal/Vice-Chancellor academic (botany) actress (2)
boss (2) boss/lawyer broadcaster curator/historian (art)
film director engineer/inventor (neon light) football manager/footballer
journalist model (fashion) model (2)/actress wrestler
obstetrician/gynaecologist poet politician

Georges Claude | Ang Lee

Horse - Libra/Libra

Academic (geography) athlete author/physician boss (2)
boss (football) politician US footballer guitarist/songwriter
novelist/biographer

Elizabeth Gaskell | Stephen Platt

Horse - Libra/Scorpio

Academic (2) (finance) academic Vice-Chancellor (U)/QC
biochemist boss civil servant climber commentator/wrestler
critic historian/diplomat editor chief school inspector judge
musician personality (TV) drummer neurologist politician (leader)

Horse - Libra/Sagittarius

Academic (architecture) author (2) boss (3) boss (insurance)
choreographer Constable (Chief) educationist engineer
pioneer (disk drive) guitarist historian/iconoclast nutritionist
physicist rugby singer/songwriter trumpeter

Colin Dexter | Alesha Dixon | Shaun Edwards | Thomas Hughes

Horse - Libra/Capricorn

Actor/singer/songwriter   Bishop   boss (2) (finance)   boss (health)
boxer   cartoonist   composer   conductor   cricketer   editor (2)
founder (holiday)   hostess   journalist (2)/editor   painter (3)
journalist/commentator   painter/sculptor   photographer
politician (leader)   swimmer

Umberto Boccioni | William Buford | Richard Harris | Sir Fred Pontin
Sir Robert Sainsbury | Dmitri Shostakovich | John L Sullivan

Horse - Libra/Aquarius

Academic (law)   actor   boss   boss (charity)   cricketer   critic
football manager   politician/governor

Béla Lugosi

Horse - Libra/Pisces

Academic (2)/philosopher   academic (biophysics)   actress/singer/composer
artist/designer   author   boss   Constable (Chief)   cosmonaut (2)
engineer/astronaut   politician   scholar/folklorist   farmer
silversmith/designer   retailer   singer

Rita Hayworth | Pavel Popovich

Horse - Scorpio/Aries

Actress   author   biographer/broadcaster   blogger   curator/lecturer
designer (fashion)   novelist   pianist   poet   politician (3)

Kazuo Ishiguro | Kelvin Klein | Dame Sybil Thorndike

Horse - Scorpio/Taurus

Actor bassist boss (2) boss (auction) marketer boxer theatre/cinema director impresario (sports) judge novelist (2) Reverend marathon runner writer/poet/mystic Admiral

Bob Hoskins | Selma Lagerlof

Horse - Scorpio/Gemini

Academic/engineer boss (acting) dramatist judge (2) secretary civil servant ethnographer surgeon teacher trainer (Nat Hunt) Maj-General/writer

Horse - Scorpio/Cancer

Academic (3) (Assyriologist) academic/epigrapher (Maya) boss (nursing) cyclist designer (fashion) politician 2-politician (leader) scholar/expert (Greek pottery) Air Marshal

Kenneth Fleetwood | Aleksander Kwasniewski | Condoleezza Rice Theodore Roosevelt

Horse - Scorpio/Leo

Actress (2) artist astronaut footballer judge president (college)/boss (lab)/tutor scientist (rocket) sculptor trainer (football team)

Stefanie Powers

Horse - Scorpio/Virgo

Actor academic (anatomy) boss (3) (lab) boss (lab) boss (design) engineer comedian novelist pianist (2) pianist/conductor sculptor violinist wrestler Admiral/aviator (naval)

J G Ballard | Big Daddy (Shirley Crabtree) | Daniel Barenboim Max Miller | Vanessa-Mae Nicholson | Jack Warner

Horse - Scorpio/Libra

Academic/novelist/poet/educationalist actor (3) critic (dance) headmaster lawyer model/actress/hotelier musicologist novelist (2) novelist/essayist philologist/translator 2-politician (leader) QC tenor

Jean Shrimpton

Horse - Scorpio/Scorpio

Actor (2) actor/director comic book artist boss (2) composer cricketer developer (real estate) entertainer (clown) golfer jockey

David Schwimmer | Tom Weiskopf

Horse - Scorpio/Sagittarius

Academic/biologist architect author (2) film director author (2) boss/surveyor civil servant dancer designer (car) economist editor evangelist footballer founder (car) engineer (2) opera/film director jockey pioneer (aeroplanes) engineer/pilot playwright saxophonist/bandleader designer (2) scientist singer writer (thriller)

Rio Ferdinand | Billy Graham | Sir Peter Hall | Soichiro Honda Alec Issigonis | Kevin Mooney Tom Weiskopf

Horse - Scorpio/Capricorn

Actress artist ballerina bombadier boss (3) (retailing) boss/engineer cartoonist composer (2) entrepreneur/boss golfer judge college master otolaryngologist/surgeon politician (leader) singer violinist/composer teacher

Spiro Agnew | Adam Ant | Leo Baxendale | Bernie Ecclestone Bubba Watson

Horse - Scorpio/Aquarius

Academic (2)   academic (applied maths)   actor/singer   astronaut
boxer   cartoonist   chef ('King of Cooks')   clerk
consultant (development infrastructure)/engineer   economist   film-maker
headmistress (2)   politician   sprinter

Primo Carnera | Michael Collins | Auguste Escoffier

Horse - Scorpio/Pisces

Academic (3) (organisational behaviour)   academic/medical college
Dean   academic (econs)   actress   boss (3) (oil)
boss/comptroller   boss/owner   film director   jockey
journalist (2)/editor   college master/QC   pianist   politician (3)
singer   tennis   Maj-General

Roman Abramovitch | Willie Carson | Linda Evans | Martin Scorsese
Geoffrey Tozer

Horse - Sagittarius/Aries

Academic (2) (government)   academic (sociology)   actor   Bishop
boss (2)   boss (TV)   magician   painter (2)   poet/editor   pop star
TV producer/personality   Rabbi   singer   writer (2)   writer (humorist)

Hanif Kureishi | Kiefer Sutherland | James Thurber

Horse - Sagittarius/Taurus

Academic/college principal   actress (voice)   athlete
banker/engineer/ civil servant   boss   comedian   film director
novelist   scientist (political)

Louis de Bernières | Ronnie Corbett | Jean-Luc Godard | Syd Little

Horse - Sagittarius/Gemini

Boss (4) boss (museum) economist engineer/inventor judge photographer (2) photographer (fashion) poet 2-politician (leader) priest psychic/healer Colonel/explorer

Nobby Clark | Billy Connolly | Hu Jintao | Jean-Claude Juncker Alfred de Musset | Peter Carl Goldmark | Léon Walras

Horse - Sagittarius/Cancer

Administrator architect boss (charity) cricketer engineer guitarist/singer historian judge politician film producer

Jimi Hendrix | Adolf Loos

Horse - Sagittarius/Leo

Academic (3)/obstetrician activist/writer actor/teacher economics adviser civil servant boss conductor designer (2) (shoe) designer (garden) author/broadcaster film producer diplomat/politician (leader) headmaster (2) headmistress magician organist/arranger poet/lecturer politician (3) politician/boss singer

Manolo Blahnik | Michael Jopling | Otto Preminger | Kurt Waldheim

Horse - Sagittarius/Virgo

Academic (2)/historian code breaker academic/oncologist author actor (2) architect athlete boss (TV) impresario metallurgist politician (2) scholar (music, languages) linguist singer/actress surgeon Air Commodore/boss

Gwyneth Dunwoody | Bouadellah Tahri

Horse - Sagittarius/Libra

Actor coach (football) cricketer footballer guitarist novelist (2) politician (leader) rugby singer/songwriter writer

Les Ferdinand | Gemma Jones | Sir Robert Menzies
Hector Hugo Munro ('Saki') | Tim Parks | Sinéad O'Connor

Horse - Sagittarius/Scorpio

Composer developer (property)/entrepreneur explorer/conservationist writer farmer film maker founder (company) publisher musician/drummer politician (3) tennis

Chris Evert | Sir Laurens van der Post

Horse - Sagittarius/Sagittarius

Activist actor (2) voice actor actor/singer (2) Archbishop martial artist hurdler journalist/editor guitarist/singer

Horse - Sagittarius/Capricorn

Architect (naval) bassist boss (2) (TV) boss/founder chef footballer judge landowner/founder (party) politician (2) singer (2) singer/songwriter (2) songwriter/producer

Nelly Furtado | Ann Gloag

Horse - Sagittarius/Aquarius

Academic (pharmacology) actress boss (2) (cars) boss cricketer (2) executive (TV) journalist Ombudsman (banking) playwright 2-politician (leader)

Leonid Brezhnev | Anna Carteret | Don Johnson

Horse - Sagittarius/Pisces

Author boss (2)/banker boss (resistance) composer/educator/linguist cricketer meteorologist politician Lord Provost skier solicitor Colonel explorer (Arctic)

John (Jack) Hobbs | Zoltán Kodály | Dame Shirley Porter Alexander Solzhenitsyn | Alberto Tomba

Horse - Capricorn/Aries

Academic (4)/philosopher academic (science/engineering) academic/classicist academic/surgeon boss/curator (gallery) composer Constable (Chief) organist/ master (choristers) 2-politician (leader) scientist/inventor solicitor

Marquess George Curzon

Horse - Capricorn/Taurus

Academic (3) (morbid anatomy) academic (surgeon) academic (science/engineering) ceramicist counsel/politician film/TV producer footballer impresario mountaineer aviator motorist (racing) engineer novelist pianist poet/critic politician (2) General

Matthew Arnold | Margaret Beckett | Lew Grade

Horse - Capricorn/Gemini

Actor (2) boss chemist/bacteriologist comedian editor headmaster playwright/dramatist politician (leader) surveyor

Giulio Andreotti | Rowan Atkinson | Louis Pasteur | Sam Wanamaker

Horse - Capricorn/Cancer

Academic/psychiatrist author (2)/critic boss (steel) chemist civil servant composer editor film director journalist/editor judge pianist (2) politician (2) politician (leader) rugby sculptor singer/songwriter film star college warden writer (comic)

Robert Duvall | Janis Joplin | Giacomo Puccini | Carol Reed

Horse - Capricorn/Leo

Academic (haematology) actress/super model astronomer/physicist boss (2) cricketer fighter (resistance) judge singer/dancer/model writer/poet Brigadier/boss (committee) Colonel

Aaliyah

Horse - Capricorn/Virgo

Academic (European studies) actress (2)/model/singer Archdeacon boss (2) boss (councils) businessman/founder diplomat DJ/actor drummer film director footballer headmistress photojournalist/ film maker politician (2) (leader) politician (Chancellor) psychiatrist QC rapper singer (3) writer(2) writer/publisher

Antoine Riboud | Mohamed Anwar Sadat | Helmut Schmidt

Horse - Capricorn/Libra

Actor (3) actress boxer dealer (art) golfer guitarist/composer jockey painter singer/actor tennis

Andy Summers | Will Young

Horse - Capricorn/Scorpio

2-Actor boxer investor journalist judge painter politician (leader) saxophonist singer (2) singer/TV producer Lieut-Colonel/campaigner Lieut-General Air Commodore/boss

Clement Attlee | Kevin Costner

Horse - Capricorn/Sagittarius

Academic author (2) boss (3) (museum) author boss (insurance) insurance broker boss (zoo) civil servant clergyman conductor engineer (2) footballer journalist horticulturalist leader (resistance) surgeon naturalist (2) politician (leader) secretary/comptroller equerry singer/musician Admiral (Fleet) Air Vice Marshal General/politician

Nick Clegg | Ferreira da Silva Eusebio | Annie Lennox
Simon Rattle | J D Salinger

Horse - Capricorn/Capricorn

Academic/Canon actor author (3) coach (football) conductor courier artist book dealer hostess charity worker Imam football manager footballer novelist playwright politician singer writer Maj-General/engineer

Lady Dupark | James Earl Jones | A N Tolstoy | Terry Venables

Horse - Capricorn/Aquarius

Actor (2) actor artist boss (2) (insurance) boss (antiquary) footballer founder/industrialist model civil servant schoolmaster/translator

Helena Rubinstein | Denzil Washington

Horse - Capricorn/Pisces

Academic (social work) hall warden barrister boss/founder breeder (racehorse) composer mathematician mediator poker politician secretary

J Edgar Hoover | Alex Salmond

Horse - Aquarius/Aries

Academic/chemist actor photographer astrologer/writer boss (2) boss (assurance) broadcaster novelist artist (2) economist/reformer manager (pop group) producer painter politician (2) politician (leader) singer

Stig Anderson | Harold Macmillan

Horse - Aquarius/Taurus

Actor/manager author/broadcaster Rabbi biologist boss (plastics) cricketer footballer pilot (ace fighter) playwright politician (3) psychiatrist rabbi/lawyer/politician

Alfred Adler | Lionel Blue

Horse - Aquarius/Gemini

Academic/barrister arbitrator astronomer/discoverer boss (2) (brewery) boss (dance band) violinist comedian composer/lyricist Constable (Chief) evangelist financier footballer computer historian conservationist journalist/editor judge minister (2) 2-politician (leader) screenwriter theologian/philosopher

Ferenc Mádl | Clyde Tombaugh

Horse - Aquarius/Cancer

Academic (2) academic (social psychology) actor boss athlete politician (2) diplomat footballer golfer judge organist politician (leader) scientist (material) engineer singer/star (music hall)

David Ginola | Robert Wagner | Boris Yeltsin

Horse - Aquarius/Leo

Academic (2)/Vice-Chancellor assistant author (2) boss (3) boss (investments) boss (TV)/ businessman comedian (2) comedian/cartoonist cricketer designer (fashion) stage designer/lecturer editor golfer guitarist librarian 2-college principal politician/economist/author singer (2) soprano surveyor General

Rick Astley | Les Dawson | Matt Groening | José-Maria Olazabal
Andrés Segovia

Horse - Aquarius/Virgo

Actor/dancer/singer comedian Constable (Chief) educationist entomologist geophysicist scientist tutor/hall principal

John Travolta

Horse - Aquarius/Libra

Actor (3) author/traveller boss (2) biologist boss (operations) Constable (Chief) cricketer engineer lawyer manager (football club) novelist painter politician (leader) singer

James Dean | Ruth Rendell | Fred Trueman

Horse - Aquarius/Scorpio

Academic (2) (history) actress author (2) boss/industrialist composer/teacher comedian disc jockey industrialist/inventor/engineer/campaigner writer/broadcaster Major/yachtsman

Tony Blackburn | Francis Galton | Emperor Kaiser William II

Horse - Aquarius/Sagittarius

Academic (Classics) artist Bishop boss (family planning) cricketer inventor lecturer pianist pioneer (eugemics)/geneticist/anthropologist politician (leader) psychotherapist singer skater typographer writer (cookery) writer (2)

Thomas Alva Edison | Jeff Koons

Horse - Aquarius/Capricorn

Academic (French) accountant/boss (2) actress bookseller/translator/publisher (2) boss (retailing) conductor/composer consultant (emergency medicine)/educator judge playwright poet college principal publisher

Rosamund Pike

Horse - Aquarius/Aquarius

Academic/co-inventor (gas laser) actor (3) actress artist ballerina consultant/writer author (4) author/commentator (sports) book binder boss (2) (orchestra) boss (prison) cricketer Ombudsman physician/writer/reformer politician (leader) writer

Claire Bloom | Gene Hackman | Henry Havelock Ellis

Horse - Aquarius/Pisces

Composer/conductor cricketer film director executive (publishing) musicologist/editor/librarian painter/graphic artist politician secretary singer/songwriter/entrepreneur writer/broadcaster/agony aunt

Gillian Ayres | Claire Rayner | King Vidor

Horse - Pisces/Aries

Actress author entertainer footballer murderer organist/boss (music) politician potter presenter (TV)/singer sculptor solicitor (2) swimmer Vice-Chancellor (U)/lecturer/barrister pacifist

Cheryl Baker | Sean Crampton | Didier Drogba | Janet Leach David Wilkie

Horse - Pisces/Taurus

Academic (2)/architect academic (physics) artist/sculptor/typographer conductor/boss (music) Constable (Chief) diplomat editor engineer model/showgirl 2-politician (leader) surfer (wind) trader (rogue) school warden

Rudolf Diesel | Eric Gill | Christine Keeler | William Lamb Nick Leeson | Pham Van Dong

Horse - Pisces/Gemini

Accountant/boss author (2) author/lyricist/singer (2) disc jockey founder (co) headmaster journalist (2)/diplomat journalist photographer pioneer (motor cars)/engineer politician sculptor singer/actor Colonel/diplomat

Gottlieb Daimler | Stuart Henry | Paul Jones | Anish Kapoor Lord Snowdon

Horse - Pisces/Cancer

Boss (2)/accountant boss/politician musician pianist/broadcaster programmer (computer) secretary sheriff singer spy war gamer/author (3) writer

Lou Costello | Arnold Dolmetsch

Horse - Pisces/Leo

Actor (4)/boss actor actor/singer actress anaesthetist boss diplomat guitarist headmaster/abbot historian judge mathematician naval officer/executive (advert) pacifist painter/designer sculptor singer (2)/model soprano tennis yachtsman

Jenny Frost | Brian Jones | Jimmy Nail

Horse - Pisces/Virgo

Actor (2) actress ambassador (2) architect bassist singer/songwriter snooker sprinter surgeon tennis

Lesley-Anne Down

Horse - Pisces/Libra

Actor (2) actress composer (3) US footballer footballer golfer headmistress musician/composer/film maker politician (leader) show jumper singer violinist Air Chief Marshal

Horse - Pisces/Scorpio

Academic (2)/Vice-Chancellor (U) baritone boss (3) boss (charity) boss (education) chaplain commentator (racing) illustrator/artist lecturer/magistrate mystic pianist/composer/property developer politician (leader) saxophonist secretary skier surgeon/otolaryngologist trade unionist writer (2) writer/broadcaster (2)

Michael Eisner | Kate Greenaway | Viktor Yushchenko

Horse - Pisces/Sagittarius

Academic (medical demography) actress boss (2)/accountant businesswoman/boss (elect) comedian novelist (2) novelist/critic politician

Horse - Pisces/Capricorn

Actor author (4)/editor/Reverend caricaturist/novelist composer librarian novelist painter pianist/teacher Pope writer/civil servant Colonel/boss/war criminal

Frédéric Chopin | Adolf Eichmann | George du Maurier
Pope Leo XIII | Mickey Spillane

Horse - Pisces/Aquarius

Actress (2) cashier (boss)/boss (personnel) Constable (Chief) cricketer editor/ businesswoman (2) entrepreneur/businessman personality (TV)/actress writer (film, theatre)

Cindy Crawford | Peter Jones | Willie Thorne | Rita Tushingham

Horse - Pisces/Pisces

Author (2)/playwright/historian author/editor boss (charity)/administrator public servant/boss (bank) comedienne showman singer snooker trainer (racehorse)

W F Cody (Buffalo Bill)

Goat - Aries/Aries

Academic/surgeon boss (3) (nursing) boss (retail) boss (museum) chef commentator cricketer diplomat politician college principal sculptor

Goat - Aries/Taurus

Academic (2)/adviser (economy) academic (maths) actor (2) author (4) boss (3) boss (engineering) conductor/boss (musical) dramatist Impresario journalist (investigative)/broadcaster judge novelist politician (leader) publicist rugby/coach chief scout sculptor singer/songwriter/musician trade unionist (2) trade unionist/politician trainer (racehorse) writer Capt/

Gutzon Borglum | Max Clifford | Roger Cook | François Duvalier Norah Jones | William Shatner

Goat - Aries/Gemini

Actor/producer auditor (2) boss (2)/consultant/researcher boss (sports) composer novelist (2) photographer politician (2) scout (chief) trainer (racehorse)

Tony Banks | Heinrich Mann | Modest Mussorgsky | Leonard Nimoy

Goat - Aries/Cancer

Academic/pharmacologist boss (3) (engineering) boss (charity) boss/engineer chemist editor/researcher guitarist/songwriter (2) pianist 2-politician (leader) songwriter

Robert Bunsen | Margaret Fingerhut | Ian Smith

Goat - Aries/Leo

Actress canoeist correspondent drummer/vocalist headmaster Moderator town planner politician politician (leader) potter/sculptor singer

Lord Tebbit

Goat - Aries/Virgo

Actor (2) artist boss (charity) diplomat (leader) drummer/vocalist (2) entrepreneur/skater/US Marine golfer hockey singer/songwriter port trader skater (2)/physician tennis college warden Rear Admiral/engineer Colonel/politician (leader)/lawyer Wing Commander/mathematician/pilot

Sophie Ellis Bextor | Ruth Madoc

Goat - Aries/Libra

Accordionist artist author/biographer boss Vice-Chancellor (U) conductor designer (fashion) ecologist/geneticist/historian journalist minister (hall) painter poet/critic politician (4) singer (3) singer/actor solicitor Vice Admiral Wing Commander/pilot

George Benson | Howard Keel

Goat - Aries/Scorpio

Academic (4)/boss (education) academic/engineer architect Bishop boss (2) (bank) choreographer/dancer ecologist/geneticist/historian horticulturalist/lecturer politician (leader) politician QC/arbitrator/author (2) record producer/singer/songwriter scientist/boss (intelligence) soprano (2) teacher/writer Air Chief Marshal

Lesley Garrett

Goat - Aries/Sagittarius

Academic (2)/epidemiologist/illustrator (2) academic/economist academic/Vice-Chancellor (U) designer (fashion) lyricist/ entertainer magistrate prebendary/priest rugby/manager violinist scientist winemaker Air Marshal Air Vice Marshal/businessman

Richard Stilgoe

Goat - Aries/Capricorn

Actor (4) actor/comedian/playwright actress (2) boss (2) boss (council) composer/musician engineer inventor chief school master poet/scholar politician (leader) politician (dictator) weatherman

Lon Chaney | Dodi Fayed | A E Housman | Kate Hudson | Eric Idle John Major | Ioannis Metaxas | Carl Wilhelm Siemens

Goat - Aries/Aquarius

Academic/chemist Academic/geoscientist/author actor (2) artist/author (3) athlete cricketer cyclist/skier explorer (polar) lacrosse player/coach model/actress pilot/author childcare pioneer politician (3) politician (leader) proprietor (newspaper)

Joseph Pulitzer

Goat - Aries/Pisces

Abbot actor (2)/singer adviser (security) boss (investment) chaplain (Fleet) civil servant correspondent (war) ecologist headmaster missionary playwright/librettist trainer (racehorse) writer/actor Vice Admiral Admiral

Amschel Rothschild

Goat - Taurus/Aries

Academic actor athlete ballerina baseballer boss (museum) film maker politician (2) Field Marshal/politician (leader) Lieut

Chow Yun-Fat | Lord Archibald Wavel

Goat - Taurus/Taurus

Academic/poet/archaeologist actress (2) administrator archaeologist (2) ballerina broadcaster/disc jockey chess player financier histopathologist novelist/dramatist politician (2) politician (leader) scientist (sleep) tycoon (media) writer (2) writer/actor

Leslie Charteris | Sharon Colyear | Katherine Hepburn Jerome K Jerome | Michael Palin

Goat - Taurus/Gemini

Academic (2) (marine zoology) actor archaeologist boss (gangsters) cartoonist chess player choreographer novelist (2) comedian journalist/editor physicist/administrator schoolmaster/scholar singer spy surveyor (church fabric) writer Rear Admiral

Andreas Baader | Dame Daphne Du Maurier | John Nunn

Goat - Taurus/Cancer

Academic (2)/economist academic (planetary sc) artist (2) boss (3) (events) boss (HSE) boss (internet) conductor broadcaster entrepreneur/boss founder (restaurant) jockey model (artists') politician (leader) presenter (TV) trade unionist/musician Brigadier/household master

Tim Martin | Debbie Rix | Sir Malcolm Sargent | Eric Schmidt David Shepherd | Desmond Wilcox

Goat - Taurus/Leo

Actress bailiff baritone boss (stds) lawyer/banker model photographer singer (2) violinist

Alexia

Goat - Taurus/Virgo

Academic (2)/Vice-Chancellor (U) academic/haematologist athlete/body builder boss (3) Constable (Chief) designer (fashion) diplomat vocalist headmaster musician (2) musician/singer painter photographer politician (2) politician (leader)

Frank Auerbach | Lonnie Donegan | Ólafur Ragnar Grimsson Donatella Versace

Goat - Taurus/Libra

Academic/historian apothecary/physician architect cricketer film star journalist (2) journalist/presenter (TV) publisher QC surveyor

W A Gropius | Patrick Minford | Kirsty Wark

Goat - Taurus/Scorpio

Academic (3) (econs) academic/principal/Vice Chancellor(2) academic/engineer Vice-Chancellor (U) correspondent film director dramatist physician physicist politician (3) politician/dictator singer/actor solicitor tennis

Pierre Curie | John Hutton | Peter McNamara | George Papadopoulos Fred Zinnemann

Goat - Taurus/Sagittarius

Academic (2)/boss academic (medical history) administrator boss (4) boss (newsagent) boss (telecoms) cartoonist conductor headmaster hockey novelist pianist politician (3) politician (leader) singer (2) Maj-General

Liberace | Iain Vallance

Goat - Taurus/Capricorn

Academic (2)/cardiologist/researcher ballerina comic/TV host drummer journalist/columnist physician politician/teacher rower singer/songwriter singer (3) singer/actress writer/speaker

Dame Margot Fonteyn

Goat - Taurus/Aquarius

Academic (2) (literature) academic/principal Bishop boss (2)/librarian (2) civil servant conductor founder (ballet)/boss ballet master illusionist librarian novelist politician (leader)

Goat - Taurus/Pisces

Academic (history) cricketer boss (2) (pharmaceutical) boss (services inspector) Chief Constable/Inspector dean designer (theatrical) gymnast lyricist pianist politician college principal registrar sculptor singer

Olga Korbut | Walter Ritchie

Goat – Gemini/Aries

Academic (2) academic/historian boss (lottery) comedian (2)
comedian/Rabbi editor entertainer GP journalist judge/QC novelist
politician (3) politician (leader) politician/accountant college principal

Imre Nagy | Lily Savage (Paul O'Grady) | Harriet Beecher Stowe

Goat - Gemini/Taurus

Academic (writing)/novelist actress boss campaigner (rights)
journalist/economist priest psychologist academic/historian/critic

Sharon Gless

Goat - Gemini/Gemini

Actor boss (5) boss (community) boss (political/military)
boss/adviser (scientific) boss (art gallery) economist politician/Reverend
politician (2) Chief Marshal

Baron John Maynard Keynes

Goat - Gemini/Cancer

Academic (geology) boss (sugar) cartoonist comedian/Rabbi
cricketer chronometer maker/author painter-etcher/watercolourist
politician (leader) politician (2) producer (TV/film) researcher worker (social)

Michael Cummins | Asif Iqbal

Goat - Gemini/Leo

Academic (2)/zoologist/Vice-Chancellor (U) actor (2) actress
author/publisher Bishop boss (2) (advert) guitarist headmaster Pope
Colonel/boss (charity)

Charles Saatchi

Goat - Gemini/Virgo

Academic (2) (architecture)/author/critic boss (newspapers)/editor boxer civil servant Constable (Chief) critic (architecture, design) diplomat/economist diver editor headmaster novelist painter (2) politician (2) proprietor/chef singer/actress teacher/author (3) writer/artist Air Marshal

Hergé | Simon Jenkins

Goat - Gemini/Libra

Academic (3) (social admin) academic (physiology) academic/political scientist actor (2)/photographer actress boss (2) civil servant designer (fashion) dramatist engineer founder (company) political scientist songwriter/musician Field Marshal

Ben de Lisi

Goat - Gemini/Scorpio

Actor (2) boss (4) boss/engineer boss (nun superior) boss (prison) chief matron clown guitarist prostitute singer

Xaviera Hollander | Richard Todd | John Wayne

Goat - Gemini/Sagittarius

Academic/Vice-Chancellor (U) actor (3)/screenwriter/director actor/scriptwriter actress ambassador archivist boss (2)/matron entrepreneur/economist headmaster judge (2) poet registrar (academic) scientist/environmentalist singer/composer Air Commodore/boss

Douglas Fairbanks Sr | Newt Gingrich | Nicole Kidman | Barry Manilow Pierre Omidyar

Goat - Gemini/Capricorn

Academic (2) (immunology) academic/scientist (computer) actress (2) ambassador arbitrator/QC architect/educator boss (police) critic (music) designer (fashion)/milliner film director/actor footballer jockey magistrate politician (leader) Speaker (politics)

Paul Gascoigne | Tim Berners-Lee | Sam Wanamaker

Goat - Gemini/Aquarius

Academic (2)/scientist (political) academic (bibliography & textual criticism) architect architect/town planner artist boss (2) (medical) boss (police) bowler college dean conductor ethnologist/explorer journalist/broadcaster Orientalist physicist pioneer (anaesthetics) politician (3) politician (leader) vocalist/songwriter/guitarist Air Marshal Lieut Colonel

Noel Gallagher | David Poole | Sir Frank Whittle

Goat - Gemini/Pisces

Academic/criminologist actress (2) boss (5)/accountant boss/consultant boss (lottery) boss (charity) boss (prison) critic (film) school inspector judge chief matron painter poet show jumper singer (2) singer/broadcaster snooker writer

Cilla Black | Virginia McKenna

Goat - Cancer/Aries

Academic (divinity)/Reverend actress/model (glamour) architect author (2) bicycle frame builder critic (literary) dancer doctor etcher mountaineer novelist/essayist/critic (2) 2-politician (leader) puppeteer saxophonist/composer/bandleader songwriter Major

Pamela Anderson | Georgie Fame | Edmund Hillary

Goat - Cancer/Taurus

Academic (2)/poet academic/historian accountant/boss (2) actor boss (museum) Constable (Chief) politician (2) rugby writer (2) writer/historian Vice Admiral/surgeon

Rupert Hambro | Marcel Proust | Jonny Wilkinson

Goat - Cancer/Gemini

Academic (radiology) ambassador boss (3)/pianist boss boss (oil) cricketer editor musician novelist singer

Franz Kafka

Goat - Cancer/Cancer

Accountant actor biologist/politician boss (3) (council) boss (pharmaceuticals) boss (procurement) boxer Vice Admiral

Jack Dempsey | W M Thackeray

Goat - Cancer/Leo

Academic (music education) Archdeacon boss (3) boss/founder (co) diplomat editor (business paper) novelist politician (3) presenter (TV/radio) table tennis tennis/coach/commentator

Goat - Cancer/Virgo

Actor (2) baseballer boss (2) (plastics) boss/banker interior designer/model driver (racing) TV host novelist singer/songwriter/actress songwriter (2) Air Marshal/Reverend Maj-General

Willem Dafoe

Goat - Cancer/Libra

Actress footballer golfer journalist/author painter/sculptor pioneer (charity) politician (2) politician/secretary college principal college principal/lecturer soldier/businessman tailor tennis Air Vice-Marshal

Arthur Ashe | Gavin Strang

Goat - Cancer/Scorpio

Academic (3) academic (jurisprudence) actor (3) actress author boss (2) (newspapers)/QC boss/footballer chess civil servant/safety investigator comedian/actor/writer diplomat engineer lawyer chief matron oncologist (clinical) 2-politician (leader) presenter (TV) psychotherapist singer tennis trainer (racehorse) General

Will Ferrell | Viktor Korchnoi | Amélie Mauresmo | Jon Pertwee Chris Serle

Goat - Cancer/Sagittarius

Academic (2)/astronomer academic (French) artist actor (2)/broadcaster/singer actor/writer/director boss (library) clerk (town) judge lyricist merchant (tea, coffee) poet/tramp songwriter

Irving Caesar | Vin Diesel

Goat - Cancer/Capricorn

Actress Bishop boss (bank) chief conductor founder (U)/economist poet/writer saxophonist singer/entertainer writer

Goat - Cancer/Aquarius

Academic (4) (textile tech) academic/medical officer academic/Vice-Chancellor (U) actress architect baseballer composer/conductor/teacher novelist/philosopher poet

Dame Iris Murdoch | Carl Orff

Goat - Cancer/Pisces

Actress boss/footballer cricketer diplomat (2) fire fighter headmaster Vice-Chancellor (U) judge rector songwriter/librettist soprano virologist/nutritionist/geneticist

Oscar Hammerstein II | Wendy Richard

Goat - Leo/Aries

Boss (2) (football) boss (oil) Vice-Chancellor (U) cricketer lawyer politician (2) colonial officer/specialist (tropical agric) printer singer (2)

Mick Jagger

Goat - Leo/Taurus

Academic (2)/chemist/Vice-Chancellor (Pro - U) academic/boss expert (civil aviation, shipping)/ businessman/civil servant lawyer mountaineer neurologist pianist politician singer/administrator/teacher songwriter/producer

Goat - Leo/Gemini

Academic/mathematician boss (3) (advertising) boss (investments) boss (tourism) 3-racing driver golfer politician representative (politics) screen writer statesman/dictator TV writer/producer/director

Benito Mussolini | Mark Weinberg

Goat - Leo/Cancer

Academic/ scientist accountant antiquarian baseballer boss (drinks) civil servant composer matron musician winemaker Maj-Gen

Goat - Leo/Leo

Academic (ship sc) author academic/mathematician/physicist boss (4) boss (film) boss (amusements) boss (councils) Dean/Very Reverend novelist/playwright poet printer (head) psychiatrist trade unionist

Goat - Leo/Virgo

Academic (2) (social institutions)   academic/biochemist   actress (2)
bandleader   Bishop   conductor   consultant (educational)
dancer/coach/choreographer   editor   pioneer (Internet)   poet (2)/ novelist
writer/therapist (sex)/poet   yachtsman

Robert Graves | Jonathan Postel

Goat - Leo/Libra

Academic/college master   architect   author/politician   boss (charity)
Constable (Chief)   illustrator   judge/recorder   super model   novelist (3)
novelist/poet   pioneer (2) (aviation)   pioneer (computer)   producer (theatre)
singer/songwriter   Maj-General

Iman | Orville Wright | Charlotte Yonge

Goat - Leo/Scorpio

Boss (3)   boss (charity)   boss (cosmetics)   boxer   cricketer (2)   diplomat
novelist   sculptor   trainer (racehorse)/jockey   yachtsman

Ken Norton

Goat - Leo/Sagittarius

Author   boss (fashion)   maker (wine)/chemist/businessman   politician (2)
politician (leader)/army chief   record producer   psychic
representative (broadcasting)   sculptor

Pervez Musharraf

Goat - Leo/Capricorn

Academic/Vice-Chancellor (U) actress/singer boss (6) boss (guerrilla) boss (oil) boss (training) boss/accountant boss (accountancy) explorer/politician pioneer (safety lift) politician (4) politician (leader) producer/director (TV) songwriter Field Marshal

Barbara Eden | Elisha G Otis

Goat - Leo/Aquarius

Academic/geneticist boss (2) (acting) boss (shipping) consultant (literary) designer judge physician/surgeon planner (urban) saxophonist

Goat - Leo/Pisces

Academic (medicine) actor (2) actor/director/producer archaeologist artist barrister boss (3) (accountancy) boss (cars) boss (charity) broadcaster civil servant Dean designer (fashion) editor fencer footballer gardener jockey musician pianist (jazz) show jumper Field Marshal

**Gabrielle (Coco) Chanel | John Humphrys | Rémy Martin
Robert De Niro**

Goat - Virgo/Aries

Architect astronaut boss (2) (aluminium) boss (2) (leisure/property) navigator church minister politician (3) politician (leader) 2-singer writer/philosopher Squadron Leader/pilot

Lord Cecil Parkinson

Goat - Virgo/Taurus

Administrator author/publisher boss educationist engineer/businessman librarian photographer politician/official (military) publisher QC/judge

"Mama Cass" Elliot

Goat - Virgo/Gemini

Academic/activist   actress (2)   actress/dancer   2-Bishop
boss (finance)   boss (cars)/business consultant   businessman/conservationist
impresario (theatrical)   industrialist   jockey   pioneer (aeronautics)
politician (4)   2-politician (leader)   singer   writer   General

Mitzi Gaynor | Peter Lilley | Ramon Magsaysay

Goat - Virgo/Cancer

Actress (2)   architect   boss (4) (energy)   boss/accountant   boss (water)
boss/banker   composer/conductor/pianist/writer   journalist   playwright
poet   politician   psychologist   singer   writer

Julio Iglesias | Jack Rosenthal

Goat - Virgo/Leo

Academic (race relations)   actor (2)   actress   boss (police)
Camera man (TV)   choreographer   composer   contralto   dealer (art)
jockey   politician (2)   politician (leader)   college principal   publisher

David Soul | Shirley Summerskill | Margaret Tyzack

Goat - Virgo/Virgo

Academic/historian   actor (2)   adviser (Government)/correspondent   boss
expert (reproductive)   hostess (colonial)   mathematician (2)/logician
mathematician/researcher/astrologer   2-politician (leader)
politician/agitator   publisher   skier

Goat - Virgo/Libra

Academic/biographer   actor (2)/voice actor   2-voice actor
boss (2) (aviation)   comedienne/writer (2)   golfer   inventor/engineer
journalist (2)   model/actress   QC   Rabbi (Chief)   writer/journalist

Goat - Virgo/Scorpio

Actor (2) actor/film director Bishop boss (TV) Vice-Chancellor (U) designer (musical instrument)/guitarist golfer journalist poet/broadcaster/playwright politician QC private secretary songwriter/bass player/vocalist

Erich von Stroheim

Goat - Virgo/Sagittarius

Academic/engineer academic/pathologist barrister/counsellor diplomat interviewer/ anchorwoman judge (2) model (fitness) politician (3) politician (leader)/orator/teacher priest singer/pianist Vice Admiral

Anne Bancroft | Jean Jaures

Goat - Virgo/Capricorn

Actor (2) actress boss (2) (news) boss (training) comptroller/solicitor editor (FT) judge novelist playwright poet/philosopher printer winemaker/wine merchant writer Capt

Larry Hagman | Michael Johnson

Goat - Virgo/Aquarius

Actor (2) actress athlete (hurdler) boss boss (3) boss (opera) climber consultant (management) cyclist designer (fashion) historian/author inspector (chief)/historian (2) novelist/poet QC/recorder writer (3)

Anthony Frodsham | Edwin Moses | Michael Ondaatje | Fay Weldon

Goat - Virgo/Pisces

Academic (2)/hepatologist academic/Vice-Chancellor (U) actress baritone clerk poet publisher writer

Sir Evelyn de Rothschild | Ernest Rutherford

Goat - Libra/Aries

Actor (2) actress boss (charity) composer (2)/pianist coordinator/civil servant cricketer/administrator designer editor jockey politician presenter (TV)/actress saxophonist/drummer singer/composer/founder (pop group) solicitor Major

Buster Keaton | Davina McCall | Franz Liszt | Philip Oakey

Goat - Libra/Taurus

Actress (3) boss (3) (association) boss (charity)/Canon boss (restaurant) composer/pianist/conductor engineer/teacher founder (2) (Meccano Engineer)/editor founder (map)/painter/author (2) physicist politician (2) statesman/diplomat wrestler writer/artist Vice Admiral

Angie Dickinson | Teresa Gorman | Charles Camille | Saint-Saëns Susan Tully | Adair Turner

Goat - Libra/Gemini

Actor/founder (theatre) boss (2) (engineering) boss (prison) Cardinal cellist Constable (Chief) jockey politician (3) 2-politician (leader) TV producer/writer rugby

Oona King | Yo Yo Ma | Juan Peron

Goat - Libra/Cancer

Academic (3) (physics)/principal (U) academic (physics) academic/immunologist actor/singer ambassador/boss (2) (MI5) athlete boss/designer/restaurateur consultant (PR) cricketer philosopher (2) theosophist/orator Field Marshal/politician (leader)

Gene Autry | Annie Besant | Ian Bishop | Terence Conran Basil D'Oliveira | Steve Ovett | Paul von Hindenburg

Goat - Libra/Leo

Actress Archbishop artiste (circus) chemist boss
co-founder (TV/films) consultant (genito-urinary medicine) cricketer
historian (architectural) microbiologist novelist photographer
politician (leader) surgeon (consultant)

Ian Chappell | Catherine Deneuve | Pierre Trudeau | Desmond Tutu

Goat - Libra/Virgo

Boss (3) (bank) boss (sports) cartoonist (polit) clerk (court)
designer (costume) diplomat driver (racing) footballer
founder (film co) goldsmith/silversmith landowner
singer/songwriter/record producer

Peter Brookes | Kimi Raikkonen | Run Run Shaw | Carole Tongue
Ne-Yo

Goat - Libra/Libra

Academic (2)/pharmacologist academic (Commonwealth) actor (2)
adviser (presidential)/spokesperson artist boss (2) politician (2)
tennis actor/film director/writer

Lech Walesa | Doris Lessing

Goat - Libra/Scorpio

Academic (physiology) activist administrator (broadcasting) ambassador
astrologer broadcaster historian politician (2)

Anna Ford | John Suthern

Goat - Libra/Sagittarius

Academic/entrepreneur/writer boss (3) boss/businessman
boss (charity) founder (advisory centre) master (history) physician
politician (leader) surgeon gynaecologist Air Chief Marshal

Goat - Libra/Capricorn

Actor (3) actor/singer actress boss (2) (politics associations)
boss/consultant (PR) commentator/author/marine officer explorer/sailor
golfer politician sports reporter Colonel

Goat - Libra/Aquarius

Actor (3) baseballer boss broadcaster/author (2) film director
footballer historian journalist/ reporter (TV) pianist writer

Chevy Chase | John le Carré | Mickey Mantle | Donald Pleasance

Goat - Libra/Pisces

Academic (2)/rector (U) academic/scientist actor (5)
actor/singer/author/composer actress artist astrologer/author (2)
barrister boss (commission) designer (sport)/administrator comedian
cricketer diplomat historian 2-politician (leader)
scientist (2) scientist (computer) writer Marshal/politician (leader)

**Diana Dors | Shammi Kapoor | John Nettles | Anthony Newley
Patrick Walker**

Goat - Scorpio/Aries

Actor (3)/writer actress author (2)/correspondent author/occultist
boss (3)/co founder boss/consultant (business) boss (bank) Major
civil servant/surveyor magistrate (boss) master (music) surgeon
trade unionist

Juhi Chawla | Letitia Dean | Lord Stanley Kalms

Goat - Scorpio/Taurus

Actress (3) actress/singer (2) boss (arts)/architect bowler
criminologist dancer/actress guitarist/singer/composer (2)
painter/composer poet (2) poetess/writer

Stephanie Powers

Goat - Scorpio/Gemini

Author boss (museum) film director/screenwriter/producer Company founder (education) lawyer magistrate manager (football) photographer/poet/painter pianist politician (leader) tennis trainer (racehorse)

Boris Becker | Dora Maar

Goat - Scorpio/Cancer

Academic/educationist/ philosopher actress boss cricketer diplomat model/designer (interior) playwright/screenwriter/speechwriter (polit) sociologist college warden

Ian Bishop

Goat - Scorpio/Leo

Actor/composer/songwriter actress (3) anthropologist Cardinal journalist painter performer (show business) publisher

Julia Roberts

Goat - Scorpio/Virgo

Academic accountant (2) actress (2) boss/accountant cricketer driver (racing) film director hairdresser painter QC singer socialist tennis Rear Admiral/boss (charity)

Billie Jean King

Goat - Scorpio/Libra

Actor/screenwriter/producer boss (2) (HR) civil servant/boss (TV) dancer (tap) diplomat film director organist/master chorister sculptor/artist Lieut-Colonel/comptroller

Goat - Scorpio/Scorpio

Academic (3) (dental surgery)/surgeon (dental) academic/toxicologist/biochemist actor (3) actress/author (2) actress/comedienne/disc jockey ambassador boss (2)/college principal/administrator boss (hosp) composer/viola player fighter (resistance)/politician (2) musician/teacher novelist statesman/orator/campaigner

Whoopi Goldberg | Bram Stoker

Goat - Scorpio/Sagittarius

Commando coach (football)/footballer etymologist footballer (2) philosopher (2) philosopher/theorist (literary) priest/scholar

Vincenzo Iaquinta

Goat - Scorpio/Capricorn

Academic (2)/educationist academic (geography) actress architect (landscape)/consultant (environment) boss diplomat (2) journalist politician (2) QC singer Vice Admiral

Baroness Joan Lestor

Goat - Scorpio/Aquarius

Academic/college master actor/playwright boss composer/pianist rhino conservationist designer (shoe) engineer (3) engineer/rifleman guru/teacher (spiritual)/musician master (music) painter (2)/art pioneer photographer/painter politician QC/recorder Rector surgeon Rear Admiral/inventor

Andrew Cohen

Goat - Scorpio/Pisces

Academic/Reverend actor author/screenwriter biochemist boss (3) boss (association) boss (IT) broadcaster/writer (investigative) editor footballer historian/politician inventor (sewing machine) car manufacturer diplomat model musician/songwriter/painter air force officer schoolmaster Air Marshal

Bill Gates | Digby Jones | Sir Ludovic Kennedy | Joni Mitchell Peter Morgan | Martin Peters | Isaac Singer

Goat - Sagittarius/Aries

Academic/physicist actress boss (Church) comedian editor entrepreneur (music) headmistress journalist photographer researcher (medical) tenor writer Admiral of Fleet

Simon Amstell | Mark Twain

Goat - Sagittarius/Taurus

Academic (2) (French)academic/physician actor (2)/choreographer actor/comic architect author (2) Bishop boss (travel) boss (2) (radio) editor (2) novelist (2) psychologist/consultant (organisational) soprano surgeon writer (travel)

Jamie Foxx | Jim Morrison | Oscar Niemeyer | Joanna Trollope Michael Unger

Goat - Sagittarius/Gemini

Author/satirist boss (sports quango) campaigner (anti-apartheid) dramatist civil servant commentator (football)/boss (films) editor/Canon model (glamour) singer (2)

Billy Idol

Goat - Sagittarius/Cancer

Actor author (3)(travel) boss businessman civil servant/QC diplomat/banker magician/musician/hypnotist painter photographer politician hall principal writer writer/artist Maj-General

Goat - Sagittarius/Leo

Academic (2) (industrial relations) academic/surgeon bookbinder broadcaster/producer (TV) civil servant composer guitarist luger model painter politician (leader) Admiral of the Fleet

Cliff Michelmore

Goat - Sagittarius/Virgo

Academic (2)/chemist academic (law)/boss (2) (tribunal) Archbishop/Primate boss (meteorology) comedian creator (Esperanto) linguist/opthalmologist cricketer geneticist headmaster guitarist naturalist novelist (2) writer

H V Rabbatts | Keith Richards | Dr Ludwig Zamenof

Goat - Sagittarius/Libra

Actress/model boss (council) Constable (Chief) composer cricketer diplomat historian musician/composer poet (2) psychiatrist vice principal/music educationist surveyor

Anna Nicole Smith

Goat - Sagittarius/Scorpio

Academic (forensic medicine) architect boss (education) outlaw poet (3) poet/art critic poet/translator/sculptor politician trade unionist warden (hall)

Billy the Kid | King George VI

Goat - Sagittarius/Sagittarius

Actor/author (2) boss (mapping) boxer commando conservationist musician/composer designer (fashion) college warden philosopher politician presenter (TV) singer/songwriter/pianist

David Kossoff

Goat - Sagittarius/Capricorn

Academic (2) (jurisprudence) academic/economist/Sovietologist author (3) composer dancer/broadcaster/actor (2) founder (biotech) headmistress judge/QC maker (harpsichord) Rabbi singer/actress tennis

Lionel Blair | Washington Irving | Rita Moreno | Frederick Pohl

Goat - Sagittarius/Aquarius

Academic author (3) banker boxer/actress body builder singer founder (publishing) cameraman cricketer engineer manufacturer/businessman (2) screenwriter/author/playwright writer/poet

Andrew Carnegie

Goat - Sagittarius/Pisces

Actor (2) actress Archbishop civil servant/boss (tax) comedian cricketer founder (design) guitarist/vocalist (2) musician conservation officer/naturalist painter politician QC/recorder mezzo soprano

Ian Botham | Georges Seurat

Goat - Capricorn/Aries

Academic (2) (botany) academic (geography) actor (2) boss (2) conductor designer (stage)/actor novelist/critic/philosopher police (boss)

Goat - Capricorn/Taurus

Academic (literature) boss designer (graphic) judge politician/activist politician (2) college principal producer (TV) writer (2) Wing Commander

Isaac Asimov | Simone de Beauvoir

Goat - Capricorn/Gemini

Academic (immunology)/pathologist actress Bishop boss (4) boss/accountant boss (secret intelligence) consultant (business)/boss film director model painter/printmaker physicist politician (leader) swimmer

Heather Mills McCartney | Matthew Webb

Goat - Capricorn/Cancer

Academic/engineer actor/comedian artist (hip hop)/actor actress (3) founder (church) mistress spiritualist trade unionist writer

Ll Cool J | Sun Myung Moon | Bill Sirs | Freddie Starr

Goat - Capricorn/Leo

Anarchist 2-banker/boss boxer diplomat engineer/author (2) footballer manufacturer (textile) novelist singer

Wilkie Collins | Joe Frazier | Sophie Tucker

Goat - Capricorn/Virgo

Actor author (2)/lawyer (2) barrister boss (3) boss (electricity) boss (weather) civil servant entrepreneur historian jockey/trainer (racehorse) (2) painter (2) politician (leader) printer singer/super model trainer (racehorse)

Mel Gibson | Albert Gore | Carla Bruni Sarkozy

Goat - Capricorn/Libra

Academic (public policy)/politician (leader) Archdeacon author/journalist campaigner (civil rights) composer consultant (engineering & metallurgical)/engineer diplomat/civil servant judge owner (racehorse) poet/psychologist (analytical) politician (3) restaurateur shopkeeper solicitor/boss (2) writer Capt/boss

Arthur Ransome

Goat - Capricorn/Scorpio

Archbishop/Cardinal boss (prison) campaigner/writer (2) coach diplomat journalist (fashion)/editor medium/clairvoyant painter (2) pilot politician (2) QC singer (2) statesman rainer (racehorse) writer/broadcaster

Angus Deayton | Henri Fantin-Latour | Clive Woodward

Goat - Capricorn/Sagittarius

Actress apothecary Bishop boss (2) boss (fire) comedian hotelier philosopher/novelist singer

Umberto Eco | Imelda Staunton

Goat - Capricorn/Capricorn

Academic (2) (Anglo-Saxon) academic/biologist actor boss (court) chef (TV)/broadcaster/bartender film director guitarist/singer(2) novelist painter politician (leader) proprietor (newspaper)/campaigner singer teacher trade unionist

Javier Pérez de Cuéllar | Federico Fellini | Keith Floyd | Joan Ruddock

Goat - Capricorn/Aquarius

Academic/accountant/adviser boss (TV) civil servant columnist driver (racing) judge mystic politician (leader) Air Vice Marshal

Jenson Button | Prof Andrew Likierman

Goat - Capricorn/Pisces

Academic/ principal (U) actor (2) actress agent (literary) (2) agent (theatrical) boss (clays) entertainer politician (leader)/journalist/editor librarian singer (2) singer/songwriter

John Denver | Ben Kingsley | Des O'Connor | Paul Young

Goat - Aquarius/Aries

Academic (public health) actor (2) agent (literary & theatrical) boss (prison) broadcaster civil servant comedian/actor entrepreneur film director guru (Vedanta) politician (2) politician (leader) QC/judge tennis tenor

John Ford | Stelios Haji-Ioannou | Manuela Maleeva | Joe Pesci Nicolas Sarkozy

Goat - Aquarius/Taurus

Actor (3) 2-actress/model adviser (diplomatic) boss (3) boss/accountant Moderator (church) boss (nursing)/nurse painter politician 3 day eventer Brigadier

Geena Davis

Goat - Aquarius/Gemini

Athlete baseballer cameraman boss (2) (elect) boss (council) footballer founder (newspaper)/editor journalist/presenter (TV) painter/critic press baron/politician tennis Air Commodore

Roberto Baggio | Colin Jackson | George (Babe) Ruth | Marat Safin Kirsty Wark

Goat - Aquarius/Cancer

Actor (2)/producer actress boss (5) (elect) boss (hotels/charity) boss (police) boss (research) broadcaster/TV presenter cameraman cyclist dancer/boss (dance) footballer headmaster singer/songwriter skater (figure) trumpeter

Hughie Green | Irina Slutskaya | Zhang Ziyi

Goat - Aquarius/Leo

Academic (Italian) actor (2)/comedian/scriptwriter actress/poker Archbishop artist boss (accountancy/consultancy) US football GP/pioneer (hospice) musician philosopher Justice/Senator solicitor

Graeme Garden

Goat - Aquarius/Virgo

Actress/model/designer (fashion) actress (2) astrologer/engineer author (3) author/broadcaster aviator boss (2) (U) consultant (management) judge model (2) murderer politician Brigadier

Anders Breivik | John Grisham

Goat - Aquarius/Libra

Actor architect boss (2) boss (cricket) golfer judge/advocate motorcyclist politician (leader) proprietor (newspaper) rugby/coach surgeon tennis vocalist General

General Thomas (Stonewall) Jackson | John Lydon (Johnny Rotten) Greg Norman

Goat - Aquarius/Scorpio

Academic (2)/botanist academic (2) (maths) artist boss editor/journalist physician/poet/anarchist pilot rugby surgeon/lecturer violinist writer

King Farouk 1 | M Stéphane Grappelli | Zane Grey

Goat - Aquarius/Sagittarius

Academic (pharmacy) banker boss (3) (engineering)
boss/solicitor consultant (mgt)/surveyor editor engineer (nuclear)
headmistress librarian novelist politician/boss Field Marshal Marshal

Charles Dickens

Goat - Aquarius/Capricorn

Academic/sociologist (radical) actor artist/sculptor boss (quango)
civil servant judge neurologist politician publisher/sportsman
singer surgeon

Goat - Aquarius/Aquarius

Academic diplomat manager (football) photographer politician/lawyer
college principal/jurist sociologist thinker/essayist writer (2)
Rear Admiral Lieut-Colonel

Alfred Ramsey

Goat - Aquarius/Pisces

Academic (Semitic languages) actor (2) actress boss boxer (2)
editor (2) executioner midwife novelist/editor physician poet
producer/director reformer (social) writer General

Gayle Hunnicutt | Gareth Hunt | Lord Swraj Paul

Goat - Pisces/Aries

Actress (2) ambassador boss (3)(TV/leisure) boss (forestry)
boss (hosp school) composer cricketer/coach distiller racing driver
headmaster

Michael Grade | Lynn Redgrave

Goat - Pisces/Taurus

Academic/zoologist author boss 2 (charity)/politician)
boss (2) (hotel)/secretary) chess cricketer judge potter sculptor
General/boss

Brian Close | Bobby Fischer | Kenneth Grahame

Goat - Pisces/Gemini

Actor (4) actor/producer/writer (4) author/journalist Bishop boss (theatre)
businessman columnist/broadcaster 2-Constable (Chief) cricketer
manager (football) novelist politician (2) politician (leader) writer/poet
Capt Lieut-Colonel

W H Auden | Timothy Laurence

Goat - Pisces/Cancer

Composer/trumpeter/bandleader critic (theatre) golfer/broadcaster/author (2)
lexicographer politician (leader) singer/guitarist/songwriter writer

Peter Alliss | Kurt Cobain

Goat - Pisces/Leo

Actress author (3) bandleader/saxophonist chef designer (fashion)
2-politician (leader) writer writer/humorist

Mikhail Gorbachev

Goat - Pisces/Virgo

Academic (conveyancing) boss (health) Vice-Chancellor (U) composer
film director dramatist/director driver (racing) footballer inventor
philosopher pianist singer/entertainer soloist (horn)/conductor
Air Vice Marshal/boss (purchasing) Field Marshal politician

Nicolas Anelka | Alexander Graham Bell | Nat 'King' Cole | Ed Balls

Goat - Pisces/Libra

Actress/singer astronomer (2) broker (insurance) racing driver rugby coach/rugby musician/composer/film producer politician (leader) publisher soprano Lieut-General

George Harrison | Giovanni Schiaparelli

Goat - Pisces/Scorpio

Actress boss (hotel) cartoonist editor expert (IR, refugee settlement) film director footballer/manager pentathlete philosopher physician scientist/historian (evangelical) trade unionist/politician

Bill Holroyd

Goat - Pisces/Sagittarius

Actress boss (5) (coal) boss (politicians' associations) boss (pharmaceuticals) boss (news) boss (telecoms/stationery) drummer librarian singer stockbroker

Rupert Murdoch

Goat - Pisces/Capricorn

Academic/physician entrepreneur/inventor priest/philosopher Provost QC/boss paralympics dressage rider singer surveyor (art) translator/writer

Lou Reed

Goat - Pisces/Aquarius

Actor/comedian athletics administrator college master composer poet politician (leader) politician (3) singer (2)/actress (2) singer/dancer/actress surgeon Maj-General/scientist

Kelsey Grammar | Ruthie Henshall

Goat - Pisces/Pisces

Academic (2)/historian (2) (religion)/writer actor/dancer (2)/singer actress (3) ballerina/actress boss (2) (IT/film) boss (charity) cricketer diplomat driver (racing) fencer musician/fiddler politician (2) surgeon/mayor teacher/historian trade unionist

Steve Jobs | Alain Prost

Monkey - Aries/Aries

Academic (zoology) actor (3) actress artist cricketer diplomat footballer pianist/teacher psychologist singer umpire (cricket)

Céline Dion | P M Glaser | Nasser Hussain | Lucy Lawless Abraham Maslow | Paul Merson | Diana Ross

Monkey - Aries/Taurus

Academic /historian actor (3) boss (bank) boss (insurance) boss (mail order) boss (construction)/engineer (2) engineer/entrepreneur boss (oil) boss (5) composer (2) general manager politician (leader) singer/guitarist/composer singer (2)

Jimmy Edwards | Peter Moores | Carl Perkins

Monkey - Aries/Gemini

Academic (2)/classicist actor (4) actor/singer actress Archbishop artist boss (2) (arts) boss (police) conductor judge politician/diplomat soprano teacher/consultant (management) trainer (Montessori teacher)

Patricia Arquette | Bette Davis | Herbert von Karajan | Omar Sharif John Suchet

Monkey - Aries/Cancer

Architect bodybuilder diplomat evangelist landowner painter/sculptor researcher (medical)/college master skier soprano Capt/astronaut

Monkey - Aries/Leo

Academic (molecular, cell biology) actress author boss (electronics) boss (3) (prison) cricketer pathologist politician (2) tennis/commentator (sports) trade unionist Admiral Capt/boss

Sue Barker | Masaru Ibuka | Isoroku Yamamoto

Monkey - Aries/Virgo

Actor (3) actress athlete Bishop boss (Industrial Relations) civil servant clarinettist/saxophonist/educator film director headmaster politician (leader) psychoanalyst representative (agric)/activist Admiral

Sonia Lannaman | Ian Messiter | Toshirô Mifune

Monkey - Aries/Libra

Academic (chemical pathology) designer (2) (glass) designer (garden)/plants man editor film director/screenwriter inventor (game) judge Colonel

René Jules Lalique | Eric Rohmer

Monkey - Aries/Scorpio

Author Bishop boss (4) (construction) boss (dairy) boss (research) boss/maker (toy) composer journalist/novelist/critic (film) missionary officer (UN) painter/etcher secretary tennis

Arthur Hailey

Monkey - Aries/Sagittarius

Academic (3)(Arctic Studies) academic (law)/QC academic/medical geographer actress boss (assurance) engineer politician (leader)/founder (political party) provost publisher/designer QC sitar player
Lieut-Commander/submariner

Joan Crawford | Arthur Griffiths | Alex Moulton | Pandit Ravi Shankar

Monkey - Aries/Capricorn

Academic (2)/dean (hospital) academic (music) architect cricketer explorer (Antarctic) keeper (museum) pilot (test) singer

Damon Albarn | Michael Atherton | James Clark Ross

Monkey - Aries/Aquarius

Actor/lawyer actress/singer/dancer (2) boss (metals) dancer/choreographer film director painter politician (leader) writer (2)
General/Commander in Chief

Liam Cosgrave | Debbie Reynolds

Monkey - Aries/Pisces

Academic (2) (language/literature) academic ((fluid mechanics) actor boss (prison) civil servant composer college master/scientist librarian/scholar judge musician pianist pilot (fighter) politician (leader) school principal singer/songwriter Group Capt

Brian McFadden

Monkey - Taurus/Aries

Academic/(2)Vice-Chancellor (u)/historian/administrator academic (law) actress (2) actor aviator (2)/writer (2) aviator/sailor/adventurer boss (3) (training) boss (finance) boss/doctor composer cricketer industrialist judge underwriter/archaeologist Brigadier/priest Wing Commander/fighter pilot Lieut-General

Steve Fossett

Monkey - Taurus/Taurus

Academic (German) boss (2) boss (property) cricketer composer
judge (2) lawyer newscaster (TV) politician (leader) Pope
screen writer writer/psychiatrist Air Marshal

Pope John Paul II (Karol Wojtyla) | Mary Robinson | Oskar Schindler

Monkey - Taurus/Gemini

Academic (3)(vet surgery) academic/college master actress (2)
actress/singer (2) astronomer/discover (He) author (2)
barrister/adviser (legal) Bishop boss (2) (music)/critic/pianist
boss/lawyer (2) boxer cricketer cryptanalyst headmaster lutenist
publicist/author teacher (drama) tenor trade unionist
resistance worker/physician Flight Lieut

Sonny Liston

Monkey - Taurus/Cancer

Academic/philologist actor boss (bank) broadcaster Constable (Chief)
designer (fashion)/founder (designer) meteorologist ventriloquist writer

Michael Fish | Valentino Garavani | Richard Madeley | Kenneth Williams

Monkey - Taurus/Leo

Academic (2) academic (zoology) activist (polit) actress artist/poet
boss (3) (appeals) boss (charity) boss (quango) film producer TV host
judge novelist/dramatist politician (leader)

Monkey - Taurus/Virgo

Academic (3)/historian academic (zoology) academic/Vice-Chancellor (U)
boss (3) (museum) boss (engineering) boss (insurance) boxer
comedian/TV host/screenwriter curator (gallery) designer
doctor/playwright/novelist journalist publisher
singer/actress/model (glamour) soldier/stockbroker Speaker (politics)

Edward Lear | Sugar Ray Leonard | Traci Lords

Monkey - Taurus/Libra

Academic/college principal actor architect/journalist boss (3) boss (milk) boss (engineering) founder (Zionism)/journalist philosopher/mathematician politician (leader) Wing Commander/boss (music)

Theodor Herzi | Colin Hope | Bertrand Russell | Harry S Truman

Monkey - Taurus/Scorpio

Abolitionist (militant) academic (2)/physicist academic (natural history) actor (2) actress/photographer administrator boss (2) comedienne/writer marketing consultant designer/decorator (interior) diplomat editor (2) farmer guru (PR)/editor industrialist producer (theatrical) rector scriptwriter (film)/producer/director singer (2) singer/songwriter sportsman tennis

Gary Glitter | Alfred Krupp | Richard O'Sullivan | Koo Stark Catherine Tate

Monkey - Taurus/Sagittarius

Composer (2) composer/pianist critic (music)/broadcaster/writer college principal rugby singer (2) socialite writer (2) Commander Maj/astronaut

Jeremy J Beadle

Monkey - Taurus/Capricorn

Actor (2) actuary author (2) broadcaster/musician Constable (Chief) designer (graphic)/film director dramatist/novelist executive (TV news) explorer/herald historian/campaigner judge painter/craftsman politician (leader)

James Barrie | Saul Bass | Christopher Patten | James Stewart

Monkey - Taurus/Aquarius

Academic (2)/designer (stage) actress Bishop broadcaster/journalist politician (2) college tutor 2-film director guitarist judge painter singer/musician surveyor (fabric)

Anouk Aimée | Francesca Annis | George Lucas

Monkey - Taurus/Pisces

Academic/flautist boss (charity) chemist/college principal Canon diplomat journalist/author pianist poet politician (leader) scientist Admiral Brigadier

Robert Browning

Monkey - Gemini/Aries

Actor/dramatist actor (3) astrophysicist author (3)/poet boss (chemicals) editor illustrator (2) illustrator/humorist keeper (records) painter physician politician (leader) producer (theatrical)/actor/author (2) publisher/bookseller QC writer/historian/critic (literary) Vice Admiral

Monkey - Gemini/Taurus

Academic (prison studies) prison governor astronomer boss/accountant diplomat headmistress journalist/author/songwriter metallurgist novelist (2) rugby surgeon snooker tennis

Ian Fleming | Sir Gerrard Peat

Monkey - Gemini/Gemini

Actor (2) boxer columnist/interviewer entertainer (voice) footballer lute maker wine merchant politician (2) politician (leader) singer trade unionist

Kylie Minogue

Monkey - Gemini/Cancer

Academic (2) actor (3) actress biographer/translator boss (5) (healthcare) boss (post) boss (health) boss/cricketer flautist/teacher footballer (US) impersonator (bird & animal) keeper (museum) lawyer physician/mayor politician rugby writer Air Chief Marshal

Elizabeth Garrett Anderson | Joe Montana | Percy Edwards
Beryl Reid

Monkey - Gemini/Leo

Academic (Turkish) actor (2)/singer actress boss (4) (charity) boss (arbitration) boss (gaming) cricketer diplomat school inspector/adviser judge/QC judge (2) musician/composer sailor singer tennis Brigadier/boss

Jason Donovan | Raymond Illingworth | Gladys Knight
Venus Williams

Monkey - Gemini/Virgo

Academic/architect/planner (city) actor/playwright adviser artist boss (2) (council) boss/manufacturer composer painter politician (2) publisher (2) reporter/publisher singer (2) writer/historian

Isaac Albéñiz | Paul Gauguin | Peggy Lee | Joseph Rowntree

Monkey - Gemini/Libra

Academic (2)/Italianist academic (literature) actor architect boss (computers/telecom) boss (cricket) boss (3) builder (railway) composer consultant (forensic seism) counsel (parliament) cricketer judge painter/etcher singer surveyor 2-Colonel

Peter Bonfield | Walter Sickert

Monkey - Gemini/Scorpio

Academic (2)/hosp consultant academic/economist/philosopher actor/dancer/choreographer author (2) Bishop boss/engineer boss (4) boxer businessman (2) church minister entrepreneur footballer judge (2) sausage maker journalist trainer (racehorse) boss (circus) Air Marshal/novelist

Monkey - Gemini/Sagittarius

Boss (3) (glass) boss (bakery/hotels) broadcaster literary critic Dean (2) editor jockey judge college principal scriptwriter/playwright solicitor Brigadier/boss (secret agents) Capt Colonel Air Marshal

Monkey - Gemini/Capricorn

Academic (midwifery/gynaecology) architect boss (shipping) cathedral Dean civil servant Constable (Chief) film producer/director/writer lawyer hall master playwright politician (2) politician/scientist yachtsman

Monkey - Gemini/Aquarius

Academic (2)/psychologist academic/dean boss/engineer college tutor lutenist politician (2) selector (equestrian) speechwriter (polit) writer journalist/press secretary

Monkey - Gemini/Pisces

Academic (US literature) banker bass boss (insurance) comedian diplomat/politician historian physicist politician (3) tennis tenor writer/broadcaster writer (2)

Harry Langdon | Ban Ki-Moon

Monkey - Cancer/Aries

Actress boss (3) (education) boss/ businessman boss (quango) composer inventor model politician provost

Eva Green | Jerry Hall | Leslie Porter | Erno Rubik

Monkey - Cancer/Taurus

Academic/politician (2) aviator (pioneer) boss (2) (builders group) boss (supermarket) journalist lawyer skater (figure) statesman surgeon/explorer

Louis Blériot | Michelle Kwan

Monkey - Cancer/Gemini

Academic (2)/linguist/expert (grammar) academic/pathologist actor athlete Bishop boss (TV)/ broadcaster harpsichordist/founder (festival) musician politician (leader)

Calvin Coolidge | David Hemery

Monkey - Cancer/Cancer

Academic/pharmacologist Bishop boss (lamps) headmaster judge politician (leader) robber solicitor Air Chief Marshal

Monkey - Cancer/Leo

Actor/film producer artist (graphic) boss (2) (sports) boss (supermarket/assurance) caddie (golf) critic (literary) guitarist/bandleader founder (anti apartheid) jockey politician (leader) psychoanalyst publisher writer

Tom Hanks

Monkey - Cancer/Virgo

Academic (3) (Anglo-Saxon) academic/archaeologist academic/linguist actress artist (botanical)/gardener boss (2) (cars) boss (health) broadcaster/politician (3) diplomat politician/businessman writer General Air Marshal

Donald Rumsfeld | Brian Walden

Monkey - Cancer/Libra

Academic (2)/Vice Chancellor academic/college master/priest ambassador artist/critic (film)/photographer author/violinist boss (3) (charity) boss (construction) boss (council/bank) breeder diplomat engineer (bloodstock)/underwriter politician (2) radiologist statesman/reformer (law)

Monkey - Cancer/Scorpio

Academic/scientist administrator boss (aircraft) contralto dramatist/dramatist explorer (Polar) footballer mountaineer philosopher QC

Roald Amundsen | Cicinho | A J Cronin

Monkey - Cancer/Sagittarius

Academic (Tibetan) animator/boss (special effects) boss (3) (water) boss (advert) comedian jockey journalist/writer missionary/scholar percussionist/maker (instrument) Air Chief Marshal

Monkey - Cancer/Capricorn

Academic (2)/engineer actor archaeologist/teacher author boxer composer (2) drummer economist TV show host/bassist judge novelist physicist 2-politician (leader) yachtsman

Niccolo Castiglioni | Vilfredo Pareto | Sir Garfield Todd

Monkey - Cancer/Aquarius

Academic/mathematician actress artist (2)/designer artist (video) boss (2) (accounts) boss (quango) cricketer golfer headmaster judge nutritionist/healer politician scientist singer/songwriter solicitor swimmer Lieut-Col General

Glenys Kinnock | W G Grace | Tony Jacklin

Monkey - Cancer/Pisces

Academic (4) (Classics) academic (history) academic (law) academic/archaeologist actress/composer boss (2) (nature council) boss/entrepreneur composer diplomat editor headmaster (2) judge painter (2) politician (2) yachtsman Colonel

Peter Blake | Gustav Mahler | Amadeo Modiglian | Peter de Savary

Monkey - Leo/Aries

Actor astrologer/author/theosophist athlete author/editor boss (2) (council) boss (investment) broadcaster headmaster keeper (public records) obstetrician

John Simpson

Monkey - Leo/Taurus

Academic (3)/architect academic/author academic/lawyer actor actress/author artist astrologer/designer boss (research) football coach judge politician(2)/lawyer politician (leader) Rabbi Major

Arthur James Balfour | Prof Charles Handy | Julia Parker

Monkey - Leo/Gemini

Actor boss (construction) bullfighter Vice-Chancellor (U) coach (rugby) Constable (Chief) geographer harpist/teacher/conductor judge midwife pianist politician (3) politician/geographer sculptor stateswoman/politician

Monkey - Leo/Cancer

Academic (2) (English) academic/neuropathologist activist actress/singer commentator (sports) dramatist educator (theological)/writer journalist judge (boss) markswoman/entertainer photographer politician (3) (leader) politician publisher statesman tennis/promoter writer Vice Admiral Squadron Leader

Salvador Allende | Henri Cartier-Bresson | Alexandre Dumas fils King Haakon VII | Annie Oakley

Monkey - Leo/Leo

Dancer/choreographer composer editor geologist judo poet politician psychologist (child) trainer (racehorse) trombonist

Jean Piaget

Monkey - Leo/Virgo

Academic (2) (English) academic/paediatrician dancer/choreographer novelist politician (2) politician (leader) theologian writer

Walter Besant | Rajiv Gandhi

Monkey - Leo/Libra

Academic/geographer activist/entrepreneur boss (2) (security) boss choreographer civil servant cricketer cyclist drummer geographer painter politician (leader) film producer writer (2)/artist writer

Raymond Poincaré

Monkey - Leo/Scorpio

Ambassador Archbishop biochemist bookseller boss (3) (foods) boss (broadcasting) boss (health body) entomologist/zoologist historian/conservationist pilot (fighter) politician (2) politician (leader) rheumatologist tennis

Tam Dalyell | Meena Pathak

Monkey - Leo/Sagittarius

Academic (2)/boss (regulatory body)   academic/historian   actress (2)   actuary   artist   author   Bishop/actor   boss (2) (bank)   boss (politics)   politician (2)   politician   boss (printing)   civil servant   librarian   singer   surgeon   trade unionist   circus animal trainer   Vice Admiral

Ray Bradbury | Frances de la Tour | Dame Angela Rumbold

Monkey - Leo/Capricorn

Academic/college rector   baritone   film director   disc jockey/broadcaster   driver (rally)   golfer   lawyer   politician/farmer/forester   rugby

Colin McRae

Monkey - Leo/Aquarius

Actress (2)   boss (3) (advertising)   boss (legal body)   boss/engineer   boss (estate agent)   botanist   judge   politician (4)   politician (leader)   politician/author   QC   singer   Lieut-General/pathologist

Gillian Anderson | Houari Boumedienne | Kim Cattrall

Monkey - Leo/Pisces

Actor (3)   adviser   author (3)   broadcaster/journalist   civil servant   dermatologist   film director/designer   footballer   headmaster (2)   headmistress   illustrator/author   painter   peacemaker   ice skater   virologist   writer/editor   writer (3)

Baroness James (P D James) | Vidia S Nalpaul | Peter O'Toole

Monkey - Virgo/Aries

Academic (2) (sedimentology)   academic/warden   actress   adviser (training)   boss (investment)   boss (2) (medical charity)   boss/designer   boss (PR)   builder (organs)   cartoonist (2)   cartoonist/author   poet   media proprietor   saxophonist/composer/conductor   singer   surgeon   writer/director

Guy Ritchie | Julia Sawalha

Monkey - Virgo/Taurus

Actor (4) actor (porn)/screenwriter actress/model actress author (2) banker caricaturist/writer critic (food) diplomat investigator (aircraft accident)

Max Beerbohm

Monkey - Virgo/Gemini

Academic (statistics) badminton Bishop boss (engineering) boxer broadcaster guitarist judge singer writer Commandant

Shirley Conran

Monkey - Virgo/Cancer

Academic (2)/physicist academic (genetics) architect/astrophysicist boss (4) boss (engineer) boss (press body) boss (water) film director Patriach record producer/songwriter/singer trainer (racehorse) writer

Lady Antonia Fraser | Barry White

Monkey - Virgo/Leo

Actress basketballer Bishop boss (3) boss/art restorer broadcaster haematologist/boss (hosp) manager (football) politician (leader) presenter (TV)/writer/singer singer (2) wrestler Commander in Chief Air Commodore

Carol Barnes | Jacqueline Bissett | Henry Campbell-Bannerman Kerry Katona | Graham Taylor

Monkey - Virgo/Virgo

Academic (Maths) boss (3) (councils) boss (consultants)/architect boss (bank) chemist civil servant comedian/musician/dancer cricketer drummer novelist ornithologist/illustrator/author politician (leader) sculptor skater (speed) wrestler

Donald Bradman | Roy Castle | Lyndon B Johnson

Monkey - Virgo/Libra

Actor (2) actor architect (consultant)/town planner author/artist basketballer boss (2) (charity) boss (construction) cyclist painter QC spymaster teacher

Chris Boardman

Monkey - Virgo/Scorpio

Actor (5) actress adviser (nursing)/nurse boss (2)/engineer broadcaster Constable (Chief) diplomat/boss (secret agent) editor film director headmaster historian/writer journalist

Monkey - Virgo/Sagittarius

Academic (2)/novelist academic (econs) actor (2)/musician actor boss (press) driver film director jockey politician (leader) QC singer Major/schoolmaster

Leslie Cheung | J Paul Getty II | Clive Lloyd

Monkey - Virgo/Capricorn

Academic (3)/engineer academic/lawyer/activist academic/college warden composer (2) composer/pianist/teacher cricketer/commentator editor judge manager (football)/footballer politician (2) politician (leader)

Anton Bruckner | Costas Karamanlis | Ray Wilkins

Monkey - Virgo/Aquarius

Academic/Vice-Chancellor (U) actor (3) actress Bishop boss (TV)/writer (2)/broadcaster conductor cricketer economist/public servant founder (opera) magician musician/cellist/artist politician QC surgeon writer/poet Lieut-Commander/specialist (mine disposal)

David Copperfield | Kareena Kapoor | Mickey Rourke

Monkey - Virgo/Pisces

Academic/painter actress (2) cricketer editor explorer/diver/photographer footballer model/actress poet/novelist saxophonist/composer Vice-Chancellor Rear Admiral/expert (anti-sub) Brigadier

Geoff Arnold | Marcel Desailly | Fay Wray

Monkey - Libra/Aries

Academic (maths) actor/film director boss (2) (body) boss editor headmaster singer musician solicitor tennis

Martina Navatilova | Jacques Tati

Monkey - Libra/Taurus

Accountant/boss (bank) actor (2) actress/novelist assistant film director Bishop boss (2) (charity) boxer church minister conductor/boss (music) Constable (Chief) novelist politician (2) rugby trade unionist Major

Eileen Chang | Carrie Fisher | Ingemar Johansson | Walter Matthau

Monkey - Libra/Gemini

Academic/economist actress (2) boss (2) (charity)/entrepreneur boss (business body) Vice-Chancellor (U) Constable (Chief) consultant (planning) film producer/actor painter/writer pianist referee (boxing) solicitor/QC tennis Rear Admiral Maj-General

J K Galbraith | Martina Hingis | Hugh Jackman

Monkey - Libra/Cancer

Actress ballerina boss (3) (industries) boss (marketing)/businessman chemist civil servant legal clerk/QC diplomat impresario musician painter politician (leader) soldier Col/businessman/boss (business body) Commander

John Entwistle | Enver Hoxha | Col Sir Tommy MacPherson

Monkey - Libra/Leo

Academic (4)/organist academic/anatomist academic/economist academic/neurophysiologist author/artist boss (petroleum) broadcaster footballer (4) gymnast headmaster (2) judge/diplomat novelist/critic (art) manufacturer (furniture) novelist pianist politician (2) politician/athlete rugby (2) stockbroker Commandant/boss

Lord Sebastian Coe | Prof J K Galbraith | Angela Rippon
Jack Rowley | Manmohan Singh

Monkey - Libra/Virgo

Boss (4) boss (investments) boss (rowing) boss (opera)/TV producer composer/musicologist footballer headmistress inventor (gyroscopic compass) politician (leader) publisher singer tennis

Elmer Sperry | Michael Stich | Gordon Sumner

Monkey - Libra/Libra

Actor architect boss editor novelist politician (2) (leader) proprietor (TV, media) statesman trade unionist Lieut-Commander (bomb disposal) General

Lord David Trimble

Monkey - Libra/Scorpio

Academic (maths)/author 2-actor/singer actor/singer actress (3) artist Bishop boss (tourism) keeper (museum) college master novelist Fleet Admiral

Greer Garson | Will Smith

Monkey - Libra/Sagittarius

Actor (2) actress author/novelist boxer college master compiler (poetry) driver (racing) Dean (church) entertainer/pianist expert (management) journalist/author poet printmaker singer/songwriter/dancer violinist

Ashanti | Mika Hakkinen | Mario Puzo | Naomi Watts

Monkey - Libra/Capricorn

Actor/film producer boss (airports) cyclist dancer headmaster historian (costume) journalist (2)/politician journalist/presenter (TV) novelist spy/civil servant tenor Vice Admiral

Michael Douglas | Anne Robinson

Monkey - Libra/Aquarius

Actor architect boss (health body)/nutritionist capt (rugby football) composer intelligence officer pianist (2) pianist/bandleader poet/writer (2) psychologist (clinical)/writer snooker teacher/reformer (education) tennis Vice-Chancellor (U) Maj-General

Jana Novotna | Ray Reardon | Ralph Vaughan Williams

Monkey - Libra/Pisces

Academic (computers, maths) actor boss (4) (advertising) boss (chemicals) boss (metals) boss (petroleum) broadcaster chemist/physicist cardiologist judge (2) physician/astronaut politician (2) QC/barrister/judge writer/archaeologist specialist (mine) stylist/businesswoman/model

Denys Henderson

Monkey – Scorpio/Aries

Astronaut bassist boss (2)/politician (2) (leader) boss (fibres) consultant (HR) judge model/actress politician principal (school) writer Maj-General/thinker

Monkey - Scorpio/Taurus

Anthropologist correspondent (war)/novelist fashion designer entrepreneur model (fitness) pianist politician (3) skater

Jerry Yang

Monkey - Scorpio/Gemini

Academic (4)/biophysicist academic (law) academic/pathologist/immunologist academic/physician actress (3) actress/clown actress/author/musician ambassador astronaut/instructor/pilot conductor director (film/theatre/opera) editor jockey/author (3) journalist photographer rugby poet singer writer/producer (TV) Lieut-Colonel

Petula Clark | Bo Derek | Dick Francis

Monkey - Scorpio/Cancer

Academic (3) (education) academic (maths) academic (medicine) actress animator/author/film director architect boss (assurance) commentator (snooker) coroner designer (car) diplomat judge psychiatrist/psychoanalyst Admiral

Hermann Rorschach

Monkey - Scorpio/Leo

Adviser (medical) boss (4) boss (sports) boss (books) boss (socks) pianist/composer/politician (leader) editor politician publisher Air Commodore Maj-General/engineer

Sophie Mirman | John G Stenhouse

Monkey - Scorpio/Virgo

Academic/paediatrician accountant actress boxer critic (book)/author (2) equestrian dressage/trainer engineer lyricist/broadcaster poet/writer

Tim Rice | Juliet Stevenson

Monkey - Scorpio/Libra

Academic (2) (biology) academic/Vice-Chancellor (U) architect boss (2) (bank) boss (quango) chancellor (U) politician (leader) editor film producer geophysicist journalist/broadcaster poet/novelist proprietor (casino) publicist writer (2) Brigadier/sportsman

Alistair Cooke | Sylvia Plath

Monkey - Scorpio/Scorpio

Academic/historian/civil servant artist boss (2) (art) boss (TV) clerk (parliament) 2-film director headmaster industrialist occultist/writer (2) singer writer/broadcaster

Lord Jenkins

Monkey - Scorpio/Sagittarius

Actor/director arts administrator boss (3) boss (cars) cricketer (2) designer (fashion) driver (racing) politician solicitor

Malcolm Bruce | Andrew Caddick | Danny DeVito | Wolfgang Joop Harry Oppenheimer | Graeme Wood

Monkey - Scorpio/Capricorn

Boss college master (2) journalist/presenter (TV/radio)/actress master (school) politician (leader) (2)/soldier politician (leader)/painter producer (record) saxophonist/flautist Rear Admiral Commander/pilot/photographer

Albert Reynolds | Kirsty Young

Monkey - Scorpio/Aquarius

Academic (3) (bacteriology)   academic (medicine)/physician
academic (child health)   anaesthetist   Archbishop   campaigner (peace)
Constable (Chief)   historian (2)   pilot (test)   politician/essayist/historian
politician (leader)   presenter (TV/radio)/driver (taxi)   rector (polytechnic)
spokesman   trade unionist

Fred Housego

Monkey - Scorpio/Pisces

Academic (3)/physicist/painter   academic/history   academic (literature)
actress   boss (4) (engineering)   boss (newspapers)   boss (nuclear)
boss (TV programmer)   comedian   naturalist   politician (leader)
trainer (racehorse)   wrestler   writer

Harry Worth

Monkey - Sagittarius/Aries

Activist (gay)   actress   artist   author   biochemist   boss (TV)
broadcaster   correspondent (foreign)   judge   politician   theologian

Monkey - Sagittarius/Taurus

Academic (biology)   actor (2)   actress   author/businessman   footballer
golfer   humorist/journalist   photographer   politician   rackets player
scholar (classical)   Admiral/boss

David Batty | Joel Chandler Harris | Lucy Liu

Monkey - Sagittarius/Gemini

Actor (2)   agent (politics)   Girl Guide   boss (2)/engineer
comedian/designer (fashion)   editor   footballer   manager (football)/boss
Moderator/writer (2)   novelist   politician (leader)

Ashley Cole | Tony Hawk | Rajendra Prasad

Monkey - Sagittarius/Cancer

Academic (2)/college master academic (cellular immunology) accountant
Bishop boss (2) (bank) guitarist/singer journalist/boss organist/composer
poet/critic/editor politician (leader) singer (2) trainer (racehorse)
Admiral

Monkey - Sagittarius/Leo

Ballerina Bishop boss/maker (carpet) composer drummer/musician
orator politician swimmer

Shane Gould

Monkey - Sagittarius/Virgo

Actor boss (4) boss (construction)/surveyor boss (quango) broadcaster
owner (gallery) politician college principal (music) soldier
solicitor/consultant (regulatory)

Jonathan King | **Keith Vaz** | **Robert Vaughn**

Monkey - Sagittarius/Libra

Actor (2) actress adviser (corporate) architect boss (TV) broadcaster
chemist journalist politician (leader) restaurateur/writer/gardener

Fiona Armstrong | **John Birt** | **General Georgy Zhukov**

Monkey - Sagittarius/Scorpio

Academic/botanist actor (2) actress boss (3) (bank) boss (TV)
boss (travel) broadcaster journalist/TV host fund manager
musician/pianist/composer politician singer
Squadron Commander/businessman

Brenda Lee

Monkey - Sagittarius/Sagittarius

Actress administrator builder (yacht) explorer footballer/Capt journalist/author judge playwright/comedian politician (2) politician (leader) Wing Commander

Jacques Chirac | John Terry

Monkey - Sagittarius/Capricorn

Academic/scholar actor boss/industrialist composer/lyricist driver (racing) expert/sportsman/journalist (2) hotelier (founder) jockey journalist/farmer physician playwright/novelist (2) poet/novelist politician (2) politician (leader) producer (TV)/presenter (2) presenter (TV) sculptor singer General

Lord Forte | Ira Gershwin | Keith Smith | Kirsty Young

Monkey - Sagittarius/Aquarius

Academic/anthropologist basketballer boss/company founder comedian/singer guitarist judge/QC musician palaeontologist politician/pastor publisher trumpeter

Quinton Hazell

Monkey - Sagittarius/Pisces

Academic (physics) actor artist boss (research) broadcaster conductor hostess judge 2-politician (leader) singer (2) singer/songwriter Lieut-Commander

Christina Aquilera | Lord Merlyn-Rees

Monkey - Capricorn/Aries

Boss (4) (airline) boss (mining) boss (publisher) boss (retail) engineer balloonist golfer 2-photographer restaurateur wrestler Air Commodore (test/fighter)

Monkey - Capricorn/Taurus

Academic/surgeon actress boss (2) mountaineer boss (historic properties) boxer Vice-Chancellor (U) comedian commentator (sports) founder (theatre) historian/author manager (footballer)/Capt (football) novelist (3) poet politician (2) rugby writer Air Marshal

Kenny Everett | Barry Goldwater | Patricia Highsmith | Marcus Rose

Monkey - Capricorn/Gemini

Astronaut boss (2) (admin) boss (retail) boxer controller (audit) diplomat/politician meteorologist/oceanographer Moderator novelist poet pianist/comedian politician (2) trainer (racehorse) Commandant Squadron Leader/navigator

Victor Borge | Wilbur Smith

Monkey - Capricorn/Cancer

Actor (2) actor/film director broadcaster business consultant/physician designer (2) designer (fashion) doctor (2)/murderer driver (racing) librarian writer

Michael Aspel | Michael Schumacher

Monkey - Capricorn/Leo

Actress Bishop civil servant clarinettist 2-comedian driver (racing) farmer/inventor (barbed wire) inventor (speed-reading) ornithologist/boss swimmer/coach vocalist Air Vice Marshal/boss (medicine)

Paul Merton | Evelyn Wood

Monkey - Capricorn/Virgo

Actor (3) actress artist/designer/conservationist boss (opera) broadcaster chemist driver (racing) inventor (2) (blast furnace)/metallurgist inventor (separate fibre from seed) 2-writer General

Frank Bough | Jack Lord | Victoria Principal | Susan Sontag
Eli Whitney

Monkey - Capricorn/Libra

Academic (2)/cardiologist academic/chemist artist boss (3) (council) boss (police) botanist/writer/broadcaster consultant (aviation) journalist maker (furniture) musician/songwriter/actor politician (3) politician (leader) restaurateur rugby sculptor singer Air Marshal/politician

David Bellamy | César | Michael Nesmith

Monkey - Capricorn/Scorpio

actor (2) boss (2) (airport) boss (prison) businessman composer diplomat drummer/bandleader engineer/sales manager horticulturist politician (2) politician (leader) college principal QC/recorder snooker solicitor star (Broadway) violinist

Colin Cowdrey | Stephen Hendry | Clive Innes | Nigel Kennedy

Monkey - Capricorn/Sagittarius

Academic (3) (Yiddish) Academic /chemist academic (psychology) anatomist/inventor (plastination) bass baritone Bishop boss (2)(football) boss (charity) singer (3) tenor writer

Gunther von Hagens | Rod Stewart

Monkey - Capricorn/Capricorn

Academic/boss (2) (research) ballerina boss/architect/planner chemist missionary novelist (2) photographer sculptor writer (gay)/humorist/performer

Quentin Crisp | Yousuf Karsh | Steve Staunton

Monkey - Capricorn/Aquarius

Actress boss (2) (oil)/editor explorer/scholar (Palestine) footballer goalkeeper intelligence linguist/ interrogator singer skier trade unionist (boss) wrestler

Batista | Suzanne Danielle

Monkey - Capricorn/Pisces

Actor artist (graphic)/printmaker/illustrator boss (4) (prison) boss (household) dancer/choreographer golfer hotelier/boss inventor (shorthand sys) musician/shop owner novelist singer/songwriter/model

Rocco Forte | Jamelia | Isaac Pitman | Dennis Wheatley

Monkey - Aquarius/Aries

Academic (2) /scholar (Thackeray) academic (psychological medicine) boss (council) commentator/correspondent conductor consultant (mgt)/accountant judge lawyer/politician/campaigner(human rights) Moderator (church) playwright politician (2) QC/recorder

Anton Chekhov

Monkey - Aquarius/Taurus

Actor astronomer 2-Bishop boss (4)/engineer boss (stats) boss (civil service) boss bullfighter pianist vocalist

Monkey - Aquarius/Gemini

Boss (4) (medical body) boss (heritage) boss (quango) boss (telecom) composer film producer QC/recorder inventor (Plimsoll line) screenwriter trainer (racehorse)

Jerome Kern | Samuel Plimsoll

Monkey - Aquarius/Cancer

Academic (epidemiology/pub health) accountant actress/dancer/singer (2) blogger/commentator/political activist cellist composer film director headmaster journalist novelist singer skier

Marti Caine | Jacqueline du Pré

Monkey - Aquarius/Leo

Actor (2) boss/engineer boss (2) designer (fashion) libertarian (civil) musician pharmacist photographer/economist politician (3) politician/farmer

Tom Selleck

Monkey - Aquarius/Virgo

Academic/ philosopher actor architect boss/founder explorer footballer GP judge lexicographer painter pioneer (photographic) skier

Akio Morita | Michael Sheen

Monkey - Aquarius/Libra

Academic/microbiologist comedian/singer (2) film director (2) film director/writer poet/novelist politician/host (TV) revolutionary/nationalist singer Vice Admiral/boss (library/opera)

Alicia Keys | Alfred Marks | Jerry Springer

Monkey - Aquarius/Scorpio

Actor (2) ambassador Archbishop boss (oil) Constable (Chief) dancer/choreographer novelist politician (4) QC/politician singer (2)/songwriter tenor/actor trade unionist

Bernie Grant | Bob Marley | Norman Willis | Elijah Wood

Monkey - Aquarius/Sagittarius

Actor (2) boss (2)(nature) boss (heritage) composer editor musician/actor politician (leader) rugby

Justin Timberlake

Monkey - Aquarius/Capricorn

Academic (3)/cardiologist academic (physics) academic/college master actress boss (law/quango) civil servant/poet dramatist/writer/painter 2-politician (leader) priest surgeon writer (2) Vice Admiral

Corazon Aquino | Mia Farrow

Monkey - Aquarius/Aquarius

Academic/psychologist actress (2) baseballer boss (2) (airports, oil) boss (gas) comedian 2-composer cricketer film director physicist/explorer (sea/air) swimmer/actor

Maud Adams | Auguste Piccard | François Truffaut

Monkey - Aquarius/Pisces

Academic/composer boss (2) (film stds) boss (Girl Guides) comedian composer (film scores)/conductor/pianist rally driver politician accounting secretary/peace activist trade unionist

Mairead Corrigan-Maguire | John T Williams

Monkey - Pisces/Aries

Academic (2)/historian academic/philosopher/broadcaster (2) actor/sailor actor (2) athlete/broadcaster boss (2) (tourism) boss (health) chamber maid composer historian monk/farmer novelist (2) singer writer

Daniel Craig | Leo Délibes | Rex Harrison | Tessa Sanderson

Monkey - Pisces/Taurus

Actor/ (2) actress/singer ambassador graphic artist author boss (3) (news) boss (regulator) boss (stds) designer (stage) diplomat/Commander goalkeeper headmaster nun/writer politician (leader) singer (2) Group Capt (bomber pilot) Lieut-General

Roger Daltrey | Patsy Kensit | Lord Nigel Lawson

Monkey - Pisces/Gemini

Boss (Stds) composer diplomat historian 2-painter publisher (music) reformer (econ)/politician (leader) sculptor singer

Lou Read

Monkey - Pisces/Cancer

Academic (4) (political sc) academic (law) academic (sociolinguistics) Archbishop artist Bishop boss (2) (housing) boss (churches) campaigner (peace) comedian designer (car) diplomat editor impresario (ballet) lecturer physician politician (2) politician (leader)

Sergei Diaghilev | Philip Oppenheim | John Updike | Max Wall

Monkey - Pisces/Leo

Academic (3)/planner academic (econs) academic/psychologist (criminal) accountant agent (insurance) artist/cartoonist athlete boss (3) (machine consultants) boss (telecoms) boss (prison) chemist composer diplomat explorer singer (4) singer/songwriter (2) singer/songwriter/actress weatherman (TV)/instructor writer General

Dame Kiri Te Kanawa | Ranulph Fiennes | Gustav Kirchoff
Lisa Loeb | Ronald Searle

Monkey - Pisces/Virgo

Boss (4) (tribunals)/QC boss (retail) boss (bank) boss (tribe) boss (recreation/museums) ballerina/teacher (ballet)/choreographer editor/critic farmer/businessman financier lawyer lawman/fighter (gun) novelist politician (leader) singer/artist tenor (2)

Berthold Auerbach | Wyatt Earp | Edward Kennedy

Monkey - Pisces/Libra

Academic (Hispanic Studies) actor/producer/director actor (2) architect bookseller (2) bookseller/politician boss (retail) broadcaster/journalist comedian designer editor headmaster novelist trainer (racehorse) physician/lecturer politician singer Maj-General

Terry Leahy | Don Maclean | John Mills | Augustus Pugin

Monkey - Pisces/Scorpio

Actress boss (4) (cigarettes) boss (2) (charity) boss/economist boss (telecommunications)/politician/solicitor horseman novelist (2) 2-politician/solicitor secretary 2-singer 2-teacher/administrator warden writer Maj-General/boss/dentist

Johnny Cash | Dame Elizabeth Taylor

Monkey - Pisces/Sagittarius

Academic (2) (materials) academic/pianist boss (2) boss (tourism) Chancellor (U) commentator (sports) composer (2) footballer founder (arts) headmaster poster girl writer Capt

Ffion Hague

Monkey - Pisces/Capricorn

Academic/economist activist (social) actor (2)/playwright actor/voice actor/writer (2) boss (3) (arts) boss (council) boss/accountant cartoonist lawyer/writer magistrate painter politician sculptor underwriter

Hank Ketcham

Monkey - Pisces/Aquarius

Actor author boss (nuclear/electric) diplomat headmaster orator painter politician (3) psychiatrist statesman tennis walker (tightrope)

Isabella Beeton | Charles Blondin | Piet Mondrian

Monkey - Pisces/Pisces

Adviser (bank) agent (politics) ambassador boss (2) (bank)/accountant boss (tax HR) broadcaster (2) composer/conductor/pianist entrepreneur hostess presenter (TV) statistician worker (social) writer/broadcaster

Karl Albrecht | Frank Muir | Bedrich Smetana

Rooster - Aries/Aries

Academic (English) boss (UN body) boss (cars) Constable (Chief) educationist school master mathematician poet/critic politician Maj-General/adjudicator (tribunals)/Recorder

Rooster - Aries/Taurus

Actor/businessman adviser (publicity) basketballer boss (bakery) diplomat founder/owner (theme park)/engineer headmaster outlaw pianist tenor

Clyde Barrow

Rooster - Aries/Gemini

Archivist astronaut boss (2) (quango) composer/pianist/conductor guitarist journalist/commentator (radio) organist scientist (polit) sculptor race walker Maj-General/boss (dentistry)

Sergei Rachmaninoff

Rooster - Aries/Cancer

Academic (2)/historian academic/surgeon (orthopaedic) anthropologist 2-baritone boss (engineering) entertainer (music hall) politician show jumper

Paul Shockemöhle

Rooster - Aries/Leo

Actor artist (2) artist (make-up) boss (quango) composer/conductor film director/politician golfer art historian songwriter/ arranger/ musician/ TV host

Severiano Ballesteros | Antony Hopkins

Rooster - Aries/Virgo

Boss (3) (bank) boss boss (cars/construction/)/engineer chief estate agent financier/banker chief matron/Capt puppeteer singer sociologist surgeon

J P Morgan

Rooster - Aries/Libra

Academic/anthropologist actor boss (hall) chatelaine civil servant croquet/barrister film producer footballer guitarist novelist/dramatist politician (2) politician/historian soldier/engineer/industrialist toxicologist trade unionist worker (youth) Commander

Cubby Broccoli | Eric Clapton | Milan Jovanovic

Rooster - Aries/Scorpio

Academic (politics) actor boss (3) (galleries) boss (telecoms) boss (football) dancer/choreographer entrepreneur (educational) goalkeeper magistrate/solicitor physicist/discoverer (X-rays) singer Air Marshal

Karren Brady | Montserrat Caballé | Wilhelm Conrad von Röntgen

Rooster - Aries/Sagittarius

Academic (civil law) actor/author actress (2) boss (2) (oil) boss (Scots clan) comedienne composer (2) composer/playwright driver (rally) photographer physicist writer Admiral

Sir Dirk Bogarde | Nick Hornby | Paddy Hopkirk | Julia Stiles

Rooster - Aries/Capricorn

Academic (medicine) artist (reggae) boss (2) boss (bank)
broadcaster rock climber 2-cricketer footballer
pianist/broadcaster/composer singer/guitarist theologian/hall principal
trade unionist vibraphonist

Joan Bakewell | Rodney Bickerstaffe | Graeme Fowler | Steve Race
Peter Tosh

Rooster - Aries/Aquarius

Actress (2) baritone biographer boss (5) (law) boss (parks)
boss (port) boss (property) boss (tourism) organist/master (choristers)
politician (4) politician (leader) vice principal/training officer
proprietor (circus) singer (2) umpire (cricket) writer
Squadron Leader/theatre director

Harold (Dickie) Bird | Gerry Cottle | Michael Heseltine
Jayne Mansfield

Rooster - Aries/Pisces

Academic/philosopher (moral) actor athlete dealer (antiques)
landowner painter philosopher politician (leader) sculptor tenor

György Lukacs

Rooster - Taurus/Aries

Academic (insurance studies) actress civil servant driver (racing)
editor/correspondent judge lawyer musician poet (2) poet/novelist
politician principal (U)/Vice-Chancellor songwriter thinker (lateral) Capt

Edward de Bono | Walter de la Mare | Rabindranath Tagore

Rooster - Taurus/Taurus

Academic/theologian actor (2) actress conductor/boss (musical) geologist historian inventor (co-, laser) judge manager (football) photojournalist priest psychologist specialist (nuclear)/spy tennis

Alan Ball | Cate Blanchett | Daniel Day-Lewis | Fred Perry

Rooster - Taurus/Gemini

Academic/historian administrator bass baritone boss (4) (films) boss/engineer boss (police) civil servant founder (school) industrialist/boss (admin-TV) neurologist photo journalist poet/composer/author singer (2)

Craig David

Rooster - Taurus/Cancer

Academic/haematologist author/conservationist boxer Vice-Chancellor commentator (sports) judge novelist (3) philosopher/writer scientist secretary (council) QC/solicitor/politician

R M Ballantyne | Dickie Davies | Soren Kierkegaard

Rooster - Taurus/Leo

Actress boss (3) (aerospace) boss (electronics) boss (charity) cricketer founder (dating) gardener musician/comedian politician (2) reformer (prison)/judge singer tennis college warden Maj-General

Renée Zellweger

Rooster - Taurus/Virgo

Academic (2) (astronomy) academic/boss (jewellery) ballerina boss (3) (engineer) boss (health) guitarist/singer (3) journalist/resistance boss librarian lyricist/instrumentalist/singer politician (2) 2-politician (leader) soprano wrestler/actor

Darcey Bussell | Dame Nellie Melba | Pete Townshend

Rooster - Taurus/Libra

Academic (3) (sociology) academic (civil engineering) academic (numismatics) ambassador (2) boss (charity) boxer civil servant diplomat eventer pathologist singer (2) Lieut-Commander/aviator Field Marshal

Zara Phillips **Bjorn Ulvaeus** **Sid Vicious**

Rooster - Taurus/Scorpio

Academic/philologist actor/hotelier astrologer/author author (2) Bishop book seller boss (9) boss (cars) cricketer interpreter philologist physicist/campaigner (civil rights) reformer (social) swimmer Vice Admiral/surgeon

Barbara Taylor Bradford | **Brian Lara** | **Andrei Sakharov**

Rooster - Taurus/Sagittarius

Academic (4) /architect academic/historian academic (medicine) academic/sculptor actor (2) bookseller boss (3) (college) boss (Islam) boss (retailing) broadcaster/breeder (pig) film director inventor (Polaroid camera) model (2)model/actress customs officer organist trainer (racehorse)

Frank Capra | **Louis Farrakhan** **Edwin Land**

Rooster - Taurus/Capricorn

Baseballer broadcaster/ breeder (pig) musician (2) musician/keyboardist QC singer (2) singer/guitarist skier 2-trade unionist

Rooster - Taurus/Aquarius

Actor (2) basketballer boss/editor/journalist comedienne composer film critic/journalist/columnist/TV personality cyclist footballer guitarist/composer novelist (2) politician (leader) rower showgirl/model writer

Rooster - Taurus/Pisces

Academic/metallurgist actor (2) actress boxer civil servant entrepreneur equestrian musician novelist physician/editor politician singer/songwriter/guitarist

Lord Ahmed | James Mason | Satyajit Ray | Sugar Ray Robinson

Rooster - Gemini/Aries

Academic/scholar (Arabic) accountant ambassador bandleader/composer boss dentist/writer economist/strategist 2-headmaster chief school inspector physicist politician (2) politician (leader) press secretary trumpeter

Alastair Campbell | J K Polk

Rooster - Gemini/Taurus

Actor (3)/singer (2) actress/author boss (political party) clergyman/antiquary cricketer industrialist/founder (cars) jeweller musician singer/actor swimmer writer Air Marshal

Joan Collins | Don Estelle | Duncan Goodhew | Armand Peugeot

Rooster - Gemini/Gemini

Academic (sociology) boss (3) boss (intelligence body) boss (U) film editor church minister film producer headmistress/cyclist/writer judge nutritionist 2-tennis urologist/surgeon

Nikolaï Davydenko | Steffi Graf

Rooster - Gemini/Cancer

Actor anthropologist boss (civil rights)/Chancellor/barrister celebrity (reality TV) Vice-Chancellor dealer (oil) footballer founder (wines/pets) guitarist inventor (smart card) judge milliner physician/researcher politician (leader) singer/teacher

Tal Farlow | Errol Flynn | Jade Goody | Pat Jennings | Suharto

Rooster - Gemini/Leo

Academic/painter/sculptor   actress (2)   boss (2) (retail)
boss /industrialist/engineer   footballer   headmistress   manager (football)
painter   politician   priest/broadcaster/author   publisher (newspaper)
tennis

Matt Busby | Anna Kournikova | Prince Philip

Rooster - Gemini/Virgo

Academic (medicine)   actress   chemist (research)   civil servant   physician
politician (leader)   singer/songwriter/guitarist   writer/translator
Maj/equerry/treasurer

Ken Livingstone | Nicola Pagett | Natalie Portman

Rooster - Gemini/Libra

Academic (engineering)   activist   artist   Bishop   boss (2)   clarinettist
2-cricketer   engineer/boss   haematologist/chemist/physician   2-headmistress
chief inspector (fire)   philosopher   physicist   politician/poet/psychiatrist
producer (record)   singer

Mike Gatting | Benny Goodman | Radovan Karadzic
Aung San Suu Kyi | Prof Eric Laithwaite

Rooster - Gemini/Scorpio

Boss (council)/town clerk   cellist   Vice-Chancellor (U)   composer (2)
conductor/composer   disc jockey   footballer   oboist   politician (2)
politician (leader) (2)   politician (leader)/Bishop
psychologist/mathematician/astrologer   community worker   Field Marshal

Derek Alun-Jones | Peter Barnes | Anthony Eden
Field Marshal Haig | Steven Norris | Zoltan Szabo | Dave Lee Travis

Rooster - Gemini/Sagittarius

Academic/zoologist actor (2) agent (theatrical)/boss (3) boss (2) (arts) boss (charity) Dean (cathedral) film director/author/comedienne grower (grape) hostess lexicographer college master musician/trumpeter politician QC runner Vice Admiral

Humphrey Lyttelton | Joan Rivers

Rooster - Gemini/Capricorn

Academic (2)/historian/boss (2) (library) academic/paediatrician actress (2) boss (books)/cryptanalyst/journalist cricketer judge philosopher QC/politician singer tennis 2-trainer (racehorse) writer Vice Admiral Maj-General

Jane Russell

Rooster - Gemini/Aquarius

Academic (chemistry) architect boss (2) (engineering) boss (church) comedian composer/conductor footballer musician pianist producer (opera)/director publisher/lawyer singer Maj-General

Richard Wagner | Brigham Young

Rooster - Gemini/Pisces

Academic (English) architect boss (quango) boxer columnist cricketer designer (2) (fashion) film producer/director/writer golfer illustrator novelist (3) Ombudsman (insurance) poet politician (2) satirist secretary (organisation) surveyor (pictures) writer/photographer/coach Capt/Lord Lieut Marshal/scout

William Aytoun | R D Blackmore | Wild Bill Hickock | Lord Tom King Gene Tunney

Rooster - Cancer/Aries

Academic (3) (medieval stained glass)   academic/boss (research)
academic/theologian (Non conformist)   actress   anthropologist
administrator (festival)   boss (3) (tech – aerospace)   boss (estate agent)
boss (museum)   broadcaster   dramatist   film maker   impersonator/artiste
judge   magnate (publishing)   manufacturer (alcoholic drinks)   novelist
pharmacologist   physician   politician (3)   politician (leader)
Speaker/politician   yachtsman   Commander/sailor

**Prof Sir James Ball | Robert Bourassa | Julian Bream | Lana Cox
Paul Ricard**

Rooster - Cancer/Taurus

Academic (2) (medicine)   boss (3)   academic/boss (insurance)
barrister/administrator   conductor (leader)   radio engineer   guitarist/lutenist
journalist   novelist   politician

Rooster - Cancer/Gemini

Actress   agriculturist   artist   Bishop   boss (2)   boss (computing)   chef
educationist   headmaster   aviation historian/curator (museum)   judge
poet   politician (2)   politician/trade unionist   Brigadier/boss
Maj-General/boss (health body)

Rex Williams | Yevgeny Yevtushenko

Rooster - Cancer/Cancer

Academic/psychologist/writer   activist   actress   boss (insurance)
composer   dressmaker/designer (fashion)   headmaster   magician   singer
snooker   tennis   theologian

Aruna Asaf Ali | Hardy Amies | Virginia Wade

Rooster - Cancer/Leo

Academic/scholar (literary) Bishop boss (bank)/accountant deputy editor editor (3) matron/nurse netballer politician

Rooster - Cancer/Virgo

Biographer boxer peace campaigner/terrorist civil servant composer (2) Egyptologist ethnologist founder (Special Olympics)/social worker keeper (museum) physician reformer (social) wrestler

Rooster - Cancer/Libra

Artist/enamelist (architectural) boss (property)/surveyor botanist/explorer cricketer critic (restaurant) drummer explorer hall master politician (3) promoter/agent rugby statesman/bookseller 2-trainer (racehorse) tutor umpire (cricket)

'Col' Tom Parker | William Henry Smith

Rooster - Cancer/Scorpio

Academic/chemist actor author boss (politics) film director footballer guitarist/songwriter/singer ice hockey novelist/screenwriter soprano (2) specialist (hosp play)

Vice Admiral

Rooster - Cancer/Sagittarius

Academic (business/finance) actress boss (3) (charity) boss (maritime) consultant (scientific) darts economist/accountant politician (leader) politician (2) tennis writer (scientific)/historian Brigadier General Lieut-Commander/master mariner/destroyer officer

John Lowe | Carly Simon | Betty Stove

Rooster - Cancer/Capricorn

Academic (politics) bank/writer (3) boss comedian/writer botanist/explorer custodian (archive) journalist judge lawyer owner (ship)/financier painter/poet/author poet (2) politician/barrister singer (2) singer/composer

Marty Feldman

Rooster - Cancer/Aquarius

Academic/historian agent (film, theatrical) boss (water company) boxer driver (racing) footballer headmaster monk/college master politician (2) politician (leader) vintner

Andrei Gromyko

Rooster - Cancer/Pisces

Academic (vehicle design) activist (political) administrator/civil servant (boss) boss (2) (accountancy) founder (Mayo Clinic)/surgeon critic (literary) industrialist librarian politician presenter (TV) psychiatrist singer/songwriter surveyor (pictures) Maj-General

Fern Britton | William James Mayo

Rooster - Leo/Aries

Academic (medicine) administrator boss (2) (insurance) boss (ports) economist editor farmer guitarist judge pianist/composer college principal printmaker/painter/sculptor sculptor (2)

Fleet Admiral | Vice Admiral | Vice Air Marshal | Támas Vasary

Rooster - Leo/Taurus

Academic/pathologist actress/writer fencer film-maker headmaster historian judge pharmacologist politician QC/Recorder Maj-General

Madhur Jaffrey | Sir Joseph Paxton

Rooster - Leo/Gemini

Academic (2)/historian (art) academic (child psychiatry) activist (polit) boss (2) (Navy) composer gardener (landscape)/architect industrialist/landowner musician Ombudsman (pensions) pioneer (electric guitar) publisher QC/boss (review panel) singer (3) singer/songwriter/actress/model soprano writer (2)

Leo Fender

Rooster - Leo/Cancer

Academic/scholar (classical) adviser (security) boss (2) (finance) boss (bank)/academic commentator designer film director/producer/writer producer (radio) trade unionist Air Marshal

John Monks | Roman Polanski

Rooster - Leo/Leo

Academic (3) (Celtic)/poet academic/geneticist architect boss (3)/surveyor boss (charity) boss/politician broadcaster/author composer/lyricist hockey (ice) lecturer (education) pianist politician (2) singer

Dame Janet Baker | Barry Norman | Richard Rogers

Rooster - Leo/Virgo

Actor/singer biologist boss (3) (engineering) boss (prison) boss (training) cartoonist dermatologist engineer promoter (mining) psychiatrist (child)/expert (drugs) stockbroker/evangelist teacher (kindergarten)/cryptographer teacher (2)

Rooster - Leo/ Libra

Academic/microbiologist bacteriologist boss (tourism) boss (4) boss (elect power) boss (brewery) Constable (Chief) guitarist police (2)/author solicitor swimmer/actress tailor (multiple) writer (2)

Sir Montague Burton

Rooster - Leo/Scorpio

Actor/comedian architect actress (2) Archdeacon ballerina barrister/QC boss (charity) bridge businesswoman conductor cricketer industrialist/consultant (design) driver (racing) headmaster 2-politician (leader) tennis writer

Roger Federer | Alex Haley | A M Juppé | Jennifer Lopez Boris Schapiro

Rooster - Leo/Sagittarius

Actress (3) actor/comic correspondent critic (art) designer (TV set) musician/expert (hi-fi) novelist pianist politician (leader)/engineer singer/actor/bandleader technologist (textile) trade unionist wrestler/actor General

Marie François Carnot | Rudy Vallee

Rooster - Leo/Capricorn

Academic (2) (thermal power) academic/geographer author/historian/journalist ambassador boss/accountant civil servant (2) theatre director journalist (2) college master/civil servant politician (2) politician/boss (TV) novelist/biographer solicitor vocalist

Northcote Parkinson

Rooster - Leo/Aquarius

Academic/epidemiologist accountant/advisor actor (2) actress astronomer author boss (construction) entrepreneur politician

Enid M Blyton | Helen Mirren | Maureen O'Hara

Rooster - Leo/Pisces

Actor artist boss (shipping) Cardinal cartoonist
creator (Star Trek)/screenwriter/producer diplomat/banker
originator (railway guides) pilot (test) proprietor (circus)

George Bradshaw | Jim Davis | Gene Roddenberry

Rooster - Virgo/Aries

Academic (German) actress/columnist/film director boss (prison)/Major
film composer/music producer stage director drummer editor
educator golfer scientist (military) wrestler writer

Max Reinhardt

Rooster - Virgo/Taurus

Architect athlete author boss (2) boss (investments)
footballer historian (social)/public servant broadcaster mathematician
novelist pilot (wartime) playwright/novelist politician

Michael Frayn | Sir Jimmy Young

Rooster - Virgo/Gemini

Actor/manager boss (3) (ballet)/dancer/choreographer
boss (medicine)/physician boss (trading) film director/producer/author (3)
judge musician navigator (wartime bomber) singer/songwriter/author/poet
teacher/writer violinist Air Chief Marshal

Van Morrison

Rooster - Virgo/Cancer

Actor/singer actress (2) boss (telecoms) Commissioner (church)
cricketer operator (tour) politician promoter singer

Mark Ramprakash

Rooster - Virgo/Leo

Academic (2) (care of elderly) academic/college master actor/writer/comedian actress (3) architect boss (aerospace) boss (bank) boss (6) boss (hall) boss (trade) cellist conductor Constable (Chief) cricketer film producer footballer headmaster impresario (theatrical) judge singer Capt/Sheriff

Stephen Fry | Rachel Hunter | Steve Shirley

Rooster - Virgo/Virgo

Academic/scholar (English) actor diplomat 2-golfer gynaecologist/embryologist naturalist/artist politician singer/pianist swimmer Wing Commander/pilot

Angel Cabrera | Bernhard Langer | David McCallum

Rooster - Virgo/Libra

Academic actor (2) artist/activist boss/accountant composer (2)/pianist/singer cricketer diplomat guitarist/singer (2)/ composer journalist/publisher judge inventor/pioneer (radio, TV) novelist satirist General Sergeant

D H Lawrence | Shane Warne

Rooster - Virgo/Scorpio

Academic (2)/designer (car) academic (biology) actress author Bishop boss (2) (chemicals)/accountant boss (law) doctor (2)/journalist GP manager(football) photographer singer/songwriter/actress/model soprano (2) translator/historian/critic

Franz Beckenbauer | Heinrich Hoffman | Beyonce Knowles
Prof Ferry Porsche

Rooster - Virgo/Sagittarius

Academic/expert (tropical medicine) actor artist boss (3)
boss (chemicals)/accountant comedian/singer(2) farmer/public servant
politician (leader) singer/songwriter

Gloria Estefan | Kwame Nkrumah | Harry Secombe

Rooster - Virgo/Capricorn

Actress (2)/stunt performer biologist boss (hall) conductor/teacher
dancer/choreographer/actress TV media executive judge
theologian/author translator (1001 Nights) writer (2)

Rooster - Virgo/Aquarius

Actor (3) actor/director cartoonist consultant (editorial)/columnist
correspondent/broadcaster librarian novelist politician
researcher (medical) scientist singer (2) singer/actor

Kate Adie

Rooster - Virgo/Pisces

Academic/conservationist (art) actor/musician author boss (2) (quango)
boss (drinks) Chaplain Constable (Chief) cricketer diplomat
gardener manager (marketing/advert) photographer poet/editor outfitter
pilot politician (leader) singer sportsman/businessman/soldier
statesman writer (2) writer/philosopher Maj-General Squadron-Leader

Austin Reed

Rooster - Libra/Aries

Boss comedian/actor/singer composer Moderator poet/writer
QC/recorder Speaker (Lords) taxi driver/killer tennis

Giuseppe F Verdi

Rooster - Libra/Taurus

Actress/comedienne actress (2) artist boss (3)/accountant boss (football) boss (excavators) composer/conductor novelist/poet singer/songwriter/record producer tennis trainer (racehorse)

Anthony Bamford | Diane Cilento | Elena Dementieva | Dawn French

Rooster - Libra/Gemini

Academic (3) (maths) academic/physician/geneticist academic/physicist boss (charity) cartoonist composer/conductor intelligence officer/soldier/police politician rheumatologist scholar (German) singer (2)/actor singer/musician trade unionist Vice-Chancellor (U)

Malcolm Arnold | Bryan Ferry

Rooster - Libra/Cancer

Actor boss (2) (train) 2-diplomat film director (2)/ film producer film director/entrepreneur/skateboarder keeper (Public Records) politician (leader) writer/entertainer Admiral/boss (oil) Maj

Robert Muldoon

Rooster - Libra/Leo

Academic (2)/theologian academic (social policy) actress Archbishop boss (police) dramatist/writer chief judge judge (2) organist pioneer (table tennis) specialist (cancer)

Rooster - Libra/Virgo

Actress (porn) actress (2) boss (chemists) dancer/choreographer politician (leader) tennis trade unionist trainer (racehorse)

Chris Cowdrey | Deborah Kerr | Paul Kruger | Serena Williams

Rooster - Libra/Libra

Actor Archbishop boss (consultant)/psychologist cricketer journalist/screenwriter (2) college master physicist Pope screen writer Air Chief Marshal Air Marshal

Niels Bohr | Lord Runcie | Pope (Paul VI)

Rooster - Libra/Scorpio

Actor baseballer coach (athletics)/athlete comedian/journalist/writer cricketer (2) cricketer/designer (set) football coach/footballer novelist (2) politician (leader) QC/barrister stylist

Rooster - Libra/Sagittarius

Academic (imperial history) astrologer/writer biologist boss (nuclear electric) consultant (heritage) cricketer geneticist headmaster (2) historian philosopher/jurist pianist principal recidivist schoolmaster zoologist

Jeff Mayo

Rooster - Libra/Capricorn

Actor boss (2) (steel) boss (airports) golfer physiologist/psychologist/physician pianist rugby statesman/explorer table tennis teacher (movement) writer Vice Admiral Colonel

Ernie Els | Fridtjof Nansen | Ivan Pavlov

Rooster - Libra/Aquarius

Actor/writer/film-maker actor (2) biologist/broadcaster/author cellist critic founder (cars) politician (2) politician (leader) tennis

Stefan Buczacki

Rooster - Libra/Pisces

Actor (3) actress founder/magnate (textiles) musician politician (2) college principal publisher singer/actor skater writer

Catherine Zeta Jones | Jayne Torvill

Rooster - Scorpio/Aries

Ambassador boss (2) (orthopaedics) composer (2) journalist/boss (resistance)/activist librarian theatre director painter pathologist (clinical) physician politician/accountant/lecturer

Francis Bacon | Johann Strauss the Younger

Rooster - Scorpio/Taurus

Actor (3) actress boss racing driver football manager novelist painter philosopher politician/obstetrician swimmer/water polo Wing Commander/controller (air traffic) Commander in Chief/General

Rooster - Scorpio/Gemini

Academic (3) (history) academic/college master academic (haematological medicine) accountant actress Vice-Chancellor (U)/engineer archaeologist boss (ballet)/doctor (2) director (artistic) physician politician

Goldie Hawn

Rooster - Scorpio/Cancer

Academic (vet physiology) boss columnist/editor/boss civil servant editor golfer physician statesman (leader) volleyball writer

Aneurin Bevan

Rooster - Scorpio/Leo

Academic (2) (psychology) academic/engineer artist
boss (3) (engineering) boss (investment) editor
producer (record)/footballer/clothing designer/rapper financier/fraudster
organist/master (choristers) poet radiologist singer (4) singer/model
singer/actress

Puff Daddy | Sarah Harding | Ezra Pound

Rooster - Scorpio/Virgo

Academic (4)/surgeon (3) academic (2)/historian academic (Hebrew)
academic/theologian actress/model architect consultant (gen mgt)
diplomat doctor/surgeon economist (land) dramatist scholar/editor
headmistress chief inspector judge politician (2) Colonel

Rooster - Scorpio/Libra

Actress architect astronaut boss (quango) composer footballer
publisher (guide book) singer/actress Admiral Rear-Admiral/surgeon

Karl Baedeker | Vincenzo Bellini | Nandita Das | Gerd Müller

Rooster - Scorpio/Scorpio

Academic (4) (physics) academic (Assyriology)
academic (cancer cytogenetics) academic (operations research)/engineer
boss (2) (shipping) boss (airline) footballer lawyer/campaigner publisher
rocker writer

Colin Marshall

Rooster - Scorpio/Sagittarius

2-Actor Bishop boss (2) (finance/admin) boss (exposition/auctioneers)
coach (football) criminal (Nazi war)/politician designer (fashion)
US footballer political scientist singer/songwriter Lieut-Colonel

Charles Bronson | Joseph Goebbels | Glenn Hoddle

Rooster - Scorpio/Capricorn

Academic (healthcare)   accountant   voice actor/comedian/screenwriter
criminal   economist   engineer   musician   playwright/boss (TV)
researcher (tornado)   viola   Air Commodore/dancer
Lieut-General   General

Reggie & Ronnie Kray | General George Patton

Rooster - Scorpio/Aquarius

Artist (2)   artist/founder (Orphism)   bass   Constable (Chief)   college dean
musician   singer (2)   soldier/rancher (cattle)
writer/consultant (management)   Lieut-Colonel (radio security)

Peter Drucker

Rooster - Scorpio/Pisces

Academic (2) (documentary papyrology)   actor   boss (bank)/banker
tap dancer   engineer   manager (football)   presenter (radio)
scholar (film)/exhibitor/publicist   singer   trainer (racehorse)
Colonel/intelligence officer

Ron Greenwood | Anni-Frid Lyngstad

Rooster - Sagittarius/Aries

Author   Vice-Chancellor (U)   civil servant/buyer   conductor   educationist
radiologist (consultant)   saxophonist   surveyor   2-Colonel
Maj/headmaster

Rooster - Sagittarius/Taurus

Academic (3) (journalism)   academic/economist   author
Vice-Chancellor (U)/lecturer   radiologist (consultant)   cornet player/bandleader
dancer/boss (ballet)   engineer   expert (bomb disposal)   guitarist
hypnotist   physiologist/writer   politician   psychiatrist   singer
trainer (racehorse)

Rooster - Sagittarius/Gemini

Mime artist/theatre director/teacher(2) athlete author/journalist/poet/screenwriter boss (bank) 2-cricketer talk show host/teacher librarian mathematician politician school principal regulator (rail)/lawyer

Rooster - Sagittarius/Cancer

Actor (2) businessman/author (2) cricketer drummer/vocalist expert (orchid)/author (2) Industrialist/commando novelist politician provost singer (2)

Donny Osmond

Rooster - Sagittarius/Leo

Actor (2) artist biographer/college principal boss (quango) comic drummer coach/manager/footballer playwright/actor/film director US footballer singer/songwriter

Rooster - Sagittarius/Virgo

Academic (geology) boss (3) (charity) boss (quango)/expert (safety) film director guitarist (2) guitarist journalist/physician/activist manager (football) musician physicist college principal QC rector (academy) singer/actor trainer (elephant)/boss (circus) Flight Lieut/consultant (agriculture)

Rooster - Sagittarius/Libra

Boss (music)/rapper broker (Government) founder (Trust) minister (church) musician physicist pianist politician singer (2)/actress Maj-General/teacher

Bette Midler | Johannes van der Waals | Jay Z

Rooster - Sagittarius/Scorpio

Academic (2) (therapeutic immunology) actor (2) astrologer author/broadcaster boss (2) (library) boss (TV/media)/lecturer broadcaster (2) novelist/critic/poet singer (3) singer/actor Commander/statesman

Billy Bragg | Jonathan Cainer | Alexander Dubcěk
Douglas Fairbanks Jr | Ford Madox Ford

Rooster - Sagittarius/Sagittarius

Actor/film director actress (2) bassist/singer cricketer fighter (resistance)/politician inventor (celluloid) mathematician model pilot (RAF) singer (4) singer/songwriter Maj-General

Natasha Bedingfield | Billy Bragg

Rooster - Sagittarius/Capricorn

Academic (2) (Greek) academic/historiographer actress (2) baseballer boss (investment) broadcaster journalist (3) journalist/ TV host/ comedian politician (leader)

Rooster - Sagittarius/Aquarius

Academic/boss (2) (surveys) author/attorney Bishop boss (investments) composer racing driver educator sound re-recording mixer novelist/designer painter singer/songwriter/dancer

Britney Spears

Rooster - Sagittarius/Pisces

Academic/founder (bioscience) Bishop boss (college)/nurse composer drummer chief economist novelist/dramatist monk/scholar (patristic) operator (wartime secret wireless) politician QC show jumper singer/actor solicitor/breeder (racehorse) Squadron Leader/author

Frances Hodgson Burnett

Rooster - Capricorn/Aries

Actor bandleader/record producer cyclist engineer/hunter (Nazi) journalist politician (2)/ writer politician (leader) publisher/editor restaurateur rugby

Tom Baker | Simon Wiesenthal

Rooster - Capricorn/Taurus

Boss (electricity) composer golfer/commentator mathematician actor naturalist/writer (2) politician publisher skier writer (children's stories)

Joy Adamson | Hugh Lofting | Clive Dunn

Rooster - Capricorn/Gemini

Baseballer Bishop boss (2) (motorcar) boss (prosecutions) drummer/record producer expert (public health) football goalkeeper GP/murderer novelist (2) pilot (test) QC/academic (law) winemaker writer/illustrator

Dr Harold Shipman

Rooster - Capricorn/Cancer

Ambassador boss (insurance) F1 engineer flight attendant/teacher football goalkeeper founder (MORI) golfer sculptor skier/author writer

Capt/Commander (destroyer)

Rooster - Capricorn/Leo

Academic (2)/geologist academic/geneticist actress (2)/singer (2) boss (2) (football) 2-headmistress politician publisher/boss inventor (speed-reading) singer/actress

Dame Gracie Fields | Dolly Parton

Rooster - Capricorn/Virgo

Actress consultant (race relations) racing driver film maker/painter headmaster journalist/ assassin/mercenary musician/composer physician/boss (quango) politician record producer/engineer singer (2) singer/songwriter extreme sportsman trumpeter

David Lynch

Rooster - Capricorn/Libra

Boss (2) boss (ballet school) cricketer editor judge Lord Lieut missionary pianist secretary (research) yachtsman Air Chief Marshal

Rooster - Capricorn/Scorpio

Academic (computing) academic/minister/philosopher actor (comedy) barrister/fighter (ace) boss/entrepreneur painter pilot (test) QC/politician (leader) surgeon violinist

Jean Chretien | Lord Hanson

Rooster - Capricorn/Sagittarius

Academic (2)/college master academic (computer science) actor boss (3) boss (assurance) boss (TV) dancer/choreographer mountaineer musician politician (leader)/psychologist Maj-General/chief engineer

Rooster - Capricorn/Capricorn

Actor (2) actress/model artist/sculptor boss (expo) dancer/artist (2) historian (garden) 2-poet priest/author singer surgeon

Richard Briers | John Paul Jones

Rooster - Capricorn/Aquarius

Academic (2)/mathematician academic/architect actress host (children's TV)/puppeteer novelist poet politician (leader) sculptor soprano surveyor

Shari Lewis | Luise Rainer

Rooster - Capricorn/Pisces

Actor (2) actress/writer (2) broadcaster (2) TV host/broadcaster illustrator/author pioneer (digital audio/video) politician singer tennis

Raymond Briggs | Dermot Murnaghan | David Nalbandian

Rooster - Aquarius/Aries

Academic/geneticist actor apothecary contralto editor engineer geographer/philosopher TV host QC/boss (healthcare) saxophonist writer/reviewer (restaurant)

Bill Bixby

Rooster - Aquarius/Taurus

Academic (library & info studies) accountant actor ambassador artist/teacher boss (4) (store) Vice-Chancellor Constable (Chief) judge (leader) novelist/dramatist officer (air force)/entrepreneur politician (2)/journalist politician (leader) singer/songwriter/dancer Capt Maj-General/engineer (boss) Air Marshal/boss Marshal/boss (police)

William Somerset Maugham | Kelly Rowland

Rooster - Aquarius/Gemini

Academic (design & computation) actor (2)/comedian adviser (2) (stds) administrator/adviser (constitutional) boss (2) (engineering) boss (diamonds) comedian (2)/actor compiler (crossword) controller (aircraft) diplomat (3) 2-diplomat (leader) editor judge politician (leader) politician (3) statesman tenor

Edith Cresson | Leslie Crowther

Rooster - Aquarius/Cancer

Academic (3)/principal (U) actor (2) actor/legal executive Bishop ceramicist/artist civil servant cricketer footballer pianist/teacher painter/teacher politician college Principal Registrar Commander/boss/banker General

Ian Salisbury

Rooster - Aquarius/Leo

Academic/economist actress contralto judge (2) pioneer (garden cities) playwright/visual artist poet socialite writer (3) Wing Commander Commander/astronaut

Paris Hilton | Ebenezer Howard

Rooster - Aquarius/Virgo

Academic (civil law) accountant/cricketer actress (2) novelist/critic oncologist singer/actor solicitor/ consultant (regulatory)

Kim Novak | Paul Hodder-Williams

Rooster - Aquarius/Libra

Academic/Vice-Chancellor baseballer boss (2) (railways) boss (accountants) boxer game show host lawyer/parliamentarian Matron novelist politician (3) politician (leader) politician (leader)/QC publisher screenwriter/director/producer show jumper

Henry 'Hank' Aaron | Carmen Miranda

Rooster - Aquarius/Scorpio

Actor (3) actress/singer/songwriter barrister civil servant cyclist/director (cycling) football manager/footballer golfer mathematician poet/critic politician (2) statesman Vice-Chancellor (U)

Minnie Driver | Sandy Lyle | Telly Savalas | Paul Schofield

Rooster - Aquarius/Sagittarius

Academic (theology) artist (2) artist/singer author (2)/poet/broadcaster diplomat/historian footballer founder (company) bed chamber maid manager (football)/coach model/stylist/designer chief press officer painter tennis venereologist writer

Yoko Ono | Bobby Robson

Rooster - Aquarius/Capricorn

Actress author (2)/comedian Vice-Chancellor legal clerk/QC composer designer (fashion) editor (3) historian journalist/broadcaster motorcyclist novelist (2)/teacher/editor ophthalmologist QC writer/broadcaster Air Commodore General/dictator

Raymond Baxter | Michael Bentine | Dick McDonald | Manuel Noriega Mary Quant | John Surtees

Rooster - Aquarius/Aquarius

Actor (2) actor/rapper boss (2) (council) boss (stores) dancer/choreographer estate agent explorer (Antarctic) politician (2) politician (UN) Brigadier/matron

Mohamed Al-Fayed | George Segal | Ernest Shackleton | U Thant

Rooster - Aquarius/Pisces

Academic (clinical oncology) bibliographer boss (4)/engineer boss (publishing) boss (HR) boss (bakery/engineering) Commissioner (estates) cricketer/farmer stunt driver mountaineer musician (2) singer/entertainer writer Air Commandant

Sacha Distel | Martin Sorrell

Rooster - Pisces/Aries

Academic (2)/anatomist academic (archaeology) ambassador
boss (2) (stores)/accountant boss (car)/industrialist chatelaine
NASCAR driver 2-journalist judge poet/art critic politician
singer/lyricist Maj-General

Giovanni Agnelli

Rooster - Pisces/Taurus

Actor/ film director baseballer radio comic conductor/pianist/arranger
golfer novelist (3)/journalist physician singer/songwriter/entrepreneur
songwriter (2)/lyricist writer Lieut-Colonel/author

Michael Campbell | LeToya Luckett

Rooster - Pisces/Gemini

Architect boss (bank) High Commissioner diplomat (2)
headmistress college master political clerk photographer politician (2)
critic/poet publisher theologian/Cardinal writer/journalist
Major/officer (artillery)

Tim Yeo

Rooster - Pisces/Cancer

Academic (2)/anaesthetist academic/haematologist actress
author/publisher/broadcaster boss (chess academy)/chess champion
businesswoman correspondent (foreign) footballer police
politician (leader) terrorist/founder (Al Qaeda) Rear Admiral/boss (ships)

Hilary Devey | Osama bin Laden

Rooster - Pisces/Leo

Academic (2)/Vice-Chancellor   academic (occupational environmental medicine)
boss (3) (nuclear)   boss (UN body)   boss/engineer   botanist/breeder (plant)
conductor/composer   expert (recording)/entrepreneur   fencer
intelligence officer   politician (leader)   singer   surgeon   tycoon
Rear Admiral/flag officer

Elkie Brooks

Rooster - Pisces/Virgo

Academic (pathology)   boss (radio)   diplomat
founder (anthroposophy)/philosopher/educationist   college principal   ruler
singer   writer

Jean-Bédel Bokassa | Beth Ditto | Rudolf Steiner

Rooster - Pisces/Libra

Actor (4)   actor/film producer   actress   composer
explorer/missionary (medical)   footballer   QC   school head   2-trade unionist
Admiral   Vice Admiral

Michael Caine | David Livingstone

Rooster - Pisces/Scorpio

Academic (2)/mathematician (2)   actor/film director/producer   actress (2)
boss (2) (power)/engineer   boss (trade unionist)   humorist/reporter/writer (2)
mathematician   pianist   solicitor/historian   scholar/Rabbi   teacher/writer
tennis

Lleyton Hewitt | Spike Lee | Ray Winstone

Rooster - Pisces/Sagittarius

Actress (2) bookseller conductor musician (2) owner (restaurant) physicist politician singer writer

Rooster - Pisces/Capricorn

Author ballerina boss (3) (finance body) boss (electric products) boss (water)/engineer diplomat driver (racing) musician/actor sculptor singer/songwriter/pianist teacher (drama) Capt Commander/submariner Vice Admiral

Malcolm Campbell | Mickey Dolenz | Nina Simone

Rooster - Pisces/Aquarius

Academic (law) actor (3) actress agent (secret) boss (3) (arts quango) campaigner dancer diplomat engineer/boss (quango) soldier/boss surgeon (neuro-otology) tenor

Enrico Caruso | Sheila Hancock

Rooster - Pisces/Pisces

Academic (humanities) boss (3) comedian conductor dancer designer (fashion) expert (Shackleton's expedition) judge politician/boss college principal/chemist singer

Jasper Carrott | Cyd Charisse | James Goldsmith
Alexander McQueen

Dog - Aries/Aries

Architect basketballer cricketer economist/editor educationist impresario (music)/promoter (concert) show jumper singer/songwriter/bassist snooker surgeon writer

John Virgo

Dog - Aries/Taurus

Actor/writer actress (2) artist ballerina/boss (3) (ballet) banker boss (petroleum) boss (broadcasting) doctor editor politician (leader) priest press secretary/adviser trade unionist writer yachtsman

Jane Asher | Gary Oldman | Antonio de Spinola

Dog - Aries/Gemini

Academic (2)/scholar (Islamic) academic (surgeon) baseballer diplomat director/screenwriter escapologist/magician gymnast physician politician (2) Vicar politician/journalist

Elmer Bernstein | Harry Houdini

Dog - Aries/Cancer

Actor (2) actress/singer Archbishop boss (3) (milk) boss (rural quango) boss (gas) composer cricketer environmentalist footballer headmaster (2) judge college master physician poet politician (leader) scholar

Robert Frost | Richard Giordano | Alan Knott

Dog - Aries/Leo

Actor author boss (foods) civil servant librarian novelist (3) politician preacher publisher/editor soprano

Dog - Aries/Virgo

Actress Bishop boss (gas) diplomat (leader) film director educationist headmaster historian (art)/curator manager (boxing) musician/composer politician (2) singer

Akira Kurosawa | Maureen Lipman

Dog - Aries/Libra

Academic (engineering) actor (2) aviator boss (3) (bank)
boss (investor)/stockbroker boss (newspapers) cartoonist composer
editor immunologist librarian (music) monk/civil servant pathologist
physicist sculptor Lieut-Commander

Richard Chamberlain

Dog - Aries/Scorpio

Actor (5) actress agent (fashion models) artist (2) boss (4) (bank)
boss (horse racing) boss (stadium) boss (science) broadcaster
civil servant headmaster (2) judge novelist/yachtswoman politician
2-politician (leader) singer (3) singer/guitarist singer/actor
surgeon (neuro) tennis college warden

Mariah Carey | Timothy Dalton | Clare Francis | Roman Herzog
Hayley Mills | Julius Nyerere

Dog - Aries/Sagittarius

Actor boss (2) (education) boss (equerry) boxer diplomat engineer
host (TV, radio) Rector rugby saxophonist trainer (racehorse)

Sir Kingsley Amis

Dog - Aries/Capricorn

Actor (2) actor/dancer architect driver (racing)
computer engineer/coin designer guitarist/vocalist/songwriter (2) politician
singer (3) singer/songwriter/composer

Dog - Aries/Aquarius

Academic/ophthalmologist agriculturist boss (2) (electricity)
Apostolic Nuncio boss (broadcasting) broadcaster car designer
engineer QC Admiral Air Marshal

Dog - Aries/Pisces

Academic (2)/sociologist academic (econs) boss cricketer editor journalist/broadcaster nursing officer politician (leader) singer (2) translator/singer

Dog - Taurus/Aries

Academic/college master anaesthetist boss (ballet) columnist/commentator/author footballer grocer industrialist politician/writer (3) publisher/novelist/historian wrestler Admiral

Sir Thomas Lipton

Dog - Taurus/Taurus

Academic (ancient thought) actor (4) actress bassist infantryman/boss (store) comedian/agent/author/journalist comic (2) college master radiologist singer/actress

Joanna Lumley | Toyah Willcox

Dog - Taurus/Gemini

Academic (2)/artist (ceramic) academic/philosopher architect boss (bank) Vice-Chancellor (U) driver (racing) footballer explorer/painter/teacher historian (art)/writer judge/QC General

Dog - Taurus/Cancer

Academic (public health) architect boss (2) (foods)/businessman boss (horses) cricketer cyclist film producer horseman musicologist/critic psephologist Capt/airman

Dog - Taurus/Leo

Academic (2)/neurologist academic (architecture) actress (3)/author (2) actress architect boss (2) (counter intelligence) diplomat golfer industrialist/boss physicist politician (leader) restaurateur cookery writer/ interior designer

Kirsten Dunst | Jim Furyk | Guglielmo Marconi

Dog - Taurus/Virgo

Actor (3) actress author (4) actress/author bandleader boss (research campaign) cartoonist cavalry officer civil servant/businessman cyclist/designer (cycling) historian (art)/writer otologist politician (leader) publisher/editor statistician (econ) tennis treasurer (law)

Shirley Mac Laine | Golda Meir | Michelle Pfeiffer | Gabriela Sabatini

Dog - Taurus/Libra

Academic/college master (2) actor author boss (2) boss (TV)/correspondent boss (Assurance)/comptroller diplomat entrepreneur headmaster/founder (school) physician tennis/administrator

Dog - Taurus/Scorpio

Actor/assassin author (2) boss (4) (health) boss (museum) boss (chemicals) boss (politics adviser) broadcaster comedian/writer film producer/creator (Godzilla) historian/diplomat judge lecturer/critic (literary) politician (2) singer volleyball General

General Sir Peter de la Billière | Baroness Hogg | John Wilkes Booth Joseph Heller | Tomoyuki Tanaka | Louis Theroux | Sandi Toksvig

Dog - Taurus/Sagittarius

Actress boss (2) (bank) boss (bank, retailing) boxer (kick) civil servant/musician cricketer economist/demographer dramatist manufacturer (perfume) Jewish minister pianist

François Coty

Dog - Taurus/Capricorn

Actress (3) anaesthetist martial artist/tennis/actor author (3) boss (3) boss (finance services) boxer cartoonist/artist curator (theatre museum) diplomat/boss engineer GP journalist judge politician (leader) publisher singer/actress treasurer writer

Candice Bergen | Cher (Cherilyn) | Henry Cooper

Dog - Taurus/Aquarius

Academic (3) (info sc) academic/numismatist academic/engineer actress archaeologist/Egyptologist architect/boss boss (3) (investors) boss/statistician diplomat founder (theatre) novelist physician politician/lawyer school principal tennis Brigadier/artilleryman

Andre Agassi | Howard Carter | Lilian Baylis | Alistair MacLean Uma Thurman

Dog - Taurus/Pisces

Actor Bishop boss (6) boss (bank) boss (museum) boss (investors) boss (prison) boss (TV) Vice-Chancellor (U) diplomat dramatist engineer/public servant engineer (2) judge magnate (packaging) naturalist/author organist/master (choristers) surgeon

Alan Bennett | Gad Rausing | Nicholas Serota

Dog - Gemini/Aries

Academic/physicist actor (3) actress actress/singer astronaut bassist engineer explorer/writer/soldier golfer historian perfumier

Paulette Goddard

Dog - Gemini/Taurus

Academic/obstetrician boss (2) (bank) boss (bank) economic consultant correspondent drummer founder (electronics) impresario (art) inventor (hovercraft) jockey model/actress singer speed skater writer

Christopher Cockerell | Millicent Martin | Michael Mates
Peter Scudamore

Dog - Gemini/Gemini

Academic/Constable (Chief) actor (2) boss (retailing) businessman cartoonist/artist drummer instructor (gliding) judge model (super)/actress/presenter (TV)/singer painter politician (2) publisher

Pietro Annigoni | Heidi Klum | Christopher Lee

Dog - Gemini/Cancer

Actor/director architect/engineer/composer archivist author/illustrator boss (prison) civil servant entrepreneur/ fashion designer footballer gynaecologist TV host/comedian murderer politician politician (leader) General

Cafu | Peter Sutcliffe

Dog - Gemini/Leo

Actress (2) agent (bloodstock) boss circus ring mistress/administrator explorer/film maker/scientist politician (leader)/creator (apartheid) politician (2) publisher/founder (publisher) singer Brigadier

Jacques-Yves Cousteau

Dog - Gemini/Virgo

Academic/educationist actress artist boss/accountant chief cashier (bank) composer diplomat film director founder (viewers' body) novelist/playwright philosopher presenter (radio) scientist wrestler Commander General

Richard Moog | Mary Whitehouse (Mrs)

Dog - Gemini/Libra

Academic (2) (engineering) academic/Vice-Chancellor (U) actress (2) anarchist boss/surveyor/consultant designer (aircraft) diplomat headmaster (2) headmistress journalist lawyer/politician politician (3) preacher/author saxophonist/pianist/composer tennis Brigadier/nurse

Wendy Craig | Justine Henin | Norman Vincent Peale

Dog - Gemini/Scorpio

Academic (medicine) actor architect bandleader/clarinettist boss (3) (insurance) boss (health) boss (politics)/businessman/accountant golfer maker (piano) novelist (2) pole vaulter trainer (racehorse) writer

G K Chesterton | Richard Frere | Phil Mickelson | Artie Shaw

Dog - Gemini/Sagittarius

Actor (3) actress/singer (4) artiste (variety)/agent (theatrical) Bishop boss (4) boss (UN) boss (telecom/advertising) boss/entrepreneur/author editor model/actress/singer mountaineer/writer poet/dramatist politician (leader) politician (2) screenwriter singer soprano wrestler/footballer

Naomi Campbell | Judy Garland | Donald Trump

Dog - Gemini/Capricorn

Academic (prehistoric archaeology) actor (4) actress boss (museum/gallery) boss (quango) boxer composer dancer/choreographer/founder (ballet) film director mountaineer singer (2)/actor vocalist/musician/guitarist

Pat Boone | Noddy Holder | George Mallory | Dame Ninette de Valois

Dog - Gemini/Aquarius

Almoner artist boss (construction) businessman/founder (Sound Diffusion) critic (music) cyclist diplomat (2) headmistress novelist singer/plasterer worker (social)

Dog - Gemini/Pisces

Boss (advertising) chemist/pharmacist journalist/broadcaster footballer/manager (football) gastro-enterologist intelligence officer/diplomat pianist politician (2) QC/politician singer

Jesse Boot | Kate Hoey | Malcolm Rifkind | Lord Maurice Saatchi Prince

Dog - Cancer/Aries

Academic/poet/critic actor (2)/musician actor/playwright businessman/boss (energy) chef softball coach theatre director philosopher politician (2) polo Lieut/politician

Dog - Cancer/Taurus

Actor (2) banker boss (2) (laboratory)/biochemist boss (museum) chemist civil servant comedienne/writer cricketer diplomat financier/author judge musician

Mark Lester | Jennifer Saunders

Dog - Cancer/Gemini

Academic/microbiologist actress boss (dance) composer jockey playwright/poet politician (4) politician (leader) Rabbi

Mollie Sugden

Dog - Cancer/Cancer

Academic (3)/historian academic (Greek) academic/economist actress boss (2) (bank) boss (music) Constable (Chief) dancer designer (fashion) educationist journalist (2) journalist/critic (art) pianist politician songwriter writer/programmer (film) Lieut-General/breeder (racehorse)

Giorgio Armani | Michael Flatley

Dog - Cancer/Leo

Academic (2) (landscape archaeology)/archaeologist academic/Dean activist/historian artist/storyteller Bishop boss designer film maker inventor(revolver)/industrialist(fashion)/musician writer (2) writer/diplomat

Samuel Colt

Dog - Cancer/Virgo

Adviser (legal)/QC boss (2) (engineering)/engineer broadcaster (radio) composer correspondent farmer journalist/boss (college) physicist politician politician (leader) sculptor Brigadier

George W Bush

Dog - Cancer/Libra

Academic (soil mechanics) actor (2) actress boss (2)/designer (fashion) boss (bank) designer (fashion) lawyer linguist/librarian pianist/critic (music) playwright/director

Pierre Cardin | Paul Smith | Sylvester Stallone

Dog - Cancer/Scorpio

Academic (pharmaceutics) archivist barrister/QC Bishop blacksmith/inventor bookseller/publisher boss (TV) boss (4) boss (engineering) couturier cricketer (2) cricketer/cricket selector dean (university) doctor/theatre film director Egyptologist politician (leader) surgeon

Ghulam Ahmed

Dog - Cancer/Sagittarius

Academic/Vice-Chancellor (U) boss (3) (oil) boss (bank) boss (industry body) businessman (2) dancer/teacher (ballet) entomologist diplomat fiddler pianist pioneer (computer)/engineer music promoter/agent soldier/public servant soldier (2) tenor

Konrad Zuse

Dog - Cancer/Capricorn

Actress astrologer baritone broadcaster historian judge model (2)/secretary pioneer (airship) politician (leader) politician (2) singer (2)/model tennis Maj-General Field Marshal

Field Marshal Horatio Kitchener | Sue Lawley | Shelley von Strunckel Ferdinand von Zeppelin

Dog - Cancer/Aquarius

Academic/orthodontist actor (2)/writer (2) architect boss (3) (publishing)/horticulturalist boss (design) boss (stats/health) hostess/collector politician (2) singer (2) tenor writer (2)/actor/film director writer/correspondent (war)

Dog - Cancer/Pisces

Academic (psychiatry) actress (2) boss (opera)/conductor art dealer economist/actor film director engineer painter tennis writer

Gustav Klimt | Jean Marsh | Ilie Nastase | Sydney Pollack

Dog - Leo/Aries

Actress athlete aviator chemist (research)/inventor designer (graphic)/typographer hurdler poet politician secretary (company)

Arthur Whitten Brown | Mary (Decker) Slaney

Dog - Leo/Taurus

Actress artist body builder civil servant/diplomat singer/pilot/disc jockey/historian novelist/playwright politician (leader) psychiatrist

Bill Clinton | Alexandre Dumas père | Miki Komori | Maria José Martinez Sanchez

Dog - Leo/Gemini

Accountant/politician (5) actress barrister boss (TV) boxer composer designer (fashion) editor founder (food) goalkeeper journalist poet/politician politician 2-politician (leader) TV producer writer/film director/scriptwriter

Connie Chung | Nicole Farhi | Alain Robbe-Grillet | Henri Nestlé

Dog - Leo/Cancer

Academic (2) (Hebrew) academic boss (coal) drummer Vice-Chancellor (U) composer designer (fashion) inventor/physicist/lawyer mountaineer politician (leader) rugby shoemaker tennis writer

Chris Bonington | Domenico Dolce | Claude Debussy
Herbert Hoover | Guy de Maupassant | Keith Moon

Dog - Leo/Leo

Acridologist   actor   author (2)/ archaeologist   boss (3) (canals)
boss (construction)   boss (electricity)   film director (2)   film director/producer
footballer/goal keeper/coach   college master   novelist   croquet
Group Capt/under Sheriff/bailiff   Colonel   Maj-General

Richard Hunting | David James

Dog - Leo/Virgo

Actress (3)   actress/bank clerk   Archbishop   author/businessman
boss (4) (bank)   boss (engineering)   boss (motor sport)/mechanic
boss (restaurants)   metallurgist   painter   poet   screenwriter/film director
singer/songwriter/actress/dancer   Vice Admiral/controller

Richard Hunting | Madonna | M. Night Shyamalan

Dog - Leo/Libra

Academic (geometry)   2-diplomat   driver (rally)   golfer
presenter (TV)/model   principal (music college)   singer
Colonel/secret agent/engineer   Air Vice Marshal

Melanie Sykes

Dog - Leo/Scorpio

Actor (2)   Attorney/author   bassist   theatre director   civil servant
designer/teacher   golfer   pilot   college principal   singer (2)/actor/entertainer
singer/songwriter/guitarist

Dog - Leo/Sagittarius

Accountant/boss (2)   actress   artist/designer   author (3)/encyclopaedist
author (2)/medium   boss (electric)   civil servant/businessman
composer/inventor (musique concrete)   conductor   footballer
photographer   politician   reporter (TV)   scholar/priest   sculptor
skater (ice)   writer/publisher

Christopher Dean | Henry Moore | Alan Shearer

Dog - Leo/Capricorn

Academic (physics) actor athlete/ research activist baseballer boss (3) (electricity) boss (forest) boss (oil) footballer lawyer/prosecutor pharmacist skater (dance) Commander Air Commodore

Norman Schwarzkopf

Dog - Leo/Aquarius

Academic (2)/historian (art)/artist academic (Chinese) athlete boss (3) (ballet) boss (education) boss (finance) creator (Skytrain)/entrepreneur engineer footballer journalist judge monk/beekeeper singer (2)/songwriter soprano tennis Lieut-General

Kate Bush | Jim Courier | Freddie Laker | Daley Thompson

Dog - Leo/Pisces

Actor (2) actor/writer artist (verbal, pictorial) boss composer dancer/choreographer journalist model/singer poet politician songwriter

Philip Larkin | Tony Robinson | William Waldegrave

Dog - Virgo/Aries

Academic (gerontology & cognitive psychology) administrator boss (3) (insurance) boss (transport) boss (museum) designer (fashion)/entrepreneur diplomat editor illustrator (book) mathematician pilot (fighter) promoter (pop) rugby statesman (leader) writer Major (pipe)

Jan Masaryk

Dog - Virgo/Taurus

Actor (2) actor 2-cricketer critic (music)/author drummer
film director/screenwriter golfer haematologist (consultant)
writer/priest (high) Missionary/nun Admiral

Darren Gough | Tommy Lee Jones | Oliver Stone
Mother Teresa (of Calcutta)

Dog - Virgo/Gemini

Academic actor (2) architect boss (bank)/banker
comedian/actor composer/conductor farmer fiddler/teacher 2-footballer
jockey journalist model (super)/actress TV/radio personality/doctor
politician singer/songwriter sociologist vocalist (2) Air Marshal

Emmanuel Petit | Claudia Schiffer

Dog - Virgo/Cancer

Academic/theologian/linguist academic (3) academic/designer (graphic)
actor (4) actress biographer/boss (2) (theatre) boss/conservationist
diplomat drummer farmer/conservationist secretary

Dog - Virgo/Leo

Academic (3) (Egyptology)/priest academic/geneticist bass (operatic)
boss (training) broadcaster composer/viola player 2-diplomat
film maker/screenwriter patriot politician producer (radio) sculptor
singer/teacher

Eric Coates | Russell Harty

Dog - Virgo/Virgo

Academic (5) (photonics)   academic (French)   academic (haematology)   academic (statistics)   academic/surgeon   author (cookery)/actress/model   boss (3)   boss (cruising)   boss (engineering)/politician   choreographer   composer   cyclist   editor (broadcast)/producer (2)   film director/producer   film producer (2)/writer (2)   theatre director   politician (leader)/reporter   runner   soprano   Vice Admiral   Lieut-Colonel/comptroller

Padma Lakshmi | John Woo | Emil Zatopek

Dog - Virgo/Libra

Academic (2) (college principal)   baseballer   intelligence officer/reporter   cricketer/founder (Wisden)   civil servant   composer   diplomat   expert (tropical medicine)   footballer   judge   long jumper   novelist   physicist/educator   poet/playwright   wine producer   scholar/archaeologist   statesman   trainer (animal)   Capt/academic (Greek)

Nathalie Coughlin | Maurice Maeterlinck | Arnold Schoenberg
Gareth Southgate | John Wisden

Dog - Virgo/Scorpio

Academic (politics & history)   actress   coach (tennis)   antiquarian/conservator/scientist   boxer   2-judge   magistrate   pastor   politician (2)   politician (leader)   singer/songwriter   swimmer   writer (2)

Barry Gibb | Billie Piper

Dog - Virgo/Sagittarius

Actor (2)/singer (2)   actor/dancer   architect   cricketer/journalist   critic (fashion)/personality (TV/radio)/designer   historian   journalist/author   politician (2)   singer/songwriter   trumpeter   writer/politician   Colonel

George Chakiris | LeAnn Rimes

Dog - Virgo/Capricorn

Academic/pathologist actor (3) adviser (banking) boss (2) (opera)/composer boss (stds)/engineer broadcaster clerk (parliament)/administrator composer critic (jazz)/author film director/writer (2) headmaster model/actress TV/radio personality/doctor poet/novelist singer (4) swimmer tennis (2)

Tim Burton | Ulrika Ericsson | Jack Hawkins | Gustav Holst Freddie Mercury | Andy Roddick | Siegfried Sassoon

Dog - Virgo/Aquarius

Academic (2) (computational theory) actress billiards boss (lab)/engineer consultant (advanced technology) economist manager (music group) novelist politician/broadcaster college principal scholar (Byzantine) skater (figure)

Brian Epstein | Sophia Loren

Dog - Virgo/Pisces

Academic (2) (German) academic/physicist/Vice-Chancellor banker chemist comedian/writer/presenter controller (TV) designer (special effects) expert (ceramics)/physician farmer/writer (2) journalist (radio) politician singer (2)/entertainer singer/poet/composer

Lenny Henry | Michael Jackson

Dog - Libra/Aries

Academic (5) (geriatric medicine) academic/designer (textile) academic (cardiology)/cardiologist academic (radiology) academic/Vice-Chancellor actor (2) agent (casting) biologist boss (3) (fire) boss (museum) boss (post) broadcaster dealer (art) racing driver editor (TV) geologist manager (football) novelist/playwright singer (3) singer/actor wrestler

Giant Haystacks (Martin Ruane) | Chris Tarrant

Dog - Libra/Taurus

Academic/actor actor (2) artist (martial) boss (investment) boss (racecourse)/accountant/consultant boss (3) botanist golfer Moderator (church) politician

Edwina Currie | George Peppard

Dog - Libra/Gemini

Academic (pharmacology) actress/model/singer/activist boss (gallery) broadcaster dramatist painter politician (leader) provost (U) singer (2)

Brigitte Bardot | Richard Carpenter | David Ben Gurion
Jean François Millet | Anneka Rice

Dog - Libra/Cancer

Actor (2) author (2)/reformer (penal) banker/boss Bishop boss (2) (engineering) boss (land quango) Vice-Chancellor (court) chaplain composer/singer (2) headmaster keeper (art) nurse playwright/author producer (musical) singer/songwriter/satirist/accordionist

Staffan Gadd

Dog - Libra/Leo

Academic (mining) actor (2) adventurer/diver/photographer actress/designer (fashion) athlete civil servant entertainer journalist/boss (charity institute) musician politician (3) politician (leader)

Max Bygraves | Diosdado Macapagal | Ian Thorpe

Dog - Libra/Virgo

Academic (2) (mining) academic (physics) actress (2) actress/singer boss (blood) clerk (parliament) cyclist doctor/writer editor judge militant/co-founder (Red Army Faction) outlaw/robber pioneer (motion pictures)/film maker politician (2) singer (2) swimmer Maj-General

Deepak Chopra | Ulrike Meinhof | Bonnie Parker

Dog - Libra/Libra

Academic (2)/archaeologist academic/scientist/astronomer Archdeacon cricketer diplomat (2) politician (3) politician/lawyer/academic politician/teacher singer/guitarist writer/anarchist Commander

Felicity Kendal

Dog - Libra/Scorpio

Actor (2) actress architect bibliographer/historian civil servant cricketer dramatist/poet musician politician (3) politician (leader) politician/boss (equality quango) psychiatrist/writer (2) QC/public prosecutor singer surgeon violinist/teacher writer

Louis Botha | Barbara Castle | Majid Khan | Helen Shapiro

Dog - Libra/Sagittarius

Actor architect aviator boss (3) boss (charity) boss (art auctioneer) film director diplomat painter singer

Nana Mouskouri | Charles Ulm

Dog - Libra/Capricorn

Actor/screenwriter artist jockey owner (circus) judge pathologist/creator (penicillin therapy) philosopher/mystic/traveller pianist college principal/boss (U) tennis trumpeter Maj-General

Matt Damon | Susan Sarandon | Billy Smart

Dog - Libra/Aquarius

Academic (3)/pathologist academic (medieval history) academic/novelist
actor/poet/musician/photographer colonial administrator 2-architect
author (2) boss (2) (music/radio) boss (law)/lawyer composer (2)
commentator/cricketer engineer footballer geologist golfer novelist
oarsman politician

George Gershwin | Viggo Mortensen | M C Pinsent
Annika Sorenstam

Dog - Libra/Pisces

Actor/film director artist Vice-Chancellor
composer/conductor/keyboard player composer (3) composer/musician
dean/provost pianist/composer politician (2) saxophonist singer
writer/broadcaster/journalist General/politician (leader) General

Paul Potts | Timothy West | Vincent Youmans

Dog - Scorpio/Aries

Academic (2)/neuropathologist academic (govt) actress (3)
boss (accountancy) chaplain (to Queen) cricketer engineer manager
musician novelist (2) poet psychotherapist/critic

Jamie Lee Curtis

Dog - Scorpio/Taurus

Barrister (2) boss (3) boss (TV) boss (packaging) conductor diplomat
fencer lawyer/intelligence officer physiotherapist politician/QC
radiologist singer lyricist skater (fig) writer/critic

Simon Le Bon | Tonya Harding

Dog - Scorpio/Gemini

Academic/engineer/geologist academic/pioneer (heart transplant) boss/ journalist/lecturer designer headmaster industrialist judge radiologist tenor 2-writer

Beryl Bainbridge | Prof Christiaan Barnard

Dog - Scorpio/Cancer

Actress (2) news anchor baseballer/coach civil servant comedian/film producer/rapper film producer (2) footballer guitarist ice hockey newsreader producer (TV) singer (3) trumpeter vocalist

Mark Austin

Dog - Scorpio/Leo

Academic (2)/petrologist/Vice-Chancellor (U) actress ambassador Archbishop boss (2) (motorcycle) boss (stadium) dramatist/novelist novelist (2) politician spy trade unionist/naval officer/solicitor (2)

Umberto Agnelli | George Blake | Kurt Vonnegut

Dog - Scorpio/Virgo

Academic (2)/archaeologist academic/U rector barrister/magistrate dancer designer/ businesswoman journalist i nventor/manufacturer (saxophone) model/polyglot/painter novelist politician (2) politician (leader) tennis

Boutros Boutros Ghali | Ken Rosewall | Adolphe Sax

Dog - Scorpio/Libra

Administrator boss gymnast host (TV)/author (2) musician/songwriter/keyboardist novelist/playwright/journalist politician singer/songwriter (2) Admiral Air Marshal

Dog - Scorpio/Scorpio

Academic (research)/boss (4) academic (mineralogy, petrology) boss (engineering) boss (newspapers) boss (TV) chemist minister/writer/theologian model/actress/director (TV) politician (leader) sculptor General/boss (prisons inspection) Air Marshal

Dog - Scorpio/Sagittarius

Academic (3) (ancient philosophy) academic (history) actress astronomer/author boss (2) (finance) boss (investments) playwright Sheriff table tennis General/author/administrator

Charles Manson

Dog - Scorpio/Capricorn

Actor (3)/director/singer actress boss (2) boss (art collection) canoeist composer designer (firearms) engineer historian (art) inventor (water turbine) college principal/educationist tennis

Georges Bizet | Tamzin Outhwaite

Dog - Scorpio/Aquarius

Academic (4) (environmental sc) academic (math physics) academic/writer (3) academic (anatomy) actor/author (2) agent (actors') comedian boss (3) (nursing)/nurse boss (charity) boxer businessman/boss driver (racing) editor musician physician/astrologer/author

Carlo de Benedetti | Ethan Hawke | Arthur Mullard

Dog - Scorpio/Pisces

Academic/pianist/composer accountant actress boss (2) boss (shipbuilding) journalist musician (2) musician/socialist novelist painter politician politician (leader) presenter (TV) spationaut/physician

Barbara Bel Geddes | Sarah Greene | René Magritte
Robert Louis Stevenson

Dog - Sagittarius/Aries

Academic/oncologist/radiologist actress/singer boss (quango)/academic (2) cellist cricketer golfer historian politician singer (3) tenor

José Carreras

Dog - Sagittarius/Taurus

Academic/college master/ geophysicist actor boss (3) (museums) boss (volunteers) civil servant/boss footballer headmaster journalist/producer philosopher /historian pioneer (frozen food) politician (leader) rugby

Clarence Birdseye

Dog - Sagittarius/Gemini

Academic (2)/economist academic (3) (architecture)/Vice-Chancellor actor/producer (2) athlete boss (hotels) critic (music) dramatist editor/lecturer/painter film producer painter (2) politician psychotherapist Rabbi rugby scholar/writer tennis

Kriss Akabusi | Anil Kapoor | C S Lewis

Dog - Sagittarius/Cancer

Academic (2) (singing)/tenor academic (philosophy) actress biochemist/politician (leader) boss (airlines) 2-inspector (chief) composer footballer jockey politician (2)/campaigner/trade unionist writer/broadcaster

Lanfranco Dettori | Chaim Weizmann

Dog - Sagittarius/Leo

Actress architect conductor/music director driver (racing) ski jumper/coach lawyer/politician (2) model playwright/poet/novelist painter politician (leader) priest rugby

Sir Winston Churchill | Emerson Fittipaldi | Lucian Freud
Charlene Tilton

Dog - Sagittarius/Virgo

Architect/principal author (2) baseballer cricketer historian
model (super)/actor nurse tennis trainer (racehorse)
writer/creator (Pinocchio)

Carlo Collodi | Ty Cobb | Stan Smith

Dog - Sagittarius/Libra

Boss (travel)/founder (Airtours) creator (Wallace/Gromit)/film maker dean (school)
harpsi-chordist/conductor director (TV) inspector (environment)
musician/composer nurse physician politician scientist

Benny Anderson | Nick Park

Dog - Sagittarius/Scorpio

Academic (education) accountant/boss actress ballerina (prima)
boss (4) (oil) boss (opera) boss (TV) boss (quango)/spokesman
creator (drama) film maker illusionist/performer physician (2)
physician/editor physicist physiotherapist presenter (TV) soprano
trade unionist writer/journalist writer (2) Lieut-General/boss (castle)

Uri Geller | Lesley Judd | Dame Alicia Markova | Diana Quick
Steven Spielberg

Dog - Sagittarius/Sagittarius

Boss/computer programmer editor golfer guitarist/songwriter/author
fashion designer murderer nurse pianist politician singer/guitarist (2)

Carl Wilson

Dog - Sagittarius/Capricorn

Actress artist athlete boss (3) boss (glass) broadcaster composer
diplomat (2) editor harmonica player/vocalist linguist/host (TV) nurse
politician Air Chief Marshal academic/engineer

Eamonn Andrews | Emil Zatopek

Dog - Sagittarius/Aquarius

Academic (3) (architecture) academic/boss (stats)/statistician academic (medicine) archaeologist Archdeacon band leader boss (3) (computers) boss (electricity) boss (civil service) embroiderer/lecturer evangelist jockey musicologist politician (leader) sprinter

Dog - Sagittarius/Pisces

Academic (2)/industrialist/administrator actor (2) actress cartoonist (created Charlie Brown, Snoopy) civil servant consultant (publishing) designer (fashion) publisher sportsman/journalist Capt

Charles Schulz | Gianni Versace

Dog - Capricorn/Aries

Actress Bishop boss dancer/choreographer doctor/musician/missionary gangster journalist/broadcaster/author novelist (2)/engineer singer/songwriter/composer Capt/navigator/air traffic controller

Sade Adu | Alphonse Capone | Albert Schweitzer | Nevil Shute

Dog - Capricorn/Taurus

Academic/therapist (occupational) actress artist boss (comics)/editor/writer novelist (2) singer (2)/actress (2) vocalist/guitarist/actress surveyor/engineer

Stan Lee

Dog - Capricorn/Gemini

Boss (3)/accountant boss (bank) boss (prison) chef/broadcaster environmentalist femme fatale/muse saxophonist/bandleader trade unionist Commodore/chief intelligence officer

Milt Jackson | Rick Stein

Dog - Capricorn/Cancer

Boss (2) (retail) boss (consumers group) diplomat founder (Time Out) golfer journalist poet politician (leader) statesman (2) writer

Dog - Capricorn/Leo

Artist astrologer author/karate expert chess criminologist/painter driver (racing) footballer psychotherapist skier scientist/environmentalist singer/actor/songwriter/instrumentalist

David Bowie

Dog - Capricorn/Virgo

Academic (econ history) actress artist (verbal, pictorial) boss (2) (fire/planning) boss (shipping) diplomat driver (rally) educationist politician (leader)/parachutist Air Commodore/boss (nursing)

Dame Maggie Smith

Dog - Capricorn/Libra

Author/teacher boss (stationery/horticulture) driver (racing) judge/QC novelist (3) snooker solicitor speed way writer

Christian Fittipaldi

Dog - Capricorn/Scorpio

Academic (2) (psycho-geriatrics) academic/historian (theatre) boss (3) (education TV) boss (theatre) boss (children) civil servant clerk (parliaments) composer counsellor/host (radio) golfer grounds man (tennis) judge/QC politician (leader) potter singer/songwriter/pianist Capt/trainer (racehorse)

Solomon Bandaranaike | Gary Barlow

Dog - Capricorn/Sagittarius

Academic (3)/cardiologist academic (botany) academic (economist)
boss (2) (electricity) cellist forester/ agriculturalist founder (theatre)
industrialist librarian college master playwright politician (leader)
snake showman/scientist squash Air Vice Marshal/boss (engineering)

David Lloyd George | Konstatin Stanislavsky

Dog - Capricorn/Capricorn

Academic (2)/Rector academic/economist actor artist
boss (4) (design) boss/entrepreneur boxer chemist (DDT) composer
economist (chief) humorist journalist/lawyer politician (2) politician (leader)
star (rock) writer/composer General/engineer (boss)

Aled Jones | Floyd Patterson

Dog - Capricorn/Aquarius

Academic (3)/physicist academic (econs)/boss (3) (U)
academic (chemistry)/consultant academic/histopathologist artist author
boss (3) (consumers' body) boss (newspapers) boss (retailing)
broadcaster/editor driver (racing) headmaster journalist/broadcaster (2)
politician

Janet Street-Porter | Prof David Shoenberg | Polly Toynbee

Dog - Capricorn/Pisces

Academic/Vice-Chancellor (U)/dean (labour law) actor (2)/dancer/singer (2)
actress (4) archaeologist racing driver journalist painter
scholar (New Testament) singer/actor

Paul Cézanne | Ava Gardner | Marianne Faithfull | Elvis Presley

Dog - Aquarius/Aries

Accountant architect brewer composer conservator/painter consultant (charitable & education) racing engineer entertainer/comedian/author judge obstetrician/gynaecologist physicist (2) pioneer (telegraphy)/physicist/inventor poet politician soprano surgeon

Charles Wheatstone

Dog - Aquarius/Taurus

Academic/ Vice-Chancellor basketballer (3) bassist cricketer model/actress mountaineer/adventurer photographer weightlifter writer/artist

Dog - Aquarius/Gemini

Academic (2) (auditory perception) academic (church history)/college master/Reverend actor (2) actress boss (2) (docks) boss (foods) comedian editor Master of the Rolls paediatrician parapsychologist/physician (2) politician primatologist/ethnologist psychiatrist scriptwriter/broadcaster worker (UN)/campaigner(social/disarmament)

Lord Denning | Hattie Jacques | Patrick MacNee | Denis Norden

Dog - Aquarius/Cancer

Academic (2)/Vice-Chancellor academic/Vice-Chancellor actor (5) actress/model architect/designer comedian boss (healthcare)/industrialist composer cricketer politician (leader)

Linda Blair | Henry Irving | Vic Reeves

Dog - Aquarius/Leo

Academic (physics) author/broadcaster 2-baseballer US footballer/mayor hockey poet/novelist (2) paratrooper politician (2) QC/recorder

Dog - Aquarius/Virgo

Academic/surgeon actor author/broadcaster boss (3) (intelligence service) boss (brewery) boss (nuclear) broadcaster (2) coach (rugby) farmer journalist/writer medical practitioner politician (2) politician (leader)

Michael Buerk | Bamber Gascoigne

Dog - Aquarius/Libra

Academic (2)/principal/Vice-Chancellor/arbitrator athlete boss (3)/founder boss (film body) boss (concert halls) composer (2) composer/violinist/conductor diplomat theatre director/poet inventor (sq bottom bag) magnate (steel) novelist playwright politician Lieut-Colonel/lecturerMaj editor/publisher

Bertolt Brecht | Anthony Hope | Carolina Kluft

Dog - Aquarius/Scorpio

Academic (2) (literature)/author academic/hall president activist (polit) bailiff golfer historian musician owner (bar) soprano Commandant

Dog - Aquarius/Sagittarius

Academic (3) (econ theory) academic/Vice-Chancellor (dep - U) academic (medicine)/physician actor boss (industrial) boss (TV) diplomat journalist intelligence officer/banker physicist/scientist physicist (2) politician (2) politician (leader) psychologist/founder (co-Gestalt) violinist/composer writer/playwright

Wolfgang Kohler

Dog - Aquarius/Capricorn

Abbess arts administrator boss (water) manufacturer (racing car) pilot film producer (opera, theatrical)/designer moderator (church) physicist politician rifle shooting Maj-General

Enzo Ferrari | Ludwig Prandtl | Charles 'Chuck' Yeager
Franco Zeffirelli

Dog - Aquarius/Aquarius

Actress (2) broadcaster boss (foods) cricketer film director diver footballer judge/barrister model/actress saxophonist singer/guitarist tennis

Joyce Grenfell | Brian Travers

Dog - Aquarius/Pisces

Academic (environmental risk assessment)/scientist actress 2-basketballer cricketer diplomat expert (marketing) footballer ice hockey politician QC/ recorder trade unionist

Charlotte Rampling

Dog - Pisces/Aries

Academic/boss (neurology) artist comedian conductor critic (literary)/private secretary dancer musician (2)/musicologist painter/sculptor pilot rugby singer/musician specialist (corp restructuring) writer General/politician

Richard Noble | Yitzhak Rabin

Dog - Pisces/Taurus

Academic (2) (plant science) author (2) boss (orchestra) Bishop Canon chemist/teacher civil servant driver (racing) economist forger (art) musician politician singer writer

Lieut-General | David Malouf

Dog - Pisces/Gemini

Actress (2) athlete author/journalist comptroller/auditor film director economist US footballer physician/mountaineer politician rugby singer (2)/actress singer/mandolinist surgeon teacher/activist

Dog - Pisces/Cancer

Actor (2) (comic) actress architect/ lighting designer boss (insurance) brewer clerk (parliament) engineer golfer painter/sculptor pilot (fighter) politician (leader) psychiatrist balloonist

Douglas Bader | Tommy Cooper | Edwin Landseer
Liza Minnelli | Ian Woosnam

Dog - Pisces/Leo

Academic (2)/college principal actress (2) boss (4) (chemicals) boss (nuclear) boss (dance)/consultant/dancer boss (Neo Nazi) farmer film director founder (wines) physicist (medical) pioneer (consumer protection)/lecturer/lawyer 2-politician (leader) trainer (racehorse) charity worker writer

Julio Gallo | Tun Razak | Miranda Richardson | Zhou Enlai (Chou En-Lai)

Dog - Pisces/Virgo

Academic/Egyptologist author (3) boss (cosmetics) journalist (sports)/fundraiser novelist pilot (fighter) yachtsman author singer

Andy Gibb | Jack Kerouac

Dog - Pisces/Libra

Academic (3)/mathematician academic (law) academic/architect actor/author actress (3) Vice-Chancellor (U) civil servant comedian/actor film maker horticulturalist musician 2-poet politician trainer (racehorse) TV producer singer/songwriter/pilot Air Chief Marshal/boss (procurement)

Charlie Higson | Rik Mayall | Gary Numan

Dog - Pisces/Scorpio

Academic/Vice-Chancellor (U) actor (4) actress artiste (variety) boss (TV) cricketer footballer horticulturist inventor (artificial dye) philosopher presenter statesman Maj-General Rear Admiral boss (education)/instructor

Lord George Bentinck | Tyne Daly | David Niven | John Noakes
Sharon Stone

Dog - Pisces/Sagittarius

Academic (physics) astronaut author (2)/poet/playwright boss (housing) businessman/administrator/politician (leader) consultant (public affairs) cyclist film director discographer college master moderator (church) writer Maj-General/equerry

Yuri Gagarin | Victor Hugo

Dog - Pisces/Capricorn

Bailiff cricketer diplomat golfer gymnast ice hockey pianist/composer pianist (2) politician (3) politician (leader) runner tennis Rear Admiral General

Robin Cook | Tomas Masaryk | Fou Ts'ong

Dog - Pisces/Aquarius

boss (2) boss (electricity)/accountant/engineer broadcaster composer editor/yachtsman journalist hotelier painter promoter (concert) singer swimmer writer (comic book)

Dog - Pisces/Pisces

Academic (2) (plastic surgeon) academic (economics) accountant/boss actress astronaut author (2) author/screenwriter cellist impresario surgeon General (charity)

Eugene Cernan | Helen Fielding | Holly Hunter

Pig - Aries/Aries

Agent (bloodstock) boss (3) (advisers/accountants) boss (films body) boss (PCs) chess/coach/football referee civil servant (head) comedian composer/musician cyclist editor (newspapers) journalist pianist playwright politician stage designer/architect tennis

Roscoe 'Fatty' Arbuckle | Jelena Doki | Sir Alan Sugar

Pig - Aries/Taurus

Academic (2)/sociologist academic/astronomer artist (mime) ballerina boss (3) (charity) boss (engineering body) boss (quango) cricketer film director journalist (TV, radio) theatre director musicologist politician (2) singer

Sir Elton John | Marcel Marceau

Pig - Aries/Gemini

Academic (5)/historian academic (continuing education) academic/surgeon/pioneer (kidney transplant) academic/surgeon (2) actor artist (2) attorney (general) boss (2) (quango) boss (foundry) musicologist painter percussionist/bandleader politician/draughtsman/engineer teacher

William Holman Hunt | Ewan McGregor

Pig - Aries/Cancer

Actress ambassador boss (petroleum) civil servant theatre/film director founder (foods) impresario novelist photographer/author surgeon/founder (antiseptic medicine)

Sir James Dewar | Joseph Lister | Sir F H Royce | Emma Thompson

Pig - Aries/Leo

Academic (3) (chemist) academic/economist (land) academic/medical scientist accountant actor architect boss (quango) boxer diplomat journalist/campaigner (political) obstetrician/gynaecologist photographer politician Air Marshal

Sean Bean

Pig - Aries/Virgo

Actor baseballer bassist boss (charity) couturier hurdler otolaryngologist poet scriptwriter singer (3) singer/songwriter/guitarist statesman/pioneer (EU) General General/author

Emmylou Harris

Pig - Aries/Libra

Actress boss (gas) caricaturist/art critic driver (racing) golfer jockey TV journalist politician record producer

Cedric Brown | Gloria Swanson | Jacques Villeneuve

Pig - Aries/Scorpio

Academic/engineer actor/composer botanist comedian/writer counsel/QC 2-guitarist politician (2)/boss (bank) politician (leader) provost/Reverend (2) rector/Reverend

Barry Cryer | Dudley Moore

Pig - Aries/Sagittarius

Academic (3)/economist academic/museologist academic/boss (engineering)/engineer architect boss (4) boss/accountant librarian/boss (services) novelist ophthalmologist politician (3) scholar General/ politician (leader) Maj/equerry

Nguyen Van Thieu

Pig - Aries/Capricorn

Academic/engineer actor (3) architect author boss (2) (health body) boss (investment) broadcaster civil servant diplomat (2) industrialist politician (leader) psychiatrist singer General

Prince Otto von Bismarck | Tom Clancy | Michael Parkinson David Tennant

Pig - Aries/Aquarius

Architect biophysicist composer Constable (Chief) coordinator/civil servant dramatist keeper (of Records) pioneer (automobile)

Walter Chrysler | Erich Mendelsohn | Tennessee Williams

Pig - Aries/Pisces

Accountant actor (2)/comedian boss (4) (council)
boss (polit communications) boss (charity) boss (dancing)
critic (art)/librettist civil servant dancer/actress interior designer
drummer painter/pioneer (Cubism)/sculptor

"Chico" Marx

Pig - Taurus/Aries

Academic (3)/matron/boss (3) (services) academic/sculptor/teacher
academic (banking/finance) auctioneer (boss) boss (publishing) librarian
playwright poet/poet translator politician (3) politician (leader) singer (2)
singer/actor writer Maj-General Air Marshal
Wing Commander/pilot (test)/explorer Lieut Col/astronaut/test pilot

John Bruton

Pig - Taurus/Taurus

Academic (Economic History) boss (3) (fire)/fireman boss (TV) conductor
economist GP headmaster photographer singer (2)/actress
singer/songwriter

Greg Dyke | Iggy Pop | Holly Valance

Pig - Taurus/Gemini

Academic (2)/Vice-Chancellor (U) actress (2) artist/teacher
boss (3) (supermarket) boss (health body) boss (purchasing)/surveyor
composer house master publisher Marshal
Major/boss (newspaper)/consultant (mgt)

William Heinemann

Pig - Taurus/Cancer

Actor boss (2) boss (shipping) coach (football) (2)/footballer cyclist dancer/actress diplomat theatre director educator (Jewish) jockey manager (football) model producer (TV) QC/barrister/playwright rugby trainer (racehorse) writer General

Jack Charlton | Bettie Page | Aaron Spelling

Pig - Taurus/Leo

Academic (2) /economist academic (public health) astronomer boss (2) (info) boss (investment) composer comptroller/solicitor cricketer/umpire film director engineer explorer golfer mathematician physician/specialist (tropical medicine) producer (theatre) publisher (music) QC Rajah singer/actor/poker surveyor (pictures) violinist breeder (dog)

James Brooke | John Speke

Pig - Taurus/Virgo

Academic/chemist actor author (2) boss (2) (recruitment) consul cricketer editor/publisher/magnate engineer industrialist/boss photographer/inventor poet potter surveyor (Queen's pictures) writer

Graham Dilley | Leslie Grantham | David Leach | Dame Ngaio Marsh
Vladimir Nabokov

Pig - Taurus/Libra

Academic (pathology) accountant/sportsman boss (3) (construction) boss (logistics) boss (secret agents) historian inventor/founder (Dyson Research) singer (2) surgeon (orthopaedic) writer Lieut-Colonel

James Dyson | Bianca Jagger | Dame Ngaio Marsh

Pig - Taurus/Scorpio

Author/playwright consultant (HR) doctor/astronaut engineer golfer novelist presenter (TV) reporter watchmaker

Anthony Trollope | Paula Yates

Pig - Taurus/Sagittarius

Ambassador boss (water) boss (4) boss (law) boss (TV) cartoonist expert (aviation)/engineer/civil servant film producer pianist/bandleader/composer pioneer (rayon manufacture) politician (4) politician (leader) politician/farmer/businessman soprano trainer (racehorse) college warden

Duke Ellington

Pig - Taurus/Capricorn

Academic (French literature) actress bandleader/musician boss (wine) comedian editor educationist headmistress inventor (record disc) philosopher politician (leader) sailor singer

Emile Berliner | Sheena Easton | Maureen O'Sullivan | Eric Sykes

Pig - Taurus/Aquarius

Architect boss expert (badger)/biologist/schoolmaster historian manager (funds) musician photographer politician (leader) writer rugby

Pig - Taurus/Pisces

Academic (papyrology) actor/ screenwriter/ film director-producer (2) author (2)/comedian/playwright boss (2) (radio quango) boss/industrialist/politician animation director/producer keyboardist politician (2) politician (leader) writer/historian

Ben Elton

Pig - Gemini/Aries

Academic (3) (international relations) academic (metallurgy) academic/geographer/planner (urban) animator (film) astrologer/author (2) 2-driver (racing) photographer flying officer Lady-in-Waiting physicist politician (leader) QC singer writer Lieut-General

Pig - Gemini/Taurus

Academic (4)/chemistacademic/composer academic(Hebrew) academic (business history) actor/writer (2) architect attorney general boss (farms) boxer school founder/headmistress lawyer lexicographer/writer politician (4) politician (leader) proprietor (newspaper)/politician show jumper tennis

Kim Clijsters | Hubert Humphrey | Ian Robert Maxwell George Osborne | Vincent Price

Pig - Gemini/Gemini

Academic (surgery) actress/comedienne actress (3) actress/broadcaster architect boss (investments) boss (resistance) chef/restaurateur diplomat editor GP inventor (Merz)/painter/poet/writer novelist (3) politician scientist Sheriff singer/songwriter writer

Norman Foster | Dame Thora Hird | Kurt Schwitters | Linda Thorson

Pig - Gemini/Cancer

Academic (4)/economist academic/scientific adviser academic/Vice Chancellor actor/writer boss (2) (IT) boss (charity) composer councillor cricketer diplomat engineer essayist/Transcendentalist/poet founder (school) consultant (2) (international econs/business) mariner (master)/teacher college mistress novelist (6) novelist/essayist painter physician pianist/composer scholar/author/historian surveyor/consultant therapist (art)

Dame Catherine Cookson | Ralph Waldo Emerson | Thomas Mann Salman Rushdie

Pig - Gemini/Leo

Academic/historian actor/comedian boss (2) (bank) boss (Fascists) composer cricketer critic/writer (2) entertainer/boxer politician (3) politician (leader) politician (leader)/lawyer QC writer

Hugh Laurie

Pig - Gemini/Virgo

Actress agent (political) boss (adviser)/scientist impressionist journalist/industrialist judge/QC neurophysiologist politician sculptor tennis

Faith Brown

Pig - Gemini/Libra

Academic actor (2) Bishop boss (arts) cellist Vice-Chancellor (U)/academic (physics)/boss clergyman/author illustrator judge politician/diplomat

Rev W Awdry | Hablot K Browne (Phiz) | Henry Kissinger | Gene Wilder

Pig - Gemini/Scorpio

Academic (2)/composer academic (civil engineering) actor artist boss (3) (culture) boss (charity) boss (opera)/composer couturier diver film star politician (2) guitarist headmaster lawyer/judge novelist (2) politician (leader)/columnist QC solicitor (2) tennis writer/broadcaster Colonel/war time secret services head/engineer General

Ronnie Wood

Pig - Gemini/Sagittarius

Academic (Portuguese) diplomat dramatist explorer judge physicist surgeon writer/broadcaster writer (3) writer/editor

Sophie Grigson | Terence Rattigan

Pig - Gemini/Capricorn

boss (2)/(banking) boss (communications) comedian/actor (2) writer playwright politician (2) rapper Chief Rabbi recorder show jumper statesman stuntman (motorcycle) model/actor

David Blunkett | Julian Clary | Eddie Kidd

Pig - Gemini/Aquarius

Academic (2)/historian (art) academic (history) author (2) author/arbiter (style) bass boss (2) (machines) boss (glass) curator (trust) editor politician singer writer Vice Admiral

Wilbert Vere Awdry | Antony Pilkington

Pig - Gemini/Pisces

Administrator astronomer/researcher basketballer radio host college master mathematician organist rapper/actor trainer (racehorse) watercolourist/teacher Major/farmer (chicken)

Pig - Cancer/Aries

Abbot actor (2) Bishop boss (2) (electrics) broadcaster Constable (Chief) politician (leader) singer (2) trade unionist Lieut-Colonel/usher to Queen Maj-General/boss/lawyer

Julian Pettifer

Pig - Cancer/Taurus

Actor/director/film producer/singer actress (2) boss/founder (advertising/PR) driver (racing) golfer historian (art)/designer journalist/biographer rugby sculptor tennis (2) Admiral

Gareth Edwards | J M Fangio | David Ogilvy

Pig - Cancer/Gemini

Academic (surgery) actress boss/businessman diplomat (2) diplomat/politician/traitor farmer physician/bacteriologist/immunologist pilot (fighter) industrialist (oil) painter politician rugby surgeon

Eikichi Itoh | Vidkin Quisling | John D Rockefeller

Pig - Cancer/Cancer

Academic/college master actor (2)/body builder basketballer biologist film director entrepreneur/writer (2) founder (theatre) actor/writer journalist surgeon

Dave Prowse

Pig - Cancer/Leo

Academic/biochemist athlete artist/film maker builder (master) footballer 2-racing driver guitarist jockey/racehorse trainer painter politician 2-politician (leader) producer (TV) scholar (German) writer

Brian May

Pig - Cancer/Virgo

Academic/nephrologist architect/Arabist boss (3) boss (hotels)/hotelier boss/architect Dalai Lama dean goalkeeper journalist/writer (doggerel) judge model/actress pianist/golfer/painter solicitor/writer (2) translator

Fabien Barthez | Mortimer Collins | Gyasto Tenzin

Pig - Cancer/Libra

Academic (2) (economics) academic/nephrologist actor/artist architect/Arabist athlete banker/politician Vice-Chancellor (U) rally driver editor model player (bridge) politician (2) singer (3) veterinarian/microbiologist

Pig - Cancer/Scorpio

Academic (2) (law) academic (dentistry) actor (3) actress archaeologist astrologer/theosopher boss (cars) composer founder (WikiLeaks)/journalist/publisher historian poet/essayist 2-politician (leader) surgeon (2) trade unionist trainer (hunting) writer

Julian Assange | James Cagney | Georges Pompidou

Pig - Cancer/Sagittarius

Academic/chemist actor bandleader Bishop boss (2) (automotive) boss (construction) politician (2) headmaster historian horticulturist microbiologist translator (chief) Rear Admiral hydrographer Vice Admiral Capt/historian

Beth Chatto

Pig - Cancer/Capricorn

Academic (pharmacy) actress boss (gas) US footballer judge church minister pianist/songwriter poet publisher solicitor writer (2) writer/journalist

Ernest Hemingway | Pauline Quirke

Pig - Cancer/Aquarius

Academic (history) actor (3) actress/singer boss (drugs)/vet designer (fashion) dealer (art) doctor journalist painter (2) TV host/producer/actress/painter

Marc Chagall | Donald Sutherland

Pig - Cancer/Pisces

Academic/psychiatrist actress/dancer/singer boss (engineering) Vice-Chancellor (U) comedian explorer footballer organist painter (2) politician skater (figure) Colonel/Panzer leader Air Chief Marshal

Ted Rogers | O J Simpson

Pig - Leo/Aries

Actor/director/screenwriter/producer author (2)/journalist author/politician broadcaster editor footballer (US) footballer/manager founder (company) musician rugby tennis theologian

Anne Hobbs | Roy Keane | Nick Ross

Pig - Leo/Taurus

Abbot actor (2)/film producer (2) actor/film producer mail artist cricketer guitarist (2)/vocalist/songwriter (2) physicist politician (leader) singer (2)/songwriter/guitarist/flautist tennis

Ian Scott Anderson | Anwar Ibrahim | Pete Sampras
Erwin Schrodinger

Pig - Leo/Gemini

Author (2) boss (3) (charity firm) boss (drinks) boss (finance) drummer editor journalist novelist politician rugby Marshal Vice Admiral

Andrew Marr

Pig - Leo/Cancer

Academic (2)/physicist academic (education)/pioneer boss (3) (consumer products) boss (quango) businesswoman/boss diplomat disc jockey/ host (talk show) headmaster college master intelligence officer pianist

Pig - Leo/Leo

Academic (molecular membrane biology) actor athlete boss (2) (museum) boss (festival)/musician cameraman designer (fashion) industrialist (2) industrialist/boss poet/novelist politician (leader)/explorer/administrator singer tennis Air Vice Marshal

Mary Joe Fernandez | Katharine Hamnett | David Walliams

Pig - Leo/Virgo

Academic (2) (government) academic/physician actor
boss (transport)/barrister creator (Mary Poppins) critic dean (music college)
designer (aircraft) murderer pilot (display)

Pig - Leo/Libra

Academic (2) (management/finance) academic (archaeology) actor/scriptwriter
barrister/politician boss (teachers/volunteers) cricketer politician (2)
rugby Field Marshal

Pig - Leo/Scorpio

Academic (internet studies)/boss (institute) actress author (3)
author/playwright Bishop boss (2) (toys) composer Constable (Chief)
drummer film director/producer founder (housing) judge painter
politician writer Brigadier/attaché Maj-General

Marcel Duchamp | Alfred Hitchcock | Keith Moon | Willy Russell

Pig - Leo/Sagittarius

Academic (stats, comp sc) actress (3) basketballer boss (cars)
broadcaster/writer conductor cricketer magician/actor college master
designer (consultant) muralist/sculptor oncologist singer

Lucille Ball

Pig - Leo/Capricorn

Academic/ philosopher actor (2) actress administrator designer (fashion)
epidemiologist/activist inventor (screw propeller)/engineer

Arnold Schwarzenegger

Pig - Leo/Aquarius

Activist/economist/writer boss (2) (religious sect) civil servant (boss) composer drummer pioneer (amplifier) poet trainer (racehorse) puppeteer/entertainer

Rupert Brooke | Rod Hull | Samuel Coleridge-Taylor

Pig - Leo/Pisces

Actor/acrobat/clown boss (pharmaceuticals) entrepreneur film director historian/writer (2)/priest novelist/poet (2) poet politician (2) politician (leader) QC/Recorder

Conrad Aiken

Pig - Virgo/Aries

Academic (2) academic (rheumatology) actor/director/producer biologist boss (2) (broadcasting) boss (publishing) civil servant cricketer cyclist flautist meteorologist politician (2) politician (leader) referee rheumatologist specialist (international relations) tennis

Richard Attenborough | Jorge Luis Borges

Pig - Virgo/Taurus

Academic (2) (engineering) academic (engineering) accountant Bishop boss boxer comedian/ presenter (TV) editor journalist model musician novelist (2) poet publicist/businessman researcher/writer/engineer Air Chief Marshal

C S Forester | Larry Grayson | Rocky Marciano | Dame Edith Sitwell

Pig - Virgo/Gemini

Actor artist/writer author boss (media) comedian (2) comedienne conductor cricketer driver (racing) inventor/designer (golf club) pilot/inventor (2) politician (2) singer/songwriter figure skater solicitor statesman

Richard Ashcroft | Karsen Solheim | Jeanette Winterson
Johnny Vegas

Pig - Virgo/Cancer

Anaesthetist artist boss (3) (bank) boss (rail)/engineer boss (water) church commissioner civil servant designer (fashion) editor engineer magistrate manufacturer (soap) novelist/politician (leader) singer tennis writer (3) writer/broadcaster

John Buchan | Goran Ivanisevic | Viscount William Lever Stella McCartney

Pig - Virgo/Leo

Academic (2) (law) actor administrator (tennis) author academic/mathematician cartoonist commentator (sports) conductor/director (music) editor science educator novelist physician/virologist physicist politician (leader) treasurer

William G Golding | Alan Weeks

Pig - Virgo/Virgo

Academic (animal husbandry) boss (2) (council) boss/founder (show) conductor/teacher diplomat TV/film director novelist/creator (Tarzan) nurse news reporter soprano Air Marshal/chief engineer

Edgar Rice Burroughs | Joan Thirkettle

Pig - Virgo/Libra

Academic/geoscientist boss (medicine) editor (fashion) judge musician/comedian painter photographer poet/scientist politician (3) politician (leader) singer General

Russ Abbot | Tessa Jowell

Pig - Virgo/Scorpio

Actor (3)/singer athlete badminton baseballer boxer coach (tennis) cricketer 2-footballer guitarist singer (3) singer/songwriter/actress/businesswoman figure skater songwriter/singer/actor swimmer writer Lieut-Commander Lieut-General

Pig - Virgo/Sagittarius

Academic/philosopher actor (2) actress composer conductor/author diplomat drummer golfer manager (football)/footballer novelist pioneer (music) politician (leader) racer (powerboat) singer/songwriter Air Marshal Wing Commander/aviator

Padraig Harrington | Stephen King | Lee Kuan Yew | Hank Williams Sr Amy Winehouse

Pig - Virgo/Capricorn

Academic (2) (Renaissance)/librarian academic/boss (2) (research) architect consultant (Info insurance) cyclist driver (racing)/commentator/businessman footballer model/actress politician physician/bacteriologist pianist /composer/arranger rugby sociologist Rear Admiral/boss (medicine)

Barbara Bach | James Hunt | Emlyn Hughes

Pig - Virgo/Aquarius

Academic/anatomist administrator boss (pharmaceuticals) chemist civil servant/town planner composer headmistress inventor poet politician (2) politician/architect reformer (social)/manufacturer (chocolate) singer

George Cadbury | Arvo Pärt

Pig - Virgo/Pisces

Actress baseballer boss/lawyer conductor cricketer diplomat/writer footballer 2-US footballer politician (2)/broadcaster politician (leader) Capt (ship)

Pig - Libra/Aries

Academic (2)/historian academic/psychiatrist actor (2)/film producer actress banker broadcaster/journalist chef/restaurateur/author designer (fashion) 2-diplomat elder (tribal) marketing executive circus performer pianist poet/translator/teacher politician college principal saxophonist/bandleader/composer screenwriter/film director singer (2)/songwriter/guitarist tenor

Marc Bolan | Robin Day | Rula Lenska | Luciano Pavarotti
Duchess of York (Sarah Ferguson)

Pig - Libra/Taurus

Academic (2)/haematologist academic/historian architect (2) architect/writer (2) barrister cartoonist comedian harpist painter pilot restaurateur wrestler writer

Le Corbusier

Pig - Libra/Gemini

Academic/dean archivist/activist biologist boss (health) diplomat diver magnate (retail)/entrepreneur mayor/solicitor (2) painter politician reformer (penal) solicitor

Theo Paphitis

Pig - Libra/Cancer

Academic/dean (medicine) boss (4) (council) boss (chemicals) boss (quango) boss (TV) prison governor politician/architect treasurer

Pig - Libra/Leo

Actor (3) actress baseballer boss (5) (airports) boss/circus performer/missionary boss (drinks) boss (health) boss (stadium) racing driver politician sports presenter promoter (holiday camp) singer (2)/artist singer/songwriter

Billy Butlin

Pig - Libra/Virgo

Academic (2) (econs) academic (biology) actor (2) actress architect athlete boss/accountant editor/film critic journalist/broadcaster painter politician/anaesthetist preacher/Reverend

Arnold Bocklin | Mark Tully

Pig - Libra/Libra

Academic (haematology)/pathologist/oncologist actor (4) actress/TV host civil servant dancer/actress/showgirl diplomat driver(rally)/businessman/sportsman golfer musician politician (leader) secretary singer

Konstantin Chernenko | Fred Couples | Donald Sinden

Pig - Libra/Scorpio

Academic/GP architect/artist commentator/TV host Constable (Chief) designer editor/journalist engineer founder (design)/designer (graphic) musician pianist singer/songwriter snooker

Johnny Mathis | Robert Stephenson

Pig - Libra/Sagittarius

Actor (2) actress artist basketballer boss (land) bowler choirmaster/organist designer (2)/decorator golfer mogul (music)/artist/author (2) politician (5) priest statesman tennis writer/scriptwriter

Simon Cowell

Pig - Libra/Capricorn

Academic (theology)/theologian/Reverend actor/writer author (2) conductor/composer US football judge musician politician (leader) sculptor singer/songwriter writer Lieut-Col/astronaut Marshal

Arnold Machin

Pig - Libra/Aquarius

Actress/singer author (2) boss/banker chef/restaurateur consultant (PR) diplomat librarian sherry merchant surfer swimmer writer Vice Admiral

Thomas Keneally

Pig - Libra/Pisces

Diplomat footballer occultist/author/mountaineer physician (consulting) politician QC show jumper signalman/grocer singer solicitor teacher

Marie Osmond

Pig - Scorpio/Aries

Academic/politician actor (3) author/activist boss (4) (council) boss (TV) boss (museum) boss (retailing) fencer goalkeeper politician (leader) trade unionist/college principal/activist trainer (racehorse) violinist

Chiang Kai-Shek | Alain Delon | Richard Dreyfuss | Nadine Gordimer Roy Rogers

Pig - Scorpio/Taurus

Academic/biologist/psychologist actor (2) actress author dancer/boss designer (hat) diplomat footballer musician/singer painter

L S Lowry

Pig - Scorpio/Gemini

Academic (cardiology) Archbishop boss (library/gallery)/librarian broadcaster chess champ/writer/educationist conductor/director (music) golfer headmaster journalist/compiler (crosswords) sculptor/artist secretary (USAF) sociologist songwriter

George Carey | Roy Lichtenstein

Pig - Scorpio/Cancer

Barrister civil servant diplomat fencer politician (2) politician/diplomat/businessman sociologist trainer (racehorse) worker (social)/reformer (social)

King Hussein (Jordan)

Pig - Scorpio/Leo

Academic (2)/anthropologist/physician academic/surgeon diplomat founder (charity) intellectual/campaigner painter (2) poet/novelist/theologian politician (4) 2-politician (leader) politician/archaeologist/explorer singer (2) singer/songwriter/guitarist skier

Hiram Bingham III | Evo Morales | Peter Noone
Chad Varah (Dr Prebendary) | Prof Magdi Yacoub

Pig - Scorpio/Virgo

Archdeacon Vice-Chancellor (U) boss (electronics) theatre director editor Lady-in-Waiting/lecturer publisher singer/actress/model

Jack Welch

Pig - Scorpio/Libra

Author chorister director (fashion) gardener humorist/TV host hurdler journalist (2) philologist/grammarian poet soldier/politician violinist/baritone Admiral

Pig - Scorpio/Scorpio

Academic (2)/historian academic/adviser (science) actor author/editor boss (bank) caricaturist cricketer engineer footballer headmistress historian painter/pioneer (art) politician TV presenter Brigadier/rugby

Peter Baring | Alexa Chung | Paul Signac

Pig - Scorpio/Sagittarius

Academic (machine intelligence) boss (2) (oil) boss/accountant economist religious minister poet film producer/director/critic/journalist singer writer/broadcaster/restaurateur

Michael Winner

Pig - Scorpio/Capricorn

Academic (3) (pathology) academic (literature)/commentator boss (2) (energy)/engineer boss (prison) designer (stage, costume) editor explorer/archaeologist golfer humorist/artist inventor/chemist rugby singer/songwriter writer/lecturer/keeper (gallery)

Bryan Adams | Léo Baekeland | Gary Player

Pig - Scorpio/Aquarius

Academic/conductor (2)/musician actor (2) actress boss (council) conductor (choral) diplomat historian (art) pilot/yachtsman politician (3) politician (leader) principal Capt/administrator Field Marshal

Bernard Montgomery

Pig - Scorpio/Pisces

Academic/physicist academic (3) academic/school director actor (4) actress astronaut boss (3) (drinks) boss (counsel) boss (law) composer engineer (2) motorcyclist head hunter/engineer jockey/trainer (racehorse) journalist (2) poet politician (leader) rugby/journalist trade unionist writer (2) writer/actor Admiral of the Fleet

Hilary Clinton | Lester Piggott | Winona Ryder | Alan Shephard Jaclyn Smith

Pig - Sagittarius/Aries

Analyst (Jungian) boss (service) engineer composer/guitarist critic (music) geneticist pioneer (rock 'n' roll)/singer/pianist writer

Little Richard (Penniman)

Pig - Sagittarius/Taurus

Academic/anatomist/adviser (medical) actor (2) actress astronaut designer (fashion) editor golfer musician physician politician college principal trade unionist Field Marshal

Jasper Conran

Pig - Sagittarius/Gemini

Academic (2) academic (modern history) Archdeacon journalist paediatrician physicist playwright/composer politician Major Marshal

Noël Coward | Christian Doppler

Pig - Sagittarius/Cancer

Academic/linguist actress archivist barrister bookseller boss (pottery) director (film/stage)/writer librarian model (glamour) pianist/composer/singer rugby

Hoagy Carmichael | David Mamet | Pat Phoenix | Lucy Pinder

Pig - Sagittarius/Leo

Actress (2) attorney (2) banker barrister boss (broadcasting) film director novelist (3) organiser (prog) poet rugby scientist sculptor tennis trade unionist

Michael Green | Richard Krajicek | Lee Remick

Pig - Sagittarius/Virgo

Ambassador   artist   boss (2) (advisory)   boss (law)   designer (garden)
journalist/philatelist   politician (leader)   soprano   sprinter

Maria Callas | Flo-Jo (Florence Griffith-Joyner) | Charles Kennedy

Pig - Sagittarius/Libra

Accountant/consultant   actress   author   boss (3) (operations)
boss (estate agent)   boss (transport)   cricketer   engineer
GP   journalist/writer   judge   musician/bandleader   politician (leader)
film producer   violinist   Lieut-Colonel/equerry

Kim Dae Jung

Pig - Sagittarius/Scorpio

Academic (2)/librarian/bibliographer   academic/Vice-Chancellor (U)
boss (2) (airport)   boss (health)   composer (2)   film director
personality (media)/writer   politician (2)   politician/probation officer
publisher (newspaper)/columnist   soprano   trainer (racehorse)
umpire (cricket)

Hector Berlioz | Phil Donahoe | Pietro Mascagni

Pig - Sagittarius/Sagittarius

Academic/physician   boss (bank)   boxer   composer
conductor/director (musical)   film maker (2)   model (super)   politician (2)
TV presenter/journalist   film & TV producer   producer (theatrical)   soldier (2)
vocalist   yachtsman   Rear Admiral

John Barbirolli | General George Armstrong Custer

Pig - Sagittarius/Capricorn

Academic (Japanese)   cartoonist   judge   novelist/activist   painter
QC/explorer (2)   novelist/poet   rugby   soldier/explorer/writer/businessman
tennis   writer (4)

Edvard Munch | Arantxa Sanchez Vicario

Pig - Sagittarius/Aquarius

Actor/film director/comedian diplomat disc jockey journalist judge pianist poet snooker/commentator Capt/flight manager

Woody Allen

Pig - Sagittarius/Pisces

Academic (landscape architecture) actor author/illustrator baseballer/manager boss (3) (retailing) boss (games) boss (trade body) calligrapher/artist caricaturist engineer (2) head hunter/engineer impersonator journalist/novelist marksman reformer singer trade unionist

Terence Beckett | Janet Brown | Boris Karloff | Joseph Whitworth

Pig - Capricorn/Aries

Actor boss (2) boss (shipbuilding) consultant (investment) coach (rugby) golfer journalist/writer (2) musician/writer painter politician (2) politician (leader) singer (2) singer/songwriter solicitor surgeon (paediatric)

Konrad Adenauer | Dido | Amanda Holden | Nigella Lawson Serge Poliakoff

Pig - Capricorn/Taurus

Agent (Br double)/spybarrister (2) boss (bank)/banker golfer magnate (hotel) novelist politician presenter (sports) solicitor Admiral

Conrad Hilton | H A R (Kim) Philby | David Vine

Pig - Capricorn/Gemini

Adviser (political) author/broadcaster baritone boss (3) (quango) boss (industries) boss (engineering) manager (racing) politician

Pig - Capricorn/Cancer

Actor (2) adviser (boss in economics) boss (3) (prison) boss (transport) boss (entertainment) designer diplomat/boss (aircraft)/banker director (artistic)/choreographer drummer footballer illustrator journalist politician singer zoologist

Pig - Capricorn/Leo

Actor/musician anaesthetist astronomer boss (3)/journalist/author boss (chemicals) boss (quango) canoeist geneticist novelist (2)

Jack London

Pig - Capricorn/Virgo

Academic (medicine)/boss actor/manager (theatre) architect baritone boss (3)/banker boss (police trainer) director (artistic) dramatist footballer magistrate/recorder statesman

General | Marshal/Commander-in-Chief

Pig - Capricorn/Libra

Actor author boss (2) (foods) boss (charity) museum curator/scholar designer (dress) glider (hang) high jumper politician producer (theatre & film) rugby

Humphrey Bogart

Pig - Capricorn/Scorpio

Academic (Armenian Studies) architect Bishop boss (2) (scouts) broadcaster cartoonist consultant (education) diplomat farmer headmistress (2) industrialist missionary politician (2)/boss (electrical) politician/journalist/economist publisher singer Commander/navigator (wartime) Capt/Lieut-Commander/schoolmaster

Pig - Capricorn/Sagittarius

Academic (physiology) activist (polit) author (3) boss (nuclear) designer (fashion) musician/writer novelist/secretary nursing officer/nurse politician (leader) rugby singer/songwriter vocalist/singer (2)

Pig - Capricorn/Capricorn

Academic (pharmaceutics) actress Bishop boss (2) (metals) boss (bank/quango/cars)/banker comedienne/singer (singer)/dancer coroner engineer (2) college master model forensic psychiatrist scientist singer writer/activist (political)

Tracey Ullman

Pig - Capricorn/Aquarius

Actor (5) actress agent/spy architect athlete biochemist boss (4) (transport)/accountant boss (publishing) boss (tobacco) boss/founder (retail) chemist cricketer critic/editor engraver (glass) footballer/manager education officer politician (2) QC solicitor theologian writer (art, design) Maj-General

Brendan Foster | Val Kilmer | H A R (Kim) Philby | Luise Rainer H G Selfridge

Pig - Capricorn/Pisces

Actor (2) comedienne composer (3)/arranger designer (aircraft) film director/screenwriter/composer/actor percussionist/drummer/composer physicist singer snooker

Thomas Sopwith | Michael Stipe | Cliff Thorburn | Wilhelm Wien

Pig - Aquarius/Aries

Academic/historian (art) boss (institute) business woman chemist consulting engineer film maker headmaster college principal singer General

Debra Meaden

Pig - Aquarius/Taurus

Astrologer baseballer boss (IT) critic/translator dealer (art) golfer headmaster journalist/historian(social) medium model/radio host 2-painter politician (2) politician (leader) playwright

Charles E.O. Carter | Jackson Pollock | Ronald Reagan

Pig - Aquarius/Gemini

Academic (2)/neurologist academic/theologian actress boss (2) (cars) boss (bank) choreographer conductor cricketer politician (2) politician/consultant (speech) TV presenter/tennis writer

Farah Fawcett | Ian Gibson | John McEnroe

Pig - Aquarius/Cancer

Academic/astronomer activist (social) announcer (radio) chancellor (U)/adviser (econ) boss (newspaper) drummer golfer musician physician politician 2-politician (leader) printer sculptor singer/ director (artistic) Air Commodore/fighter pilot

Dan Quayle

Pig - Aquarius/Leo

Academic (4) (law) academic (biochemistry) academic/chemist academic/physicist accountant/boss (4) boss (electronics) boss (charity) boss (investment) boss (stockbroker) composer jockey (2) jockey/breeder (horse) missionary politician (3) provost (U)/mathematician shoemaker/breeder(cattle)/conservationist singer/actor/politician deputy Speaker (Lords) writer

Sonny Bono | Jean Muir

Pig - Aquarius/Virgo

Academic (Eng law) actor (2)/designer/director legal adviser boss (quango) chemist chorister/director (music) dancer/actor doctor/inventor (medical) driver (rally)/inventor (Gatsometer speed detector) footballer photographer company secretary

Mikhail Baryshnikov | Eva Braun

Pig - Aquarius/Libra

Academic (6) (surgery) academic/college master/historian academic (Irish history) academic (music) academic (Persian) academic/college principal actor/manager (actor) boss (electricity)/engineer broadcaster college president musician/teacher/restorer (musical instruments)

Pig - Aquarius/Scorpio

Academic (2)/chemist academic (surgery) actress (2) boss (3) (research)/college principal boss (parks) industrialist/politician/boss (engineering) judge novelist (2) pilot (test) college principal singer (2) wrestler writer yachtsman

Amanda Holden | Michael Hutchence | Merle Oberon | Jules Verne

Pig - Aquarius/Sagittarius

Author ballerina boss (water)/engineer cartoonist coach (football) comedian composer (2) pianist Admiral/scientist Group Capt/specialist (air armaments)

Sven-Göran Eriksson | Johan Ludvig Runeberg

Pig - Aquarius/Capricorn

Academic (oncology)/boss (research) actress boss (2) (design) boss/detective Constable (Chief) footballer golfer lawyer/historian leader (religious) novelist/poet politician (leader) QC/judge surfer writer/humorist/critic Brigadier Capt/jockey Field Marshal

Steve McManaman

Pig - Aquarius/Aquarius

Academic/college president actress bookseller boss (5) (council) boss (prison) boss (airport, oil) editor farmer judge physicist politician (2) politician (leader) company secretary trade unionist Maj-General/boss (medical services) Maj-General Maj-General/boss

Christina Foyle | Megawati Sukarnoputri

Pig - Aquarius/Pisces

Academic (Hungarian Studies) actress boss (5 (publishing) boss boss (technology) boss (intelligence/spy) boss (opera/theatre) composer cricketer diplomat judge pianist politician secretary soprano Lieut-General

Arthur Rubinstein | Ann Sothern

Pig - Pisces/Aries

Actress administrator boss (police) chef/restaurateur illusionist novelist oceanographer/navigator philosopher politician (2) politician (leader) producer (radio)

Derren Brown | Jean Harlow | W J Locke | Anton Mosimann

Pig - Pisces/Taurus

Academic (2)/physicist actress Archbishop civil servant clown (circus) compose/pianist diplomat poet singer wine writer/lecturer

Sandie Shaw

Pig - Pisces/Gemini

Actor advocate/QC author boss (trust) diplomat headmaster journalist (2) judge model (fashion) politician rapper/TV star writer

Fabio Lanzoni | Ben Okri

Pig - Pisces/Cancer

Actress (2) actress administrator (theatre) Archbishop author ballerina/coach boss (TV) guitarist journalist officer (naval)

Emily Blunt | Rachel Weisz

Pig - Pisces/Leo

Academic (2) (public admin/policy) academic/paediatrician actor (2) Bishop boss (2) (finance)/surveyor boss (supermarket) climber composer/singer (2) politician/actor politician/soldier/author (2) rector (institute) soprano wrestler writer/poet/screenwriter

Pig - Pisces/Virgo

Academic (US & Eng literature) Archbishop astrologer boss (3) (china) boss (police) boss (tribunals) composer conductor/musicologist discoverer/ physiologist founder (Scientology)/writer (2)/creator (Dianetics) high jumper hockey illustrator inspector (sen chief - education) poet/novelist/librettist politician (2) college president/financier singer Air Vice-Marshal/bomber fighter pilot

Kiki Dee | Dick Fosbury | Ron L Hubbard | Cardinal Basil Hume Vaughan Williams

Pig - Pisces/Libra

Astronomer/TV presenter   author (2)   chemist   conductor   editor
film director   manager (football)   performer (TV)   writer/broadcaster

Brian Clough | Lord Paul Condon | Patrick Moore

Pig - Pisces/Scorpio

Academic/endocrinologist   Boss (6) (shipping)   boss (circus troupe)
boss (TV)   boss (museum)   boss/owner   consultant (wine)/journalist
model/photographer   politician (3)   politician/boss (quango)   promoter (sports)
squash   statesman   Group Capt/bomber pilot

Penny Lancaster | Roland Rat | Alan Yentob

Pig - Pisces/Sagittarius

Academic (2)/biologist   academic   ballerina   barrister/industrialist/historian
boss (hotels)   boss (insurance)   designer (fashion)/inventor (miniskirt)
dramatist/nationalist   entrepreneur   soldier/poet (2)
poet/broadcaster/songwriter   model   politician   secretary   singer
trade unionist   tennis   Flight-Lieut/navigator

Pam Ayres | Gabriele D'Annunzio | André Courrèges

Pig - Pisces/Capricorn

Actor   architect/designer   artist/critic   astronaut   barrister/businessman
boss (dairy)   guitarist   bank manager   musician/trumpeter
politician (leader)   Public Prosecutor/QC   QC/recorder   singer/songwriter
skater   tennis   violinist

Pig - Pisces/Aquarius

Actor/writer   actress (2)   bookseller/publisher   engineer
headmaster   photographer   politician (2)   presenter (TV)/glamour model
solicitor

Melinda Messenger

Pig - Pisces/Pisces

Actress college master composer engineer personality (TV) politician secretary (2) secretary/controller singer/guitarist soprano (2) 2-writer

Glenn Close

CHAPTER 4

NOTABLE BUSINESS OR ROMANTIC RELATIONSHIPS

This Chapter has some real life evidence to support the tendencies for compatibility or incompatibility between various star signs, as detailed in Chapters 1 & 2. It makes interesting reading to note that there has to be some astrological attraction, at least initially, to establish a relationship. Like most relationships, other factors, including complacency or distractions could appear, thereby ending a relationship unexpectedly.

A number of couples who are famous in the business or public arena have been chosen to show their extent of compatibility with some explanation based on the earlier chapters.

Where available, their Ascendants would be mentioned. Otherwise, only their Chinese signs, Sun/Moon signs are given. Please note that the dates of births are in format of month/day/year.

As expected, I could not confirm definitely all the events mentioned in the chapter, as that would not be feasible. Apart from my astrological inferences, most of the information was obtained from freely available information and public reports.

Sir Paul McCartney (6.18.42 - water Horse, Gemini/Leo, Pisces Ascendant)

a) Linda McCartney (9.24.41 - metal Snake, Libra/Scorpio, Scorpio Ascendant).

Both Paul and Linda have the air Sun signs of Gemini and Libra respectively, a highly compatible combination for good communications. Also both have watery Ascendants which would ensure good emotional closeness, at least in their outwardly interactions.

"She was a really funny lady, very witty. A delicious sense of humour. She was happy. So I use that now. I balance every sad moment with a happy moment. That kind of helps day to day. It helps me get through." Paul.

b) **Heather Mills** (1.12.68 water Horse, Capricorn/Gemini) married 2002, divorced 2008

"You can be a litigant in person. It's not easy, but just make sure you do all your research, save yourself a fortune....Beatrice only gets £35,000 a year - so obviously she's meant to travel B class while her father travels A class, but obviously I will pay for that." Heather

Heather's quotes confirmed the importance of money and being not trusting to a typical Capricorn.

Paul Newman (7.27.54 wood Horse, Leo/Cancer)
Joanne Woodward (2.27.30 metal Horse, Pisces/Aquarius)

As Horses, both would value their independence. Leos tend to be romantic and loyal. Pisceans would appreciate good consideration and sensitivity and her Moon in Aquarius would accentuate her need for some independence.

"Being married to Paul is being married to the most considerate, romantic man....to be married to a man who makes you laugh every day, ah, now that's a real treat." Joanne.
You can't spend a life time breathing down each other's necks." – Paul.

Syd Little (12.19.42 water Horse, Sagittarius/Taurus)
Eddie Large (6.25.41 metal Snake, Cancer/Cancer)

Famous as the Little & Large comedy double act, Syd Little was dubbed the serious, 'straight man', typical of Sagittarians. Eddie Large played the 'funny man', making impressions, a natural talent for Cancerians, a master of moods and the empathic Snake. This showed how two fairly different characters could make a successful partnership.

Sarah Ferguson (10.15.59 - earth Pig, Libra/Aries, Scorpio Ascendant)

Prince Andrew (2.19.60 - metal Rat, Aquarius/Scorpio, Leo Ascendant)

The Pig and Rat combination did not show a particularly strong bond but the Western signs did.

Libran and Aquarians can be soul mates as both are Air. Arians and Aquarians can sometimes get on too. There was the Aries Moon and Leo Ascendant link and Scorpio Moon and Scorpio Ascendant attractions. As some of the elements were of the fixed category, there could have been some friction too.

"We grow together, and we support each other no matter what, through everything, together....I think there's no finer man than him. I've never met a finer man." - Sarah. The couple married in 1986 but divorced in 1996, although they have remained good friends. "But whether they will remarry still appears to be a matter for speculation."

Silvio Berlusconi (9.29.36 fire Rat, Libra/Pisces, Virgo Ascendant)

With 3 'weaker' signs of Libra, Pisces and Virgo, one could definitely expect some volatility in his relationships.

a) Carla Dell'Oglio (9.12.40 – metal Dragon, Virgo/Aquarius, Pisces Ascendant) - married from 1965 to 1985.

Very strong multiple compatibility and attractions here between Rat/Dragon, common Virgo and Pisces – thus explaining their 25 year long marriage.

b) Veronica Lario (7.19.56 fire Monkey, Cancer/Sagittarius, Capricorn Ascendant) – married 1990, divorced in 2009

The pair of Rat and Monkey was basically strong but the flirtatious nature of Libra could have been unbearable for the sensitive Cancerian, even though her Moon was in freedom loving Sagittarius.

"I am convinced that at this point it would be more dignified to stop here.... I cannot stay with a man who frequents minors."- Lario.

c) Mike Bongiorno (5.26.24 – wood Rat, Gemini/Pisces)

Mike had been a close friend with Silvio for many years; not surprising as both are Rats, with their Moons in emotional Pisces, plus the natural compatibility of Libra with Gemini.

Halle Berry (8.14.66 fire Horse, Leo/Cancer, Taurus Ascendant)

a) David Justice (4.14.66 - fire Horse, Aries/Aquarius) – married 1992, acrimoniously divorced 1997, allegedly there was a string of restraining orders against him related to domestic violence

A rather fiery relationship was plausible, especially between the fixity of Leo and Taurus, with the aggressiveness of Aries. Aquarius Moon would also add a touch of coolness. "But the two reportedly barely saw one another (not surprised as both were Horses) and when they did there were allegations of abuse by David."

b) Eric Benet (10.15.66 **-** fire Horse, Libra/Scorpio). Married 2001 and divorced 2005, Benet admitted to at least ten extramarital affairs in the two year marriage. Another Horsey relationship – thus proving that like does attract like! Although there was a Scorpio Moon, it was not enough to restrain the wayward Libran Sun.

Bette Davis (4.5.08 - earth Monkey, Aries/Gemini, Scorpio Ascendant)

a) Harmon Nelson (7.5.07- fire Goat, Cancer/Taurus), divorced after 6 yrs.

b) William Grant Sherry (7.12.14 –wood Tiger, Cancer/Pisces) - divorced after 5 yrs.

c) **Gary Merrill** (8.2.15 –water Rabbit, Leo/Taurus – divorced after 10 yrs.

Above did confirm that Monkeys might not get on too well with Tigers and Goats. The watery Cancer for 2 husbands was probably helped by the Scorpio Ascendant. The fire affinity between the Suns in Aries and Leo had probably enhanced the moderately weak Monkey – Rabbit tie.

Queen Victoria (5.24.1819 – earth Rabbit, Gemini/Gemini, Gemini Ascendant)

Prince Albert (8.26.1819 – earth Rabbit, Virgo/Scorpio, Ascendant Virgo)

Similarity obviously had proved to be attractive between the 2 earth Rabbits, thus getting the quiet reassurance from each other. Gemini and Virgo were generally known for good general intelligence and to foster responsive communications.

Billy Connolly (11.24.42- water Horse, Sagittarius/Gemini, Libra Ascendant)

Pam Anderson (7.1.67 – fire Goat, Cancer/Aries, Gemini Ascendant)

Good complements with the fire element (Sagittarius Sun and Aries Moon) and the air element (Libra Ascendant and 2 Geminis). The fact that they had 5 children would indicate the Cancerian's focus on her home/family.

David Cameron (10.9.66 – fire Horse, Libra/Leo, Ascendant Libra)

Samantha Cameron (4.18.71 – metal Pig, Aries/Capricorn)

There is a predictable attraction between Libra and Aries; hence twice the dosage as David's Ascendant is also Libra. The fire link between Leo and Aries would further support the relationship. The normally ambitious thinking Capricorn would definitely enjoy the huge career potential as the PM's wife.

Elizabeth Taylor (2.27.32 - water Monkey, Pisces/Scorpio, Sagittarius Ascendant), married 8 times.

a) **Michael Wilding** (7.23.12 – water Rat, Cancer/Scorpio) married 5 years.

One can see a strong combination of Monkey/Rat and the perfect watery trios of Pisces, Scorpio and Cancer. Being more than twice her age when they married, it was commented that he was like a father but they remained good friends after the divorce.

b) **Richard Burton** (11.10.25 - wood Ox, Scorpio/Virgo, Aries Ascendant)

Not surprising that they married twice as the water connection was very strong between Pisces Sun and Scorpio Sun/Moon. Also a natural compatibility existed between fiery Sagittarius and Aries.

c) **Eddie Fisher** (8.10.28 – earth Dragon, Leo//Gemini) married 5 years.

A strong link existed between Monkey and Dragon and also between both fire signs of protective Leo and fun loving Sagittarius.

Note: Husband Mike Todd was omitted due to uncertainty of his DOB.

Cher – Cherilyn Sarkisian (5.20.46 – fire Dog, Taurus/Capricorn, Cancer Ascendant)

Sonny Bono (2.16.35 – wood Pig, Aquarius/Leo, Libra Ascendant)

On the surface, there was not much evidence of strong compatibility, except for the admiration that each might value in some of their basic characteristics. Both would exhibit good tenacity, natural pleasantness and goodwill; hence their effort to perform together after their divorce (married for 10 years). Both had elements which suited the stage, singing and welcome the limelight.

John Lennon (10.9.40 - metal Dragon, Libra/Aquarius, Aries Ascendant)

Yoko Ono (2.18.33 – water Rooster, Aquarius/Sagittarius, Libra Ascendant)

A very strong natural attraction existed, especially from Western astrological perspectives. There were the air and fire complements of similar Libra Sun/Ascendant, Aquarius Sun and Moon and the fiery Aries Ascendant and Sagittarius Moon.

Muhammd Ali (1.17.42- metal Snake, Capricorn/Aquarius, Leo Ascendant)

Angelo Dundee (8.30.20 – metal Monkey, Virgo/Pisces) - the lifelong business/boxing trainer.

Good rapport between Snake and clever Monkey was expected. There was also the earthy synergy between Capricorn and Virgo, an observant teacher.

Nicole Scherzinger (6.29.78 – earth Horse, Cancer/Taurus, Virgo Ascendant) split after 5 year romance.

Lewis Hamilton (1.7.85 - wood Rat, Capricorn/Cancer)

"Lewis has been working 24/7 to win Nicole back and even though she's not materialistic he's splashing the cash big time to try to dazzle her back into his arms."
"Nicole is still really angry Lewis was unprepared to commit to marriage, but he's desperate to get her back and says this time he'll pop the question and be a great family? man." – important to her as she would naturally be a family oriented Cancerian.

They were basically compatible with his Cancer Moon and her Cancer Sun, her Taurus Moon and his Capricorn Sun. Her Virgo Ascendant would make her feel closer too but his Capricorn streak might add some hesitant caution to his ambitious make up. However, a Horse and Rat is not naturally ideal.

Russell Brand (6.4.75 - wood Rabbit, Gemini/Aries, Capricorn Ascendant), 14 month marriage.

Katy Perry (10.25.84 – wood ~Rat, Scorpio/Scorpio, Libra Ascendant)

A Rat/Rabbit was not perfect and the only obvious rapport came from his Sun Gemini and her Libra Ascendant. Otherwise, she could be too overpowering with her passionate Scorpio Sun/Moon combo versus his more traditional Capricorn Ascendant.

"Some of it's the fame, but I think getting married is — you've got a whole other person that you've got to make as important as you," Russell

"He's a very smart man, and I was in love with him when I married him....I felt a lot of responsibility for it ending, but then I found out the real truth, which I can't necessarily disclose. I keep it locked in my safe for a rainy day," Katy (a secretive double Scorpio showing her protective element).

Ant - Anthony McParlin (11.18.75 - wood Rabbit, Scorpio/Taurus)
Dec - Declan Donelly (9.25.75 - wood Rabbit, Libra/Taurus)

They are held together mainly because of their common wood Rabbit personality and subconscious Moon in Taurus.

"I've never wanted to work alone since we started together." Dec; indicating his preference for partnership, a common Libran trait.

Paul Daniels (4.6.38 – earth Tiger, Aries/Gemini, Pisces Ascendant)

Debbie McGee (10.31.58 – earth Dog, Scorpio/Libra)

Strong Tiger and Dog couple, enhanced by their watery combination of Pisces and Scorpio. Paul's Aries Sun would add sizzle to their relationship.

"He was so charismatic. There was so much chemistry. I'm not ashamed to tell people that we have a good sex life – we always have had." Debbie – important for Scorpios, and normally for Arians too.

Margaret Thatcher (10.13.25 - wood Ox, Libra/Leo, Scorpio Ascendant – piercing eyes)

Ronald Reagan (2.6.11 - metal Pig, Aquarius/Taurus, Sagittarius Ascendant)
A natural empathy existed between her Libra Sun and his Aquarius Sun, against an amenable bond between an Ox and a Pig.

"I knew that I was talking to someone who instinctively felt and thought as I did. This was not just a matter of politics, but "about a philosophy of government, a view of human nature," Margaret. "Of the two, Thatcher was more fiercely loyal and Reagan more likely to play the henpecked husband", one observed.

Demi Moore (11.11.62 – water Tiger, Scorpio/Taurus, Pisces Ascendant)

a) **Bruce Willis** (3.19.55 – wood Goat, Pisces/Capricorn, Virgo Ascendant) married 10 years.

Not the best in relationship between a Tiger and Goat, but this seemed to be more than compensated with the strong Scorpio and Pisces combination and helped by the 3 earth signs of Taurus, Capricorn and Virgo.

"He was worried about her (addiction) and wanted her to get better....Many of her friends did the same thing, but she just wouldn't listen." – not surprising with her strong Scorpio/Taurus combination. "Moore and Willis aren't the only divorced couple in Hollywood who have remained close after splitting up."

b) **Ashton Kutcher** (2.7.78 – earth Horse, Aquarius/Aquarius, Gemini Ascendant) – split after 6 years on his alleged cheating.

A strong Tiger and Horse duo but fairly weak on Western astrology as it was a water plus air combo.

"Ashton wants her to know he is there for her and supports her no matter what."

David Copperfield (9.16.56 – fire Monkey, Virgo/Aquarius, Virgo Ascendant)

Claudia Schiffer (8.25.70 – metal Dog, Virgo/Gemini, Scorpio Ascendant)

Although an average Monkey/Dog relationship, both had Sun in Virgo and Moons in air signs, thus giving above average strength in their bond.

David Bowie (1.8.47 - fire Dog, Capricorn/Leo, Aquarius Ascendant)

Iman Abdulmajid (7.25.55 – wood Goat, Leo/Libra)

A relatively stable pairing mainly based on traditional values and mutual support. There's the air connection and common Leo (fixed) link.

Marilyn Monroe (6.1.26 - fire Tiger, Gemini/Aquarius, Leo Ascendant – lioness' mane)

a) **Arthur Miller** (10.17.15 - wood Rabbit, Libra/Aquarius, Libra Ascendant)- married 5 years.

Basically, it was a compatible and intense relationship with both Sun and Moon and his Ascendant. However, her Leo Ascendant, which needed much attention without criticism was a problem.

" married another father figure - the intellectual playwright Arthur Miller."
"He was impressed by her sensitivity and her sense of reality; she responded to his gentleness."

b) **Joe DiMaggio** (11.25.14 - wood Tiger, Sagittarius/Pisces, Sagittarius Ascendant) married 9 months.

Two married tigers would probably make a tempestuous relationship. Also, Joe's fiery elements could be too much for Marilyn's changeable, airy elements but her Leo and his Sagittarian Sun and Ascendant would offer some attraction.

"...even though they still harbored love for one another. She knew the relationship would never work."

Madonna (8.16.58 - earth Dog, Leo/Virgo, Aquarius Ascendant)

a) **Sean Penn** (8.17.60 - metal Rat, Leo/Cancer, Sagittarius Ascendant) married 4 years.

A warm relationship between Dog and Rat but strong intensity expected between two fixed and proud Leos. Sean's Moon in Cancer should add some emotions to the cool and enigmatic Aquarian Ascendant of Madonna.

"....it was evident that this union was a colossal clash of egos".
"Each seems to remain unaccountably fascinated by the other; Penn worshipped her, in an almost obsessive way.
"Madonna has said privately that the fireworks between them were unlike anything she's ever experienced, before or since...."

b) **Guy Ritchie** (9.10.68 – earth Monkey, Virgo/Aries) married 8 years.

A good Dog/Monkey union and where her Virgo Moon was his Sun. Also, good attraction existed between his Arian Moon and her Aquarian Ascendant.

"She's branded him 'emotionally retarded'."

Lucille Ball (8.6.11 – metal Pig, Leo/Capricorn, Capricorn Ascendant)

Desi Arnaz (3.2.17 - fire Snake, Pisces/Cancer, Cancer Ascendant), married 20 years.

Snakes and Pigs would not normally get on very well, especially when one was hard metallic and the other hot tempered.
Desi was probably charming and emotional; quite opposite to the controlling, dignified Lucille who had to rely on Desi's business skills.

"....a volatile interplay of alcoholism, infidelity—and a surpassing love that endured for nearly 50 years."
"She thought that having a baby would hold them together."
", but Desi was the brains. He was the staunch one. Lucy just deferred to him.... we heard a lot of loud arguing and cursing and glass."

shattering and screaming, and we were scared.... Desi was the love of Lucy's life. It was romantic, passionate, everything you could imagine in a love affair, and she was deeply hurt by what happened. They had tried like three times to get a divorce, but Lucy had always stopped it. "

Bonnie Parker (10.1.10 – metal Dog, Libra/Virgo)

Clyde Barrow (3.24.09 – earth Rooster, Aries/Taurus, Leo Ascendant)

Natural attraction was expected between Libra and Aries; also the Moon affinity in earthy Virgo and Taurus, whilst Clyde's Leo would take the lead.

"The attraction was instantaneous....They were both people who wanted other's approval. They wanted glamour, they wanted excitement. They found in each other the things they were looking for."

Pierre Curie (5.15.1859 - earth Goat, Taurus/Scorpio, Pisces Ascendant)

Marie Curie (11.7.1867 - fire Rabbit, Scorpio/Pisces, Capricorn Ascendant)

A very strong bond existed between the Goat and Rabbit.
Both had the inquisitive and tenacious Scorpio, backed by intuitive Pisces in their Ascendant and Moon. Also Marie's Capricorn Ascendant would add fuel to their ambitious efforts.

Steve Jobs (2.24.55 – wood Goat, Pisces/Pisces, Virgo Ascendant)

Steve Wozniak (8.11.50 - metal Tiger, Leo/Cancer, Virgo Ascendant)

Apparently, not a very strong affinity could be expected between a Goat and a Tiger. Both shared a Virgo Ascendant, which would be important as far as work ethic and fastidiousness were concerned. Steve would probably be the 'softer' personality of the two. Also, water was present in their basic signs; more prevalent in Steve, thus some natural empathy.

"We've always been friends. Can you find anyone who's ever seen us argue? We're not close friends, but never had any falling-out." Wozniak

Anna Kournikova (6.7.81 - metal Rooster, Gemini/Leo)

Enrique Iglesias (5.8.75 – wood Rabbit, Taurus/Aries), dated for 12 (?) years

On the face of it, there were no strong indications of compatibility except for their fiery Moon signs. But were things said or happened in private though?

"I've never really thought marriage would make a difference". Enrique
"I believe in commitment. I believe in being open and trusting each other and respecting each other completely." Anna

Johnny Depp (6.9.63 – water Rabbit, Gemini/Capricorn, Leo Ascendant)

Vanessa Paradis (12.22.72 – water Rat, Capricorn/Cancer, Sagittarius Ascendant) partner for 14 years.

Rabbit and Rats tend to get on fairly well. Both had a fiery Ascendant and similar Capricorn for Moon in one and Sun in the other, thereby explaining a fairly long partnership.

"Love is not just about butterflies and fairy tales." Vanessa
" ....woman who's been good to you... She's a great mommy and a great woman..admitted he still 'loves' his ex and mother of his two children." Johnny

Ted Turner (11.19.38 – earth Tiger, Scorpio/Libra, Sagittarius Ascendant)

Jane Fonda (12.21.37 - fire Ox, Sagittarius/Leo, Capricorn Ascendant – work ethic with outwardly self control) married for 10 years.

An interesting relationship, which had a strong basic, fiery attraction between a Sagittarian Ascendant and Sun but also underlying tensions from a more volatile Tiger and intense Scorpio. Her more traditional influence from Capricorn and steady Leonine Moon might be causing some irritations later on. Her Moon's need for continual reassurance might even exhaust the strong Scorpio. Feeling 'free' would have been a strong natural urge for her.

"..staying together for a decade despite his rampant cheating which she discovered early on in their relationship. Fonda, 74, later claimed it was only after the $40million divorce that she felt free for the first time in her life."

"The couple had behaved like a 'pair of lovesick teenagers' at first , There were times leading up to and even after the divorce when she wanted to share with me (daughter, Mary) some of the things Ted was doing that destroyed their relationship." He feels differently and that her decision to leave was devastating. 'She's as opinionated as me, if not more. In areas like the status of women, she probably was even a little stronger than me. The U.S. TV mogul said that he longs for the intimacy they shared together and that he is lonely without her, even though they do still speak once a month on the phone."

Humphrey Bogart (12.25.1899 – earth Pig, Capricorn/Libra, Taurus Ascendant)

Lauren Bacall (9.16.24 – wood Rooster, Virgo/Taurus, Cancer Ascendant)

A medium strength relationship would have existed between the Pig and Rooster.

However, his Taurean Ascendant and her Taurean Moon, together with his earthy Capricorn and her earthy Virgo could have boosted the relationship. Her Cancerian Ascendant could fit well with her emotional Pig.

"I hope Bogie knew how much I loved him, how much he meant to me, how I highly valued him. I've had another life since then, but he was my first love, and you never forget your first love." - Lauren
"When he saw me at the beginning of the day and when he called me on the telephone, his first words were always 'Hello, Baby.' My heart would literally pound." - Lauren

Letter to Lauren from Bogie**:** *"Baby, I do love you so dearly and I never, never want to hurt you or bring any unhappiness to you - I want you to have the loveliest life any mortal ever had. It's been so long, darling, since I've cared so deeply for anyone that I just don't know what to do or say. I can only say that I've searched my heart thoroughly these past* *two weeks and I know that I deeply adore you and I know that I've got to have you. We just must wait because at present nothing can be done that would not bring disaster to you."*

"She's a real Joe. You'll fall in love with her like everybody else." - Humphrey

Liv Tyler (7.1.77 - fire Snake, Cancer/Capricorn, Cancer Ascendant)

Joaquin Rafael Phoenix (10.28.74 – wood Tiger, Scorpio/Aries), break up after 3 years, and had at least 7 celebrity relationships.

A fairly strong attraction would have existed between Snake and Tiger. The key link was her watery Cancer Sun and Ascendant with his watery Scorpio Sun. His Arian Moon would inject the additional passion.

"We hit it off immediately...every once in a while you find an actor that, with one word, can sum up eight different emotions. She absolutely nailed that....at a certain point, I think we stopped evolving with each other, stopped progressing, and made a very mature decision to move on, even though there was still a great love there". Rafael on LIV

Bill Clinton (8.19.46 – fire Dog, Leo/Taurus, Libra Ascendant)

Hilary Clinton (10.26.47 – fire Pig, Scorpio/Pisces, Leo Ascendant)

Pigs and Dogs are normally of average compatibility.
The obvious link was between Bill's Sun in Leo and Hilary's Leo Ascendant. On the whole, Hilary would be a more passionate and emotional person, when compared to Bill's somewhat more inflexible and flirtatious/fun loving nature.

Imelda Marcos (7.2.29 – earth Snake, Cancer/Taurus, Scorpio Ascendant)

Ferdinand Marcos (9.11.17 – fire Snake, Virgo/Cancer, Cancer Ascendant)

There was almost a perfect and highly devoted combination of two Snakes, earthy and watery signs. Both had watery Ascendants, one with a Cancer Sun and the other Cancer Moon.

" she thinks he was the best thing that ever happened to the Philippines." Imelda

Ronald Reagan (2.6.11 – metal Pig, Aquarius/Taurus, Sagittarius Ascendant)

Nancy Reagan (7.6.21 – metal Rooster, Cancer/Leo, Libra Ascendant)

A fairly good match existed between a Pig and a Rooster.
His Aquarius Sun should match well with her airy Libran Ascendant and his Sagittarian Ascendant could appeal to her Moon in Leo.

Wallis Simpson (6.19.1896 – fire Monkey, Gemini/Libra, Aquarius Ascendant)
King Edward 8 (6.23.1894 – wood Horse, Cancer/Pisces, Aquarius Ascendant)

The obviously main reason for this significant case was that both had an Aquarian Ascendant, which would imply deep and common similarity in their basic outlook. This was enhanced by his attraction to her sexy Gemini Sun and Libran Moon. Overall, they could have been a highly interactive couple.

"With the price of losing the crown. King Edward 8 became the Duke of Windsor and married his beloved Wallis Simpson. The famous couple lived happily together for 35 years."

Angelina Jolie (6.4.75 – water Rabbit, Gemini/Aries, Cancer Ascendant)

Brad Pitt (12.18.63, water Rabbit, Sagittarius/Capricorn, Sagittarius Ascendant), together since 2005 with 3 own children.

The obvious link would come from their common water Rabbit sign, predisposing them to be equally sensitive.
There was also her Arian Moon attraction to his Sagittarian Sun and Ascendant.

"Brad Pitt and Angelina Jolie can't keep their eyes off each other at the LA Salt premiere in 2010."

"Angelina Jolie credited her "loving and supportive" partner Brad Pitt when talking about her mastectomy to the New York Times."

Liam Gallagher (9.21.72 - water Rat, Virgo/Pisces
Noel Gallagher (5.29.67 – fire Goat, Gemini/Aquarius,

Rats and Goats do not normally get on well together.
Liam had earth and water in his Sun and Moon whereas Noel had just air in both; thus explained the lack of affinity for each other.

These two brothers were well known for their intense conflicts and feuds within the group, Oasis.

Barry Gibb (9.1.46 – fire Dog, Virgo/Scorpio, Libra Ascendant)

Maurice Gibb (12.22.49 – earth Ox, Sagittarius/Aquarius, Scorpio Ascendant)

Robin Gibb (12.22.49 – earth Ox, Sagittarius/Aquarius, Scorpio Ascendant)

Barry have had disputes with Maurice and Robin. This was not surprising as Maurice and Robin had virtually identical astrological profiles.

Although the ox and dog should get on well, the Western signs predicted otherwise. Barry's earthy Sun sign of Virgo and his airy Libran Ascendant could be at odds with the others' fiery, independent loving Sagittarius and their strong, watery Scorpio.

Kylie Minogue (5.28.68 – earth Monkey, Gemini/Gemini)

Dannii Minogue (10.20.71 – metal Pig, Libra/Scorpio)

It had been rumoured that there was some sibling rivalry between Kylie and Dannii.

Astrologically speaking, a Pig may not get on too well with a Monkey. Also, as both Sun signs were of the air element, they should be reasonably compatible although some monkey tricks could abound to add some tension.

Prince Charles (1.14.48 – earth Rat, Scorpio/Aries, Leo Ascendant – proud bearing)

a) **Princess Diana** (7.1.61 – metal Ox, Cancer/Aquarius, Sagittarius Ascendant)

It's a well known and somehow tragic piece of royal history between Prince Charles and Princess Diana.

An entrepreneurial Rat does not always see eye to eye with the resolute Ox.

However, in this case, there would have been strong compatible elements for a good relationship. Her homely Cancer should go well with his watery Scorpio and both their Ascendants were fiery. But her strong need to outshine him in public and need for independence could upset his stronger, demanding personality (for full appreciation).

b) **Camilla – Duchess of Cornwall** (7.17.47 – fire Pig, Cancer/Cancer, Leo Ascendant)

There was a similar but more empathic relationship here, as compared to Princess Diana's. Camilla would naturally be more sensitive/protective and somewhat more tactful in not 'competing' for the limelight in public with Prince Charles. As both their Ascendant was Leo, their basic outlook to life could be fairly similar too.

Catherine Zeta Jones (9.25.69 – earth Rooster, Libra/Pisces, Sagittarius Ascendant)

Michael Douglas (9.25.44, wood Monkey, Libra/Capricorn, Scorpio Ascendant) – separated due to 'family/health stresses' after 13 years' marriage. However, there has been talk about a possible reconciliation.

Many would have surmised about this pair's compatibility and age difference. The attraction between a Rooster and a Monkey would not be naturally strong.

However, both shared the Libran Sun and her Piscean Moon would have attracted his Scorpio Ascendant.

"Zeta-Jones was "totally" in love but was "concerned" that Douglas had cheated on his first wife repeatedly – probably due his passionate Scorpio Ascendant. Douglas also got a confidentiality clause from Zeta-Jones, barring her from ever revealing personal details of their marriage – probably important to a secretive Scorpio who had suspicions on a Sagittarian/Libran ability to keep mum on personal matters.

Evan Williams (3.31.72 – water Rat, Aries/Libra) – entrepreneur/boss for Blogger, Twitter etc.

Biz Stone (3.10.74 – wood Tiger, Pisces/Libra,) – creative Director at Twitter.

Sun in Aries and Moons in Libra could work well if there was some tolerance. With both their Moons in communicative Libra, things could work out well at a subconscious level.

Queen Elizabeth II (4.21.26, fire Tiger, Taurus/Leo, Capricorn Ascendant – dedicated and traditional)

Prince Philip (6.10.21 - metal Rooster, Gemini/Leo, Capricorn Ascendant), married for over 65 years.

Traditionally, Tigers and Roosters are not compatible.

As both their Ascendants were in traditional Capricorn and shared a karmic Leonine Moon, it would forecast a stable relationship, mainly based on trust and discipline.

"She never looked at anyone else."

"Cherish Lilibet? I wonder if that word is enough to express what is in me.....the only 'thing' in this world which is absolutely real to me." Prince Philip

"Philip is an angel—he is so kind and thoughtful.....he has, quite simply, been my strength and stay all these years." Queen Elizabeth

Daniel Craig (3.2.68 – earth Monkey, Pisces/Aries)
Rachel Weisz (3.7.70 - metal Dog, Pisces/Pisces)

It's an OK relationship between a Monkey and a Dog.

There were multiple similarities between the Sun and Moon signs through the romantically inclined Pisces. Daniel's Arian Moon would add a bit more spice to their apparent dreaminess. Rachel's ex-husband, Darren Aronofsky, had a cooler Aquarian Sun with influence from a Sagittarian Moon.

John Major (3.29.43 – water Goat, Aries/Capricorn, Capricorn Ascendant)

Edwina Currie (10.13.46 – fire Dog, Libra/Taurus, Leo Ascendant)

A natural attraction would be expected between a Goat and a Dog.

Similarly, Edwina's Libran Sun and fiery Leonine Ascendant would be drawn to John's Arian Sun. John's Capricornian (Machiavillian?) Ascendant and Moon could explain his regret over the 4 year long affair. Not surprisingly, Mrs Norma Major (2.12.42) had an Aquarian Sun and a Capricornian Moon, thus helping to explain her apparent forgiveness.

"However, she says that after his arrival in 10 Downing Street she "appeared to have been forgotten".
"She admitted she was hurt not to be mentioned in the index of Mr Major's autobiography... claims in the diaries that her love for Mr Major persisted after he became prime minister in 1990, "dominating her life".
"Described her former lover as having "quite a Machiavellian streak about him".

Ben Cohen (3.18.51 metal Rabbit, Pisces/Cancer), co-founded Ben & Jerry (ice-cream)

Jerry Greenfield (3.14.51 - metal Rabbit, Pisces/Gemini), co-founded Ben & Jerry

Ben and Jerry shared at least 55% of their personality traits due to them being a metal Rabbit with Sun in Pisces.
"and were childhood friends."

Bill Hewlett (5.20.13 – water Ox, Taurus/Sagittarius, Capricorn Ascendant)

David Packard (9.7.12 – water Rat, Virgo/Cancer, Capricorn Ascendant)

There should be some, not huge compatibility between an Ox and a Rat. The driving, key factor came from the earthy (hence more stable) combination of their ambitious Capricorn Ascendant, Bill's steadfast Taurean Sun and David's meticulous Virgoan Sun. Their Moons in Sagittarius and Cancer would have added the elements of curiosity and tenacious imagination.

"Bill and Dave clicked because they had similar personality types with an insatiable curiosity.....they were driven by accomplishment, not egos."

Larry Page (3.26.73 - water Ox, Aries/Capricorn), co-founded Google.
Sergey Brin (8.21.73 - water Ox, Leo/Taurus), co-founded Google.

Two Oxen would have achieved much via their persistent diligence.

With their fiery, opinionated Suns in Aries and Leo, things could get rather heated up at times; to be probably slowed down by their earthy Moons in Capricorn and Taurus.

"At the beginning both had a hard time gelling with each other, since they never seem to agree on a single topic. According to Brin, "they are both obnoxious"

"I want to be looked back on as being very innovative, very trusted. " Sergey

"We are targeting innovation..." Larry

Adolf Hitler (4.20.1889 – earth Ox, Taurus/Capricorn, Libra Ascendant)

Eva Braun (2.6.12 – metal Pig, Aquarius/Virgo, Capricorn Ascendant)

Both had two earth and 1 air influences from their basic signs, thus inducing good mutual attraction.

"Eva happened to be standing on a ladder which gave them both a good vantage point: he looked at her legs, she looked down at his face, they each liked what they saw."
"There is no evidence that the relationship between Hitler and Eva Braun was other than a normal one, except that the pleasures that she provided him were those of domesticity and relaxation rather than eroticism."
"She was unconcerned with personal advancement or advancement of her family, spending her time instead floating about, changing her clothes seven times a day, waiting for her Führer to call."

William Procter (12.7.1801 – metal Rooster, Sagittarius/Capricorn), co-founded Procter & Gamble.

James Gamble (4.3.1803 – water Pig, Aries/Virgo), co-founded Procter & Gamble.

Although they met as brothers-in-law, a Rooster normally gets along well with a Pig. William's Sagittarian Sun should be ideal with James' innovative, Arian Sun. Also, their earthy Moons in disciplined Capricorn and industrious Virgo would make things even better.

Tiger Woods (12.30.75 - wood Rabbit, Capricorn/Sagittarius, Virgo Ascendant)

Elin Nordegren (1.1.80 - earth Goat, Capricorn/Gemini), divorced after Tiger's indiscretion.

A well matched couple between a Rabbit and a Goat.
This would be enhanced by both having their Suns in Capricorn, and boosted with another earthy Virgoan Ascendant of Tiger's. However, his Sagittarian Moon could have given him the urge to be free and be happy go lucky.

<u>**ABBA Group:**</u>

Agnetha Fältskog (4.5.50 – metal Tiger, Aries/Scorpio, Leo Ascendant)

Björn Ulvaeus (4.25.45 – wood Rooster, Taurus/Libra), married to Agnetha for 9 years.

On the surface, not the best of astrological combinations but it might be a case of a fiery, dominating personality in Agnetha with a more amenable Björn.

'I don't think I'm very good at judging people. Sometimes I get a bad feeling but not very often...Björn and I have dealt with the heartbreak. It is amicable. In love, there are so many ups and downs," Agnetha

Anni-Frid Lyngstad (11.15.45 – wood Rooster, Scorpio/Pisces)
Benny Andersson (12.16.46 – fire Dog, Sagittarius/Libra), married to Anni-Frid for 3 years but had lived together as a test marriage for 9 years.

Two fairly opposite personalities existed here; again a stronger, more emotional Anni-Frid with a more flexible, fiery Benny.

"Benny had given her a new sense of security and she had started to enjoy life."

"What I wish for most is to be harmonious and happy and open, taking things as they come. Deep inside I'm really a thinker...there would be occasional tensions and frictions... naturally I was depressed, how do you think one feels going through a divorce from a man you love" Anni-Frid

CHAPTER 5

INDEPENDENT QUOTES AND FINAL COMMENTS

This chapter contains some third party quotes made on people, thereby confirming some of the descriptions pertaining to the key traits of the star signs already described in earlier chapters. Each combination consists of the Chinese sign, Western Sun /Moon signs, which gives a fairly unique profile of the individual. Assuming that the authors of these obituaries are not professional astrologers, it is quite amazing as to how accurately they could describe these profiles by inadvertently using some terms of the stereotypical astrological traits.

Many of these are taken from publications and articles ("From others") available to the general public. All quotes from obituaries are from The Daily Telegraph (used under licence) and their dates of publication are given in case you wish to read the whole article.

Craigie Aitchison (born 1.13.26, painter, **wood Ox, Capricorn/Capricorn**)

"..his spare but powerfully evocative style remained more or less unchanged for 50 years... conformed to no school or fashion.....a gentle and whiskery man... a lonely figure in 20th-century art... converted a ruined farmhouse...... it was precisely that quality of innocent spontaneity that admirers so liked in him... a regular visitor to the Tate, where he would attempt to copy works of art."

Richard Barker (born 7.17.39, headmaster, **earth Rabbit, Cancer/Cancer**)

"..quiet persistence and careful planning the transition to full co-education was implemented with ease... worked out a "scoring system" – known as the "Barker conversion formula" ....developed the business studies A-level course... edited a successful series of books."

Claude Blair (born 11.30.22, museum curator, **water Dog, Sagittarius/Aries**)

"embodied the tradition of curators who were at once competent generalists and serious specialists....combine acute visual observation with documentary evidence...quick to spot potential... could be unsparing in criticism of inaccuracy or pretentiousness... published around 200 articles and wrote, co-wrote or edited 10 books... a warm-hearted man and a bon vivant who relished travel... publish and research energetically."

Very Reverend Keith Jukes (born 2.18.54, **wood Horse, Aquarius/Virgo**)

"...his proven gifts as a pastor and conciliator were in much demand..... reputation as a troubleshooter.... immediately set about restoring financial controls and stability to the Cathedral... in and through all these crises, Jukes exercised a warm, pastoral touch.... earned their affection and respect by his gifts of hospitality and sense of fun... his pastoral and administrative gifts helped to stabilise a difficult and over-stretched team....

Berthold Beitz (born 9.26.13, industrialist, **water Ox, Libra/Leo**)

"...his autocratic air and ability to switch in an instant from chilly and overbearing to warm and charming....

many Germans criticised him for his pride, but then he had plenty to be proud about.... Beitz was recognised as "Righteous Among the Nations" by Israel's Yad Vashem Holocaust memorial... "My motives were not political, they were purely humane, moral motives,".... employed his unconventional approach to management to reorganise Krupp... credited with making the first, crucial contact...
© The Daily Telegraph 1.8.13

Professor John Burrows (born 6.4.35, historian, scholar, **wood Pig, Gemini/Cancer**)

"....graduated with a double First, took a doctorate.....had little time for modern fads....boisterous, funny, infuriating and subversive, he loved rich food, wine, conversation and parties of all kinds... disliked committee work... his most recent work, the elegant and witty *A History of Histories."*
© The Daily Telegraph 27.12.09

Lord Buxton of Alsa (born 7.15.18, farmer, naturalist, TV executive, **earth Horse, Cancer/Libra**)

"...created nature reserves... never afraid to speak his mind... love of field sports... made more than 250 wildlife films...his conduct during this action won him an immediate MC.... became president of the Falkland Islands Foundation, a conservation body fighting to preserve the birds threatened by a depletion in their food supply due to overfishing."
© The Daily Telegraph 3.9.09

Leonie Cohn (born 6.22.17, radio producer, broadcaster, **fire Snake Cancer/Leo**)

"insatiable intellectual curiosity....persistence... her resilience ensured... formidably intellectual... few producers had matched Leonie Cohn's fierce loyalty to ideas and contributors... took an active part in local affairs"
© The Daily Telegraph 1.9.09

Merce Cunningham (born 4.16.19, choreographer, dancer, **earth Goat, Aries/Scorpio**)

"....revolutionised modern dance....impatient with the quest to discover meaning in art...tirelessly innovative...remained endlessly inventive and inquisitive... while the dance was superb, the music could be surplus to requirements... new ways of perceiving and experiencing the world... artistic maverick and the gentlest of geniuses."

© *The Daily Telegraph* 27.7.09

Kim Dae-jung (born 1.6.24, President, **water Pig, Capricorn/Capricorn**)

"a former dissident whose opposition to successive dictatorial regimes led to him being described as the Nelson Mandela of Asia.... arrested as a "reactionary capitalist" ....a devout Roman Catholic....personal and political courage.... skillfully exploiting the sense of national crisis... set an example of tolerance... commercial acumen... argued for liberal reforms and a policy of reconciliation with North Korea and the Soviet Union... pursued his "Sunshine" policy of engagement with communist North Korea ....a populist politician with a gift for oratory".

© The Daily Telegraph 18.8.09

Simon Dee (born 7.28.35, disc jockey, talk show host, **wood Pig, Leo/Cancer**)

"....lived the sex, drugs and rock-and-roll dream ....making (and spending) prodigious amounts of money... a quick-witted but bumptious arriviste.... "naïve" interviewing style.... tiresome, stubborn and bloody-minded....becoming too big for his boots... believed he was bigger than the BBC that had created him.... bickered with his production staff, demanded guest-list approval and threw tantrums... sacking from his Radio 2 show for disobeying an instruction.. in court for assaulting a bailiff..... smashed a lavatory seat"

© The Daily Telegraph 30.8.09

General Sir Patrick Howard-Dobson (born 8.12.21, **metal Rooster, Leo/Sagittarius**)

"...an able commander and an outstanding staff officer, also a talented all-round sportsman head boy... captain of cricket...a shrewd judge of people...friendly and compassionate, his interest and enthusiasm were greatly valued... Intelligent and well-read, he had a great gift for getting along with and getting the best out of people from all walks of life..."

© The Daily Telegraph 20.12.09

Vic Chesnutt (born 11.11.64, singer, songwriter, **wood Dragon, Scorpio/Aquarius**)

"....almost completely paralysed after a drunken car crash ...eccentric, engaging songs... toured the world in a wheelchair... autobiographical accounts of addiction, self-hatred with unexpected humour and tenderness...'I am ambivalent towards human beings,' he said. 'It's ugly, but true. I am always at extremes, from 'I'm a lover' to 'I'm despicable, toxic trash'. '.... battle with depression and made several attempts at suicide."

© The Daily Telegraph 1.2.10

Jack Ellory (born 6.18.20, flautist, **metal Monkey, Gemini/Cancer**)
"...His tone was none the less lyrical, sonorous and energetic ....sharp sense of humour...a great raconteur and enjoyed regaling his family and friends with anecdotes... youngest member of Guards' band...as a teenager, he won scholarships to both Trinity College and The Royal College of Music"..."

© The Daily Telegraph 20.8.09

Guillermo Endara (born 5.12.36, President of Panama, **fire Rat, Taurus/Capricorn**)

"...affable but bland... to get to power, he demonstrated courage and determination... refused to back down "one inch"..... a particularly bright pupil at school... extremely able practitioner of labour law.. his second, very public, hunger strike.....'I like eating and have a big appetite'...many thought Endara somewhat dull... a portly widower whose appetite gave him the nickname 'Honey Bun'...'Happy Fatty'.

© The Daily Telegraph 2.10.09

Keith Floyd (born 12.28.43, TV chef, restaurateur, bartender, army officer, **water Goat, Capricorn/Capricorn**)

"genial chef... tore up the old formalities of television cookery....over 15 years Floyd produced 19 series...wrote more than 20 cookbooks... raffish charm and contagious enthusiasm...roguish charm... had writing talent and, determined to make it as a hack ....prone to depression and grumbled incessantly about the burden of fame... despite his charisma, wit, charm and frequent generosity, Floyd was also known for his temper tantrums, towering immodesty and bouts of maudlin despair....

poured his cupful over the carpet .. astute judgment.... regard his diners with ill-disguised contempt ...perfectionist Floyd... bon vivant style and turbulent relationships... four marriages."

© *The Daily Telegraph* 9.15.09

Gani Fawehinmi (born 4.22.38, lawyer, human rights campaigner, **earth Tiger, Taurus/Capricorn**)

"..At the price of frequent beatings, repeated imprisonment and almost incessant intimidation, he continued to mount legal protests.... his fearless, relentless (human rights) campaigning.....the people's lawyer...he said: 'What I believe in, I pursue intensely. I put my life on the line..... I am proud to be a confrontationist"...uncompromising attitude and boundless energy... his style could be abrasive.... upset some of his supporters.....no great team player or pragmatist...brilliance in the courtroom, legal expertise and knowledge... common touch and immense popularity... married two wives, with whom he had 14 children."

© *The Daily Telegraph* 6.10.2009

Joan Furbank (born 9.2.17, florist, **fire Snake, Virgo/Pisces**)

"...A woman of boundless energy and generosity, and always immaculately chic.... Joan often wrote their letters home.... a tireless worker for good causes.... excellent cook and a generous hostess... unnecessary to spend large amounts of money to produce a stunning display...."

© *The Daily Telegraph* 5.11.09

Jade Goody (born 6.5.81, reality TV celebrity, **metal Rooster, Gemini/Cancer**)

"her gobby, ignorant trajectory in the *Big Brother* .....boyfriend chipped in: 'She's a sex-crazed, lying, two-timing drunken tart'...viewers, it seemed, warmed to her malapropisms, guilelessness and obvious vulnerability... acquired, cheated on and discarded several boyfriends... branded a racist bully ("Shilpa Poppadom")...once biting off a chunk of another girl's earlobe... tactless "motor mouth"....opened a beauty salon (Ugly's)...

© *The Daily Telegraph* 22.3.09

Patrick Hannan (born 9.26.41, journalist, broadcaster, **metal Snake, Libra/Sagittarius**)

"....admired for his authority, erudition and wit... lateral thinker... despite his incisive mind, he remained a man of modesty and charm... admired for his authority, erudition and wit ......penetrating and provocative... broadcaster of great gusto .....duly impartial..."

© The Daily Telegraph 12.10.2009

Sir Denis Henry (born 4.19.31, judge, **metal Goat, Aries/Taurus**)

"...great skill and intelligence…solicitous and slightly diffident demeanour… his advocacy was always of the highest order......a formidable opponent…a low golf handicap…slight shyness belied a quiet self-confidence…a lively and gregarious character... constant sparkle in his eye.".

© The Daily Telegraph 14.4.10

Don Hewitt (born 12.14.22, TV director, **water Dog, Sagittarius/Libra**)

"...Gifted with the common touch and unashamedly anti-intellectual... "I operate by my guts and my fingertips," he boasted... unorthodox – "show-bizzy" – television techniques... "Lots of dazzle, lots of pace - noted a CBS president... instinctive understanding of the television medium.... strong visual sense thrice married"

© The Daily Telegraph 23 10 2009

From others: "an intense and combative man."

Jimmy Hoseason (born 11.6.27, holiday entrepreneur**, fire Rabbit, Scorpio/Aries**)

"...maths lecturer... ravel trade pioneer... foresight... kept abreast of the latest management thinking... zero-tolerance of mediocrity....shrewd to recognise the potential of "woman power"...under his chairmanship the firm proved to be recession-proof."

© The Daily Telegraph 15.11.2009

Thomas Hoving (born 1.15.31, museum director, author, **metal Horse, Capricorn/Sagittarius**)

"....charismatic... a gifted connoisseur, scholar, aesthete, diplomat, fund-raiser, executive and conciliator... he admitted, to be effective, had to be 'part gunslinger, legal fixer, accomplice smuggler, anarchist and toady'. "My collecting style was pure piracy,"..'I got a reputation as a shark"... frequent school expulsions for cheek and breaches of discipline.. became an independent consultant.."

© The Daily Telegraph 11.12.09

Tomaz Humar (born 2.18.69, mountaineer, **earth Rooster, Aquarius/Pisces**)

"..rebelled against his disciplinarian father...his desire for fame and publicity turned many climbers.against him...ignoring the team leader's orders to return to base... attributed his success to new age therapies... risked his life by climbing solo on a dangerous peak, but expected others to risk their lives for him."

© The Daily Telegraph 19.11.09

Bishop Abel Muzorewa (born 4.14.25, **wood Ox, Aries/Sagittarius**)

"...powerful orator and proved a tough negotiator... by nature I am a non-violent person... UN Peace Prize for outstanding achievement in human rights for his opposition to minority rule... mild-mannered man... proved as militant as the more radical nationalist guerrilla leaders."

© The Daily Telegraph 9.4.10

Professor Humphrey Kay (born 10.10.23, haematologist; doctor, **water Pig, Libra/Libra**)

"....inspirational pioneer ....deft diplomatic skills.... Kay was its first administrator... "Aden - a happy, peaceful place, where one learned to etc... a born naturalist with an enthusiastic, inquiring mind and a keen eye...a passion for opera, ballet and music....an accomplished musician and poet... he would sing".

© The Daily Telegraph 4.12.09

Sir Ludovic Kennedy (born 11.3.19, interviewer, investigative writer; **earth Goat, Scorpio/Pisces**, Scorpio Ascendant, Leo MC)

"...urbane presenter... combined his laconic, humorous style with a rage for justice that made him a formidable investigator... specialised in ferreting out truth, pursuing almost-lost causes and bringing to light what seemed to him to be miscarriages of justice... campaigned for the release of the Birmingham Six and other IRA suspects... "distrust all those in whom the urge to punish is strong"... he also championed atheism, republicanism, voluntary euthanasia and fox-hunting... he had suffered for more than 20 years from anxiety neurosis... extremely highly strung... published a steady stream of books about crime, the law and miscarriages of justice

© The Daily Telegraph 19.10.09

From others: "rigorous and charismatic interviewer....articulate his powerful and provocative views....ability to see through to the truth of a story....ardent and often outspoken campaigner....stern, schoolmasterly gaze, always as his own man...believe that an interviewer should be courteous but incisive....highly protective of his family".

Irving Kristol (born 1.22.20, thinker, essayist, **earth Goat, Aquarius/Aquarius**)

"Depression-era American student radical turned reactionary, and was often described as the "godfather" of the American neoconservative movement; many credited him with helping to transform the political landscape of the United States in the late 20th century...his aim was "to convert the Republican Party etc... instrumental in nurturing writers who shared the same anti-liberal establishment ethos as he did... played an important role in shaping neoconservative links with the world of think tanks and pressure groups.... it is necessary to have "permanent revolution" to sustain an activist ideology"

© The Daily Telegraph 20.9.09

From others: ".coordinator of a vast movement......exceptionally able editor in conceptualising original ideas for serious articles...able controversialist, but much of his thinking was negative"

Professor Claude Levi-Strauss (born 11.28.08, social anthropologist; **earth Monkey, Sagittarius/Capricorn**, Virgo Ascendant, Gemini MC)

"....his work inspired a school of academic followers.....capacity for creating complex intellectual jigsaws... deadpan voice, and with a deadpan expression.....book sprang out of depression... highly original interpretation of data...views were never predictable... give lectures, write articles. love of music.. "I like tree..animals...but I am not very fond of humans"."

© The Daily Telegraph 3.11.09

Sir David Lean (born 3.25.08,film director – **earth Monkey, Aries/Sagittarius**)

"....his distant manner...I have hardly ever been bored in my life...a self-contained, supremely self-confident personality... rigorously eschewed small-talk.... universally respected for his technical mastery and the editorial skills..."hardly ever been bored in my life... I work like mad when I work, but I also love doing nothing.".... never stopped planning new projects.... married five times."

© *The Daily Telegraph* *17.4.91*

Professor Sir Hugh Lloyd-Jones (born 9.21.22, Greek scholar, Capt, **water Dog, Virgo/Virgo**)

"...gate keeper for a particular style of traditional scholarship.....at his best when probing the unexamined assumptions of others or challenging fashionable beliefs...his barbs were more frequently directed at transatlantic scholars who attempted to impose Freudian or Levi-Straussian theories on Greek myth and literature...professed himself a "conservative with very little intrinsic belief in the goodness of human nature"... as a teacher, Lloyd-Jones was encouraging, demanding and sometimes waspishly indiscreet about his academic colleagues... passion of his own intellectual convictions"

© *The Daily Telegraph* 5.10.09

Ian Norrie (born 8.3.27, bookseller, author, **fire Rabbit, Leo/Libra**)

"....busy journalist and author......held so many forcefully expressed opinions that he was known (sometimes with a hint of asperity) as "the Sage of Hampstead"... shrewdly observed his customers' range of tastes... had a brusque side... disgraced himself by becoming a pacifist... author of vigorous comic novels... generous employer who befriended his staff.."

© *The Daily Telegraph* *9.11.09*

Robert Novak (born 2.26.31, columnist, broadcaster, **metal Goat, Pisces/Gemini**)

"..known as the "Prince of Darkness" on account of his pessimistic outlook... his scowling, unvarnished style made him something of a Washington institution.... does not trade in witty prose or expansive

theories... takes particular glee in inciting – or at least enabling – inter- and intraparty warfare... Novak's administration sources had acted illegally.... Novak was seen as rumpled and grouchy.... enjoyed an enviable reputation for working the phones.... after swearing on air, he walked off the set during a political debate."
© The Daily Telegraph 19.8.2009

From others: "a difficult, pugnacious figure...controversial/maverick views.... long record of controversial disclosures...nicer in person than his television persona...suspended by CNN for unacceptable outburst"

Major-General Ken Perkins (8.15.26, **fire Tiger, Leo/Scorpio**)
"...shouted at his ADC: "Don't run – generals don't run! Just move briskly!"..... a proficient boxer, he captained the team.... had flown 214 sorties and engaged 470 targets....awas awarded a DFC... on retiring from the Army in 1982, Perkins joined British Aerospace as military adviser.... he rose through the ranks to command one of the most prestigious units in the British Army... some who thought that Perkins might have climbed higher were it not for his uncompromising nature: he was never afraid to go out on a limb or to ruffle feathers by questioning the official line...
© The Daily Telegraph 10.11.09

From others: "Don't run – generals don't run! Just move briskly!"..... his uncompromising nature":

Sir Bob Phillis (born 12.3.45, media executive, **metal Rooster, Sagittarius/Scorpio**)
"hard-working.. ITN's workforce halved during his tenure, but its finances were greatly strengthened... invaluable and supportive...well-liked throughout his industry... could be tough... amiable demeanour of a favourite schoolmaster... introduced a business focus to a newsgathering organisation... lectured"
© The Daily Telegraph 23.12.09

Sir John Quicke (born 4.20.22, agriculturalist, cheese maker, **water Dog, Aries/Aquarius**)

".....an innovative farmer...enjoyed a rich spiritual life...ability to see both sides of the argument...created one of the first large dairy herds... combined respect for tradition, innovation and good practice to create a successful farming business.....created national collections of magnolias, azaleas and berberis... to the end of his life Quicke retained his intellectual curiosity".

© The Daily Telegraph 04 Jan 2010

Prof John Ramsden (born 11.12.47, historian, **fire Pig, Scorpio/Scorpio**)

"....a key historian... incessant inquisitiveness about history...qualified at night-school as an accountant...hugely productive academic career... practical...a lively and intellectually resourceful undergraduate.... enthusiasm for his subject, always brimming over in his conversation... man of firm beliefs... interests were extremely broad....a career of enormous energy... retentive memory... drive and energy had been sparked, in part, by the incessant inquisitiveness about history.....his characteristic combination of blunt speech and kindness to individuals... his learning could, on occasion, be intimidating."

© The Daily Telegraph 21.10.09

From others: "produced lucid penetrating accounts..meticulous research..well organised enthusiasm."

Commander Sir Miles Rivett-Carnac, Bt (born 2.7.33, merchant banker, **water Rooster, Aquarius/Cancer**)

"....a popular divisional officer, highly numerate, his sound judgment of people and cheerful willingness to undertake any difficult task...appointed captain of the large fleet destroyer analytical mind and business sense... left the Navy to make a new start in the financial world... instrumental in restoring the finances of its charitable arm..."

© The Daily Telegraph 6.10.09

Rafael Caldera (born 1.24.16, President of Venezuela, **wood Rabbit, Capricorn/Taurus**)

"...an august and respected politician... running for the presidency aged only 31.... active in an anti-communist youth movement.... espousing social justice based on conservative values, wove together elements of Left and Right..... quickly resigned to set up his own centre-Right party.... he quickly buttressed his position with a series of consensus-building moves..... a devout Roman Catholic and the holder of many honorary degrees.... elected president aged 77.

© The Daily Telegraph 18.1.10

From others: "...ambitious...soon fell out with...honest and austere man."

Prof Simon Thirgood (born 12.6.62, ecologist, **wood Tiger, Sagittarius/Aries**)

"Among Thirgood's many gifts was his ability to see how scientific inquiry could be developed into pragmatic policy for managing the environment.... he indulged his love of mountaineering.... responsible for a wide range of projects in Africa..... published more than 100 scientific papers on an astonishing diversity of subjects.... had a keen eye for the absurd, and could be very entertaining when confronted by windy scientific presentations which he regarded as self-indulgent.... always focused on the most useful and important questions.... constantly injecting humour and encouragement into proceedings.... had little time for bureaucracy... an active outdoorsman.."

© The Daily Telegraph 9.9.2009

From others: "..morale-boosting disposition...a wise, at times caustic judge of others' works...generous with his time..spoke persuasively.."

Rear-Admiral "Sam" Salt (born 4.19.40, submariner, businessman, head of sales/marketing, **metal Dragon, Aries/Scorpio**)

"...quiet and economical with his words... enthusiastic leadership... ability to motivate people...astute decision making... when appropriate he could be indiscreet... he needled the French.....some skill at stone-engraving and painting..."

© The Daily Telegraph 6.12.09

Paul Samuelson (born 5.15.15, economist; **wood Rabbit, Taurus/Gemini**)

"...person of analytical ability...perceptive... gave the world a common language with which the complexities of world markets can be discussed and understood...normally ebullient..."My finger," he said, "has been in every pie."... a prolific writer and commentator... "I was born as an economist"... consultant to the United States Treasury... refused all offers of a government post, feeling that it would prevent him from writing and speaking freely... had six children.. "I had expected a scrumptious meal," Samuelson later complained. "We had franks and beans."

Randal Sadleir (born 5.6.24, colonial administrator, **wood Rat, Taurus/Aquarius**)

"...participating in Swahili radio broadcasts... enthusiasm... joined the jubilant crowd racing through the streets...as "Mr Problems" who adjudicated disputes, supervised dam building and inspected schools and hospitals as well as acting as magistrate, coroner, registrar and policeman... "You're neither civil nor servile", Sir Edward Twining (governor) told him."

Pat Thompson (born 6.6.20, tutor of college, **metal Monkey, Gemini/Aquarius**)

"...He had little time for putting individuals in categories.... Credulity was to be undermined, and flights of fancy or overblown prose would simply provoke the comment: "Too much Wardour Street.".... Thompson always lectured without notes... regularly taught for 20 hours a week.... not a man for indecision, and colleagues could find him unaccommodating; but a touch of cussedness was something he polished...

From others: "....lively seminars, ruthless as administrator and in argument, even offensive....urbane manner belied temperamental volatility.."

Michael Thornely (born 10.21.18, headmaster, **earth Horse, Libra/Taurus**)

"...reputation for musical and theatrical productions...his steadiness successfully preserved the ethos of the school...burdens of extended office had inevitably taken a toll on his health".

© The Daily Telegraph

David Vine (born 1.3.36, sports presenter, **wood Pig, Capricorn/Taurus**)

"...affable front man for many popular BBC television shows.... the versatile Vine was renowned as a safe pair of hands... reliable, unflappable, at ease with off-the-cuff improvisation..... he enjoyed the occasional dig in the ribs... after his retirement he underwent triple heart by-pass surgery, and later continued working as a consultant for the BBC."

© The Daily Telegraph 12.1.2009

From others: "true and utter gentleman at all times...professionalism and dedication.... enterprise... attention to detail..."

Dinah Williams (born 7.23.11, organic farmer, **metal Pig, Cancer/Gemini**)

Profoundly shocked by the repressive and damaging effect of Stalin's farm collectivism..... An outspoken opponent of chemical fertilisers.... passionate about the role of nutrition in health and the importance of good food.... had little time for doctors, preferring to rely on naturopathic treatments..."

© The Daily Telegraph 23.10.2009

From others: "pioneer/matriarch of organic farming....quietly spoken.....in conversation she is direct... was an inspiration...her steadfastness and integrity..one of her sayings –"the whiter the bread, the sooner you're dead"."

Sir Oliver Wright (born 3.6.21, diplomat, **metal Rooster, Pisces/Aquarius**)

"..swarthy good looks and physical presence of actors....a man of

sensitive politicaoxariesl antennae... Foreign Secretary relies on him greatly, especially in speech writing.. his knowledge of personalities and politics at the centre proved an invaluable asset... proved a most suitable Ambassador...
© The Daily Telegraph 6.9.2009

From others: "...very lovable human being....outstanding ability to work with others...got things done...more interested in common sense and practical results than finer points of analysis...ability to get to what he saw as the essentials of a situation.... valued the sureness of his judgement and sense of proportion.."

Final Comments

Astrology has always been given space by some newspapers, be it as horoscopes in their supplements/magazines or as occasional articles. Over the years, I did manage to have a few letters published in their Letters section. They are reproduced below to indicate some degree of general acceptability and popularity of astrology as a credible science, at the very least for public debate.

'Split Personality:
Mr Alan Howarth's defection to Labour should hold little surprise to those who are acquainted with the fundamentals of astrology. The theory suggests that he may exhibit dual personalities due to his Sun being in Gemini, the twins. His Moon is in Aquarius, which may predispose him to unconventional behaviour. One should also consider the possibility of unpredictable antics which are often associated with the Chinese Monkey.'
(The Daily Telegraph 13.10.1995)

'SERPENT:
Paul Britton's explanations for Hamilton's atrocity at Dunblane seem plausible, psychologically. However, astrologically speaking, Hamilton was apparently born as a Chinese Snake, which is known to bitterly avenge lifelong grudges. Hence "*Caveat Serpens*".'
(The Sunday Times 24.3.1996)

'In the Stars:
You justifiably questioned the future of the coalition ("Will magic last?", Focus election special, last week) asking if it had "any chance of going the distance". The answer may lie in astrology. The prime minister and his deputy are fiery Chinese Horses that should gallop nicely together. As a Capricorn, Clegg has a diplomatic approach that will echo Cameron's Libran preference for minimal conflict and fair play.'
(The Sunday Times 23.5.2010)

'End of Labour:
We have faced an interesting astrological dilemma. Nick Clegg's preference for diplomacy as a Capricorn is mirrored by David Cameron's sense of fair play and conflict avoidance as a Libran. But how would this potential indecision have panned out with Gordon Brown's fishy input as a Piscean? As like attracts like, my money has been on a Lib-Con pact.'
(The Independent 12.5.2010)

'Tiger Woods:
We should not be too surprised by Tiger Woods' spitting and swearing. Astrology may help to explain his actions. As a Chinese Rabbit/Cat, he has a natural tendency to act independently, irrespective of what's expected as acceptable behaviour. He is also a Capricorn, whose kind is known for their strong suspicion of others and occasional obnoxiousness. On the plus side, many Capricorns have succeeded in eventually reaching the top by sheer hard work and disciplined approach, with disbelief in taking short cuts. But he will definitely be attracted to money. His Ascendant sign in Virgo should imbue him with the essential physical skills to play golf well.'
(Daily Mail 15.2.2011)

It will become obvious to the critical reader that matching the 'best' jobs to the star sign(s) requires a combination of excellent astrological knowledge, some intuition, practical experience and worldly facts.

Many of those listed in this book have more than one main job or vocational interest. This may be attributed to the complex nature of personality, which has several components that can influence career choice. Also, the roles might be fashioned by circumstances, personal experiences, family background and genes –factors that should be considered as relevant.

However, as you progress with increasing exposure to the above key elements, you will detect a fairly distinct pattern associated with each unique combination of star signs. It can become a fascinating lifelong hobby or even a serious vocation to associate various signs to certain personalities.

Chapter 4 can form the basis for starting to understand why some genuine 'couples' have bonded well. Again, other factors, such as physical attraction and the right 'gelling' chemistry would have played their important roles.

The attraction between the similar and the opposites may well exist. However, for centuries, Global Astrology (Western and Chinese) has been proven to be a useful tool for predicting successful partnerships and relationships.

Some relationships have really sparked off amidst much publicity but have sadly ended in acrimonious divorces. The examples given in Chapter 4 should prove illuminating.

It is important for you to study in detail and understand the comments made on the various signs in Chapters 1 & 2. This will help you fully appreciate what each sign and sign combination will be in terms of likely personality and behaviour. You may well be seeking specific behavioural traits in your partner. Some traits could put you off from considering certain signs. You 'must' also bear in mind that some of the more intelligent/knowledgeable (of Global Astrology) or chameleonic signs can or will temporarily mask their negative aspects, thereby presenting them as highly attractive persona.

In this book, I have attempted to create a unique record of celebrities, past and present, their professions and astrological details. Hence you can now check out and have a more accurate understanding of your personality and temperament. Do their professions resonate with you personally? Should you delve deeper into his/her biography? Thus, this information should help you to research further along astrological lines or for pure personal satisfaction.

From the information, it should be fairly conclusive that astrology is here to stay. It is an intriguing subject that can provide useful indications and good predictions for your ideal career. **Everyone** has the free will to decide but to ignore one's fundamental leanings (or tendencies in astrological speak) may seem unwise. This amounts to working against the grain?

There will always be sceptics. If there were no sizeable grains of truth within astrology, it would not have lasted these 2 millennia for the Chinese Lunar calendar (2.6 millennia for Western astrology, which apparently started in Babylon). To pinpoint exact characteristics for each sign might sound implausible. This book has done exactly that, mainly based on actual observations and research at a more fundamental level.
Astrology is a vast subject full of minutiae of details and fascinating information. Much of the latter would seem fairly hard to prove. For those who are sceptical about astrology and are keen on scientific proofs, Gunter Sachs's book is an excellent source. He concluded that: "We have proved it – there is a correlation (between star signs and human behaviour and predispositions)". It will probably take several lifetimes to fully understand all aspects of Western and Chinese astrology. One should study the subjects with reputable astrologers.

By studying the key traits listed in this book, you would now have as your framework 24 basic elements, which you can use to construct complex profiles of individuals using the Sun, Moon and Chinese signs. Ideally, adding the Ascendant or Rising sign should give you at least 70% of anyone's personality profile. Hopefully, your own further research into the horoscopes of your favourite celebrities or even the eccentrics would reveal fascinating information.

One interesting situation involves identical twins. It happens that I am married to a twin. Does it mean that both twins should be following the same career and be equally successful? Research done by some has shown that the events and abilities could be surprisingly similar. However, one can conclude that <u>similar abilities, preferences and trends</u> could be found but these would not appear exactly as astrology is not an exact science. The birth chart supposedly maps out predispositions only, not specific events. With similar conditioning and known physical environments, events might be more predictable.

As many astrologers will happily testify, it is impossible to be 100% precise in linking astrology with successful careers. I have attempted to simplify astrology for the layperson so that there are discernible patterns of digestible facts, which could offer good reassurance to those who seek these. This book is only a guide and other relevant factors (historical era, race, religion, geological areas, customs, education and social status etc.) should be considered.

My intention is to give everyone concerned, a relatively simple means to know oneself with good precision and to use this book as a guide to pick a suitable profession for good career success. You will realise that many professions are common to some signs. This is to be expected since many jobs would require specific types of personalities, skills and temperaments. The advanced alternative is to use detailed astrological analyses, which go into complex, intellectually challenging interpretations (midheaven/MC, houses, aspects etc), and possibly extinguishing any glimmer of interest in astrology in some people. It would be more difficult to confirm these correlations too. Hopefully, this book would offer pragmatic career guidance and engender further interest in astrology as a useful science.

Astrology has played a major role in my own life and you too can definitely benefit from its implications!

Finally, it is so easy, and almost a cliché to say that experiencing an unsuitable job (career) or smarting from an incompatible relationship can be wasteful of time and a drain on emotional energies.

Why not be smarter by using the wisdom of Global Astrology to lead a more successful and happier life?

Bibliography

The New International Ephemerides 1900-2050 by St Michel 1993

Love, Sex and Astrology by Teri King,
Allison & Busby Ltd (London) 1972

The Handbook of Chinese Horoscopes
by Theodora Lau,
Souvenir Press 1979

Astrology and Health by Sheila Geddes, The Aquarian Press 1981

The New Astrology by Suzanne White, The Pan Books 1987

How to Use Vocational Astrology for Success in the
Workplace by Noel Tyl, The Llewellyn Publications

Successful Career Planning With Astrology by Rupert J Sewell,
The Aquarian Press 1985

Star Signs by Emily Bolam & Caroline Ness, The Albion Press 1994

The Ascendant – Your Karmic Doorway by Martin Schulman,
Samuel Weiser Inc 1993

Work Your Stars by Matthew Dr Matt Abergel, Simon & Schuster 1999

The Modern Text Book of Astrology by Margaret E Hone.
L N Fowler & Co Ltd 1980

Astrology – 30 Years Research by Doris Chase Doane,
American Federation of Astrologers Inc 1979

The Principles of Astrology by Charles E. O. Carter,
The Theosophical Publishing House Ltd 1971

The Astrology File by Gunter Sachs, Orion 1998

Birth Signs – The Unique New Guide to Your Planetary Influences
by Debbie Frank, Vermilion (London) 1992

Understanding Astrology by Sasha Fenton, The Aquarian Press 1991

Sun & Moon Signs by Marisa St Clair, Index 1999

Synastry by Ronald Davison, Aurora 1983